Translation and Global Asia

Asian Translation Traditions Series • 1

Translation and Global Asia
Relocating Networks of Cultural Production

EDITED BY

Uganda Sze-pui Kwan

and

Lawrence Wang-chi Wong

翻譯研究中心
Research Centre for Translation

中文大學出版社
THE CHINESE UNIVERSITY PRESS

Asian Translation Traditions Series
Series Editor: Lawrence Wang-chi Wong
Series Assistant: Stephanie Cheuk Wong

Translation and Global Asia: Relocating Networks of Cultural Production
Edited by Uganda Sze-pui Kwan and Lawrence Wang-chi Wong

ISBN: 978-962-996-608-9

Published by:

Research Centre for Translation
Institute of Chinese Studies
The Chinese University of Hong Kong
Sha Tin, N.T., Hong Kong
Fax: +852 2603 5110
E-mail: rct@cuhk.edu.hk
Website: www.cuhk.edu.hk/rct

The Chinese University Press
The Chinese University of Hong Kong
Sha Tin, N.T., Hong Kong
Fax: +852 2603 7355
E-mail: cup@cuhk.edu.hk
Website: www.chineseupress.com

Printed in Hong Kong

Cover image: Asiae Novo Descriptio Auctore Jodoco Hondio [A new description of Asia], by Jodocus Hondius (1563–1612), dated 1610.

Series Editor's Preface

Asian countries have long histories of translation, though research in this field has remained fragmented and obscure. As a result, their rich translation traditions remain largely unexplored. This state of affairs leaves much to be desired, as studies on the richness of translational activities throughout history in this region will undoubtedly yield valuable information on Asia and, on a larger scale, the whole world. From the Turkish Ottoman Empire to the colonial rule in Asian societies, more academic research is needed to examine the impact translation had on the highly diversified Asian societies and cultures.

To promote and enhance high-quality research in the translation traditions of Asian countries, the Research Centre for Translation (RCT), The Chinese University of Hong Kong publishes the present Asian Translation Traditions Series. It aims to attract scholars of translation studies as well as various related disciplines to contribute to the field, and to fill the current vacancy of English publications on translation history. The series will be especially valuable to Western scholars with limited access to works and materials in the Asian languages.

Edited volumes and monographs by single or multiple authors are included in the series' publishing scope. Volumes in the series can focus on a topic relating to translation traditions of one single Asian country, or cover multiple countries for comparison. To ensure the highest possible academic standard, all book manuscripts will undergo a double-blind review process, which is closely monitored by the Academic Committee. The committee comprises distinguished and renowned international scholars who would also advise on the focus and orientation of the series.

The RCT is a research unit at the Institute of Chinese Studies, The Chinese University of Hong Kong. Established in 1971, it aims to promote

Chinese literature internationally through translation and to foster pioneering research in Asian translation studies. It is now one of the foremost research centres in translation and translation studies in Asia. The centre has published since 1973, *Renditions*, the very successful journal of Chinese literature in English, and a new academic journal, *Studies in Translation History*, which was launched in June 2011 and is jointly published with Fudan University Press in Shanghai. It is the first of its kind and publishes high-quality papers on Chinese translation history.

Asian Translation Traditions Series welcomes submissions from all researchers and scholars. It is our sincere wish that, together with your support, we can help push the boundaries of research in Asian translation history.

Lawrence Wang-chi Wong
Series Editor, Asian Translation Traditions Series

Contents

Acknowledgements

The present volume is a collection of articles selected from the papers presented at the Fourth Asian Translation Traditions (ATT) Conference held in Hong Kong from 15–17 December 2010, which was jointly organized by the Research Centre for Translation (RCT), The Chinese University of Hong Kong, and the College of Humanities, Arts and Social Sciences, Nanyang Technological University, Singapore.

Since the conference series' inception in 2004 by Dr Eva Hung, former RCT Director, the ATT conferences aspire to be an international forum for the researchers and scholars of Asian Translation Studies. The conferences are held biennially in different countries in order to allow the interaction of knowledge at a regional and international level. They aim to explore the richness and diversity of non-Western discourses and practices of translation, focusing on translational exchanges among non-Western languages, and the change and continuity in Asian translation traditions. The three-day ATT4 Conference was a great success. We must thank the members of the Organizing Committee of the conference, namely Professors Alan Kam Leung Chan, Max Ko-wu Huang, James St. André, and Judy Wakabayashi, as well as all the participants of the conference from different parts of the world, including mainland China, Taiwan, Hong Kong, India, Japan, Singapore, Malaysia, the Philippines, Thailand, Iran, Israel, Turkey, Australia, Canada, the US, the UK, and others. We would like to thank in particular Professor Su Guaning, former President of Nanyang Technological University, for approving a generous funding to support the event. Sponsorship also came from the Institute of Chinese Studies, The Chinese University of Hong Kong, and we would like to express our gratitude to Professor Jenny So, who was then the Director of the Institute.

The present volume is the first title of the Asian Translation Traditions Series published by the RCT and The Chinese University Press (CUP). Special thanks should go to the members of the Academic Committee of the series, Professors Susan Bassnett, Joshua Fogel, Rachel Harrison, Peter Kornicki, Joachim Kurtz, and William Tay. The same should also go to the two reviewers of the manuscripts who have provided invaluable comments for further improving the papers. The editorial team of the CUP has done a wonderful job in helping at different stages the smooth publication of the book. We are immensely grateful.

Last but not least, we would like to take this opportunity to thank our colleagues at the RCT, and give our thanks in particular to Olivia Wui Sze Lui. They are no doubt a highly devoted, passionate, meticulous, and professional team, sharing and working hard towards a common goal of promoting translation and translation studies. For the ATT4 Conference, they had spent a lot of time and made the best efforts to make it a success. It goes without saying that the publication of the present volume owes much to their hard work. Our very sincere thanks.

Uganda Sze-pui Kwan
Lawrence Wang-chi Wong

Introduction

Uganda Sze-pui KWAN

The name "Asia" is of ancient origin. It was created by the ancient Greeks, to whom "Asia" referred to a great land mass opposite to Europe. The geographical delineation of this land mass was founded on the ancient Greeks' worldview, epistemological interest, and psychological attitude. It was of course also limited by technological level in the maritime era. Ever since the name "Asia" was constructed by the European other, the signified content of Asia has never ceased to evolve. It changed considerably when the Ottoman Empire and the Russian Empire were formed. It became more defined, covering the Mongol Empire to the north, the Mughal Empire to the south, and the Chinese Empire to the east, with Japan at its eastern end. The term "Asia" as the name of the whole land mass remains unchanged over time, though political regimes within have changed from empires to nation-states, from colonial settlements to sovereign countries. Although Asia has always been viewed by the Europeans as ancient, mysterious, incomprehensible or even rather unified with shared civilization or cultural beliefs,[1] there is in fact a great variety of people, ethnicity, languages, and cultural systems, etc., which forms competing goals, uneven developments, and potentialities.

In the twenty-first century, a completely new notion of Asia emerged. Asia has become a synonym for new commercial market,[2] hyper-quick capital flows, unexplored natural resources, and unprecedented intercultural

1 Amitav Acharya, "Asia Is Not One," *Journal of Asian Studies* 69, no. 4 (November 2010), pp. 1001–1013.

2 James E. Rauch, "Does Network Theory Connect to the Rest of Us? A Review of Matthew O. Jackson's *Social and Economic Networks*," *Journal of Economic Literature* 48, no. 4 (December 2010), pp. 980–986.

dynamics. The perception of Asia seems to have swung from one extreme to the other, changing from ancient relics to future power. Of course, neither of these perceptions do justice to Asia. This notion of Asia is essentially a product of Orientalism which has governed the Western historiography since the seventeenth century. As Henk Wesseling cogently argues, world history has often been viewed by the Westerners as the study of the West and the "rest."[3] The real Asia is always in motion. Its mobility and fluidity are directed by thousands of networks. These networks are formed by both tangible materials and intangible beliefs. There are economic, religious, political, as well as intellectual networks. The power flow can be from top down, but it also can be from bottom up. In this book, we will see that translation is the hub that connects the multifaceted networks undergirding the East and the West, the traditional and the modern, the first and third world structures, the national and the leftist. Translator is not only an interface but also an active agent that opens up new frontiers between them.

In order to see how Asia made its impact upon the world and how knowledge about Asia was produced, we will put the focus on the synergies circulating between Asia and other parts of the world by means of translation. In so doing, we also challenge past historical accounts when they only serve to glorify a single teleological modernity.[4] This book collects some of the most innovative research on the history of translation in Asia. Many papers in it are based on detailed historical investigations, since it is only through a firm grasp of Asian's own traditions, instead of a survey type of study, that we can offer an alternate view to the Eurocentric representation of Asia.

In section one, we place China at the centre of the stage as one of the key players in Asia. The focus here is on China, or the cultural factors constituting China. We avoid using the term "Chineseness" because

3 Henk Wesseling, "Overseas History," in *New Perspectives on Historical Writing*, ed. Peter Burke (University Park, Pa.: Pennsylvania State University Press, 1992), p. 9.

4 Duara Prasenjit, *The Crisis of Global Modernity: Asian Traditions and a Sustainable Future* (Cambridge: Cambridge University Press, 2014).

the essentialism underlying this term carries with it effects of inclusion and exclusion on the discussion of cultural identity and ethnicity in the Chinese Empire.[5] China had always regarded herself as a powerhouse to its tributary states. The sense of Chinese (or Han) supremacy had made her unwilling to learn foreign languages for the purpose of cultural exchange. Apart from Buddhist translation, in the long history of Chinese translation, the absorption of foreign knowledge had only served political purposes. The three papers in the first section demonstrate the delicate use of translation. It was used as a means to fulfil political aims—to control and Sinicize the barbarians. Joshua Fogel shows some early attempts by the scholar-gentry of the Ming dynasty to introduce Japanese poetry into China. Although they had begun with the paradigmatic purpose to gather intelligence for China's maritime security, Japanese poems were selected, translated, and absorbed into the Chinese learning system through various kinds of translation technology. Scholars creatively used sound, script and shape to create topolects and chronolects to understand the Japanese language. This creative absorption laid a solid foundation for including Japanese poetry into Chinese learning. Although it cannot be compared with the wholesale absorption of Japanese knowledge after the Sino-Japanese War in 1895, when the Chinese intellectuals started viewing Japanese learning as a shortcut to modern Western knowledge, early attempts to decode the Japanese language were probably a latent social force in the Zhejiang province for the future modernization of China in the last decades of the nineteenth century. Jae-ho Shin's paper places the translation of *Xiaojing* (Book of filial piety) in highly politically charged environments—the frontiers of China in Tuoba Wei (386–534) and Mongol Yuan in the year of 1307. Confucianism had long been appropriated for political ends. Such appropriation can easily be traced back to the Han dynasty and can still be seen in the recent use of the Confucian Institute as a soft power to extend Chinese influence. Shin's work not only makes an examination of a rarely discussed text, the *Xiaojing* in Uighur script,

5 Allen Chun, "Fuck Chineseness: On the Ambiguities of Ethnicity as Culture as Identity," in *Boundary 2* 23, no. 2 (Summer, 1996), pp. 111–138.

but also contextualizes translation activities inside larger political concerns. In the same vein, Lawrence Wong's paper is focused on the handling of business with barbarians. He approaches the matter from the perspective of the linguists and interpreters, and demonstrates how ethical issues of interpreters were closely related to the xenophobia of the Qing court in the eighteenth- and nineteenth-century China.

In section two, the attention shifts from East Asia to Inner Asia, focusing first on North Korea and then on Tibetan literature. Theresa Hyun's work gives a detailed account of the broad reception of Western European literature in the Democratic People's Republic of Korea in the high time of the Cold War. Because of the cultural isolationism policy of North Korea, literary translator Im Hak-Su could exert an influence by creating linguistic markers to localize foreign literature, which resulted in some unprecedented cultural collision. Similarly, Georgios Halkias' paper is focused on the process of absorbing the foreign into the local, seen in Buddhist literature. The authoritative nature of religious literature always hinders the translator's freedom to make imaginative adaptations. Hence knowledge production tends to shift to the by-products created alongside it—loan words, lexicon, bilingual dictionaries, etc. The multicultural translation brought forth from India and China enriched the cultural platform of Buddhist translation in imperial Tibet. Contrary to Halkias' paper, Corazon Villareal discusses the sublimation and enrichment of the aesthetical elements in the dedicated translator, Rolando Tinio (1937–1997). On the surface, Corazon Villareal's quest is simple, which is to demonstrate the functions and *skopos* of the translations of this Filipino poet, dramatist, director, actor, critic, essayist, and educator. However, by using a pun of the playwright as the research topic, Villareal leads us to a simple but monumental question: "*May Katwiran Ba?*" (Was there a reason to translate?). It is resonant with the name of the artist's play *May Katwiran ba ang Katwiran?* (Does reason have its reason?). Tinio's avant-garde attempt to introduce new elements in theatre translation, such as bringing in provocative content and creating new jargon, had hugely electrified the audience and had a long-term effect on the formation of the post-colonial identity of the vernacular literature in Philippine.

The three papers in section three are concerned with representation and appropriation of foreign literariness in the making of national literature in South Asia. In the process of absorbing foreign elements, societies in this area generated a special discourse to define themselves and the others. Both E. V. Ramakrishnan and Megha Pansare situate the literary scenes in the socio-political turmoil of India. Translation was used as a political tool. Though its function was not only that of a propaganda tool, the translated text was used to generate social discourse to aid the struggle for national freedom and to consolidate the national building process by borrowing Russian national literature through the skilful choice of using local languages. Phrae Chittiphalangsri takes another path. She attempts to bring to light the prominent motif of translation—what is created by the clash of canonical literature. How was new literariness accentuated in early Thai literature when the literary scene was unsatisfied with existing literary technique and the literary conceptualization of the "real" (verisimilitude)? Phrae Chittiphalangsri not only dissects genre and literary skills, but also takes a rather idiosyncratic path to reveal the creative use of pseudotranslation to consolidate the sense of the "real" under the impulse of making her own literary canon in the post-colonial Thailand.

The last section is concerned with the ethics of translation. While translation can open up avenues of political, social, and gender possibilities, it is also a Pandora's Box, which is shown in many historical junctures. Translation does not always fulfil the presumed goals and intents. It also causes collision of interests of different stakeholders. The betrayal of translation is rampant if the society is polarized by different social elements, and information flow is embargoed and hence easily hijacked by the course of information transmission. But who has the right to do it? Who is sensitive enough to catch the very moment of translating delicate information? Language is a form of power, and social elite is always catching the early wind of the paradigmatic change. Nazry Bahrawi's paper examines the Malay translation of a sociological treatise *The Myth of the Lazy Native* written by a contemporary Malaysian social elite Syed Hussein Alatas (1928–2007) to decolonize the imperialist imagination of the native in Malaysia. For a long time, the hybrid faces of the Asian natives in colonial literature converged into one single image—idleness, indolence, slothfulness, inactivity, and sluggishness. Although we understand that the stereotypical other is created to justify the colonial discourse of "the white man's burden," we have to ask who are the real lazy-bones here if the multifaceted indigenous people are compressed into one single cultural representation? Nazry Bahrawi's choice of work, *The Myth of the Lazy Native*, therefore produces a metatextual performativity to destabilize one of the most important postcolonial themes. Uganda Kwan's paper takes the historical commonality of two twin cities (Hong Kong and Singapore) in the nineteenth century to examine the betrayal of translation. The British Empire is usually seen as a powerful hegemonic machinery to coerce the indigenous. It does not, however, appear to be so powerful when we see how the colonial government was crippled by mistranslation and untrustworthy interpreters when the colonizer first set foot in the new colonies. Who could not speak before the subaltern was silenced in the fractures of histories?

The volume presents a wide range of topics, covering literary, religious, diplomatic, and political translation in Asian translatorial praxis—China, Mongolia, Japan, Korea, the Philippines, Malaysia, Thailand, Singapore, Hong Kong, and India—which are previously marginalized in Western translation studies. Through crossing the boundaries of text and translator, the rigidity of power structure in a society or state is shifted and destabilized. Translation is therefore an activity that is always full of transformative power and mobile potentialities. In the course of making new networks, the very act of translation diffuses the linearity and unidirectional traffic of power. It then forms new network upon the old, be it a social, religious, intellectual, linguistic or historical one.

Disembodiment and Dissemination: The Chinese Factor

Japanese Poetry in Chinese Translation from the Ming Period

Joshua FOGEL

While Japanese study of China and annotated translations from the Chinese have been an ongoing phenomena since Japan first adopted Chinese characters, for many cultural and social reasons, Chinese study of Japan has been a less well-developed field. There have nonetheless been four eras in which the Chinese have demonstrated considerable interest and even built the beginnings of scholarship concerned with things Japanese: the late Ming (more specifically the Jiajing 嘉靖 and Wanli 萬曆 reigns), the decade from the first Sino-Japanese War (1894–1895) through the Russo-Japanese War (1904–1905), the 1930s and first half of the 1940s (from the Manchurian Incident of 1931 through the conclusion of World War II), and the present period (roughly the past 30 years).[1] With the exception of the last of these, in each of the first three eras, it was war that elicited a heightened Chinese interest in Japan—even the final contemporary period (as with the others) might be understood as Chinese interest aroused by a desire to know a potential enemy.

---

1 This view is shared with Wu Anlong 武安隆 and Xiong Dayun 熊達雲, *Chūgokujin no Nihon kenkyū shi* 中国人の日本研究史 [History of Chinese Japanology] (Tokyo: Rokkō shuppan, 1989), pp. 14–16; Watanabe Mitsuo 渡辺三男, "Chūgoku kobunken ni mieru Nihongo: *Kakurin gyokuro* to *Sho shi kaiyō* ni tsuite 中國古文獻に見える日本語：鶴林玉露と書史會要について" [Japan as seen in old Chinese documents: The *Helin yulu* and the *Shu shi huiyao*], *Komazawa daigaku kenkyū kiyō* 駒澤大学研究紀要 [Bulletin of studies from Komazawa University] 15 (March 1957), pp. 155–156. Wang Yizhong cites a total of 81 Chinese works from the Ming period about Japan, and there were certainly many more; see Wang Yizhong 王以中, "Mingdai haifang tuji lu 明代海防圖籍錄" [Texts on coastal defence and maps from the Ming period], *Qinghua zhoukan* 清華週刊 [Qinghua weekly] 37, no. 9–10 (May 1932), pp. 141–162.

The essay that follows emerges from the first of these periods, the least well studied anywhere.[2] After a brief discussion of pre-Ming traces of Japanese writings in Chinese texts, I focus on a corpus of medieval Japanese poems translated, annotated, and explicated in Chinese in an utterly magnificent edition. Sadly, we know next to nothing about how this work was done or much of the specific background.

Prior to the late Ming, there were any number of efforts over the centuries in which Chinese authors attempted to represent Japanese proper nouns in particular—in fact, such efforts predate the transmission of any written language to Japan. Only in the Ming, though, did Chinese writers try to come to terms with aspects of the Japanese language that distinguished it from Chinese; in other words, to see Japanese as a significant entity in its own right and not just a kind of crippled Chinese. For example, the existence of the *kana* syllabaries were not unknown before the Ming, but it was only in the late Ming that Chinese scholars began to study them seriously, to explain Japanese grammar by parsing the structure of the Japanese sentence, and preparing long lists of words with Chinese pronunciation guides.

All too often taken as a transparent vessel, language reflects, contains, and indeed transports the social, political, and cultural contexts of its speakers and writers. Prior to the twentieth century, virtually all educated Japanese, Koreans, Vietnamese, and others inhabiting what I have called the Sinosphere[3] looked to China for moral, political, and cultural leadership, and they understood that mastery of the written Chinese language was an essential part of the package of becoming a civilized people. Knowing Chinese thus became a definitional index to the level of one's erudition, and given the close linkage between knowledge and morality in Sinic culture, knowledge of Chinese thus became a basic part

2 See Joshua A. Fogel, "Chinese Understanding of the Japanese Language from Ming to Qing," in *Sagacious Monks and Bloodthirsty Warriors: Chinese Views of Japan in the Ming-Qing Period*, ed. Joshua A. Fogel (Norwalk: EastBridge, 2002), pp. 63–87.

3 See Joshua A. Fogel, *Articulating the Sinosphere: Sino-Japanese Relations in Space and Time* (Cambridge, MA: Harvard University Press, 2009), pp. 4–5.

of one's self-cultivation and broader elite social cohesion.

Chinese, however, rarely made the effort to learn a foreign language prior to the tail end of the Qing empire, and those who did were often seen as decidedly odd. For example, when the Qing scholar Weng Guangping 翁廣平 (1760–1843) introduced his study of Japan and the Japanese, the *Wuqi jing bu* 吾妻鏡補 (Commentary on the *Azuma kagami*), he virtually apologized for being a man who "by nature enjoys strange books."[4] The obvious exceptions are marked by the conquest dynasties of Yuan and Qing, at which time a fair number of Chinese perforce learned Mongolian and Manchu, respectively. In these instances, power politics dictated language acquisition, and refusal to do so might be seen as a form of proto-nationalism. Otherwise, there was simply little or no cultural capital to be gained by Chinese attempting to acquire a foreign language—any foreign language—while there was vast cultural capital associated with other East Asians acquiring Chinese. To the extent that they evinced any interest in Japan at all, elite Chinese would have seen it solely as a function of how well they judged the efforts of Japanese scholars and writers to compose Chinese poetry and prose, write commentaries on the Confucian classics, and in these ways contribute to a larger Sinic cultural endeavour.

As the foregoing should readily indicate, language was inextricably bound up with culture in the minds of East Asians, never simply a linguistic or political concern. This is, of course, still true in many parts of the world today. That the Chinese felt self-sufficient with literary Chinese was, to be sure, something they shared with other East Asian elites, and it is a quality that set each apart from his fellow nationals of the lower classes. Because of a shared sense of culture within East Asia, Chinese and Japanese (and Korean and Vietnamese) scholars might have

4 Cited in Wang Baoping 王寶平, "*Wuqi jing bu* zhuzhe Weng Guangping kao 吾妻鏡補注者翁廣平考" [A study of Weng Guangping, author of the *Wuqi jing bu*], in *Zhong-Ri wenhua luncong—1996* 中日文化論叢—1996 [Essays in Sino-Japanese culture—1996], ed. Hangzhou daxue Riben wenhua yanjiusuo 杭州大學日本文化研究所 and Kanagawa daigaku jinbungaku kenkyūjo 神奈川大學人文學研究所 (Hangzhou: Hangzhou daxue chubanshe, 1996), pp. 156–157.

felt a stronger cultural and hence personal attraction to one another and the civilization all were creating together than they would have to peasants in their home countries.

The first reference to a Japanese word in a Chinese text appears in the section on the "people of *Wa*" (*Woren* 倭人), the ancient name for "Japan," in the *Wei zhi* 魏志 (Chronicle of [the kingdom of] Wei) by Chen Shou 陳壽 (233–297). The *Han shu* 漢書 (History of the [Former] Han) and the *Hou Han shu* 後漢書 (History of the Later Han) both have extremely brief mentions of "*Wa*/*Wo*," but it is not until the *Wei zhi* that we get an extended treatment. The famous passage there contains numerous Japanese proper nouns: toponyms, official titles, a handful of personal names such as that of the female sovereign Himiko 卑彌呼, and a whole host of state or country names within what are now the islands of Japan.[5] These are not treated in any linguistic fashion but simply as renderings of foreign words. Given the fact that the *Wei zhi* was composed at a time prior to the use of Chinese characters (to say nothing of any native written language) in Japan, this transcription of these early Japanese words in Chinese characters marks the first time that any Japanese words were ever written down—at least as far as we know from the evidence before us now.

Later dynastic histories that contain treatises on either "*Wo*" or "*Woren*" frequently include similar Chinese-character transcriptions for Japanese

5 The literature on this section from the *Wei zhi* is one of the most commented upon pieces of writing in all of Japanese scholarship, comprising hundreds of books and far more articles. There are even books about all the books and articles within this scholarly literature. For annotated translations, see Ishihara Michihiro 石原道広, *Yakuchū Chūgoku seishi Nihon den* 訳註中国正史日本伝 [Treatises on Japan from the Chinese dynastic histories, translated and annotated] (Tokyo: Kokusho kankōkai, 1975), pp. 14, 18, 22; Wang Xiangrong 汪向榮 and Xia Yingyuan 夏應元, *Zhong-Ri guanxi shiliao huibian* 中日關係史料匯編 [Collection of historical materials on Sino-Japanese relations] (Beijing: Zhonghua shuju, 1984), pp. 8–13, 18–21. See also the early English translation in Ryusaku Tsunoda and L. Carrington Goodrich, *Japan in the Chinese Dynastic Histories* (Pasadena: P. D. and Ione Perkins, 1951), pp. 14, 16, 20; and more recently in J. Edward Kidder, *Himiko and Japan's Elusive Chiefdom of Yamatai: Archaeology, History, and Mythology* (Honolulu: University of Hawai'i Press, 2007).

proper nouns. These would include the listing of the "five kings" of *Wa* and their embassies to various Chinese courts, given in the entry on *Wo*/*Wa* in the *Song shu* 宋書 (History of the Liu-Song dynasty). In each case, the "Japanese" king was requesting investiture within the ritual system surrounding the Chinese court. The entry on *Wo* in the *Sui shu* 隋書 (History of the Sui dynasty) includes the names of the kings of *Wa* and various Japanese place names as well.[6]

Thus far, we have looked solely at the standard, official history or *zhengshi* 正史. Certain private collections of poetry and prose also include, on occasion, reference to something Japanese or cite Japanese terms in Chinese-graph renderings. The Chinese monk Yichu 義楚 (Mingjiao Dashi 明教大師) from the Five Dynasties era (907–960) incorporated a section on "States, settlements, prefecture, and towns" in his *Shishi liutie* 釋氏六帖 (Six models of Buddhism). In it he included a subsection on Japan, which he certainly never visited, that carries the following note about Mount Fuji: "Over 1,000 *li* to the northeast is a mountain by the name of Fuji.... A single flower soaring on high, its summit is covered in mist."[7] There are many similar notes in middle-period and early modern Chinese literature, including as many as several hundred such in Chinese poetry of the Tang period (618–907), and interestingly this is not the first mention of a Japanese mountain in a Chinese text. The entry on "Japan"

6 Wang Xiangrong and Xia Yingyuan, *Zhong-Ri guanxi shiliao huibian*, pp. 31–32, 44–45; Ishihara Michihiro, *Yakuchū Chūgoku seishi Nihon den*, pp. 25–26, 49, 50; Tsunoda and Goodrich, *Japan in the Chinese Dynastic Histories*, pp. 29–30, 40. See also Watanabe Mitsuo, "*Zuisho* Wakokuden no Nihongo hitei 隋書倭国伝の日本語比定" [Identifying Japanese words in the "Treatise on Japan" in the *Sui shu*], *Komazawa kokubun* 駒沢国文 5 (October 1966), pp. 1–8.

7 Yichu 義楚, *Shishi liutie* 釋氏六帖 [Six models of Buddhism], in vol. 5 of *Xiandai Foxue daxi* 現代佛學大系 [Modern compendium on Buddhism] (Taibei: Mile chubanshe, 1982), p. 433. It is not known precisely but believed that, because he had not travelled to Japan himself, Yichu gained this information from a Japanese monk, Kanpo 寛輔 (Kōjun Daishi 弘順大師) who travelled to China in 958; see Wang Xiangrong, "Guanyu *Riben kao* 關於《日本考》" [On the *Riben kao*], in *Zhong-Ri guanxi shi wenxian lunkao* 中日關係史文獻論考 [Essays on documents in the history of Sino-Japanese relations] (Beijing: Yuelu shushe, 1985), p. 242.

in the *Sui shu* of several centuries earlier refers to Mount Aso 阿蘇山, which occasionally still appears in the news as an active volcano.[8]

All of the above notwithstanding, prior to the Song era we can point to no effort on the part of the Chinese to say anything about the Japanese language itself. Luo Dajing 羅大經 (Jinglun 景綸, *jinshi* 進士 or metropolitan graduate of 1226), a Southern Song scholar and poet from Luling 廬陵 (in what is now Jiangxi Province), notes in his important diary, *Helin yulu* 鶴林玉露 (The glittering dew drops of Helin), of a meeting he had as a young man in Zhonglu 鐘陸, Zhejiang Province, with a visiting Japanese monk called Ankaku 安覺 (1160–1242). Ankaku, it turns out, was a Rinzai Zen 臨濟禪 (Linji Chan) monk who came from the Kōshōji 香正寺 in Chikuzen 筑前 domain and was originally known as Shikijō Ryōyū 色定良祐. He was said to be a brilliant young man who, reportedly, had mastered the entire massive Buddhist canon by the age of 20; he then travelled to China shortly after the year 1200 and stayed there for more than 10 years. He spent his time in China memorizing the Buddhist texts that comprise the canon and returned to Japan in 1214.[9]

8 Ishihara Michihiro, "Chūgoku ni okeru Nihon kan no tanshoteki keitai: Zuidai izen no Nihon kan 中國における日本觀の端緒的形態：隋代以前の日本觀" [The emergence of views of Japan in China: Views of Japan before the Sui era], *Ibaraki daigaku bunrigakubu kiyō (jinbun kagaku)* 茨城大学文理学部紀要（人文科学）[Bulletin of the Liberal Arts and Sciences Department of Ibaraki University, Humanities Division] 1 (March 1951), p. 203; Ishihara Michihiro, "Nichi-Min tsūkō bōeki o meguru Nihon kan: Mindai no Nihon kan (ni) 日明通交貿易をめぐる日本觀：明代の日本觀（二）" [Views of Japan surrounding Japanese-Ming communications and trade: Views of Japan in the Ming era, part 2], *Ibaraki daigaku bunrigakubu kiyō (jinbun kagaku)* 5 (March 1955), p. 20.

9 Luo Dajing 羅大經, *Helin yulu* 鶴林玉露 [The glittering dew drops of Helin], *juan* 16, pp. 5b–6a (repr., Shanghai: Shanghai shudian chubanshe, 1990); Ishihara Michihiro, "Chūgoku ni okeru rinkōteki Nihon kan no tenkai: Tō, Godai, Sō jidai no Nihon kan 中國における隣好的日本觀の展開：唐・五代・宋時代の日本觀" [The development of a friendly view of Japan in China: Views of Japan in the Tang, Five Dynasties, and Song periods], *Ibaraki daigaku bunrigakubu kiyō (jinbun kagaku)* 2 (Feburary 1952), pp. 53–54; Watanabe Mitsuo, "Chūgoku kobunken ni mieru Nihongo," p. 157, citing works such as the *Nihon Bukkyō jinmei jisho* 日本佛教人名辭書 [Biographical dictionary of Japanese Buddhism] and the *Honchō kōsō den* 本朝高僧傳 [Biographies

Luo briefly recounts Ankaku's career to date and describes something of the Japanese language that Ankaku taught him. He notes 20 Chinese terms and their Japanese translations which are given in Chinese-character transcriptions (see Figure 1–1).

日本國僧
予少年時於鍾陵(原本作陵從諸本改)邂逅日本國一僧名安覺自言離其國
已十年欲盡記一部藏經乃歸念誦甚苦不舍晝夜每有遺忘則
叩頭佛前祈佛陰相是時已記藏經一半矣夷狄之人異教之徒
其立志堅苦不退轉至於如此朱文公云今世學者讀書尋行數
墨備禮應數六經語孟不曾全記得三五板如此而望有成亦已
難矣其視此僧殆有愧色僧言其國稱其國王曰天人國王安撫
曰牧隊通判曰在國司秀才曰殿羅罷僧曰黃榜硯曰松蘇利必
筆曰分直墨曰蘇彌頭曰加是羅手曰提眼曰媚口曰窟底耳曰
弭弭面曰皮部心曰毋兒脚曰又兒雨曰下米風曰客安之鹽曰
洗和酒曰沙嬉(以上僧言其國等九十六字諸本無)

Figure 1–1

of eminent monks of our era]; Zhang Yaqiu 張雅秋, "Cong *Helin yulu* zhong de yize shiliao kan Songdai Zhong-Ri wenhua jiaoliu 從《鶴林玉露》中的一則史料看宋代中日文化交流" [Song-era Sino-Japanese relations as seen from the historical material in the *Helin yulu*], in *Zhong-Ri wenhua luncong—1996*, pp. 205–206. I have followed this last essay by Zhang Yaqiu (p. 208) for Ankaku dates, although Watanabe offers slightly different ones. Wang Yong 王勇 refers to pieces of this sort about Japan in the Tang, Five Dynasties, and Song eras as the "prehistory of Chinese Japanology" in his essay, "Chūgoku ni okeru Nihon kenkyū no zenshi 中国に於ける日本研究の前史" [The prehistory of Japanese studies in China], in *Zhong-Ri wenhua luncong—1991* 中日文化論叢—1991 [Essays in Sino-Japanese culture—1991], ed. Hangzhou daxue Riben wenhua yanjiusuo and Kanagawa daigaku jinbungaku kenkyūjo (Hangzhou: Hangzhou daxue chubanshe, 1991), pp. 132–146.

The first three are political terms for which Ankaku gave not transcriptions but actual Japanese translations (or, at least, Japanese equivalents), and the fourth term is a mixture of direct translation and Chinese graphs used to render Japanese morphemes. The remaining 16 are single-character terms given in Chinese which are followed by Japanese pronunciations approximated by Chinese characters. This process is known among Japanese linguists as *kan'yaku* 漢譯 (*hanyi*) or *on'yaku* 音譯 (*yinyi*). For example, in the image above, the Chinese term *yu* 雨 (rain) is followed by two graphs (in contemporary Mandarin pronunciation) which read *xiami* 下米, an approximation for Japanese *ame* (rain); Chinese *tou* 頭 (head) is followed by *jiashiluo* 加是羅 which approximates the Japanese term for head, *kashira*.[10]

In all such cases, one must not forget that we are comparing contemporary pronunciations of Chinese and Japanese terms. Chinese and Japanese topolects and chronolects have undoubtedly changed dramatically over the eight centuries since this exchange took place, and this is the intellectual juncture at which trained linguists can make a great contribution. Nonetheless, even the ear of an untrained linguist can easily detect the equivalencies in Luo's list. That said, Luo's enumeration was the only one of its kind prior to the Ming era.

It would not be until the Ming period that the two Japanese *kana* syllabary alphabets were introduced to Chinese readers, and Ming-era texts about Japan would expand Luo Dajing's word list many times over. We have no extant Chinese-language texts about Japan or the Japanese language for the Yuan period, but the Mongol conquest certainly would have exposed elite Chinese, especially those who served in its government, to the Mongolian language. The Mongols themselves had only acquired a

10 Luo Dajing, *Helin yulu*, *juan* 16, pp. 5b–6a. For a more detailed and specialized study of just one of the terms in this text, see Asayama Shin'ya 朝山信彌, "Kakurin gyokuro no 'ōbō' nado ni tsuite 鶴林玉露の黃榜などについて" [On the expression "huangbang" in the *Helin yulu* and other matters], *Kokugo kokubun* 國語國文 [Language and literature] 7, no. 12 (December 1937), pp. 116–120; see also Arisaka Hideyo 有坂秀世, "Jōdai ni okeru sagyō no tōon 上代に於けるサ行頭音" [Initials in the *sa*-line in antiquity], *Kokugo to kokubungaku* 國語と國文學 [Studies in Japanese language and literature] 13 (January 1936), p. 96.

written language, based on the Uighur script, a few decades prior to their conquest of the Song. At its height, the Mongol empire stretched from the Pacific coastline all the way to the Middle East, terrain covering countless ethnic groups, civilizations, and languages.

Indeed, the early Ming author, Tao Zongyi 陶宗儀 (1329–1410), who would first introduce the *hiragana* syllabary into China, noted that its graphs were "like Mongolian."[11] He probably meant that, unlike Chinese characters, they were fairly simple and squiggly. His work was entitled *Shu shi huiyao* 書史會要 (Essentials in the history of calligraphy) and it bears an author's preface dated 1376, only eight years after the Ming expulsion of the Mongols from China. Tao lived in Huangyan 黄岩, Zhejiang Province from his birth through the early years of the Ming. He was a gifted scholar especially in the field of calligraphic studies; although he passed the *jinshi* examinations, he never served in office, turned down several offers of posts, and devoted himself to teaching.

The *Shu shi huiyao* runs to nine fascicles, presenting a history of calligraphic styles from antiquity through the Yuan era. One portion of the eighth fascicle is interestingly concerned with the styles of calligraphy of "foreign lands" (*waiyu* 外域)—including Sanskrit, Uighur, Arabic, and Japanese. Following a short explanation of Japanese calligraphy, Tao explains with great clarity the *hiragana* syllabaries in the *i-ro-ha* order (comparable to A-B-C in languages written with the Roman alphabet). Beneath each *kana* graph is a Chinese character approximating the Japanese pronunciation of that graph; the *sa*, *ta*, and *ha* rows of the Japanese syllabary alphabet are each accorded two pronunciations, although the reason is not explicitly provided.[12]

---

11 Tao Zongyi 陶宗儀, *Shu shi huiyao* 書史會要 [Essentials in the history of calligraphy] (n.p.: 1376).

12 Tao Zongyi, *Shu shi huiyao*; Watanabe Mitsuo, "Chūgoku kobunken," pp. 159–162; Watanabe Mitsuo, "Minjin ni yoru Nihon gobun rikai no keika 明人による日本語文理解の経過" [How Chinese of the Ming era came to understand the Japanese language], *Tsurumi joshi tanki daigaku kiyō* 鶴見女子短期大学紀要 [Bulletin of Tsurumi Junior College] 1 (March 1962), p. 100; Hamada Atsushi 濱田敦, "Kokugo o kisai seru Mindai Shina bunken 國語を記載せる明代支那文獻" [Chinese

There were similar works, by way of comparison, prepared by Koreans in which the Japanese syllabaries were paired with their approximate *han'gŭl* equivalents as pronunciation guides. The earliest such Korean text is the *Yongbi ŏch'ŏng ka* 龍飛御天歌 (Songs of flying dragons) by Kwŏn Che 權踶 (1387–1445), Chŏng In-ji 鄭麟趾 (1396–1478), and others. It appeared in 1445, one year prior to the celebrated proclamation announcing the invention of *han'gŭl*, making it the earliest known text to make use of the Korean alphabet as well. The most famous early text in this genre introducing Japanese syllabaries, published a few decades after the invention of *han'gŭl*, was the *Irop'a* 伊路波 (I-ro-ha) of 1492.[13]

For his part, Tao then provides a listing of 10 words with Japanese pronunciations given in *kana*. He claims that he gained all of this knowledge of the Japanese language from a Japanese Buddhist monk by the name of Kokkin Taiyō 克金大用 who was then in China, although

---

documents of the Ming dynasty which record Japanese terms], *Kokugo kokubun* 10, no. 7 (July 1940), pp. 10–11; Ogawa Tamaki 小川環樹, "*Sho shi kaiyō* ni mitaru 'iroha' no Kanji taion ni tsuite 書史會要に見たるいろはの漢字對音について" [On the corresponding Kanji phonemes for "*i-ro-ha*" as seen in the *Shu shi huiyao*], *Kokugo kokubun* 16, no. 5 (September 1947), pp. 311–320; Arisaka Hideyo, "*Sho shi kaiyō* no 'iroha' no onchū ni tsuite 書史会要の「いろは」の音註について" [On the phonetic transcription of the Japanese syllabary alphabet in the *Shu shi huiyao*], *Gengo kenkyū* 言語研究 [Language studies] 16 (August 1950), pp. 1–13. Hamada Atsushi ("Kokugo o kisai seru," p. 11) has demonstrated that these pairs represent voiced/unvoiced pairs in the Wenzhou dialect which would be included in the Wu dialect group in which Tao's native speech would also have fallen. On the Japanese side, Japanese linguists trying to reconstruct the pronunciation of *kana* in the medieval period have used Tao's work to this end; see, for example, Hashimoto Shinkichi 橋本進吉, "Hagyō shiin no hensen ni tsuite 波行子音の變遷について" [On changes in the consonants in the *ha*-line], in *Kokugo on'in no kenkyū* 國語音韻の研究 [Studies in Japanese phonetics] (Tokyo: Iwanami shoten, 1950), pp. 33–35.

13 See Ōtomo Shin'ichi 大友信一, *Muromachi jidai no kokugo onsei no kenkyū: Chūgoku shiryō ni yoru* 室町時代の国語音声の研究：中国資料による [Studies in Japanese phonetics of the Muromachi period, based on Chinese materials] (Tokyo: Shibundō, 1963), pp. 40–41; Kamei Takashi 亀井孝, Ōfuji Tokihiko 大藤時彦, and Yamada Toshio 山田俊雄, *Nihongo no rekishi 4: Utsuriyuku kodaigo* 日本語の歴史、4：移りゆく古代語 [The history of Japanese, vol. 4: The changing ancient language] (Tokyo: Heibonsha, 1976), p. 406.

no other sources presently known provide any information about such a person. Buddhist monks, as we saw in the case of Ankaku, continue to play a seminal role in this cultural transmission between Japan and China.

Tao's presentation of the elements of the Japanese syllabary alphabet is done with extremely assiduousness to the sound system of both tongues. Coming from southeastern Zhejiang—between Ningbo and Wenzhou—his own dialect would have fallen within the Wu dialect grouping, and he wrote the *Shu shi huiyao* while living in the Songjiang 松江 region, also within the Wu dialect area. Thus, while he would most likely have also been a speaker of the standard capital Mandarin of his day, Tao's native dialect and hence his readings for the Chinese-character renderings of the Japanese syllabaries do in fact reflect Wu pronunciations.[14] With no information about his Japanese informant, we cannot judge anything about what dialect he might have brought to the informed explanation of *kana*.

There is no indication in Tao's work that Japan had another, comparable syllabary alphabet in addition to *hiragana*, and only roughly 180 years later would the *katakana* syllabary alphabet be introduced to Chinese readers. We are now much later in the Ming period, and concern with the real Japan (or what many took to be "Japan") was high in many Chinese minds because of the pirate raids along the southeast Chinese coastline. These were the actions of the *Wakō* 倭寇 (*Wokou*) or "Japanese" pirate attacks that devastated many communities in the region. In 1556 Yang Yi 楊宜, governor of Zhejiang, ordered Zheng Shungong 鄭舜功 (1522–1566?, originally from Xin'an 新安, Guangdong) to travel to Japan and appeal to the authorities there to put a halt to pirate activities. Soon after arriving, Zheng was arrested in Bungo 豊後 domain on the island of Kyushu by Ōtomo Yoshishige 大友義鎮 (Sōrin 宗麟, 1530–1587) and held there—not imprisoned though held under a form of mild house arrest—for as long as six or seven months. He would remain in Japan for over a year, during which time he had considerable experience interacting with the Japanese people and observing their ways and habits; he returned to China in 1557

14 Ōtomo Shin'ichi, *Muromachi jidai no kokugo*, pp. 64–66.

in the company of a monk by the name of Tokuyō Seiju 德陽清授, another Rinzai Zen sect follower, this time from the great Daitokuji 大德寺 temple complex.[15] Upon his return to China, Zheng wrote up his observations in a work of encyclopedic proportions under the title *Riben yijian* 日本一鑑 (A mirror on Japan) in 16 fascicles.

Among many other things, the *katakana* syllabaries were introduced in the *Riben yijian*, and the method used by Zheng closely followed that used by Tao for *hiragana*. Aside from a small number of what appear to be transcriptional errors, Zheng not only presented *katakana* in a clear manner for literate Chinese, but he also clearly attempted to use characters that suggested the origins of the *kana* graph in question. He referred to them a "*Huawen Wozi*" 華文倭字 (literally, Chinese writing, Japanese graphs). After presenting *katakana*, he similarly arranged the *hiragana* syllabaries which he called "*Wozi Wo*" 倭字倭 (he probably meant "*Wozi Woyin*" 倭字倭音 or, literally, Japanese characters and Japanese pronunciation).[16] It is unclear if he actually understood the relationship

15 Ōtomo Shin'ichi, *Muromachi jidai* (pp. 415–417), gives slightly different dates, and he notes as well that Tokuyō Seiju spent time at the Zhiping 治平 Temple in Maozhou, Sichuan—altogether four years in China.

16 See Zheng Shungong 鄭舜功, *Riben yijian* 日本一鑑 [A mirror on Japan], *juan* 4–5 (n.p.: Beijing reprint of Wendiange 文殿閣 text, 1939). See also Watanabe Mitsuo, "Minjin ni yoru Nihon gobun rikai no keika," pp. 101, 106; Tomioka Kenzō 富岡謙藏, "*Nihon ikkan* kaidai 日本一鑑解題" [An introduction to the *Riben yijian*], *Geibun* 藝文 [Art and literature] 5, no. 9 (September 1914), pp. 257–258; Akiyama Kenzō 秋山謙藏, *Nis-Shi kōshō shi kenkyū* 日支交渉史研究 [Studies in the history of Sino-Japanese interactions] (Tokyo: Iwanami shoten, 1941), pp. 604, 605, 607; Ishihara Michihiro, "Mindai Nihon kan no ichi sokumen 明代日本観の一側面" [One perspective on Japan in the Ming era], *Ibaraki daigaku bungakubu kiyō (bungakka ronshū)* 茨城大学文学部紀要（文学科論集）[Bulletin of the Faculty of Letters of Ibaraki University, essays from the Literature Division] 1 (January 1968), pp. 9, 14, 15; Watanabe Mitsuo, "Minmatsu no Nihon shōkaisho: *Nihon ikkan* ni tsuite 明末の日本紹介書：日本一鑑について" [An introductory text on Japan from the late Ming: *Riben yijian*], *Komazawa daigaku kenkyū kiyō* 13 (March 1955), pp. 144–169; Ōtomo Shin'ichi, *Muromachi jidai*, p. 471; Wang Xiangrong, "Cong *Jinglüe fuguo yaobian* kan renchen kang-Wo zhanshi 從《經略復國要編》看壬辰抗倭戰事" [The anti-"Japanese" war of 1592 as seen from the *Jinglüe fuguo yaobian*], in his *Zhong-Ri guanxi shi wenxian lunkao*, pp. 264–288.

between the two sets of syllabaries, for these designations would possibly indicate otherwise. As noted earlier, the late-Ming texts about Japan contained lengthy lists of Japanese words with Chinese-character pronunciations appended, and the *Riben yijian* has the longest of them all: 3,399 words in total. This number would not be surpassed until the modern compilation of bilingual dictionaries.

The inclusion of such lengthy word lists, an innovation of the late-Ming period, specifically the Jiajing (1522–1566) and Wanli (1572–1629) reigns, became a standard feature of works purporting to explain things Japanese in China. As we shall shortly see, several of these texts also offered highly inventive ways of explaining elements of Japanese grammar as well. They were all compiled as a consequence of the potential and real threat posed by military intrusions from "Japanese" pirates, many not most of whom, we now know, were Chinese operating out of bases in Japan and by the armies of Hideyoshi 秀吉 (1536/7–1598) at the end of the seventeenth century.

There were as well government efforts in this area going back to the early Ming. To facilitate contacts with foreign states bringing tribute to the Ming court, an Interpreters' Institute (Huitong guan 會通館) was charged by the court with preparing word lists for the languages spoken by the people who comprised these foreign embassies. The institution was founded in the Yuan dynasty to deal with the many foreign emissaries, provide them with housing, proper clothing, and transport while in the capital, and supervise their movements there. These lists are known as a group as *Huayi yiyu* 華夷譯語 (Sino-foreign vocabularies). The earliest such official list was compiled on orders from Ming Taizu 明太祖 (Zhu Yuanzhang 朱元璋, 1328–1398), founder of the dynasty; it was a Sino-Mongolian list prepared by Qoninči (fl. 1376–1394), a Mongol also known by the Chinese name Huo Yuanjie 火原潔, and Mašāīh Muhammed (Mashayihei Mahama 馬沙亦黑馬哈瑪), begun in 1382 and completed six years later. Then, in 1407 the Translators' Institute (Siyi guan 四夷館) was founded with the express purposes of translating documents that came to court in foreign languages and training future translators.

Glossaries of this sort for Japanese, referred to generally as *Riben jiyu* 日本寄語 (Japanese vocabularies), date to the early fifteenth century. Six of them remain extant, each proving pronunciation guides for roughly 520–560 terms. For example, one list comprised of 521 terms breaks down into the following categories: astronomy (42), geography (43), times of the year and seasons (37), flora (52), fauna (45), palaces and mansions (14), implements (68), people (47), personal affairs (51), the human body (20), clothing (20), foods (30), precious items (19), literature and history (10), voice and countenance (9), numbers (24), directions (11), and common usage terms (20). In general, these groupings resemble those of later texts, but undoubtedly because their primary purpose was state-to-state communication, they tend more to emphasize official discourse.[17]

---

17 Michele Ruggieri and Matteo Ricci, *Dicionário Português-Chinês*, ed. John W. Witek, S. J. (Lisbon: Biblioteca Nacional; Portugal: Instituto Português do Oriente; San Francisco: Ricci Institute for Chinese-Western Cultural History, University of San Francisco, 2001), p. 180; Kyōto daigaku bungakubu 京都大学文学部 [Faculty of Letters, Kyoto University], ed., *Sanshū Nihon yakugo* 纂輯日本訳語 [Compiled Japanese vocabularies] (Kyoto: Kyōto daigaku kokubungakkai, 1968), pp. 215, 217–229; Watanabe Mitsuo, "Minjin ni yoru Nihon gobun rikai no keika," pp. 104–105; Hamada Atsushi, "Nihon kigo kaidoku shian 日本寄語解讀試安" [A plan for explicating the Japanese translation terms], *Jinbun kenkyū* 人文研究 [Studies in the humanities] 2, no. 1 (January 1951), pp. 19–59; Asai Keirin 淺井惠倫, "Kōhon Nihon yakugo 校本日本譯語" [Japanese terms in translation, annotated], in *Andō kyōju kanreki shukuga kinen ronbunshū* 安藤教授還暦祝賀記念論文集 [Essays in honour of the sixtieth birthday of Professor Andō] (Tokyo: San'yōdō, 1950), pp. 1–56; Ishihara Michihiro, "Mindai ni okeru Shinajin no Nihon kenkyū 明代における支那人の日本研究" [Studies of Japan by Chinese on the Ming period], in *Tō-A shi zakkō* 東亞史襍攷 [Essays on East Asian history] (Tokyo: Seikatsusha, 1944), pp. 211–214; Ōtomo Shin'ichi, "*Nihonkan yakugo* no seiritsu, kokugo on'in shiryō to shite no kachi 「日本館訳語」の成立、国語音韻資料としての価値" [The formation of the *Ribenguan yiyu*, its value as material on Japanese phonetics], *Kokugogaku* 国語学 [Studies in the Japanese language] 43 (March 1961), pp. 31–42; Watanabe Mitsuo, "Ka-i yakugo oyobi *Nihonkan yakugo* ni tsuite 華夷訳語および日本館訳語について" [Sino-foreign vocabularies and the *Ribenguan yiyu*], *Komazawa daigaku kenkyū kiyō* 18 (March 1960), pp. 120–135; Watanabe Mitsuo, "Ka-i yakugo oyobi *Nihonkan yakugo* ni tsuite (shōzen) 華夷訳語および日本館訳語について（承前）" [Sino-foreign vocabularies

These official vocabulary lists were not known or available beyond the government's precincts which severely limited their influence. The first text composed privately—not for official use—which included a word list of the sort we have been discussing was also inspired by the threat of pirate activity: *Riben kao lüe* 日本考略 (Brief study of Japan) by Xue Jun 薛俊.[18] As its title indicates, this work was only one fascicle in length, but it is generally thought to be the first specialized text about Japan by a Chinese, and it is the first to have the term "Riben" 日本 (Japan) in its title. It appeared in 1523, the second year of the Jiajing reign, and would influence all subsequent Ming-era works on Japan. Although he would later hold higher education posts as assistant instructor (*xundao* 訓導) in Changzhou

and the *Ribenguan yiyu*, continued], *Komazawa daigaku kenkyū kiyō* 19 (March 1961), pp. 15–31; and the extremely technical, detailed essay by Nakano Miyoko 中野美代子, "Nihon kigo ni yoru 16 seiki Teikai onkei no suitei, oyobi Muromachi makki kokugo on ni kansuru jakkan no mondai 日本寄語による16世紀定海音系の推定、および室町末期國語音に關する若干の問題" [Reconstructing Dinghai dialect of the sixteenth century on the basis of Japanese translation terms, and various issues concerning the pronunciation of Japanese in the late-Muromachi period], *Tōhōgaku* 東方學 [East Asian studies] 28 (July 1964), pp. 100–120. We have one entire Japanese vocabulary meticulously analyzed word for word in Ōtomo Shin'ichi and Kimura Akira 木村晟, *Nihonkan yakugo, honbun to sakuin* 日本館訳語、本文と索引 [The *Ribenguan yiyu*, text and index] (Tokyo: Rakubunsha, 1968). On the Siyi guan in English, see Norman Wild, "Materials for the Study of the Ssû I Kuan (Bureau of Translation)," *Bulletin of the School of Oriental and African Studies* 11 (1943–1946), pp. 617–640. For a work in English on the *Riben jiyu*, see the much older essay by Joseph Edkins, "A Chinese and Japanese Vocabulary of the Fifteenth Century," *Transactions of the Asiatic Society of Japan* 10 (1882), pp. 1–14; and the rejoinder by Ernest Satow, "Notes on Dr. Edkins' Paper, 'A Chinese and Japanese Vocabulary of the Fifteenth Century,'" *Transactions of the Asiatic Society of Japan* 10 (1882), pp. 15–38. The establishment of a training institute for interpreters and translators underwent a similar process in Korea. In 1276 the T'ongmun'gwan 通文館 [Translators' institute] was opened to train experts in spoken and written Chinese only; when the Yi dynasty was founded in 1392, it was replaced by the Sayŏgwŏn 司譯院 [Interpreters' institute], and in about 1414 a Waehakch'ŏng 倭學廳 [Japanese studies office] was set up to train Japanese-language interpreters and translators. See Ōtomo Shin'ichi, *Muromachi jidai*, pp. 39–40, citing the *Sejong sillok* 世宗實錄 [Veritable records of King Sejong]. Among the many texts used to train experts in Japanese was the *Irop'a* mentioned earlier.

18 Also sometimes referred to as *Ribenguo kao lüe* 日本國考略.

and instructor (*jiaoyu* 教諭) in Fuliang, Xue Jun was still a student in the Dinghai county school when the Dinghai District Magistrate, Zheng Yuqing 鄭余慶 ordered him to compose a work of some sort that brought together the known information about Japan and shed light on that land and its people, as well as to offer any ideas he might have to the military on how best to deal with the pirates assailing the Chinese coast. Xue notes early in his work that there had been fighting and consequent destruction earlier in 1523 in Ningbo between men under the command of the Ōuchi 大内 envoy, Kendō Sōsetsu 謙道宗設, and the Hosokawa 細川 envoys, Rankō Zuisa 鸞岡端佐 and Song Suqing 宋素卿 (d.1525), but it had not reached as far as Dinghai. Xue never actually visited Japan, meaning that his work reflects no direct knowledge of circumstances there.[19]

The late Professor Wang Xiangrong (1920–2006), who studied the *Riben kao lüe* and its sources in depth, argues that it would not have been a particularly significant work had it not been China's first such specialized text on Japan. Its most important innovation was the inclusion of a listing

19 Wang Xiangrong, "Zhongguo diyibu yanjiu Riben de zhuanzhu: *Riben kao lüe* 中國第一部研究日本的專著：《日本考略》" [China's first specialized study of Japan, the *Riben kao lüe*], in *Zhong-Ri guanxi shi wenxian lunkao*, pp. 222–223, 224, 230; Kyōto daigaku bungakubu kokugogaku kokubungaku kenkyūshitsu 京都大学文学部国語学国文学研究室 [Departments of Japanese Language and Japanese Literature, Faculty of Letters, Kyoto University], comp. and ed., *Nihon kigo no kenkyū* 日本寄語の研究 [Studies of Japanese vocabularies] (Kyoto: Kyōto daigaku kokubungakkai, 1965), p. 1; Watanabe Mitsuo, "Minjin ni yoru Nihon gobun rikai no keika," p. 104; Akiyama Kenzō, "Mindai ni okeru Shinajin no Nihongo kenkyū 明代に於ける支那人の日本語研究" [Studies of the Japanese language by Chinese in the Ming era], *Kokugo to kokubungaku* 10, no. 1 (January 1933), p. 9; Miao Fenglin 繆鳳林, "Mingren zhu yu Riben youguan shiji tiyao sizhong 明人著與日本有關史籍提要四種" [Four historical texts concerning Japan written by Chinese of the Ming period], *Jiangsu shengli guoxue tushuguan* 江蘇省立國學圖書館 [National studied library of Jiangsu Province] 2 (1929), pp. 1–4; Fukushima Kunimichi 福島邦道, "*Nihon kigo* gokai「日本寄語」語解" [Explanation of the words in the *Riben jiyu*], *Kokugogaku* 36 (March 1959), pp. 69–78. Although his dates remain unknown, there is a biography of Xue Jun in the *Ming shi* 明史 [History of the Ming dynasty], *juan* 207; he later acquired the prestige title Wenlinlang 文林郎 [gentleman-litterateur].

of 357 Japanese words with *kan'yaku* readings, and this very list would be repeated in other late-Ming texts virtually verbatim (errors included).[20]

One text from the middle of the Wanli era of the Ming that marks that apex of Chinese interest in all things Japanese dates to the end of the sixteenth century. The *Riben kao* 日本考 (Study of Japan) in five fascicles was the work of two military men, Li Yangong 李言恭 (1541–1599, then at work in the military headquarters of the Capital Training Division) and Hao Jie 郝傑 (then serving as right Censor-in-Chief); under another title, *Riben fengtu ji* 日本風土記 (Account of the customs of Japan), it was appended to the *Quan-Zhe bingzhi kao* 全浙兵制考 (Study of the military institutions of Zhejiang), a work by another military man, Hou Jigao 侯繼高 (a regional commander to whom it is frequently and incorrectly attributed). The book was first published some time between the seventh lunar month of 1592 and the tenth month of 1593, just as the armies of Hideyoshi were invading the mainland for the first time; in the eleventh month of 1593, Li presented their work to Song Yingchang 宋應昌 (1536–1606), military commissioner in charge of combating the invading forces from Japan. Li had apparently been sent by Song to Japan in an effort to prevent Japan from attacking further. His experiences there and travelling along the Korean peninsula en route to Japan, the interviews he carried out, and the acquisition of information about Japan and its language enabled him and Hao to present a much more current picture of the archipelago and its culture.[21]

---

20 Wang Xiangrong, "Zhongguo diyibu yanjiu Riben de zhuanzhu," pp. 232–233; Xue Jun, *Riben kao lüe* (n.p.: Deyueyi zang ed., 1831), pp. 16b–23a. The earliest extant edition of the *Riben kao lüe* dates back to 1530 with a preface by Wang Wenguang 王文光. On the various editions of this work and their differences, large and small, see Kyōto daigaku bungakubu kokugogaku kokubungaku kenkyūshitsu, comp. and ed., *Nihon kigo no kenkyū*, pp. 2–17. On the origins of the term *jiyu* 寄語 [vocabulary], with its *locus classicus* in the *Liji* 禮記, see Watanabe Mitsuo, "Minjin ni yoru Nihon gobun rikai no keika," p. 104.

21 Watanabe Mitsuo, "Minjin ni yoru Nihon gobun rikai no keika," p. 107; Wang Xiangrong, "Guanyu *Riben kao*," pp. 245–246, 248, 252–254; Ishihara Michihiro, "Mindai ni okeru Shinajin no Nihon kenkyū," p. 213. Li's biography can be found in fascicle 126 of the *Ming shi*, and Hao's in fascicle 221. The confusion concerning

It is especially interesting that, although the impetus to compiling this book was the threat of war with Japan—not with "Japanese" pirates, but large armies landing on the Korean peninsula—one-half of the book is centrally concerned with language. The first fascicle of the text includes the names of the Japanese islands with Chinese-character readings; the second fascicle lists roughly 70 terms concerned with Japanese customs and practices. In both cases, the material appears to have been lifted entirely from an earlier text, *Chouhai tubian* 籌海圖編 (Illustrated essay on maritime defence, 13 fascicles) by Zheng Ruozeng 鄭若曾 (1505–1580). The third fascicle introduces the *hiragana* syllabaries in cursive form, arranged in *i-ro-ha* order and followed by Chinese graphs for pronunciation (some of these appear to reflect the eastern Zhejiang topolect of the late Ming). The fascicle also includes 39 Japanese *waka* 和歌 (a 31-syllable poetic form) with a complex system of explanation to be explained in detail below.

The fourth fascicle is concerned solely with the Japanese language. It includes a word list of between 1,140 and 1,186 (depending on which edition of the work is consulted). The number of terms is only about one-third of those in the *Riben yijian*, but the classification of terms indicates a greater degree of sophistication—a full 56 categories, more than any text of the time. Fascicle five is considerably shorter and includes much miscellaneous information of a social and cultural nature in no particular order and with no particular reason for inclusion.[22]

One of the most extraordinary features of the entire text appears right at the beginning of fascicle four, a long Chinese-style poem with four-line

---

two incarnations of the text is discussed by Hamada Atsushi, "Kokugo o kisai seru," pp. 22–25, and in greater detail in Ōtomo Shin'ichi, *Muromachi jidai*, pp. 489–496; and Wang Xiangrong, "Guanyu *Riben kao*," p. 260.

22 See Li Yangong 李言恭 and Hao Jie 郝傑, *Riben kao*, ed. Wang Xiangrong and Yan Dazhong 嚴大中 (repr., Beijing: Zhonghua shuju, 1983), passim; Watanabe Mitsuo, trans. and annot., *Shinshū yakuchū Nihon kō* 新修譯註日本考 [*Riben kao*, revised translation with annotations] (Tokyo: Shintensha, 1985). See also Watanabe Mitsuo, "Minjin ni yoru Nihon gobun rikai no keika," pp. 107–108; and Wang Xiangrong, "Guanyu *Riben kao*," p. 260.

stanzas, each line seven characters in length, entitled "Qieyin zhengshe ge" 切音正舌歌 (Poem on correct pronunciation). In poetic form it delineates the different ways in which Chinese characters are used and pronounced in Japanese. Even more extraordinary is the passage within it describing the use of grammatical particles in Japanese, something entirely alien to Chinese grammar and something which would not be addressed again in a Chinese text for nearly three centuries.[23]

Let us now take a closer look at several of the 39 *waka* which were drawn from various medieval Japanese poetry collections. The authors added to each poem the following six explanatory tools: (a) a four-character title in Chinese; (b) a Chinese-character reading corresponding to the *kana* value (the *kun* 訓 or native reading) beside each Chinese character in the text; (c) *huyin* 呼音 or Japanese pronunciation (using Chinese characters) for each of the characters in the poem that stand in their own right; (d) *dufa* 讀法 or reading in an all Chinese-character rendering for each poem (effectively combining b and c); (e) *shiyin* 釋音 or explanatory guide to the meaning and function of every element in the poem, a technique, according to the *Dai Kan-Wa jiten* 大漢和辭典 (Great Chinese-Japanese dictionary) of Morohashi Tetsuji 諸橋轍次 (1883–1982), used in translating ancient poems and songs into *Kanshi* 漢詩 or Chinese-language poems; and (f) *qieyi* 切意 or a Chinese poetic rendition of the poem's overall meaning. What follows is an example of one such poem extracted from the *Shūi waka shū* 拾遺和歌集 (Waka collection of gleanings), a lengthy imperial collection of poems compiled at the very beginning of the eleventh century. This one, whose author is unknown, is listed as number 50 (according to modern enumeration) in the first fascicle named "Haru" 春 (Spring).[24]

23 Li and Hao, *Riben kao*, pp. 140–141; Watanabe Mitsuo, trans. and annot., *Shinshū yakuchū Nihon kō*, pp. 205–207.

24 Li and Hao, *Riben kao*, pp. 112; Watanabe Mitsuo, trans. and annot., *Shinshū yakuchū Nihon kō*, pp. 174–175.

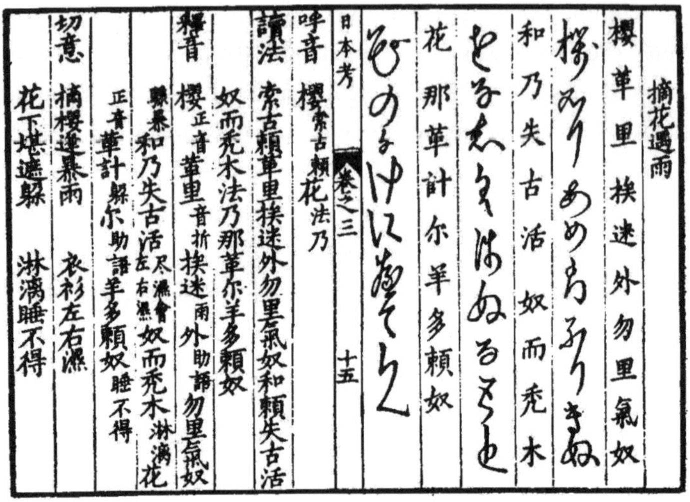
摘花遇雨
櫻革里挨迷外勿里氣奴
櫻かりあめはふりきぬ
和乃失古活奴而禿木
をなしくはぬるとも
花那革計尔羊多頼奴
花のかげにやてらん
日本考 巻之三 十五
呼音 櫻索古頼 花法乃
讀法 索古頼革里挨迷外勿里氣奴和頼失古活
奴而禿木法乃那革尔羊多頼奴
釋音 櫻正音 革里音折 挨迷雨 外助語 勿里氣奴
驟暴 和乃失古活尽濕會左右濕 奴而禿木淋漓 花
正音 革計躲 尔助語 羊多頼奴睡不得
切意 摘櫻逢暴雨 衣衫左右濕
花下堪遮躲 淋漓睡不得

Figure 1–2. From *Riben kao*, 3:15.

(a)

摘花遇雨

(b)

櫻革里埃迷外勿里氣奴和乃失古活奴而禿木花那革計尔羊多賴奴

櫻かりあめはふりきぬをなしくはぬるとも花のかげにやてらん

(c)

櫻	花
索古賴	法乃

(d)

索古賴革里埃迷外勿里氣奴和賴失古活奴而禿木法乃那革尔羊多賴奴

(e)

櫻	革里	埃迷	外	勿里氣奴	和乃失古活	奴而禿木	花
正音	音折	雨	助語	驟暴	尽濕會左右濕	淋漓	正音

革計	尔	羊多賴奴
躲	助語	睡不得

(f)

摘櫻逢暴雨、衣衫左右濕、花下堪遮躲、淋漓睡不得

The colossal amount of work that would have gone into such an effort must have required not only time but considerable knowledge of both languages and their poetry. Poetry is, of course, one of the most difficult literary genres to translate—perhaps the most difficult—and this method of explication not only translates but also explains each and every graph and their role in the poem. There was not, of course, a single Chinese reference work of any kind available at the time to assist in the process.

In addition to the 39 *waka* in fascicle three of the text, fascicle five contains some 12 *kouta* 小歌 (ballads or ditties) under a section entitled "Shan'ge" 山歌 (mountain songs), most of which date to the Muromachi period (1338–1573). Using a format similar to that used for the *waka*, the authors provide the following information in explicating each song (save the first one): (a) a four-character title in Chinese; (b) a Chinese-character reading corresponding to the *kana* value in Japanese; (c) *shiyin*; and (d) *qieyin*. The explication of the second *kouta* breaks down as follows:[25]

(a)
夫歸妻接

(b)
一多濕那禿那耶和一多濕那禿那耶他賣里油米各打推（搖）屋繪箔一單彈可尼
いしとの　殿　やおいとしの　殿　や賜れ　　弓　肩 よ　　　　靭　戴　　こうに

(c)
一多濕小肝・禿那丈夫・和一多濕大小肝・他賣里遞來・油米弓・各打肩・屋繪箔箭袋・一單彈可頂在頭上・那搖尼皆助語

(d)
小肝丈夫・大小肝丈夫・遞弓來・放在我肩上・箭袋頂在我頭上

As we saw earlier, the characters used to render Japanese pronunciation in this song reflect the Zhejiang topolect of the late Ming. In addition, one should note that *waka* and *kouta* are now frequently difficult to parse,

25 Li and Hao, *Riben kao*, pp. 237–238; Watanabe Mitsuo, trans. and annot., *Shinshū yakuchū Nihon kō*, pp. 306–307.

making these explanations by Li and Hao over 400 years afterward still a helpful tool, but especially so for linguists.[26] Unfortunately, we do not know how it is that Li and Hao acquired such knowledge; even if they had a host of highly educated Japanese informants, not likely to be found among the Japanese prisoners of war met along the Korean peninsula, the effort was Herculean.

There are other texts from the late Ming era that discuss Japan or offer a short listing of Japanese words with Chinese-graph transcriptions, but nothing compares to those discussed above, in particular the *Riben kao*. As contacts between Chinese and Japanese decreased over the course of the next few centuries, a result as much of foreign policy decisions on both sides as the peace that prevailed before Meiji 明治 times, Chinese writing about Japan declined sharply. There was one major text written in the Qing period by Weng Guangping (see above), but his fascicle on the Japanese language marked a sharp retrogression from late Ming efforts.

These writings from the late Ming were not lost or forgotten in later times, but they were not used to build a native Chinese tradition of Japanology. It was only after China's defeat in the Sino-Japanese War of 1894–1895 that many Chinese awoke to the idea that Japan might be worth a second look. Even then, the first major writings on Japan by Chinese—almost all of them associated with the first Chinese Missions established in the early Meiji era: Huang Zunxian 黃遵憲 (1848–1905), Yao Wendong 姚文棟 (1852–1927), and Yang Shoujing 楊守敬 (1839–1915) among them—were written on the basis of little or no knowledge of the Japanese. They were still working on the assumption that all that was worthy of notice could be acquired through a monolingual knowledge of Chinese, and most of the interlocutors in Japan—holdovers from the earlier late-Tokugawa period who retained a love for writing in Chinese—confirmed them in this bias. It would still be awhile before modern Chinese would return to a level reached by their great predecessors in the late Ming period.

26 Ōtomo Shin'ichi, *Muromachi jidai*, pp. 503, 505, 513, 546; Watanabe Mitsuo, "Minjin ni yoru Nihon gobun rikai no keika," pp. 110–112.

Bibliography

Akiyama, Kenzō 秋山謙藏. "Mindai ni okeru Shinajin no Nihongo kenkyū 明代に於ける支那人の日本語研究" [Studies of the Japanese language by Chinese in the Ming era]. *Kokugo to kokubungaku* 國語と國文學 [Studies in Japanese language and literature] 10, no. 1 (January 1933), pp. 1–38.

———. *Nis-Shi kōshō shi kenkyū* 日支交涉史研究 [Studies in the history of Sino-Japanese interactions]. Tokyo: Iwanami shoten, 1941.

Arisaka, Hideyo 有坂秀世. "Jōdai ni okeru sagyō no tōon 上代に於けるサ行頭音" [Initials in the *sa*-line in antiquity]. *Kokugo to kokubungaku* 國語と國文學 [Studies in Japanese language and literature] 13 (January 1936), pp. 90–103.

———. "*Sho shi kaiyō* no 'iroha' no onchū ni tsuite 書史会要の「いろは」の音註について" [On the phonetic transcription of the Japanese syllabary alphabet in the *Shu shi huiyao*]. *Gengo kenkyū* 言語研究 [Language studies] 16 (August 1950), pp. 1–13.

Asai, Keirin 淺井惠倫. "Kōhon Nihon yakugo 校本日本譯語" [Japanese terms in translation, annotated]. In *Andō kyōju kanreki shukuga kinen ronbunshū* 安藤教授還曆祝賀記念論文集 [Essays in honour of the sixtieth birthday of Professor Andō]. Tokyo: San'yōdō, 1950, pp. 1–56.

Asayama, Shin'ya 朝山信彌. "Kakurin gyokuro no 'ōbō' nado ni tsuite 鶴林玉露の黃榜などについて" [On the expression "huangbang" in the *Helin yulu* and other matters]. *Kokugo kokubun* 國語國文 [Langauge and literature] 7, no. 12 (December 1937), pp. 116–120.

Edkins, Joseph. "A Chinese and Japanese Vocabulary of the Fifteenth Century." *Transactions of the Asiatic Society of Japan* 10 (1882), pp. 1–14.

Fogel, Joshua A. "Chinese Understanding of the Japanese Language from Ming to Qing." In *Sagacious Monks and Bloodthirsty Warriors: Chinese Views of Japan in the Ming-Qing Period*, edited by Joshua A. Fogel. Norwalk: EastBridge, 2002, pp. 63–87.

———. *Articulating the Sinosphere: Sino-Japanese Relations in Space and Time.* Cambridge, MA: Harvard University Press, 2009.

Fukushima, Kunimichi 福島邦道. "*Nihon kigo* gokai「日本寄語」語解" [Explanation of the words in the *Riben jiyu*]. *Kokugogaku* 国語学 [Studies in the Japanese language] 36 (March 1959), pp. 69–78.

Hamada, Atsushi 濱田敦. "Kokugo o kisai seru Mindai Shina bunken 國語を記載せる明代支那文獻" [Chinese documents of the Ming dynasty which record

Japanese terms]. *Kokugo kokubun* 國語國文 [Language and literature] 10, no. 7 (July 1940), pp. 7–45.

———. "Nihon kigo kaidoku shian 日本寄語解讀試安" [A plan for explicating the Japanese translation terms]. *Jinbun kenkyū* 人文研究 [Studies in the humanities] 2, no. 1 (January 1951), pp. 19–59.

Hashimoto, Shinkichi 橋本進吉. "Hagyō shiin no hensen ni tsuite 波行子音の變遷について" [On changes in the consonants in the *ha*-line]. In *Kokugo on'in no kenkyū* 國語音韻の研究 [Studies in Japanese phonetics]. Tokyo: Iwanami shoten, 1950, pp. 29–45.

Ishihara, Michihiro 石原道広. "Mindai ni okeru Shinajin no Nihon kenkyū 明代における支那人の日本研究" [Studies of Japan by Chinese on the Ming period]. In *Tō-A shi zakkō* 東亞史襍攷 [Essays on East Asian history]. Tokyo: Seikatsusha, 1944, pp. 211–214.

———. "Chūgoku ni okeru Nihon kan no tanshoteki keitai: Zuidai izen no Nihon kan 中國における日本觀の端緒的形態：隋代以前の日本觀" [The emergence of views of Japan in China: Views of Japan before the Sui era]. *Ibaraki daigaku bunrigakubu kiyō (jinbun kagaku)* 茨城大学文理学部紀要（人文科学）[Bulletin of the Liberal Arts and Sciences Department of Ibaraki University, Humanities Division] 1 (March 1951), pp. 187–206.

———. "Chūgoku ni okeru rinkōteki Nihon kan no tenkai: Tō, Godai, Sō jidai no Nihon kan 中國における隣好的日本觀の展開：唐・五代・宋時代の日本觀" [The development of a friendly view of Japan in China: Views of Japan in the Tang, Five Dynasties, and Song periods]. *Ibaraki daigaku bunrigakubu kiyō (jinbun kagaku)* 茨城大学文理学部紀要（人文科学）[Bulletin of the Liberal Arts and Sciences Department of Ibaraki University, Humanities Division] 2 (February 1952), pp. 30–59.

———. "Nichi-Min tsūkō bōeki o meguru Nihon kan: Mindai no Nihon kan (ni) 日明通交貿易をめぐる日本觀：明代の日本觀（二）" [Views of Japan surrounding Japanese-Ming communications and trade: Views of Japan in the Ming era, part 2]. *Ibaraki daigaku bunrigakubu kiyō (jinbun kagaku)* 茨城大学文理学部紀要（人文科学）[Bulletin of the Liberal Arts and Sciences Department of Ibaraki University, Humanities Division] 5 (March 1955), pp. 14–28.

———. "Mindai Nihon kan no ichi sokumen 明代日本観の一側面" [One perspective on Japan in the Ming era]. *Ibaraki daigaku bungakubu kiyō (bungakka ronshū)* 茨城大学文学部紀要（文学科論集）[Bulletin of the Faculty of Letters of Ibaraki University, essays from the Literature Division] 1

(January 1968), pp. 1–39.

———. *Yakuchū Chūgoku seishi Nihon den* 訳註中国正史日本伝 [Treatises on Japan from the Chinese dynastic histories, translated and annotated]. Tokyo: Kokusho kankōkai, 1975.

Kamei, Takashi 亀井孝, Ōfuji Tokihiko 大藤時彦, and Yamada Toshio 山田俊雄. *Nihongo no rekishi 4: Utsuriyuku kodaigo* 日本語の歴史、4：移りゆく古代語 [The history of Japanese, vol. 4: The changing ancient language]. Tokyo: Heibonsha, 1976.

Kidder, J. Edward. *Himiko and Japan's Elusive Chiefdom of Yamatai: Archaeology, History, and Mythology*. Honolulu: University of Hawai'i Press, 2007.

Kyōto daigaku bungakubu 京都大学文学部 [Faculty of Letters, Kyoto University], ed. *Sanshū Nihon yakugo* 纂輯日本訳語 [Compiled Japanese vocabularies]. Kyoto: Kyōto daigaku kokubungakkai, 1968.

Kyōto daigaku bungakubu kokugogaku kokubungaku kenkyūshitsu 京都大学文学部国語学国文学研究室 [Departments of Japanese Language and Japanese Literature, Faculty of Letters, Kyoto University], comp. and ed. *Nihon kigo no kenkyū* 日本寄語の研究 [Studies of Japanese vocabularies]. Kyoto: Kyōto daigaku kokubungakkai, 1965.

Li, Yangong 李言恭, and Hao Jie 郝傑. *Riben kao* 日本考 [Study of Japan]. Edited by Wang Xiangrong 汪向榮 and Yan Dazhong 嚴大中. Reprint, Beijing: Zhonghua shuju, 1983.

Luo, Dajing 羅大經. *Helin yulu* 鶴林玉露 [The glittering dew drops of Helin], *juan* 16, pp. 5b–6a. Reprint, Shanghai: Shanghai shudian chubanshe, 1990.

Miao, Fenglin 繆鳳林. "Mingren zhu yu Riben youguan shiji tiyao sizhong 明人著與日本有關史籍提要四種" [Four historical texts concerning Japan written by Chinese of the Ming period]. *Jiangsu shengli guoxue tushuguan* 江蘇省立國學圖書館 [National studied library of Jiangsu Province] 2 (1929), pp. 1–18.

Nakano, Miyoko 中野美代子. "Nihon kigo ni yoru 16 seiki Teikai onkei no suitei, oyobi Muromachi makki kokugo on ni kansuru jakkan no mondai 日本寄語による16世紀定海音系の推定、および室町末期國語音に關する若干の問題" [Reconstructing Dinghai dialect of the sixteenth century on the basis of Japanese translation terms, and various issues concerning the pronunciation of Japanese in the late-Muromachi period]. *Tōhōgaku* 東方學 [East Asian studies] 28 (July 1964), pp. 100–120.

Ogawa, Tamaki 小川環樹. "*Sho shi kaiyō* ni mitaru 'iroha' no Kanji taion ni tsuite 書史會要に見たるいろはの漢字對音について" [On the corresponding Kanji phonemes for "*i-ro-ha*" as seen in the *Shu shi huiyao*]. *Kokugo kokubun* 國語國文 [Language and literature] 16, no. 5 (September 1947), pp. 311–320.

Ōtomo, Shin'ichi 大友信一. "*Nihonkan yakugo* no seiritsu, kokugo on'in shiryō to shite no kachi 「日本館訳語」の成立、国語音韻資料としての価値" [The formation of the *Ribenguan yiyu*, its value as material on Japanese phonetics]. *Kokugogaku* 国語学 [Studies in the Japanese language] 43 (March 1961), pp. 31–42.

———. *Muromachi jidai no kokugo onsei no kenkyū: Chūgoku shiryō ni yoru* 室町時代の国語音声の研究：中国資料による [Studies in Japanese phonetics of the Muromachi period, based on Chinese materials]. Tokyo: Shibundō, 1963.

Ōtomo, Shin'ichi 大友信一, and Kimura Akira 木村晟. *Nihonkan yakugo, honbun to sakuin* 日本館訳語、本文と索引 [The *Ribenguan yiyu*, text and index]. Tokyo: Rakubunsha, 1968.

Ruggieri, Michele, and Matteo Ricci. *Dicionário Português-Chinês*. Edited by John W. Witek, S.J. Lisbon: Biblioteca Nacional; Portugal: Instituto Português do Oriente; San Francisco: Ricci Institute for Chinese-Western Cultural History, University of San Francisco, 2001.

Satow, Ernest. "Notes on Dr. Edkins' Paper, 'A Chinese and Japanese Vocabulary of the Fifteenth Century.'" *Transactions of the Asiatic Society of Japan* 10 (1882), pp. 15–38.

Tao, Zongyi 陶宗儀. *Shu shi huiyao* 書史會要 [Essentials in the history of calligraphy]. N.p.: 1376.

Tomioka, Kenzō 富岡謙藏. "*Nihon ikkan* kaidai 日本一鑑解題" [An introduction to the *Riben yijian*]. *Geibun* 藝文 [Art and literature] 5, no. 9 (September 1914), pp. 256–259.

Tsunoda, Ryusaku, and L. Carrington Goodrich. *Japan in the Chinese Dynastic Histories*. Pasadena: P. D. and Ione Perkins, 1951.

Wang, Baoping 王寶平. "*Wuqi jing bu* zhuzhe Weng Guangping kao 吾妻鏡補注者翁廣平考" [A study of Weng Guangping, author of the *Wuqi jing bu*]. In *Zhong-Ri wenhua luncong—1996* 中日文化論叢—1996 [Essays in Sino-Japanese culture—1996], edited by Hangzhou daxue Riben wenhua yanjiusuo 杭州大學日本文化研究所 and Kanagawa daigaku jinbungaku kenkyūjo 神奈川大學人文學研究所. Hangzhou: Hangzhou daxue chubanshe, 1996, pp. 150–160.

Wang, Xiangrong 汪向榮. "Cong *Jinglüe fuguo yaobian* kan renchen kang-Wo zhanshi 從《經略復國要編》看壬辰抗倭戰事" [The anti-"Japanese" war of 1592 as seen from the *Jinglüe fuguo yaobian*]. In *Zhong-Ri guanxi shi wenxian lunkao* 中日關係史文獻論考 [Essays on documents in the history of Sino-Japanese relations]. Beijing: Yuelu shushe, 1985, pp. 264–288.

———. "Guanyu *Riben kao* 關於《日本考》" [On the *Riben kao*]. In *Zhong-Ri guanxi shi wenxian lunkao* 中日關係史文獻論考 [Essays on documents in the history of Sino-Japanese relations]. Beijing: Yuelu shushe, 1985, pp. 239–263.

———. "Zhongguo diyibu yanjiu Riben de zhuanzhu: *Riben kao lüe* 中國第一部研究日本的專著：《日本考略》" [China's first specialized study of Japan, the *Riben kao lüe*]. In *Zhong-Ri guanxi shi wenxian lunkao* 中日關係史文獻論考 [Essays on documents in the history of Sino-Japanese relations]. Beijing: Yuelu shushe, 1985, pp. 218–238.

Wang, Xiangrong 汪向榮, and Xia Yingyuan 夏應元. *Zhong-Ri guanxi shiliao huibian* 中日關係史料匯編 [Collection of historical materials on Sino-Japanese relations]. Beijing: Zhonghua shuju, 1984.

Wang, Yizhong 王以中. "Mingdai haifang tuji lu 明代海防圖籍錄" [Texts on coastal defence and maps from the Ming period]. *Qinghua zhoukan* 清華週刊 [Qinghua weekly] 37, no. 9–10 (May 1932), pp. 141–162.

Wang, Yong 王勇. "Chūgoku ni okeru Nihon kenkyū no zenshi 中国に於ける日本研究の前史" [The prehistory of Japanese studies in China]. In *Zhong-Ri wenhua luncong—1991* 中日文化論叢—1991 [Essays in Sino-Japanese culture—1991], edited by Hangzhou daxue Riben wenhua yanjiusuo 杭州大學日本文化研究所 and Kanagawa daigaku jinbungaku kenkyūjo 神奈川大學人文學研究所. Hangzhou: Hangzhou daxue chubanshe, 1991, pp. 132–146.

Watanabe, Mitsuo 渡辺三男. "Minmatsu no Nihon shōkaisho: *Nihon ikkan* ni tsuite 明末の日本紹介書：日本一鑑について" [An introductory text on Japan from the late Ming: *Riben yijian*]. *Komazawa daigaku kenkyū kiyō* 駒澤大學研究紀要 [Bulletin of studies from Komazawa University] 13 (March 1955), pp. 144–169.

———. "Chūgoku kobunken ni mieru Nihongo: *Kakurin gyokuro* to *Sho shi kaiyō* ni tsuite 中國古文獻に見える日本語：鶴林玉露と書史會要について" [Japan as seen in old Chinese documents: The *Helin yulu* and the *Shu shi huiyao*]. *Komazawa daigaku kenkyū kiyō* 駒澤大学研究紀要 [Bulletin of studies from Komazawa University] 15 (March 1957), pp. 155–163.

———. "Ka-i yakugo oyobi *Nihonkan yakugo* ni tsuite 華夷訳語および日本館訳語について" [Sino-foreign vocabularies and the *Ribenguan yiyu*]. *Komazawa daigaku kenkyū kiyō* 駒澤大学研究紀要 [Bulletin of studies from Komazawa University] 18 (March 1960), pp. 120–135.

———. "Ka-i yakugo oyobi *Nihonkan yakugo* ni tsuite (shōzen) 華夷訳語および日本館訳語について(承前)" [Sino-foreign vocabularies and the *Ribenguan yiyu*, continued]. *Komazawa daigaku kenkyū kiyō* 駒澤大学研究紀要 [Bulletin of studies from Komazawa University] 19 (March 1961), pp. 15–31.

———. "Minjin ni yoru Nihon gobun rikai no keika 明人による日本語文理解の経過" [How Chinese of the Ming era came to understand the Japanese language]. *Tsurumi joshi tanki daigaku kiyō* 鶴見女子短期大学紀要 [Bulletin of Tsurumi Junior College] 1 (March 1962), pp. 98–114.

———. "*Zuisho* Wakokuden no Nihongo hitei 隋書倭国伝の日本語比定" [Identifying Japanese words in the "Treatise on Japan" in the *Sui shu*]. *Komazawa kokubun* 駒沢国文 [National literature from Komazawa] 5 (October 1966), pp. 1–8.

———, trans. and annot. *Shinshū yakuchū Nihon kō* 新修譯註日本考 [*Riben kao*, revised translation with annotations]. Tokyo: Shintensha, 1985.

Wild, Norman. "Materials for the Study of the Ssû I Kuan (Bureau of Translation)." *Bulletin of the School of Oriental and African Studies* 11 (1943–1946), pp. 617–640.

Wu, Anlong 武安隆, and Xiong Dayun 熊達雲. *Chūgokujin no Nihon kenkyū shi* 中国人の日本研究史 [History of Chinese Japanology]. Tokyo: Rokkō shuppan, 1989.

Xue, Jun 薛俊. *Riben kao lüe* 日本考略 [Brief study of Japan]. N.p.: Deyueyi zang ed., 1831.

Yichu 義楚. *Shishi liutie* 釋氏六帖 [Six models of Buddhism]. In vol. 5 of *Xiandai Foxue daxi* 現代佛學大系 [Modern compendium on Buddhism]. Taibei: Mile chubanshe, 1982.

Zhang, Yaqiu 張雅秋. "Cong *Helin yulu* zhong de yize shiliao kan Songdai Zhong-Ri wenhua jiaoliu 從《鶴林玉露》中的一則史料看宋代中日文化交流" [Song-era Sino-Japanese relations as seen from the historical material in the *Helin yulu*]. In *Zhong-Ri wenhua luncong—1996* 中日文化論叢—1996 [Essays in Sino-Japanese culture—1996], edited by Hangzhou daxue Riben wenhua yanjiusuo 杭州大學日本文化研究所 and Kanagawa daigaku jinbungaku kenkyūjo 神奈川大學人文學研究所. Hangzhou: Hangzhou daxue chubanshe, 1996, pp. 205–212.

Zheng, Shungong 鄭舜功. *Riben yijian* 日本一鑑 [A mirror on Japan], *juan* 4–5. N.p.: Beijing reprint of Wendiange 文殿閣 text, 1939.

Translation and Sinicization: *Xiaojing* Translation in Tuoba Wei and Mongol Yuan

Jae-ho SHIN

Introduction

On the twenty-first day of the fifth month of 1307, Prince Khaishan, a young hero of the steppe war against Khaidu, formally came to power and succeeded Temür, the deceased Khaghan of the Yuan Ulus. Khaishan's grasp of the khaghanship, which ended the three months' interregnum after Temür's death, led to a deviation from the pattern of rule established by his great-grandfather, Khubilai.[1] Rather than a ruler of a sedentary state, Khaishan was a typical nomadic monarch and, as such, did not trust the bureaucratic apparatus at Yuan's capital, Khanbaliq (a.k.a. Dadu).[2] Considering his background, there is a passage from *Yuan shi* 元史 (History of Yuan) concerning *Xiaojing* 孝經 (Book of filial piety) that attracts our attention. The new Khaghan issued a decree on the distribution of the Confucian classic only about three months after his enthronement:

> On the day of *xinhai* 辛亥, then Assistant Director of the Right[3] in the Secretariat, Bolod Temür, offered a copy of *Xiaojing* that he had translated by means of the national script. [The emperor] decreed: "Since this work contains the subtle teaching of Confucius, from princes and dukes down

1 Hsiao Ch'i-ch'ing, "Mid-Yuan Politics," in *The Cambridge History of China*, vol. 6, *Alien Regimes and Border States, 907–1368*, ed. Herbert Franke and Denis Twitchett (Cambridge, New York, and Oakleigh: Cambridge University Press, 1978), pp. 507–508.

2 Ibid.

3 According to *Yuan shi*, Youcheng 右丞 (rank 2a), or Assistant Director of the Right, was the fourth highest position in the Secretariat. See Song Lian 宋濂 et al., *Yuan shi* 元史 [History of Yuan], vol. 85 (Beijing: Zhonghua shuju, 1976), p. 2122.

> to common people, all ought to act according to it." He also ordered the Central Secretariat to cut woodblocks and print the text and to distribute it to his subordinate kings and those below them.[4]

The translation of *Xiaojing* and its distribution could be seen as an example of Confucianization,[5] or sinicization, in a conquest dynasty. Even though filial piety itself is a universal value, Confucian filial piety was regarded as something unique in traditional China; indeed, it was thought of as a critical yardstick by which to contrast civilized Chinese people with their neighbouring "barbarians."[6] Therefore, it is very tempting to argue that Khaishan, one of the most steppe-oriented of all Yuan rulers, in fact attempted to sinicize his empire by inculcating the Confucian morality in the Mongol people. Plausible as this may sound, however, there remains an unmistakable incongruity. Filial piety has been expressed in diverse forms by different cultures. The Mongol people were no exception: they practised it in their own manner. In fact, the debates over widow remarriage and levirate exemplify how much the family ethics of the Mongolian society, including the mores of filial piety, differed from those of Han-Chinese society, and how conservative the Mongols were in their steppe tradition of family ethics.[7] For this reason, it is curious as to why Khaishan ordered to distribute *Xiaojing* among his own people at the beginning of his reign.

The aim of this paper is to provide an explanation for the launch of Khaishan's *Xiaojing* project in 1307 in relation to the issue of sinicization. To this end, I will depend mainly on two approaches: the understanding

4 Song Lian et al., *Yuan shi*, vol. 22, p. 486.

5 Miya Noriko 宮紀子, *Mongoru jidai no shuppan bunka* モンゴル時代の出版文化 [Cultural policy and publishing activities during the Mongol period] (Nagoya: Nagoya Daigaku Shuppankai, 2006), p. 69. She sees Khaishan's *Xiaojing* project as a starting point of the revival of Confucianism which was actually designed by Ayurbarwada and Confucian scholars under his aegis.

6 Sima Qian 司馬遷, *Shi ji* 史記 [Records of the grand historian], vol. 110 (Beijing: Zhonghua shuju, 1982), pp. 2899–2900.

7 Jennifer Holmgren, "Observations on Marriage and Inheritances Practices in Early Mongol and Yuan Society with Particular Reference to the Levirate," *Journal of Asian History* 20, no. 2 (1986), pp. 169–192.

of *Xiaojing* as a text of political ideology and the comparison of the roles the book played in the two conquest empires of the Mongols and the Tuoba Xianbei 拓跋鮮卑.

In ancient China, the *Xiaojing* was more than a textbook on Confucian filial piety. Like many other Chinese "classics," the *Book of Filial Piety* was also a book of political philosophy,[8] and even of magic words.[9] Therefore, *Xiaojing* policies in Chinese history should be viewed in their political context. In fact, the political mobilization of *Xiaojing* was not a rare phenomenon in Chinese history; most dynasties, including those of nomadic origin, tried to distribute the book so long as they did not ignore Confucianism. Thus, in order to elucidate the hallmark of Khaishan's *Xiaojing* policy, I will compare it with the Xianbei 鮮卑 version of *Xiaojing* published during the Tuoba Wei 拓跋魏 period (fourth to sixth centuries CE). Tuoba Wei was never a typical Chinese dynasty, but it showed another nomadic attitude to the Han-Chinese culture which was quite different from that of the Mongol empire. Making a comparison between these two cases of *Xiaojing* translation will, I expect, illuminate the reason why Khaishan ordered to distribute its Mongolian version in 1307 and also clarify the characteristics of the Mongol approach to Confucianism in relation to the issue of sinicization.

Political Implication of *Xiaojing* in Ancient China

Xiaojing, or *Book of Filial Piety*, is a Confucian classic consisting of conversations on filial piety between Confucius and his student, Zengzi 曾子. The conversation between these two historical figures, however, does not guarantee when and by whom the book was actually authored. At least as early as the Song period, scholars began to doubt if Confucius, or Zengzi,

8 Watanabe Shin'ichirō 渡辺信一郎, *Chūgoku kodai kokka no shisō kōzō: Sensei kokka to ideorogī* 中国古代国家の思想構造：専制国家とイデオロギー [The intellectual structure of ancient Chinese states: Despotic states and the ideology] (Tokyo: Azekura Shobō, 1994), pp. 170–258.

9 Yoshikawa Tadao 吉川忠夫, *Rikuchō seishinshi kenkyū* 六朝精神史研究 [Intellectual history of the Six Dynasties period] (Kyoto: Dōhōsha, 1984), pp. 547–567.

was the real writer of the text. For instance, Zhu Xi 朱熹 sneeringly criticized that Confucian scholars of the Qi and Lu kingdoms during the late Warring States period counterfeited the book to exploit the authority of Confucius and Zengzi. Today most scholars agree that *Xiaojing* was compiled during the transitional period between the late Warring States period and the early Han dynasty.

Xiaojing, like other Confucian classics, suffered from the book-burning policy of the First Emperor 始皇帝 of the Qin dynasty. The two extant versions actually resurfaced during the Han dynasty. These are the *New Text Xiaojing* 今文孝經 discovered in the early Han period and the *Old Text Xiaojing* 古文孝經 that came to light during the reign of Emperor Wu 武帝 (r. 141–87 BCE) respectively; they show only ignorable difference in substance. Later, Emperor Xuanzong 玄宗 (r. 712–756 CE) of the Tang dynasty, following the format of the new text version which has 18 chapters, synthesized the two versions to publish *Yu zhu Xiaojing* 御注孝經 (*Xiaojing* with imperial commentaries) with his own comments. This edition became the standard version of *Xiaojing* and remained influential until Zhu Xi wrote *Xiaojing kan wu* 孝經刊誤 (Corrections to *Xiaojing*) in 14 chapters in 1186. For example, the Jin dynasty required civil service examinees to study with the royal version.[10]

Xiaojing, with its role as a textbook to encourage filial piety within a family, has multilayered meanings in ancient China. The most intriguing one is its having been regarded as being imbued with magical qualities. When the Yellow Turban rebels threatened the Han court during the late second century CE, Xiang Xu 向栩, a Han courtier, argued that the revolt would disperse on its own if the court ordered a general to recite lines from *Xiaojing*.[11] Also the Han people believed that the text could be used to exorcize evil spirits.[12]

---

10 Toqto'a (Tuotuo) 脫脫 et al., *Jin shi* 金史 [History of Jin], vol. 51 (Beijing: Zhonghua shuju, 1982), p. 1131.

11 Fan Ye 范曄, *Houhan shu* 後漢書 [Book of Later Han], vol. 81 (Beijing: Zhonghua shuju, 1982), p. 2694.

12 Yi Sŏngkyu 李成珪, "Handae Hyokyŏng ŭi pokŭp kwa kŭ inyŏm 漢代『효경(孝經)』의 普及과 그 理念" [The ideology of *Xiaojing* and government policy of encouraging the filial piety in Han China], *Han'guk sasangsa hak* 韓國思想史學 [The study of Korean history of thought] 10 (1998), p. 188.

Such belief in the supernatural potential of the book continued during the period of the Southern and Northern Dynasties. *Xiaojing* was, along with the *Laozi*, the *Prajñāpāramitā Hṛdaya Sutra* (i.e. the *Heart Sutra*), and the *Saddharma Pundarika Sutra* (i.e. the *Lotus Sutra*), one of preferred funerary items to bury with the deceased in the Southern Dynasties.[13] In this manner, *Xiaojing* became a sort of religious scripture in Tuoba Wei. Chinese archaeologists recently discovered tombs of Xianbei nobles in northern China, whose murals were painted with the motifs of famous stories of filial sons, such as that of the mythical sage-king Shun 舜.[14] Dien, citing Sun Ji's interpretation, explains that the use of the filial son stories on the coffins is "to be attributed to the almost religious significance the *Xiaojing* or Confucian *Classic of Filial Piety* achieved at this time."[15] In short, *Xiaojing* was not only a book of worldly family ethics, but conveyed a sort of religious value as well, at least until the period of the Northern and Southern Dynasties.

Our focus in this paper, however, is the political message in *Xiaojing*. Along with the *Analects of Confucius* and the *Book of Odes*, *Xiaojing* occupied the highest position in the hierarchy of Confucian classics until the Han dynasty in that these books were believed to contain the gist of Confucianism.[16] Confucian ethics, however, was never restricted as only a frame of reference for individual activity; it was a political ideology at the same time. Confucian filial piety was no exception. As mentioned above, the *Book of Filial Piety* was compiled sometime between the late

13 Yoshikawa Tadao, *Rikuchō seishinshi kenkyū*, pp. 556–562.

14 Guyuanxian wenwu gongzuozhan 固原縣文物工作站, "Ningxia Guyuan Bei Wei mu qingli jianbao 寧夏固原北魏墓清理簡報" [Preliminary report on the excavation of a tomb of Northern Wei in Guyuan, Ningxia], *Wenwu* 文物 [Cultural relics], no. 6 (1984), pp. 49–50; Sun Ji 孫機, "Guyuan Bei Wei qiguanhua yanjiu 固原北魏漆棺畫研究" [Study of the painting on a Northern Wei lacquered coffin in Guyuan], *Wenwu*, no. 9 (1989), pp. 39–40.

15 Albert Dien, "A New Look at the Xianbei and Their Impact on Chinese Culture," in *Ancient Mortuary Traditions of China*, ed. George Kuwayama (Los Angeles: Far Eastern Art Council, Los Angeles County Museum of Art; Honolulu: University of Hawai'i Press, 1991), p. 47.

16 Yi Sŏngkyu, "Handae Hyokyŏng ŭi pokŭp kwa kŭ inyŏm," p. 191.

Warring States period and the early Han dynasty.[17] That is, the text and its messages are the product of the transitional period when the strong emperorship supported by bureaucrats was reorganizing the traditional clan-based society into a uniform one under the power of a single emperor.

It was the Han government that comprehensively mobilized Confucian filial piety for the purpose of strengthening the emperorship.[18] In contrast to its predecessor, Qin, the Han court maintained both a centralized local administration system and semi-independent appanages. The appanages, though first rewarded to meritorious vassals, were distributed to the princes of the Han royal family after the bloody purge of the vassals. The Han court, therefore, had to struggle continuously to control these potentially dangerous powers and finally succeeded in making them nominal sinecures by Emperor Wu's reign. However, the Han court could not eliminate all centrifugal forces beyond its governmental authority: local magnates, such as *san lao* 三老 (Three elders), who would ultimately become the semi-independent local military elites in the chaotic years of the late Han period, survived. For this reason, the Han government needed ideological devices as well as a strong administrative apparatus to control the centrifugal forces within its territory.[19]

The reason *Xiaojing* became significant in the Han court is that it provided a model of statecraft centred on the throne. The keyword of *Xiaojing* is no doubt filial piety. However, this universal value transformed into specific political ethics when it was categorized according to five social orders: the filial piety of the son of Heaven (*tianzi* 天子), that of princes of states (*zhuhou* 諸侯), that of high ministers and great officers (*qingdafu* 卿大夫), that of inferior officers (*shi* 士), and that of common people (*shuren* 庶人). The notion of hierarchically stratified filial piety demanded that each group follow its particular norm. For example, while the filial piety of the son of Heaven is to rule all under Heaven, that of princes of states is how to maintain

17 Itano Chōhachi 板野長八, *Chūgoku kodai ni okeru ningenkan no tenkai* 中国古代における人間観の展開 [Development of the views on human nature in ancient China] (Tokyo: Iwanami Shoten, 1972), pp. 211–227.

18 Ibid.; Watanabe Shin'ichirō, *Chūgoku kodai kokka no shisō kōzō*, pp. 233–258.

19 Yi Sŏngkyu, "Handae Hyokyŏng ŭi pokŭp kwa kŭ inyŏm," pp. 191–203.

their wealth and noble standing. Concretely, the book advises the princes to be "frugal and careful in their expenses" and avoid becoming arrogant. In the same manner, the filial piety for high ministers and great officers is to "preserve their ancestral temples" by following the laws of ancient sage kings, whereas inferior officers can embody their filial piety with the loyalty to their ruler and the obedience to their seniors. Only the filial piety of common people is on how to nourish their parents. In summary, *Xiaojing* stipulated the social norms for each social status, which was what the Han court had craved to distribute in order to confirm and stabilize the status quo of the empire.

Furthermore, *Xiaojing* sanctified the emperorship by converging the filial piety on the emperor, the son of Heaven. On its ninth chapter, "The Government of the Sages 聖治," it reads,

> Of all (creatures with their different) natures produced by Heaven and Earth, man is the noblest. Of all the actions of man there is none greater than filial piety. In filial piety there is nothing greater than the reverential awe of one's father. In the reverential awe shown to one's father there is nothing greater than the making him the correlate of Heaven. The duke of Zhou 周公 was the man who (first) did this. Formerly the duke of Zhou at the border altar sacrificed to Houji 後稷 as the correlate of Heaven, and in the Brilliant Hall he honoured King Wen 文王, and sacrificed to him as the correlate of God. The consequence was that from (all the states) within the four seas, every (prince) came in the discharge of his duty to [assist in those] sacrifices.[20]

The supreme filial piety, therefore, can be embodied only by the emperor, the son of Heaven, who holds the mandate of Heaven; semi-independent princes are permitted just to assist him in the process of the embodiment. In other words, filial piety as norms of diverse social strata focuses on the emperor—the representative of Heaven in the world—who substantiates

20 James Legge, trans., "Hsiāo King," in *The Sacred Books of China: The Texts of Confucianism* (Oxford: The Clarendon Press, 1879), pp. 476–478. Chinese names in original translation were re-Romanized with *pinyin* in this quote.

the ultimate filial piety with which he rules the empire.[21] Following the logic of *Xiaojing*, in principle the Han emperor was a kind of religious despot under the auspice of Heaven. And in order to keep imperial princes and local powers under control, the central power in Chang'an and later Luoyang tried to instill the ideology of hierarchy with the Han emperor atop into his subjects by means of *Xiaojing*.

In this sense, *Xiaojing* emerged as a text of political ideology of the ancient Chinese empire. The necessity of the text, such as the need to maintain stratified society and control centrifugal powers, however, survived the Han dynasty. The political role of *Xiaojing* was also mobilized by nomadic dynasties in northern China. In next section we will focus on the role of *Xiaojing* in the late fifth-century Tuoba Wei.

Sinicization Policies and the Xianbei-version *Xiaojing* in Tuoba Wei

On the "Monograph of Canons and Books" in *Sui shu* 隋書 (Book of Sui), the compiler catalogued versions of *Xiaojing* still extant in the early Tang period. Last on the list, he referred to a volume of Xianbei vernacular *Xiaojing* 國語孝經 as follows:

> When Tuoba Wei transferred its capital to Luoyang, Tuoba people were not yet proficient in Chinese language. Emperor Xiaowen 孝文帝 (r. 471–499) ordered Kexiling 可悉陵, the marquis of Houfu, to translate the heart of *Xiaojing* by means of the barbarian (i.e. Xianbei) language and to educate the (Tuoba) people (with the book). It is called the vernacular *Xiaojing*.[22]

Since the capital was removed in 493, the vernacular edition of *Xiaojing* may have been published between 493 and 499, during the last phase of Emperor Xiaowen's reign.

21 Chung Ho-hun 鄭豪薰, "Chuja *Xiaojing kan wu* wa kŭ sŏnggyŏk 朱子『孝經刊誤』와 그 성격" [The formation of Zhu Xi's *Xiaojing kan wu* and its political significance], *Tongbang hakji* 東方學志 [The journal of Eastern studies] 106 (2002), pp. 79–80.

22 Wei Zheng 魏徵 et al., *Sui shu* 隋書 [Book of Sui], vol. 32 (Beijing: Zhonghua shuju, 1984), pp. 934–935.

Emperor Xiaowen is well known for a series of his sinicization policies, collectively known as "Taihe Reforms." Facilitated by the "anti-barbarian" sentiment of the Chinese Empress-Dowager Feng 馮太后 (442–490), the emperor tried to "bring the country closer to the dowager's and the young emperor's ideal of a Han-Chinese, Confucianized bureaucratic monarchy ruling an ordered, aristocratic society. To this end, Xianbei ways had to be rejected as far as possible."[23] For example, Xianbei clothing, the use of steppe tongues at court, and shamanistic practices and native cults were prohibited; Chinese surnames were adopted in lieu of traditional Xianbei surnames;[24] the internal imperial court system, *neichao* 內朝, comparable to the Mongol *kessig*[25] and the imperial inspector system were reformed;[26] and the tribe dissolution policy, which was first decreed by Emperor Daowu 道武帝 (r. 386–409), was reconfirmed during Emperor Xiaowen's reign.[27] The strong sinicization drive was for strengthening the emperorship by checking the military powers in the Wei court. The emperor aimed to concentrate as much power as he could in his hands by replacing the traditional power-sharing practices of the steppe with the Chinese ruling system centring on strong emperorship.[28]

What must be remembered here, however, is that all the sinicization policies were not successful over the whole gamut of his empire. If anything, scholars recently agree that it seems to have been effective in some geographically restricted areas, such as the new capital, Luoyang, and its environs. For example, the equal-field system, a means through

23 William John Francis Jenner, *Memories of Loyang: Yang Hsüan-chih and the Lost Capital (493–534)* (Oxford: Clarendon Press; New York: Oxford University Press, 1981), p. 28.

24 David B. Honey, "Stripping off Felt and Fur: An Essay on Nomadic Sinification," *Papers on Inner Asia* 21 (1992), p. 20.

25 Kawamoto Yoshiaki 川本芳昭, *Gi Shin Nanbokuchō jidai no minzoku mondai* 魏晋南北朝時代の民族問題 [Ethnic issues in the period of disunity] (Tokyo: Kyūko Shoin, 1998), pp. 188–227.

26 Ibid., pp. 228–251.

27 Ibid., pp. 124–186.

28 Valerie Hansen, *The Open Empire: A History of China to 1600* (New York: Norton, 2000), p. 181.

which the Tuoba Wei court was able to have a direct hold on peasants, did not become firmly established beyond the region immediately surrounding the capital because of the lack of a stable local administrative structure.[29] Moreover, the tribe dissolution policy could not satisfactorily liquidate the traditional tribal society. The traditional privilege of noble groups such as the "Ten Surnames 十姓" and the centrifugal chieftainship were the issues at hand for Emperor Xiaowen when he enforced the sinicization policies.[30] Especially, the Xianbei people in the northern border regions of the empire, in particular elite units of hereditary soldiers stationed there, were still proud of and keen to conserve their traditional customs, which continued until the collapse of the dynasty.[31]

It was natural, therefore, that the Xianbei customs and language re-emerged after succeeding Tuoba dynasties were founded in the wake of the spilt of the Northern Wei (534) triggered by a series of rebellions of nomadic military commanders following the "Revolt of the Six Garrisons 六鎮之亂" in 523. The Western Wei 西魏 (535–556, later Northern Zhou 北周 [557–581]), especially, restored the traditional non-Han-Chinese naming custom that Emperor Xiaowen had outlawed in 496, and this shows the limit of the Taihe sinicization policies 太和改制.[32] Likewise, the attempt to emulate the Han-Chinese cultural elements for the purpose of undergirding the Tuoba emperorship never went smoothly; it was a troublesome process resisted by many antagonists, including even the emperor's heir apparent, and ultimately led to the collapse of the dynasty. It was during the difficult process of building the Han-Chinese-style power structure that the emperor ordered the publishing of the Xianbei vernacular *Xiaojing*.

Now let us return to the matter of the publication of the Xianbei vernacular *Xiaojing*. Unfortunately, we have no more than the above-excerpted

29 Hansen, *The Open Empire*, p. 180.

30 Kawamoto Yoshiaki, *Gi Shin Nanbokuchō jidai no minzoku mondai*, pp. 143–159.

31 Honey, "Stripping off Felt and Fur," pp. 22–23; Kawamoto Yoshiaki, *Gi Shin Nanbokuchō jidai no minzoku mondai*, pp. 173–178; Hansen, *The Open Empire*, pp. 182–183.

32 See Albert Dien, "The Bestowal of Surnames under the Western Wei-Northern Chou: A Case of Counter-Acculturation," *T'oung Pao* 63 (1977), pp. 137–177.

information on the version. The lack of relevant data notwithstanding, it is possible to set up a hypothesis on Emperor Xiaowen's underlying intention on the basis of some clues found in the history of Northern Wei.

First and foremost, Emperor Xiaowen possibly ordered the translation and distribution of *Xiaojing* for his political agenda. As we have seen, both the Han and Tuoba Wei courts faced similar problems—maintaining stratified social structure and checking strong centrifugal elites. And Emperor Xiaowen pursued the Han-Chinese model in order to eradicate from his empire the traditional concept of "Khan as a *primus inter pares*" of the steppe world. Thus, it is not unreasonable to think that he attempted to follow the precedent of the Han dynasty. He is thought to have intended to provide his Xianbei subjects with the idea of an inviolable sovereign, the one and only legitimate representative of the prime filial piety to Heaven, by means of diffusing the message in *Xiaojing*.

More fundamentally, the emperor mobilized *Xiaojing* for reasons beyond his political renovation—the total Confucianization of the Xianbei society. Let us give consideration to his tribe dissolution policy. He actively accepted the Han-Chinese-style kinship order and social caste structure as paragons in order to deconstruct the tribal connection that was still strong after Emperor Daowu's first attempt. For example, the five grades of the mourning system, *wufu* 五服 (the rule on the sphere of mourning for the dead), a quintessence of Han-Chinese kinship customs, was made as a principle when Emperor Xiaowen forced the reorganization of the Xianbei's tribal nexus into a Chinese one.[33] Besides, the emperor even advocated the "three-year mourning period" practice,[34] a significant symbol of Confucian filial piety. In other words, Confucian—to be exact Han-Chinese—filial piety was at the core of his project to redesign the empire's entire social topography, in which the Xianbei vernacular *Xiaojing* was intended for permeating Confucian values into Xianbei society.

33 Kawamoto Yoshiaki, *Gi Shin Nanbokuchō jidai no minzoku mondai*, pp. 159–165.

34 Wei Shou 魏收, *Wei Shu* 魏書 [Book of Wei], vol. 7 (Beijing: Zhonghua shuju, 1984), part 2, p. 179.

Conclusively, Emperor Xiaowen attempted the total Confucianization in not only the political sphere but also the societal sphere of his empire for the purpose of fortifying his emperorship. The vernacular *Xiaojing* was a source from which the emperor and his court supplied their Xianbei people with Confucian filial piety—the gist of the Han-Chinese kinship ethics on which the Taihe Confucianization drive hinged. The emperor tried to redesign his empire according to the model of the Chinese empire, and *Xiaojing* was used as a sort of guidebook for the sinicization.

Khaishan's *Xiaojing* Distribution Policy in 1307

Referring to the first encounter between the Mongols and *Xiaojing*, Cleaves introduces the funerary inscription by Wang E 王鶚 in memory of Li Chi Chang 李志常 (or Li Chih-ch'ang, 1193–1278), which shows Li taught Ögedei Khan's heir apparent, Güyüg, the *Book of Changes* 易經, *Book of Odes* 詩經, *Book of Documents* 書經, *Daodejing* 道德經, and *Xiaojing*[35] in 1229. Based on the inscription, we can know that *Xiaojing* was available to the Mongols already in the early thirteenth century. Setting aside the doubt whether or not Li's teaching was meaningfully influential to the Mongol elites, however, we note some interesting facts in this first encounter. Li was a student of Qiu Chuji 丘處機, a Daoist priest also known as Changchun 長春 (1148–1227), who is famous for his audience with Chinggis Khan in 1219. Furthermore, the curriculum for the future Khaghan Güyüg bespeaks that Li faithfully followed the syncretistic teachings of the Quanzhen-sect Daoism 全真教 in which *Daodejing*, *Xiaojing*, and the *Heart Sutra* were in particular emphasized as leading to the real Dao by its founder, Wang Chongyang 王重陽 (1113–1170).[36] Accordingly, the *Xiaojing* in Li's book list may have been accepted as

35 Francis W. Cleaves, "The Eighteenth Chapter of an Early Mongolian Version of the *Hsiao Ching*," *Harvard Journal of Asiatic Studies* 45, no. 1 (1985), pp. 225–227.

36 Arthur Waley, "Introduction," in *The Travels of an Alchemist*, by Li Chih-ch'ang, trans. Arthur Waley (London: Routledge and Sons, 1931), pp. 13–16; Herbert Franke, "The Chin Dynasty," in Franke and Twitchett, *The Cambridge History of China*, vol. 6, p. 317; Miya Noriko, *Mongoru jidai no shuppan bunka*, p. 67.

a Daoist textbook by the early Mongol elites rather than a Confucian classic. At least, apparently the introduction of *Xiaojing* during Ögedei's reign does not directly lead to Confucianization.

Not until 1244 did *Xiaojing* become a Confucian text among the Mongol elite. In the biography of Wang E in *Yuan shi*, we read that Wang, the former *jinshi* 進士 of Jin dynasty, lectured to then-prince Khubilai about *Xiaojing*, *Shu* (*jing*), *Yi* (*jing*) "as well as the ways of regulating a household and of governing a country and the change of affairs of all ages."[37] Although Wang's curriculum does not differ greatly from Li's one, given Wang's philosophical tendency, it can be said that now *Xiaojing* was approached from the Confucian perspective. Certainly the topic between Khubilai and Wang, "the ways of regulating a household and of governing a country and the change of affairs of all ages," implies an attitude different from the tone of the conversation between Chinggis Khan and Qiu Chuji 25 years before.[38] Wang's "lecture" to Khubilai may have been given through interpreters because Khubilai's knowledge of Chinese was poor.[39]

Thereafter, *Xiaojing* continued to circulate among the Mongols: Khubilai's heir apparent, Zhenjin 眞金 (a.k.a. Chingkim, 1243–1292), was taught the book,[40] and the School for the Sons of the State (*Guozixue* 國子學) also included *Xiaojing* in its curriculum in 1287.[41] In both cases—especially in the latter case—an edition in Chinese was used.[42] In early fourteenth

37 Song Lian et al., *Yuan shi*, vol. 160, p. 3756. Cleaves assumes that "the ways of regulating a household and of governing a country" alludes *The Great Learning* [*Daxue* 大學]. See Cleaves, "The Eighteenth Chapter of an Early Mongolian Version of the *Hsiao Ching*," p. 227.

38 "Then he [Chinggis Khan] asked him [Qiu Chuji]: 'Adept, what Medicine of Long Life have you brought me from afar?' The Master replied: 'I have means of protecting life, but no elixir that will prolong it.' The Emperor pleased with his candour, and two tents for the Master and his disciples set up the east of his own." Li Chih-ch'ang, *The Travels of an Alchemist*, p. 101.

39 Herbert Franke, "Could the Mongol Emperors Read and Write Chinese?" *Asia Major* 3 (1952), pp. 29–31.

40 Song Lian et al., *Yuan shi*, vol. 115, p. 2888.

41 Ibid., vol. 81, p. 2029.

42 Zhenjin was a pupil of Chinese Confucians and interested enough in Chinese culture to ask his son Abači to study Chinese writing. However, he did not ask all of his

century, *Xiaojing* gained a foothold in the Yuan court: Khaishan's brother and heir apparent, Ayurbarwada, ordered to print an illustrated *Xiaojing* along with *Daxue yanyi* 大學衍義 and *Lienü zhuan* 烈女傳 just a few weeks after Khaishan's rise to the throne.[43] Even Khaishan himself, when he honoured his queen-mother, issued a decree in which a passage from *Xiaojing* was quoted.[44] These cases bespeak that Chinese-version *Xiaojing* was familiar to some degree to some within the inner circle of the Tuluid dynasty.

It is still unclear, however, why Khaishan in 1307 ordered the publishing and distribution of the Mongolian *Xiaojing* in 'Phags-pa script instead of any version in Chinese which was already available to him. It may be reasonable to think that his aim was to distribute the ideas in the book beyond the relatively restricted range of the Mongol people who were familiar with literary Chinese. Fortunately, we can get useful clues from the Mongolian version of *Xiaojing* written in Uighur script.

Introduced first by Walter Fuchs in 1946, the *Xiaojing* in Uighur script has drawn the attention of several eminent scholars.[45] This copy has neither a preface nor a colophon, so it is impossible to pin down where and when it was printed. However, according to de Rachewiltz's grammatical analysis of the text, the extant copy is likely a later reprint from the original blocks carved in the Yuan period and its first translation

---

sons to do so; "his eldest son Kamala was not able to read and had to rely on an oral translation of the *Tzŭ-chi t'ung-kien* into Mongol." See Franke, "Could the Mongol Emperors Read and Write Chinese?" p. 31. Concerning the School for the Sons of the State 國子學, its role was to teach the meaning of [Confucian] classics and correct its pronunciation and interpretation 講授經旨，是正音訓, which implies that the *Xiaojing* in the curriculum was a Chinese version. Song Lian et al., *Yuan shi*, vol. 81, p. 2029.

43 Song Lian et al., *Yuan shi*, vol. 24, p. 536.

44 "Zun Huangtaihou zhao 尊皇太后詔" [A decree to honour Imperial Queen Mother], in *Da Yuan shengzheng guochao dianzhang* 大元聖政國朝典章 [Dynastic institutions of the sagely administration of the Great Yuan], vol. 1, *Zhaoling* 詔令 (Taipei: Wenhai chubanshe, 1964), p. 38. This decree was possibly written by Yan Fu 閻復 (1236–1312). See Miya Noriko, *Mongoru jidai no shuppan bunka*, p. 72, n20. However, it is questionable if Khaishan was aware that *Xiaojing* was quoted in the decree.

45 Igor de Rachewiltz, "The Preclassical Mongolian Version of the *Hsiao-ching*," *Zentralasiatischen Studien* 16 (1982), pp. 7–109. Especially pp. 14–23.

in manuscript form goes back possibly as early as the mid-thirteenth century.[46] Therefore, we can think that the *Xiaojing* in Uighur script had already appeared before the founding of the School for the Sons of the State and circulated within the Mongol and, probably, *Semu* 色目 elites. Then, the book in Uighur script was likely published in 1307, coupled with the new 'Phags-pa script version.[47] So we may assume that the *Xiaojing* in 'Phags-pa script as well as in Uighur script stemmed from different intellectual settings from the School for the Sons of the State which is thought to have had a relatively strong Han-Chinese tradition.[48]

This assumption can be underpinned by an examination of the *Xiaojing* versions preferred after the Song dynasty. The *Xiaojing* in Uighur script consists of 18 chapters, which follows the format of the *New Text Xiaojing* 今文孝經. The *New Text Xiaojing* had been the standard format until the twelfth century. For example, both the *Xiaojing* with imperial commentaries (*Yu zhu Xiaojing*) and the version in the *Commentaries on the Thirteen Classics* (*Shisanjing zhushu* 十三經注疏) follow the format of the *New Text Xiaojing*. Therefore, it can be said that the *Xiaojing* in Uighur script succeeded the Han-Tang Confucianism, or the pre-Neo-Confucian tradition.

Seen from this perspective, we note that Khaishan's decree to distribute *Xiaojing* deviated from the mainstream of Confucianism in the mid-Yuan period. The Neo-Confucian intellectuals from the newly-conquered southern provinces grew to dominate the intellectual terrain of the Yuan society, replacing the older generation of influential northerners from the late thirteenth century (1270s–1280s).[49] The reinstitution of the civil

46 de Rachewiltz, "The Preclassical Mongolian Version of the *Hsiao-ching*," pp. 17–19.

47 Ibid.

48 The *Elementary Learning* [*Xiaoxue* 小學] and the Four Books in the curriculum of the School for the Sons of the State were Zhu Xi's version. William Theodore de Bary, *Neo-Confucian Orthodoxy and the Learning of the Mind-and-Heart* (New York: Columbia University Press, 1981), p. 48. It is uncertain, however, if the *Xiaojing* used in the school was also his *Xiaojing kan wu* 孝經刊誤 [Corrections to *Xiaojing*].

49 John Dardess, "Did the Mongols Matter? Territory, Power, and the Intelligentsia in China from the Northern Song to the Early Ming," in *The Song-Yuan-Ming Transition in Chinese History*, ed. Paul Jakov Smith and Richard von Glahn (Cambridge and London: Harvard University Press, 2003), pp. 130–131.

service examination during the 1310s, adopting Zhu Xi's interpretation as the canonical textbook for examinees, reveals the increasing influence of Neo-Confucians in the Yuan court.[50] The Neo-Confucians, however, dismissed the value of *Xiaojing* as a Confucian classic. Zhu Xi criticized that then-existing *Xiaojing* editions embodied misunderstandings of the Han dynasty literati and that it was fallacy to interpret *Xiaojing* with the notion of the "governance with filial piety 孝治論."[51] In other words, Zhu Xi denied the basic understanding of *Xiaojing* of the Han-Tang Confucianism, prescribing thereafter how scholars should understand the text in Neo-Confucian tradition. As Neo-Confucians became puissant in the Yuan court, therefore, the authority of *Xiaojing* waned; the Yuan, and its successors as well, did not require civil service examination candidates to be well acquainted with *Xiaojing*. For these reasons, here we can conclude that Khaishan's *Xiaojing* distribution policy had little to do with then prevailing Neo-Confucianism, but more with the tradition of the Han-Tang Confucianism, considering not only its eighteen-chapter structure but also his emphasis on *Xiaojing* itself.

Steering away from the influence of Neo-Confucianism, Khaishan's aim in the *Xiaojing* policy probably had something with the traditional understanding of *Xiaojing*—the view that sees it as a source of political ideology supporting the idea of an inviolable sovereign. Then, how can we locate his *Xiaojing* project in his whole line of policy? Traditionally, historians have made a harsh evaluation of Khaishan's reign. For example, under the rubric of "Administrative Anomalies," the chapter on mid-Yuan politics in *The Cambridge History of China* says that "apparently in order to court support for his authority, he (Khaishan) granted nineteen princely titles in 1307 and 1308 alone, fourteen of which were princes of the first rank (*i-tz'u wang*).... Of the fourteen recipients, only two were the sons of the khaghans, thus totally disregarding Khubilai's unwritten law that only

50 de Bary, *Neo-Confucian Orthodoxy and the Learning of the Mind-and-Heart*, pp. 50–60; Dardess, "Did the Mongols Matter?" pp. 130–131.

51 Chung Ho-hun, "Chuja *Xiaojing kan wu* wa kŭ sŏnggyŏk," pp. 80–81.

the sons of khaghans could be made princes of the first rank."[52] Generally speaking, the appanages and various privileges following the titles are thought to have led to the financial deterioration as well as the rise of semi-autonomous powers in his empire.

However, Khaishan's generous bestowal of princely titles can be seen as a strategy to place the northern steppe powers under the influence of the central government in Khanbaliq. "By awarding them fiefs for the most part named after, and nominally identified with, territorial divisions inside China," as Dardess pointed out, Khaishan introduced "a new and more precisely graduated scale of princely ranks of Chinese origin through which the emperor could control promotions and demotions."[53] It is largely agreed that Khaishan showed interest in the steppe world in order to be the great khaghan of the Yeke Mongol Ulus, not the emperor of the Yuan dynasty.[54] He did not concentrate on China proper as his brother Ayurbarwada would do in the next decade. However, it is also true that Khaishan did not unreservedly advocate the pre-dynastic steppe tradition, either. If anything, he extended the central bureaucratic network over Mongolia with which he could to some degree check the steppe princes.[55] Furthermore, his reliance on the Turkic forces, whose members were free from the tribal bonds of the Mongols, was certainly a deviation from the Mongol tradition.[56] Therefore, Khaishan's policies that historians considered "deviate" or "anomalous" were the aftermath of his project to control the Mongol princes and to stabilize his authority as a khaghan. His interest in *Xiaojing* was not likely to be exceptional.

52 Hsiao Ch'i-ch'ing, "Mid-Yuan Politics," p. 508.

53 John Dardess, *Conquerors and Confucians* (New York: Columbia University Press, 1973), p. 25.

54 Sugiyama Masaaki 杉山正明, *Mongoru teikoku no kōbō* モンゴル帝国の興亡 [The rise and fall of the Mongol empire] (Tokyo: Kōdansha, 1996). Translated by Rim Daehui et al. as *Monggol segye jeguk* (Seoul: Sinsŏwŏn, 1999), pp. 321–323.

55 Dardess, *Conquerors and Confucians*, pp. 24–25.

56 Lee Yonggyu, "Seeking Loyalty: The Inner Asian Tradition of Personal Guards and Its Influence in Persia and China" (Ph.D. dissertation, Harvard University, 2004), pp. 240–273.

The Mongolian *Xiaojing* in 1307 may have been a sort of ideological leverage to exalt Khaishan's authority among the Mongols. More concretely, it seems to have been for infusing the Mongol princes with the image of an inviolable khaghan. On the surface, Khaishan ordered his court to distribute the book to "his subordinate kings and those below them" so that "from the princes and dukes down to the common people, all ought to act according to it [i.e. the teaching of Confucius]." However, his main target was apparently the Mongol ruling elite, such as princes and kings, because it is doubtful whether non-elite Mongol people could read either Uighur or 'Phags-pa scripts. Thus Khaishan tried to spread pre-Neo-Confucian political ideal by distributing *Xiaojing*, disregarding other elements of Han-Chinese family ethics. So his distribution of the classic of the "governance with filial piety" and the generous bestowal of princely titles to the princes were the two wings of his project to embrace them in his control. At any rate, the princes had in principle the right to elect their khaghan, and Khaishan could not ignore their privilege. Even Khubilai could not strip the Ochigin of their traditional privilege after he had quelled Nayan's rebellion.[57] Khaishan's dependence on the Turk military machines also reveals that he was unable to force their Mongol retainers to give up the traditional tribal connection. As long as he could not disarm the potentially menacing princes, it was reasonable for him to embrace the princes into khaghan-centred hierarchy and strengthen ideological propaganda for the khaghanate.

In conclusion, *Xiaojing*, just as it did during the Han and Tuoba Wei dynasties, primarily worked as a text of political ideology at the Khaishan's court in 1307. *Xiaojing* was to provide the vassal kings under the Mongol khaghan with their respective role model, elevating Khaishan from *primus inter pares* among the Golden Family to an inviolable sovereign. Therefore

57 Yoon Eunsook 尹銀淑, "Kubilai kan ŭi chung'ang chipkwŏnhwa e daehan tongdojewangdŭl ŭi daeŭng: 'Nayan panran'ŭl chungsim ŭro 쿠빌라이칸의 중앙집권화에 대한 東道諸王들의 대응 —'나얀 반란'을 중심으로—" [The reaction of eastern feudal lords to Qubilai Qa'an's centralized authoritarian rules: Focus on the Nayan rebellion], *Chung'ang Asia Yŏnn'gu* 中央아시아研究 [Central Asian studies] 8 (2003), pp. 29–50.

we can say that Khaishan's *Xiaojing* project was deliberately employed in the context of political history in his reign, distanced from the mainstream of the Yuan Confucianism. Thus it was natural that the project did not survive after his demise in 1311. Although the civil service examination was resumed during the reign of Ayurbarwada, *Xiaojing* never returned to its previous status and the principle of "governance with filial piety" which Khaishan designed to plant in his empire was not taken as seriously as before.

Conclusion

Khaishan's decree in 1307 to distribute *Xiaojing* was a political tactic to strengthen his throne. Although he was a war hero, since he needed to distinguish himself from other Mongol princes, he tried to imbue them with the Confucian model of emperorship. For this reason, the seemingly odd link between the steppe hero and the Confucian classic was forged.

Xiaojing was not only a text on family ethics but also acted as a way of legitimating the emperor-centred hierarchy under pre-Neo-Confucian tradition. Compiled when early Chinese empires emerged, it reflects the ethos of early Confucians supporting a centralized emperorship. The book was therefore on the core of the far-flung political propaganda in the Han dynasty for the purpose of stabilizing the status quo and buttressing the authority of the son of Heaven. Thus the Han dynasty was known as a period of the "governance with filial piety."[58]

During the late phase of the Tuoba Wei, *Xiaojing* played another significant role—acting as a textbook for sinicization. In addition to elevating the emperorship among centrifugal Xianbei leaders, Emperor Xiaowen employed it to sinicize Tuoba's traditional tribal relation. That is, when the emperor planned to rearrange his empire in accordance with the Han-Chinese social order, the book functioned as the source of Chinese family, political, and social ethics. The publication of the Xianbei-version *Xiaojing* during the reign of Emperor Xiaowen symbolizes the book's importance in his sinicization process.

58 Yi Sŏngkyu, "Handae Hyokyŏng ŭi pokŭp kwa kŭ inyŏm," pp. 183–186.

The *Xiaojing* distribution policy in 1307 was also under the tradition of the Han-Tang Confucianism. It did not signify the simple revival of ancient statecraft, however; it exemplifies some characteristics of the Mongol attitude toward the Han-Chinese culture. That Khaishan employed the traditional Chinese way to strengthen emperorship means that Confucianism penetrated into the court of the steppe hero to some degree. But I would like to stress the fact that it stepped aside from the mainstream of the Chinese intellectual tradition in the early fourteenth century: it mobilized the Han-Tang Confucian tradition which was already out-of-fashion as of 1307. There seems to have been a particular current of Confucian scholarship among the Mongol elites and *Semu* intellectuals which remained separate from the Chinese intellectual trend to some extent. That is, Khaishan's order to distribute *Xiaojing* in 1307 was not the unconditional imitation of Chinese culture but a sort of Mongolization of Confucianism.

At the same time, the comparison of the *Xiaojing* translation and distribution policies sheds light on the difference between these two conquest dynasties. In Mongol Yuan, unlike in Tuoba Wei, the impact of the decree by Khaishan in 1307 was not intended to reach beyond the political sphere of the empire. This difference was partly because the notion of "governance with filial piety," the core of the pre-Neo-Confucian *Xiaojing* interpretation, was denied by Zhu Xi and his pupils whose thoughts dominated the Yuan society. More important, however, it reveals that the Mongols' attitude toward Chinese culture was selective. Unlike Emperor Xiaowen of Tuoba Wei who distributed *Xiaojing* as a part of his all-angle sinicization campaign, Khaishan did not enforce any special sinicization policy along with distributing the Confucian canon. For Khaishan, the *Xiaojing* translation in 1307 was no more than a simple expedient for his political goals, not the first step toward the total Confucianization of the Mongol society. This difference between these two dynasties well demonstrates that the translation of Confucian classics in China's neighbouring nomadic societies cannot always be understood as a yardstick of sinicization; rather it may have been the result of selective efforts to deal with the politics of the steppe world.

Bibliography

Chung, Ho-hun 鄭豪薰. "Chuja *Xiaojing kan wu* wa kŭ sŏnggyŏk 朱子『孝經刊誤』와 그 성격" [The formation of Zhu Xi's *Xiaojing kan wu* and its political significance]. *Tongbang hakji* 東方學志 [The journal of Eastern studies] 106 (2002), pp. 71–106.

Cleaves, Francis W. "The First Chapter of an Early Mongolian Version of the *Hsiao Ching*." *Acta Orientalia Academiae Scientiarum Hungaricae* 36 (1982), pp. 69–88.

———. "The Second Chapter of an Early Mongolian Version of the *Hsiao Ching*." In *Documenta Barbarorum: Festschrift für Walter Heissig zum 70*, edited by Klaus Sagaster and Michael Weiers. Wiesbaden: O. Harrassowitz, 1983, pp. 272–281.

———. "The Eighteenth Chapter of an Early Mongolian Version of the *Hsiao Ching*." *Harvard Journal of Asiatic Studies* 45, no. 1 (1985), pp. 225–254.

———. "An Early Mongolian Version of the *Hsiao Ching*." Chapters 3–6, *Mongolian Studies* 14 (1991), pp. 117–143; 15 (1992), pp. 137–150; 16 (1993), pp. 19–40; 17 (1994), pp. 1–20.

———, trans. *An Early Mongolian Version of the Hsiao Ching*. Bloomington, Indiana: Mongolia Society, 2001.

Da Yuan shengzheng guochao dianzhang 大元聖政國朝典章 [Dynastic institutions of the sagely administration of the Great Yuan] (a.k.a. *Yuan dianzhang* 元典章). Taipei: Wenhai chubanshe, 1964.

Dardess, John. *Conquerors and Confucians*. New York: Columbia University Press, 1973.

———. "Did the Mongols Matter? Territory, Power, and the Intelligentsia in China from the Northern Song to the Early Ming." In *The Song-Yuan-Ming Transition in Chinese History*, edited by Paul Jakov Smith and Richard von Glahn. Cambridge and London: Harvard University Press, 2003, pp. 111–134.

de Bary, William Theodore. *Neo-Confucian Orthodoxy and the Learning of the Mind-and-Heart*. New York: Columbia University Press, 1981.

de Rachewiltz, Igor. "The Preclassical Mongolian Version of the *Hsiao-ching*." *Zentralasiatischen Studien* 16 (1982), pp. 7–109.

———. "More about the Preclassical Mongolian Version of the *Hsiao-ching*." *Zentralasiatischen Studien* 19 (1986), pp. 27–37.

Dien, Albert. "The Bestowal of Surnames under the Western Wei-Northern Chou: A Case of Counter-Acculturation." *T'oung Pao* 63 (1977), pp. 137–177.

———. "A New Look at the Xianbei and Their Impact on Chinese Culture." In *Ancient Mortuary Traditions of China*, edited by George Kuwayama. Los Angeles: Far Eastern Art Council, Los Angeles County Museum of Art; Honolulu: University of Hawai'i Press, 1991, pp. 40–59.

Fan, Ye 范曄. *Houhan shu* 後漢書 [Book of Later Han]. Beijing: Zhonghua shuju, 1982.

Franke, Herbert. "Could the Mongol Emperors Read and Write Chinese?" *Asia Major* 3 (1952), pp. 28–41.

———. "Chinese Historiography under Mongol Rule: The Role of History in Acculturation." *Mongolian Studies* 1 (1974), pp. 15–26.

Franke, Herbert, and Denis Twitchett, eds. *The Cambridge History of China*. Vol. 6, *Alien Regimes and Border States, 907–1368*. Cambridge, New York, and Oakleigh: Cambridge University Press, 1978.

Guyuanxian wenwu gongzuozhan 固原縣文物工作站. "Ningxia Guyuan Bei Wei mu qingli jianbao 寧夏固原北魏墓清理簡報" [Preliminary report on the excavation of a tomb of Northern Wei in Guyuan, Ningxia]. *Wenwu* 文物 [Cultural relics], no. 6 (1984), pp. 49–56.

Hansen, Valerie. *The Open Empire: A History of China to 1600*. New York: Norton, 2000.

Ho, Ping-ti. "Lo-yang, A.D. 495–534: A Study of Physical and Socio-Economic Planning of a Metropolitan Area." *Harvard Journal of Asiatic Studies* 26 (1966), pp. 52–101.

Holmgren, Jennifer. "Observations on Marriage and Inheritances Practices in Early Mongol and Yuan Society with Particular Reference to the Levirate." *Journal of Asian History* 20, no. 2 (1986), pp. 127–192.

Honey, David B. "Stripping off Felt and Fur: An Essay on Nomadic Sinification." *Papers on Inner Asia* 21 (1992), pp. 1–39.

Itano, Chōhachi 板野長八. *Chūgoku kodai ni okeru ningenkan no tenkai* 中国古代における人間観の展開 [Development of the views on human nature in ancient China]. Tokyo: Iwanami Shoten, 1972.

Jenner, William John Francis. *Memories of Loyang: Yang Hsüan-chih and the Lost Capital (493–534)*. Oxford: Clarendon Press; New York: Oxford University Press, 1981.

Kawamoto, Yoshiaki 川本芳昭. *Gi Shin Nanbokuchō jidai no minzoku mondai* 魏晋南

北朝時代の民族問題 [Ethnic issues in the period of disunity]. Tokyo: Kyūko Shoin, 1998.

Lee, Yonggyu. "Seeking Loyalty: The Inner Asian Tradition of Personal Guards and Its Influence in Persia and China." Ph.D. dissertation, Harvard University, 2004.

Legge, James, trans. "Hsiāo King." In *The Sacred Books of China: The Texts of Confucianism*, edited by James Legge. Oxford: The Clarendon Press, 1879, pp. 449–488.

Li, Chih-ch'ang. *The Travels of an Alchemist: The Journey of the Taoist Ch'ang-ch'un from China to the Hindukush at the Summons of Chingiz Khan.* Translated by Arthur Waley. London: Routledge and Sons, 1931.

Miya, Noriko 宮紀子. *Mongoru jidai no shuppan bunka* モンゴル時代の出版文化 [Cultural policy and publishing activities during the Mongol period]. Nagoya: Nagoya Daigaku Shuppankai, 2006.

Sima, Qian 司馬遷. *Shi ji* 史記 [Records of the grand historian]. Beijing: Zhonghua shuju, 1982.

Song, Lian 宋濂 et al. *Yuan shi* 元史 [History of Yuan]. Beijing: Zhonghua shuju, 1976.

Sugiyama, Masaaki 杉山正明. *Mongoru teikoku no kōbō* モンゴル帝国の興亡 [The rise and fall of the Mongol empire]. Tokyo: Kōdansha, 1996. Translated by Rim Daehui et al. as *Monggol segye jeguk* (Seoul: Sinsŏwŏn, 1999).

Sun, Ji 孫機. "Guyuan Bei Wei qiguanhua yanjiu 固原北魏漆棺畫研究" [Study of the painting on a Northern Wei lacquered coffin in Guyuan]. *Wenwu* 文物 [Cultural relics], no. 9 (1989), pp. 38–44.

Tao, Jing-shen. *The Jurchen in Twelfth-century China: A Study of Sinicization.* Seattle: University of Washington Press, 1977.

Toqto'a (Tuotuo) 脫脫 et al. *Jin shi* 金史 [History of Jin]. Beijing: Zhonghua shuju, 1982.

Watanabe, Shin'ichirō 渡辺信一郎. *Chūgoku kodai kokka no shisō kōzō: Sensei kokka to ideorogī* 中国古代国家の思想構造：専制国家とイデオロギー [The intellectual structure of ancient Chinese states: Despotic states and the ideology]. Tokyo: Azekura Shobō, 1994.

Wei, Shou 魏收. *Wei Shu* 魏書 [Book of Wei]. Beijing: Zhonghua shuju, 1984.

Wei, Zheng 魏徵 et al. *Sui shu* 隋書 [Book of Sui]. Beijing: Zhonghua shuju, 1984.

Yi, Sŏngkyu 李成珪. "Handae Hyokyŏng ŭi pokŭp kwa kŭ inyŏm 漢代『효경(孝經)』의 普及과 그 理念" [The ideology of *Xiaojing* and government policy of encouraging the filial piety in Han China]. *Han'guk sasangsa hak* 韓國思想史學 [The study of Korean history of thought] 10 (1998), pp. 183–221.

Yoon, Eunsook 尹銀淑. "Kubilai kan ŭi chung'ang chipkwōnhwa e daehan tongdojewangdŭl ŭi daeŭng: 'Nayan panran'ŭl chungsim ŭro 쿠빌라이칸의 중앙집권화에 대한 東道諸王들의 대응—'나얀 반란'을 중심으로—" [The reaction of eastern feudal lords to Qubilai Qa'an's centralized authoritarian rules: Focus on the Nayan rebellion]. *Chung'ang Asia Yŏnn'gu* 中央아시아研究 [Central Asian studies] 8 (2003), pp. 29–50.

Yoshikawa, Tadao 吉川忠夫. *Rikuchō seishinshi kenkyū* 六朝精神史研究 [Intellectual history of the Six Dynasties period]. Kyōto: Dōhōsha, 1984.

"*Chouban yiwu*" (Handling the Affairs of the Barbarians): Translators in the Translation History of the Eighteenth to Nineteenth Century China

Lawrence Wang-chi WONG

While it is a simple fact that all translation activities are undertaken by translators, little attention has been paid to them, because people generally put most of the emphasis on the products, that is, the translations. This is understandable for the general readers, as the only item they actually encounter is the translation works. However, for translation history scholars, without a thorough knowledge of the "agents," whose hard labour brings about the products, they will not be able to have a comprehensive and accurate understanding of the various aspects of the translation activities that have taken place, inclusive of the products. The present paper studies a major and yet neglected phenomenon in the translation history of the eighteenth to nineteenth century China, the translators. It is not a discussion on individual translator's works or activities. Rather, we will look at the translators as a phenomenon, focusing on their social, cultural and even political position at a very special time and spatial frame in Chinese history: the eighteenth to nineteenth century, when the British attempted to force open the tightly-closed door of Imperial China. During these early contacts between two great powers of distinctively different languages, cultures and ideologies, tensions and even conflicts were almost unavoidable. While we may expect the translators/interpreters to play a vital and difficult role in negotiating the differences, their tasks were made complicated by one important traditional concept in China: foreigners were uncivilized barbarians from afar. "*Chouban yiwu*" 籌辦夷務 (handling the affairs of the barbarians) was the term used in the nineteenth century by the Qing court when they had to deal with the Westerners.

I

Since ancient times, the Chinese had developed a kind of superiority complex over their neighbours. The word *yi* 夷 or *manyi* 蠻夷 appeared in writings dated back to the Zhou 周 dynasty about three thousand years ago. At the very early stage, the focus might have been on the geographical difference: people who lived outside the central kingdom (*Zhongguo* 中國) or the Central Plain (*Zhongyuan* 中原) were called *yi* or *manyi*. However, as some historians have correctly pointed out, since the Spring and Autumn period (*Chunqiu* 春秋, 770–746 BCE), when China was not a united country and the various states were frequently at war with one another and in particular against the neighbouring tribes, there began an emphasis on the differences in culture. As the Chinese were in general more advanced and better developed in the arts of civilization, and very often, militarily too, they felt superior to the steppe nomadic tribes in the surrounding regions. By labelling these tribal people *yi*, the uncivilized barbarians, the Chinese were able to distinguish themselves from the others, justifying their claim to rule over all places "under the Heaven" (*tianxia* 天下). All the other states could at most maintain a kind of lord-vassal relationship with the Son of Heaven (*tianzi* 天子). They were the tributary states to pay tributes to China on a regular basis. In short, the traditional Chinese world order, for a very long period of time, was, as John K. Fairbank (1907–1991) summarises, Sinocentric, hierarchical and non-egalitarian.[1]

When the Europeans came to China in the sixteenth century, they were taken as *manyi* in no different way. Lydia Liu, in her famous work *The Clash of Empires: The Invention of China in Modern World Making*,[2] argues that the interpretation of *yi* as equivalent to "barbarian" was but a "super-sign"—*yi*/barbarian—created by the British. To her, it was Charles

---

1 John K. Fairbank, ed., *The Chinese World Order: Traditional China's Foreign Relations* (Cambridge, MA: Harvard University Press, 1968).

2 Lydia H. Liu, *The Clash of Empires: The Invention of China in Modern World Making* (Cambridge, MA and London: Harvard University Press, 2004), p. 31.

Gutzlaff (1803–1851), a Prussian missionary, who in 1832 first made a protest to the Chinese officials about the use of *yi* on the Westerners, after which the British became more and more critical and intolerable towards this term and the Chinese attitude. She quotes Robert Morrison (1792–1834), the first Protestant missionary to China, for support. In his *A Dictionary of the Chinese Language*, the first Chinese-English bilingual dictionary published in 1815, Morrison defined *yiren* 夷人 as "a foreigner," referring to "a distant man; one from remote parts." Robert Morrison even suggested that *yi* was in fact "the more respectable term" than *fan* 番.[3] This seems authoritative enough. However, what Lydia Liu probably does not know, or at least she has not mentioned is: Robert Morrison himself had a clear understanding of the derogatory nature of the use of the word among the Chinese at that time. In 1821, 11 years before Gulzlaff made the protest, Morrison wrote the following lines in an article openly published in the *Chinese Repository*:

> [T]he Chinese word *E* 夷 [*yi*] which is usually translated *foreigners*, but which conveys, in addition to *not belonging to China*, an idea of inferiority, resembling the word *barbarian* as anciently used by the Greeks.[4]

Then in 1827, when he had to explain the use of *yi* to the Supercargoes of the East India Company, he stated categorically that *yi* "is a dubious word, never used by ourselves."[5] Clearly, he was deliberate in avoiding the term, because he was aware that it had this inferiority connotation. This explains why he would prefer to translate *yi* as "a foreigner" in his dictionary.

3 Robert Morrison, *A Dictionary of the Chinese Language*, vol. 1 (Macao: East India Company Press, 1815), p. 61.

4 Eliza A. Morrison, "Narrative of an Affair between a Watering Party of Seamen, from the *Topaz*, an English Frigate, and the Chinese Inhabitants of Lin-tin Island, Situated above Macao, in the Passage from the Sea to the Anchorage at Whampoa, Interspersed with Remarks on the Current Affairs of Canton, 1821–2," in *Memoirs of the Life and Labours of Robert Morrison, DD*, vol. 2 (London: Longman, Orme, Brown, Green and Longmans, 1839), p. 31.

5 H. B. Morse, *The Chronicles of the East India Company Trading to China, 1635–1834*, vol. 4 (London: Oxford University Press, 1926), p. 152.

There are more other evidences to prove that the British, or the Westerners in general, were aware of the disparaging use of the word *yi*. Long before the British established their trading post in Guangzhou, in the Ming dynasty, the Jesuit missionaries were clear about how they were treated by the Chinese. Matteo Ricci (1552–1610) recorded in his memoir that the Chinese took all Westerners as uncivilized and illiterate barbarians, "as though there was no room for doubt that they differ but little from the beasts of the field and the forest," "scarcely ever do they give them a title more honourable than they would assign to their demons."[6]

As for the British, they had indeed filed a petition, if not a protest, to the local authorities in Guangzhou against the use of *yi* much earlier than Gutzlaff did. In November 1814, George Thomas Staunton (1781–1859), representing John F. Elphinstone (1778–1854), Supercargo of the East India Company, in a meeting with a senior Chinese official, registered his discontent towards the use of *yi* for the British.[7] This kind of feeble protest would not change the attitude of the Chinese. Thus we saw in the Chinese writings of that period all kinds of barbarians: the British Barbarians, the French Barbarians, the Dutch Barbarians, the Portuguese Barbarians, etc. Regardless of their nationalities, they were all the same seen as inferior, uncivilized barbarians from the peripheral distant lands. Even the first formal embassy sent by Great Britain to China in 1783, under Lord George Macartney (1737–1806), was taken as a tributary mission from a barbarian state afar. The state letter sent by the Chinese Emperor Qianlong 乾隆 (1711–1799; r. 1736–1795) to King George III (1738–1820; r. 1760–1820) was written in such an arrogant and conceited kind of language that the

6 Louis J. Gallagher, SJ, trans., *China in the Sixteenth Century: The Journals of Matthew Ricci: 1583–1610* (New York: Random House, 1953), pp. 88–89. In various other places of this work, there are similar complaints. Ibid., pp. 167, 201, 447.

7 Liang Tingnan 梁廷枏, *Yue haiguan zhi* 粵海關志 [Records of the Guangdong customs] (Shaoguan: Guangdong renmin chuban, 2002), p. 555. But Liang Tingnan got the date wrong. It was not the 15th year of Jiaqing 嘉慶, which was 1810; but the 19th year of Jiaqing, that was 1814. See also John Robert Morrison, *Chinese Commercial Guide, Consisting of a Collection of Details Respecting Foreign Trade in China* (Canton: Albion Press, 1834), p. 40.

European Jesuit translators decided there was a need to make major changes to the text in order to make it acceptable to the British.[8] They removed "any offensive turn of phrase" and "insert[ed] all the terms of respect for the King of England."[9] It was not until the Second Opium War that the British were able to insert a clause in the Treaty of Tientsin (1858) to assert that "henceforward, the character 'I' 夷 (barbarian), shall not be applied to the Government or subjects of Her Britannic Majesty in any Chinese official document issued by the Chinese Authorities either in the Capital or in the Provinces."[10]

It was under this framework of Westerners as barbarians that the Chinese translators operated in the eighteenth to nineteenth century.[11]

---

8 The Chinese version of the letter can be found in "Daqing huangdi gei yingjili guowang chiyu 大清皇帝給英吉利國王勅諭" [The imperial edict from the Emperor of Great Qing to the King of England], in *Yingshi Majia'erni fanghua dang'an shiliao huibian* 英使馬戛爾尼訪華檔案史料匯編 [A collection of historical materials on the Macartney Embassy to China], ed. The First Archive of Chinese History (Beijing: Guoji wenhua chuban gongshi, 1996), pp. 165–166. A relatively faithful translation is done by J. L. Cranmer-Byng, "Lord Macartney's Embassy to Peking in 1793: From Official Chinese Documents," in *Britain and the China Trade, 1635–1842*, selected by Patrick Tuck, vol. 7 (London and New York: Routledge, 2000), pp. 134–137.

9 Alain Peyrefitte, *The Collision of Two Civilizations: The British Expedition to China in 1792–4*, trans. Jon Rothschile (London: Harvill, 1993), pp. 288–289. For a discussion of the translation issues and translators in the Macartney Mission, cf., Wang Hongzhi 王宏志 (Lawrence Wang-chi Wong), "Majia'erni shihua de fanyi wenti 馬戛爾尼使華的翻譯問題" [Translation in the Macartney Embassy to China], *Zhongyang yanjiuyuan jindaishi yanjiusuo jikan* 中央研究院近代史研究所集刊 [Bulletin of the Institute of Modern History, Academia Sinica], no. 63 (March 2009), pp. 97–145.

10 "Treaty of Tientsin," in *Treaties, Conventions, etc., between China and Foreign States*, vol. 1 (Shanghai: Inspector General of Customs, 1917; repr., New York: AMS Press, 1973), p. 419.

11 For a more thorough treatment of the *yi* concept towards the Westerners in the eighteenth-century China, see Lawrence Wang-chi Wong, "Barbarians or Not Barbarians: Translating *Yi* in the Context of Sino-British Relations in the Eighteenth and Nineteenth Centuries," in *Towards a History of Translating: In Commemoration of the 40th Anniversary of the Research Centre for Translation, CUHK*, ed. Lawrence Wang-chi Wong, vol. 3 (Hong Kong: Research Centre for Translation, The Chinese University of Hong Kong, 2013), pp. 293–387.

II

In the eighteenth to nineteenth century, the only activity permitted for the Westerners in China was trading, which had been confined to just one port, Canton (Guangzhou) since 1757. Anxious to keep the barbarians under good control, the Chinese authorities imposed very tight control over the trade practices and activities of the Westerners in this city at the southern tip of the Empire, notoriously known as the Canton system among the Western traders.[12] The Chinese officials, however, would not trouble themselves with the "barbarian affairs" directly; and all dealings were handled through the so-called Hong merchants, who hired a group of people known as *tongshi* 通事 for communication with the foreigners.

Generally, people translate *tongshi* as linguists,[13] including the authoritative H. B. Morse (1855–1934).[14] Cranmer-Byne argues that there should be a distinction between "linguists" and "interpreters": "The word 'interpreter' generally indicates a reasonable degree in verbal translation from one language into another, but the attainments of these 'linguists' were of a low grade, most of them not having progressed beyond the most elementary stage."[15] Nevertheless, there was no such distinction in Chinese eyes at those days—the one term that had been applied to all was "*tongshi*," and they were the Chinese translators/interpreters serving the Westerners in the eighteenth to nineteenth century. It has to be pointed out that at the early stage very few

12 For a general account of the Canton system, cf., John K. Fairbank, *Trade and Diplomacy on the China Coast: The Opening of the Treaty Ports, 1842–1854* (Stanford: Stanford University Press, 1969), pp. 39–53; Immanuel C. Y. Hsu, *The Rise of Modern China* (Hong Kong: Oxford University Press, 1975), pp. 189–219. For Canton trade, cf., Paul A. Van Dyke, *The Canton Trade: Life and Enterprise on the China Coast, 1700–1845* (Hong Kong: Hong Kong University Press, 2005). In Chinese, a classical work on the Thirteen Cohongs in Guangzhou is Liang Jiabin 梁嘉彬, *Guangdong shisanhang kao* 廣東十三行考 [A study of the Thirteen Hongs in Guangdong] (Shanghai: Guoli bianyiguan, 1937).

13 For example, see William C. Hunter, *The "Fan Kwae" at Canton before the Treaty Days, 1825–1844* (London: Kegan Paul, Trench, & Co, 1882); Fairbank, *Trade and Diplomacy on the China Coast*; Van Dyke, *The Canton Trade.*

14 Morse, *The Chronicles of the East India Company Trading to China*, 5 vols.

15 Cranmer-Byng, "Lord Macartney's Embassy to Peking in 1793," p. 122.

Westerners could master Chinese and act as translators/interpreters. Apart from the fact that Chinese was to them an extremely difficult language, requiring, as Gordon Cumming (1837–1924) puts it, "a head of oak, lungs of brass, nerves of steel, a constitution of iron, the patience of Job, and the lifetime of Methuselah" to learn it,[16] the major obstacle came from the Qing authorities. It was generally believed that the Chinese were strictly forbidden to teach their language to foreigners. Reportedly, there were cases that the Chinese instructors were beheaded for violating this law.[17] Robert Morrison also claimed that his two Chinese instructors lived in such fear of detection and torture that at least one of them, if not both, carried poison all the time so that "life might rather be ended than the pains of a Chinese prison suffered."[18] Thus, throughout the eighteenth and the first half of nineteenth centuries, there were just a handful of Westerners, mostly missionaries, who had some command of the Chinese language,[19] leaving the traders little choice but to count on the *tongshi* from the Chinese side for translation and interpreting services.

Unfortunately, these *tongshi* were not qualified as translators/interpreters by any standard. In the first place, they did not receive any formal training in foreign language. The general Chinese, in particular the literati, were not eager to learn any foreign language. Not to say the dangers they might face for knowing a foreign language, which will be explained shortly, what advantage would it bring them to acquire the language of the barbarians? Only those who were engaged in and profited from foreign trade might, for practical reason, somehow pick up some bits of foreign languages during the course of their work. William Hunter (1812–1891), an American trader who had spent several years in Guangzhou from 1825 and had a lot of

16 Gordon C. F. Cumming, *Wanderings in China*, vol. 2 (Edinburgh and London: William Blackwood and Sons, 1886), p. 54.

17 Hunter, *The "Fan Kwae" at Canton before the Treaty Days*, p. 60.

18 Marshall Broomhall, *Robert Morrison: A Master-Builder* (London: Church Missionary Society, 1924), p. 55.

19 For example, there were James Flint (who in 1759 went to Tianjin to complain about the trading practices in Guangzhou and was imprisoned for three years in Macao), M. Galbert, George Thomas Staunton (1781–1859), and later Charles Gutzlaff, Robert Morrison, John Francis Davis (1795–1890), and William Hunter.

first-hand experiences to deal with this group, categorically said that the *tongshi* "knew nothing of any language but their own."[20] There might be exaggeration, as the majority of these *tongshi* at that time should somehow manage to communicate with the Westerners with a kind of "Pidgin English." This special "language" was, as Hunter suggested, a Chinese invention, "by cleverly making himself familiar with *sounds* of foreign words, and conforming them to his own monosyllabic mode of expression, at the same time using simple Chinese words to express their meaning."[21] It was a mixture of English, Portuguese, Italian and even Malay words, with lots of local additions, spoken in the Chinese syntax. This was basically incomprehensible to an average British, although it was used in all aspects of life, ranging "from table-talk to homicide and philosophy."[22]

However, some *tongshi* might not really master Pidgin English well. Hunter reported a trial case in which a Lascar seaman was accused of entering Chinese territory unlawfully after a shipwreck. The chief *tongshi*, Old Tom, who virtually knew not a slightest bit of the language, made up the questions and answers for interrogation with the assistance of a trunk and box-maker who managed to pick up some foreign language. The whole situation was pathetically farcical.[23]

To make the situation more difficult, apart from interpreting, *tongshi* were also responsible for preparing and providing written translations. It was explicitly stipulated as a rule, dated back to 1757, that Westerners could not directly send letters or petitions to the Chinese authorities and all communications had to be made through the Hong merchants and *tongshi*. This posed an insurmountable problem, as virtually no Chinese *tongshi* could master written English. Worse still, *tongshi* were not only poor in foreign languages, many of them could not write well in Chinese either. Traditionally, traders and merchants, seen as greedy and voracious people who were concerned with making profits and money only, were at the lowest

20 Hunter, *The "Fan Kwae" at Canton before the Treaty Days*, p. 50.

21 Ibid., p. 61.

22 Fairbank, *Trade and Diplomacy on the China Coast*, p. 13.

23 William C. Hunter, *Bits of Old China* (London: Kegan Paul, Trench, & Co., 1855), pp. 21–30.

stratum in society. They did not receive solid traditional Chinese education in preparation to entering officialdom. We cannot expect them to translate competently even into their own language. It is therefore not surprising to find in the documents of the East India Company records of complaints against the quality of the translation. To cite just one example:

> The difficulty in obtaining a faithful interpretation of a letter by means of the Merchants is almost insurmountable, it being only by general expressions that we can at any time render ourselves intelligible.[24]

There were other issues too. In the first place, the so-called professional ethics of the *tongshi* were severely questionable. In the trial case of the Lascar seaman just mentioned, the box-maker, assistant to the chief *tongshi*, did not really interpret for the seaman although he was able to do so. Instead, during the entire course of interrogation, he kept on selling his goods to the poor seaman. The interest of the seaman was not his concern at all. But a more serious and fundamental problem lied in the relationship between the *tongshi* and the Chinese officials.

As stated, *tongshi* was part of the Canton system set up by the Qing government to keep the Westerners under control when they came to trade in Canton. Clearly, translating and interpreting was only part of their duties, and they had other more important obligations, especially in the eyes of the Chinese officials. We do not intend to go into details the trading aspect of the *tongshi*'s work.[25] In short, they were the key link or the middlemen between the Western traders and the Chinese merchants as well as the authorities. However, this was by no means an easy job. The Chinese authorities in Guangzhou imposed many unreasonable rules and restrictions on the Westerners;[26] and there were various kinds of levies, fees and financial

24 Morse, *The Chronicles of the East India Company Trading to China*, vol. 3, p. 7.

25 For a detailed presentation of *tongshi*'s role in the Canton trade, cf. Van Dyke, *The Canton Trade*, in particular chapter 5, pp. 77–93.

26 William Hunter reported in details the regulations in his book. Clearly, these regulations were made clear to the foreigners in Guangzhou at that time. Hunter, *The "Fan Kwae" at Canton before the Treaty Days*, pp. 28–30.

exploitation. It was the *tongshi* and the compradors to implement all these rules and collect the charges. They were also held responsible for examining the goods that the Western traders brought in, ensuring that there was no illegal product. In this way, they played very much the role of the customs. Further, the *tongshi* had to take good care of the daily living of the foreigners in Guangzhou. The supply of daily provisions was conducted through the compradors who were employed by the *tongshi*; and all employment of Chinese servants and workers by the foreigners had to be done through the *tongshi* too. Even if the Westerners wanted to go out for a walk (it was stipulated that foreigners could not enter the city of Guangzhou, but were allowed to go out for a walk at some scenic spots two times every month), the *tongshi* had to accompany them. In short, the *tongshi* had to ensure that the foreigners would behave well and act according to the wish of the Chinese authorities. Everything should be under good control and nothing should go wrong. But this was a most challenging task. Far away from home, eager to make quick money, living and working under severe rules and pressure, these Western traders could be reckless, unrestrained and wild, not to say that there were obvious cultural differences in terms of behaviour and manner. These traders often fought with the Chinese to demand better treatment and living conditions, and at the same time they fought against each other for greater trade benefits. Throughout the years, there were constant frictions and unhappy events. Sometimes the Western traders would even try to bypass the Hoppo and petition to more senior officials who happened to be around. This usually had serious consequences, because it was an indication that the barbarians were not under effective control.

With this policy of the Chinese authorities to control the barbarians through controlling the Chinese who were in contact with the Westerners, the *tongshi* were under severe pressure and highly venerable. One very effective measure adopted by the authorities against any misconduct was to remove all *tongshi* from the factories, as it virtually meant a suspension of trade and supply of daily provisions. This might not harm the *tongshi* too badly, except for short-term economic losses. It was taken as the last resort and would only be employed when the situation was critical. More often, the authorities would pressurize the *tongshi* in order to force the Western traders into compliance. There are many records in the documents of the East India Company that *tongshi* were arrested, put in chains to see the Westerners or parade the factories, or even beaten up in front of the Western traders. For instance, as early as in 1689, the Hoppo and Captain Heath of the *Defence*, the biggest British cargo ship ever sailed to China, could not agree on the port fee. The *tongshi* came abroad in tears and told them that "he would be bamboo'd to death if they did not comply."[27] Then in 1699, the *Macclesfield* refused to depart Guangzhou when the trading season was over because he had not collected the full amount promised for his goods. Before long, the *tongshi* of the Supercargo, Mr Douglas, was brought to his house in chain and demanded the ship to leave.[28] Then there was one case in 1810, the *tongshi* was imprisoned and put to exile for over a decade, after the Selection Committee of the East India Company complained that they were troubled by the bankruptcy of a Hong merchant, Gnewqua. The British traders were so sympathetic with this poor *tongshi*, Ashing 亞城 (Wu Acheng 吳亞城) that they put this in their records:

> [W]e learn with extreme regret that the Manderins [*sic*] are proceeding with great violence in the persecution of Ashing and also in the examination of Gnewqua and Ponqua. Ashing seems the particular object of their cruelty and they have been practiced to such a degree that tho' he long persisted in a fair statement of the Facts he is said ultimately from extreme suffering to have been compelled to declare whatever the Mandarins thought proper to dictate and in this way has been made to confess much matter injurious to the H'ble Company and disgraceful to its representatives in China.[29]

Clearly, in the eyes of the Chinese authorities, this was a powerful weapon to force the foreigners into compliance, as the relationship between the traders and the *tongshi* was in general cordial, and the Westerners usually would not

27 Morse, *The Chronicles of the East India Company Trading to China*, vol. 1, p. 82.
28 Ibid., pp. 96–97.
29 Ibid., vol. 3, p. 148.

want the *tongshi* and compradors who worked for them suffered too badly. With all these, we have to accept the argument that "being able to effectively negotiate, persuade and pacify were skills more important to the linguists' careers than being able to interpret foreigners' actions correctly or translate their intentions accurately."[30] In other words, there was not the need, from the *tongshi*'s point of view at least, to possess language proficiency or the ability to translate accurately. In fact, given the difficult situation they might face, they would rather sacrifice accuracy in translation or interpretation in favour of maintaining good relations with the Chinese authorities and the Westerners. Even though they might be able to translate accurately, they would not do so if they knew that an accurate translation might offend the officials. Morse recorded this kind of thinking of the English Supercargoes on the Chinese merchants and the *tongshi*:

> That the Chinese will assert falsehoods the most gross, and even perjure themselves when their own interests are at stake, or their pockets are likely to be affected, we have too frequent evidence of, to doubt, ...[31]

He correctly related this "difference of mental outlook" to interpreting:

> Not only was the pidgin English of the merchants and linguists of the most elementary character, but their interests were not identical with those of the Company, and they were too timid to be trusted to interpret exactly any phrases which might be unpleasing to the ears of the officials.[32]

It was in effect a power structure issue, more than a language or translation problem.

But nevertheless, it does not mean that the *tongshi* would be in a better position if they could maintain close and cordial relations with the Westerners. On the contrary, getting too close to the barbarians could be dangerous, as they would be viewed with extreme scepticism by the Chinese that they would collude with these unreliable barbarians to harm the interest of the

30 Van Dyke, *The Canton Trade*, p. 78.

31 Morse, *The Chronicles of the East India Company Trading to China*, vol. 3, p. 31.

32 Ibid.

country. In fact, people who knew a foreign language and worked closely with the foreigners would easily be labelled as *hanjian* 漢奸, traitor to the Chinese. Arthur Waley (1899–1966), in his much referred book *The Opium War through Chinese Eyes*, gives an illuminating definition on *hanjian*:

> Over and over again in the documents of this period there occurs the term *Han-chien* [*hanjian*], meaning literally "Chinese evil-doers", as opposed to *I-chien* [*yijian* 夷奸], "foreign evil-doers". It was applied, long before the War, to Chinese who entered the service of foreigners, learnt foreign languages, corresponded with foreigners or made friends with them in any way. There were, of course, licensed compradors and interpreters who theoretically were not *Han-chien*; but they were under constant suspicion, as were also the licensed guild-merchants, through whom the foreigners conducted their trade. After the war started, whole new classes of *Han-chien* arose: those who obtained maps and sea-charts for the enemy, who passed on political and military information to them, acted as pilots, worked as craftsmen on board foreign warships and so on. Later the expression became a term of abuse for anyone who favoured appeasement rather than war to the death, it often being assumed that, if he did so, it must be because he was in the foreigners' pay.[33]

While he seems to be making a distinction between the various kinds of *hanjian*, it is astonishing to see how broad the scope of *hanjian* was: it virtually included anyone who had come into the slightest connection with the foreigners in whatever capacity. Even worse, people were, as Waley suggested, "under constant suspicion" of being *hanjian* even if they did not fall exactly into any of the categorizations.

We may briefly look into one case during the First Opium War, about a *tongshi* from Guangdong named Bao Peng 鮑鵬, who was solicited as interpreter by Qi Shan 琦善 (1790–1854), imperial commissioner sent by the Emperor to negotiate a peace treaty with the British. Unfortunately, even before peace terms were reached, both Bao Peng and Qi Shan were in

33 Arthur Waley, *The Opium War through Chinese Eyes* (London: George Allen & Unwin, 1958), p. 222.

trouble. Qi suffered heavy punishment for agreeing to, without the approval of the Emperor, among other unfavourable terms, cede Chinese territory to the British. This is easily understandable. But even the *tongshi*, Bao Peng, who was supposedly acting as an interpreter, was sentenced for permanent exile in the far and remote Xinjiang and would not be pardoned even if there were a general amnesty. This sentence was much stiffer than the standard penalty. Why was this so?

No doubt, from what is available, Bao was not a respectable or amiable character. John Elliot Bingham, who had taken part in the Opium War and had personally known Bao Peng, made a vivid description of Bao Peng in his "narrative of the expedition to China":

> On one of his [Bao Peng's] trips to Macao, he had visited his old master, Mr. Dent, and then went to see his late fellow-servants, who very soon began to jeer him on his increased consequence, when jumping up with his right arm extended, and hand clenched, he thus broke forth:– "You thinkee my one smallo man? you thinkee my go buy one catty rice, one catty fowl? No! my largo man, my have catchee peace, my have catchee war my hand, suppose I opee he, makee peace, suppose I shutee he, must makee fight." It loses much in relating: the fellow's manner must be seen to be understood.[34]

He also said Bao was a "most intolerable liar,"[35] always making up stories and excuses to squeeze money.[36] However, repulsive Bao Peng might have been, his behaviours were, unfortunately, not untypical of those of most of the *tongshi* or the compradors in Guangzhou at that time. This should not have been a contributing factor for the severe sentence he received.

On this case, the Board of Punishments, the highest judiciary department, made a comprehensive report to the Emperor after thorough investigations. It stated clearly that they had interrogated Bao Peng very seriously and they did not cover that physical torture had been applied for

34 J. Elliot Bingham, *Narrative of the Expedition to China, from the Commencement of the War to Its Termination in 1842*, 2nd ed., vol. 2 (London: Henry Colburn, 1843), pp. 40–41.

35 Ibid., vol. 1, p. 249.

36 Ibid., pp. 256–257.

several times.[37] From what was presented in the memorial, no irregularity was noted that would mire Bao Peng into such a predicament. There was no mentioning of any treacherous act. In the end the sentence suggested by the Board of Punishments was based on a "technicality" that he had acted as a comprador without a proper licence, thus having "illicit intercourse with the foreigners."[38] They were very explicit that he was not implicated to any other crime. It was a pity for Bao that they decided to impose the maximum penalty, just because it was a critical moment in the fight against the British. What is even worse, despite this objective investigation and report which confirms his innocence, Bao Peng has been considered an agent working for the British, hence a *hanjian* by both his contemporaries and later historians. However, no concrete evidence has ever been provided to prove this serious charge. Clearly, he was the kind of people who "were under constant suspicion" as *hanjian*, simply because of his service to the enemies in the capacity of *tongshi*.

After this Bao Peng case, no *tongshi* or interpreter from China would further be involved in the peace negotiation with the British. Qi Ying 耆英 (1787–1858), who succeeded Qi Shan as negotiator, did not bring any *tongshi* along. The Qing court was satisfied with the situation that the negotiation would be conducted without any interpreters from their own side. Hence, for the final stage of the peace settlement, negotiation was mainly carried out with the interpretation service of John Robert Morrison (1814–1843), Chinese Secretary and Chief Interpreter for the British. In fact, both the English and Chinese versions of the Treaty of Nanking were prepared and provided by the British. Without a qualified translator/interpreter from their own camp, there was no way for the Chinese to know what was exactly written in the English version of the Treaty. This is unthinkable in modern diplomacy, as the British interpreter would never be neutral. He would definitely uphold British interest over that of the Chinese.

---

37 "Xingbu zouzhe 刑部奏折" [Memorial from the Board of Punishments], in *Yapian zhanzheng* 鴉片戰爭, vol. 3 of *Zhongguo jindaishi ziliao congkan* 中國近代史資料叢刊 [Corpus of materials on Chinese modern history], ed. Qi Sihe 齊思和 et al., vol. 3 (Shanghai: Shanghai renmin chubanshe, 1955), p. 382.

38 Waley, *The Opium War through Chinese Eyes*, p. 243.

III

Although it was disastrously defeated in the First Opium War, both militarily and diplomatically, the Qing court did not learn any lesson. For another 20 years, no attempt was ever made to train translators/interpreters for better communication with the West. It was after another more catastrophic defeat at the Second Opium War in 1859–1860 that they saw the need and established the first Western language training school, the Tongwenguan 同文館 (Institute of Common Languages). Students were recruited to learn English, French, German, and Russian. Formally starting class in 1862, the Tongwenguan eventually trained up the first generation of Chinese translators/interpreters for diplomatic intercourses with the European countries.

No doubt, it was out of very practical need that the Chinese were forced to train up translators/interpreters. A clause in the peace treaty of the Second Opium War, Treaty of Tientsin (1858), stipulated that "[a]ll official communications addressed by the Diplomatic and Consular Agents of Her Majesty the Queen to the Chinese Authorities shall, henceforth, be written in English. They will for the present be accompanied by a Chinese version, but, it is understood that, in the event of there being any difference of meaning between the English and Chinese text, the English Government will hold the sense as expressed in the English text to be the correct sense."[39] A good team of translators/interpreters was in desperate need.

Significantly, the chief architect for establishing the Tongwenguan, Prince Gong 恭親王 (Yi Xin 奕訢, 1833–1898), was a man who had a very different view towards the West. In a report to the Emperor on the ways to deal with the Westerners, he indicated that there had to be a change in strategy because the situation they faced was not the same as that of the past, when they only had to deal with the neighbouring tribes. One particular observation he made about the Westerners was that they were reasonable, reliable and trustworthy. They could be bound by treaty terms. "By good faith and justice we can still

39 *Treaties, Conventions, etc., between China and Foreign States*, p. 418.

win them over and control their nature."[40] It was reported that he was once asked by the French interpreter if he considered the Westerners "a barbarous people." His reply was most direct and positive: "I never thought so, because, having no acquaintance with your true character, I had no fixed opinion; but now, most certainly, I do not."[41] In fact, we can tell that Prince Gong had a genuine respect for some Westerners. One thing which marked him out from the other senior ministers in the Qing court was that he had no hesitation in employing Westerners to his service. The most well-known example is Robert Hart (1835–1911), who worked as Inspector General of China's Maritime Customs for almost half a century since November 1863. Prince Gong was quoted to have said that if we had a hundred Harts, things would be easy. He even called him "*Wo-mun-tee Ha-ta* 我們的赫德"—"the Hart of us."[42] W. A. P. Martin (1827–1916), who was appointed as the Chief Instructor (which he preferred it to be referred to as President) of Tongwenguan, also reported the "uncommonly gracious" manner that Prince Gong greeted him: "always taking both my hands in his, after the cordial manner of the Tartars, in marked contrast with the rigid salute of the Chinese, which even between intimate friends consists in each shaking his own hands at a respectful distance."[43] This should not be surprising. After all, he was the one who concluded the Treaty of Tientsin, which stipulated that the word *yi* should no longer be used in all future official exchanges with the British.

Despite the powerful patronage from Prince Gong, the operation of the Tongwenguan was not as smooth as one might have thought. While it seems natural and undisputable to appoint foreign instructors to teach foreign languages, Prince Gong encountered problems in doing so

40 Yi Xin et al., "Tongchou yangwu quanju zhuoni zhangcheng liutiao 通籌洋務全局酌擬章程六條" [A draft scheme of six items for the overall management of foreign affairs], in *Di'erci yapian zhanzheng* 第二次鴉片戰爭 [The Second Opium War], ed. Qi Sihe et al., vol. 5 (Shanghai: Shanghai renmin chubanshe, 1978), p. 340.

41 D. F. Rennie, *Peking and the Pekingese during the First Year of the British Embassy at Peking*, vol. 1 (London: John Murray, 1865), p. 182.

42 Ibid., p. 264.

43 W. A. P. Martin, *A Cycle of Cathay, or China, South and North with Personal Reminiscences* (New York, Chicago, and Toronto: Fleming H. Revell Co., 1900), pp. 294–295.

for Tongwenguan. At the very initial stage, they just wanted to recruit instructors from Guangzhou, some Chinese who might be able to speak English. Such an attempt was doomed to fail, as no qualified language instructor could ever be found from the pool of *tongshi* and foreign trade merchants there. This delayed the whole process, and Tongwenguan was not able to start classes until almost two years later, in June 1862, when the court finally approved to hire a British, J. S. Burdon (1826–1907) to be the first instructor at the Institute. Nevertheless, even this most reasonable move had to be justified by several memorials to the Emperor; and one very important point stressed in the memorials was these foreign instructors were honest and subservient. Further, they were put on probation for a period of one to two years, while at the same time, Chinese instructors were appointed to keep a vigilant eye on them. With this, it is no surprise that when Prince Gong tried to introduce Astronomy and Mathematics to the curriculum, the opposing voices were extremely strong. He was severely condemned for sending the Chinese scholars to taking the barbarians as teachers. "Why the barbarians? Why do we have to honour the barbarians as our teachers?" he was challenged.[44] His opponents argued that only those who were inferior in "intention and conduct" would honour the barbarians as teachers. This is the famous "Tongwenguan Controversy of 1867."[45] Although the court ultimately approved the establishment of the School of Mathematics and Astronomy, it was but a bitter victory for Prince Gong. The number of applications to the Institute for several years was extremely low and they were not able to recruit good students. In 1869, there were only two students for the whole English section, eight for the French, and the biggest number was in the Russian section, eighteen.[46]

---

44 "Wo Ren zouzhe 倭仁奏折" [Memorial of Wo Ren], in *Yangwu yundong* 洋務運動 [Self-strengthening Movement], ed. Zhongguo shixue hui 中國史學會, vol. 2 (Shanghai: Shanghai renmin chubanshe, 2000), p. 30.

45 A precise account of the event can be found in Liu Kwang-ching, "Politics, Intellectual Outlook and Reform: The T'ung-wen Kuan Controversy of 1867," in *Reform in Nineteenth-century China*, ed. Paul A. Cohen and John E. Schrecker (Cambridge, MA: Harvard University Press, 1976), pp. 87–100.

46 Xiong Yuezhi 熊月之, *Xixue dongjian yu wan Qing shehui* 西學東漸與晚清社會 [The

In fact, the quality of the students had always been a problem, especially in the first decades. The most critical issue lied in the fact that the students would not be able to sit for the civil examination (*keju* 科舉) and were hence deprived of the opportunity to climb high in officialdom. Further, in the early years, only Manchu were admitted. This policy not only limited the number, but also adversely affected the quality, because the Manchu had been a privileged class for so long that they would not be eager to work hard and learn a foreign language for a living. More importantly, people generally still had a low opinion towards translators/interpreters. They saw them not too different from the traditional *tongshi*, even though they were officially trained at a government institute as part of the modernization programme. As late as 1886, 24 years after the establishment of the Tongwenguan, Prince Qing 慶親王 (Yi Kuang 奕劻, 1838–1918), who replaced Prince Gong to take charge of foreign affairs, said the following in a memorial to the Emperor: "The good ones [students of the Tongwenguan] will act as diplomats, the poor ones may serve as interpreters."[47] This reflects the mentality and attitude of the Qing court at the highest level. There was severe social pressure too. One English instructor of the Tongwenguan reported in the *North China Herald* that people despised those who enrolled at the school.[48] One graduate even gave detailed description as to how the whole family was looked down upon or isolated by the relatives because one member of the family went to study at the Tongwenguan.[49] As a result, although Tongwenguan offered very favourable terms to attract the students, including lodging, food and a substantial stipend (no tuition fees, of course), there was no way to attract good students; and those who enrolled were not serious about class.

---

dissemination of Western learning and the late Qing society] (Shanghai: Shanghai renmin chubanshe, 1994), p. 304.

47 *Yangwu yundong*, vol. 2, p. 66.

48 *North China Herald*, 25 January 1870, quoted from Knight Biggestaff, "The T'ung-wen Kuan," in *The Earliest Modern Government Schools in China* (Ithaca: Cornell University Press, 1961), p. 140, n106.

49 Qi Rushan 齊如山 (1877–1966), *Qi Rushan huiyilu* 齊如山回憶錄 [Recollections of Qi Rushan] (Taibei: Zhongyang wenwu gongyingshe, 1956), pp. 27–28.

IV

Apart from the officially trained translators/interpreters in Tongwenguan and other government institutes, there was a group of people who got involved in translation in the second half of the nineteenth century, the so-called treaty-port intellectuals. This is a term coined by the American historian Paul Cohen in his study of Wang Tao 王韜 (1828–1897) to label those traditional Chinese men-of-letters who moved to and lived in the coastal treaty ports newly opened by the Treaty of Nanking after the Opium War.[50] They had all received traditional Chinese education, well prepared to take the traditional examinations in hope of climbing high in the ladder of officialdom. Many of them might have already held the *xiucai* 秀才 title. But most reluctantly they were forced by reality, mainly poverty, to give up this plan and took up new kinds of jobs related to the Westerners. One particular job relevant to our discussion here is for them to assist the Westerners, mainly missionaries, to translate Western works into Chinese. These missionaries had come to China and learned Chinese for a few years. They needed to hire educated Chinese to assist them to translate or prepare religious writings in Chinese.[51]

As they worked very closely with the Westerners, treaty-port intellectuals were among the earliest Chinese to have first-hand contacts with all the new things brought in by the West. After China had repeatedly been defeated and started to see the need to strengthen itself by learning from the West, these

---

50 Paul A. Cohen, *Between Tradition and Modernity: Wang T'ao and Reform in Late Ch'ing China* (Cambridge, MA: Harvard University Press, 1974), p. 16.

51 There were different forms of collaboration between the Westerners and their assistants, depending very much on how well they knew each other's language. The "standard method of composition" "amounted to a kind of dictation; the foreigner gave an oral rendering in Chinese that the assistant took down and reworked into a readable draft, which the foreigner then checked for misunderstandings." Another method is for the missionaries to make their own drafts and the assistants were responsible for polishing them. See Patrick Hanan, "Chinese Christian Literature: The Writing Process," in *Treasures of the Yenching: Seventy-fifth Anniversary of the Harvard-Yenching Library*, ed. Patrick Hanan (Cambridge, MA: Harvard-Yenching Library, 2003), pp. 261–283.

people began to be seen as a progressive force in the earliest modernization process of China. However, the modernization process of the late Qing was a slow one, and it took quite some time for people to recognize the contributions of the treaty-port intellectuals. Before this happened, they were under severe pressure. People have long over-emphasized the constructive role played by the treaty-port intellectuals in China's modernization, but on the other hand largely neglected the dark side of their psychology to operate "on the fringes."[52]

Wang Tao was one of the earliest Chinese who were employed by the Westerners in Shanghai to assist them to translate Western works into Chinese. In 1849, following the footsteps of his father, Wang Tao started to work for the London Missionary Society Press, under Walter Henry Medhurst (1796–1857) and Alexander Wylie (1815–1887), until he was forced to flee to Hong Kong in 1862 for his involvement with the Taiping Rebellion. In other words, he had acted as a translator or as an assistant for translation in Shanghai for 13 years. This is no doubt a considerably lengthy period. Expectedly, the Missionary Society Press in Shanghai translated mostly religious works, which were alien to Wang Tao's traditional training. But they also translated many other scientific writings that were subsequently of great use to China in the so-called Self-strengthening Movement.[53] In other words, Wang Tao was a pioneer in introducing the modern West to China. Further, after fleeing to the British colony of Hong Kong, where he lived for as long as 23 years, he continued to work mainly as an assistant to James Legge (1815–1897) in his translation of the Chinese classics. He

---

52 Paul Cohen depicts a rather rosy picture of the treaty-port intellectuals, as if there was a rapid and smooth transition to success:

> Operating on the fringes of the Chinese world, the work of these men at first seemed to be little relationship to the main stream of events in China. But, in time, a convergence developed between what they had to offer and what China needed. And, as this happened, they gradually acquired a modicum of status and self-respect.

Cohen, *Between Tradition and Modernity*, p. 16.

53 Between 1844 and 1860, the London Missionary Society Press in Shanghai published altogether 171 titles, out of which 138 were religious writings and 33 were related to Western sciences. Cf. Xiong Yuezhi, *Xixue dongjian yu wan Qing shehui*, p. 188.

was also one of the earliest Chinese to travel widely in Europe, as he was invited to visit UK and Europe for over two years as early as 1867. Then in 1874, he started the *Xunhuan ribao* 循環日報 in Hong Kong, the first Chinese newspaper, and acted as its Chief Editor. Publishing articles after articles on China, he was considered as an expert on the so-called *shiwu* 時務 (current affairs) and the West. He also visited Japan in 1879 for four months. In 1884, he was allowed to end his exile and go back to Shanghai, as a renowned reformer to head the Shanghai Polytechnic Institute and Reading Room. Clearly, all the experiences and knowledge he gained during his years working closely with the Westerners became an invaluable asset, at a time when China became very eager to learn from the West.

However, in the early years when he worked with the Westerners in Shanghai as a translator, Wang Tao was extremely unhappy about this job. In the private letters to his close friends and relatives, he made all kinds of bitter complaints. Like all employees do, he complained that the working hours were long and the pay was not high. He grumbled about the living and working condition. But judging from the available materials, this was not true. We see in his own diaries that he went out for chats or drinks with friends quite freely even in the midst of work. On the other hand, he earned very good salaries for this job, certainly good enough to make him stay on with this "unpleasant" job. He also criticized the quality of the drafts made by the missionaries, that they were so poor that even a resurrected Confucius would not be able to improve them. This might be true, as the several missionaries that he worked with had learned Chinese just for a few years. Overall, Wang Tao did not gain any satisfaction out of the job.

But this was not the key issue. The greatest problem for Wang Tao was that he had to work for the Westerners to earn his living. As a traditional man-of-letters, he had wanted to take the civil examination and become a senior official. It was very promising at the beginning, when he got the *xiucai* title at the age of 17; and it was reported that the examiners were very much impressed by his essays.[54] However, he failed to pass the *juren* 舉人

54 Wang Tao, "Taoyuan laomin zizhuan 弢園老民自傳" [An autobiography of the old man Wang Tao], in *Taoyuan wenlu waibian* 弢園文錄外編 [Additional essays of

examination a year after, and this constituted a severe blow to him. He fell sick for several months. Then after his father had passed away, as the eldest son of the family who had to shoulder the burden, Wang Tao was forced to take up the job offered to him by Medhurst. In a number of letters, he explained to his friends and relatives that he reluctantly took up the job for the salary.[55] It should be stressed that even after he had started working in Shanghai, he sat for the examination again in 1856 and 1859. Although he failed in all these attempts, he obviously had not really given up hope. Working for the Westerners in China was not a preferable career option.

Worse still, as a man-of-letters of the traditional kind, Wang Tao firmly believed that the Westerners were uncivilized barbarians. In his letters and diary written in the early years, he always unfailingly referred to the Westerners as barbarians. He had no hesitation to quote the famous racist saying from *Zuozhuan* 左傳, "those who are not of my kin must have a different heart" (*feiwo zulei, qixin biyi* 非我族類，其心必異).[56] Since he had worked with the Westerners for some time, he was regarded as, and in fact he spoke like, an expert in foreign affairs. But the picture he drew about the encroachment of the Westerners was extremely negative. He saw it a deadly threat to China, both politically and culturally. Holding a traditional negative view about trade and commerce, Wang Tao argued that China would not be benefited from opening trade to the West, rather it would suffer from further exploitations. He even cited the case of India for reference. With the opening of Shanghai and other treaty ports, all strategically situated, the whole of China was exposed to foreign invasion and there was no way for China to cope with the Westerners if hostilities broke out again.[57] Although he took part in translating scientific writings and apparently had quite a good grasp of their ideas, he, as argued by Cohen, took a deprecatory view of Western science.[58] To him, the West outperformed the

Wang Tao] (Shanghai: Shanghai shudian chubanshe, 2002), p. 269.

55 Wang Tao, "Taoyuan laomin zizhuan," p. 269; Wang Tao, *Taoyuan chidu* 弢園尺牘 [The letters of Wang Tao] (Beijing: Zhonghua shuju, 1959), pp. 11, 67.

56 Wang Tao, *Taoyuan chidu*, pp. 90, 92.

57 Ibid., p. 4.

58 Cohen, *Between Tradition and Modernity*, p. 27.

Chinese in technology, but there was nothing to be proud of, as technology was of the lower realm. On the other hand, the Dao 道 of China was much more superior and should be valued. Ultimately, the Chinese Dao would win over the Western technology. For this reason, he had, in particular, grave concern with the spread of Christianity, as it would affect the minds of the people. He worried that traditional Chinese culture and values would be overturned. This would bring disastrous damage to Confucianism.[59] The Chinese might become barbarous as well. However, one firmly established fact is that Wang Tao was actually baptized, although he never mentioned this in any of his writing.[60] He not only tried to cover this up,[61] he even criticized his friends for getting too close to the missionaries.[62]

With this traditional Chinese thinking, Wang Tao was in great pain when he had to work with the Westerners as a translation assistant. Understandably, he felt in particular bad that he had to assist translating religious works. In one diary entry, he recorded how one of his friends Guan Sifu 管嗣復 (?–1860), who was also working as a translation assistant to Medhurst, refused to help translating religious writings. Wang Tao felt shameful that he could not take a firm stance like his friend.[63] To him, he had sold himself to the barbarians. It was a fatal mistake that he had committed when he was young, and there was no way he could change his fate then. He sensed very strong social pressure and repeatedly said that he could not face his relatives and friends.[64] (At the same time, however, he blamed his friends and relatives for not stopping

59 Wang Tao, *Taoyuan chidu*, p. 27; Wang Tao, *Wang Tao riji* 王韜日記 [Diaries of Wang Tao], eds. Fang Xing 方行 and Tang Zhijun 湯志鈞 (Beijing: Zhonghua shuju, 1987), p. 98.

60 Cohen, *Between Tradition and Modernity*, pp. 20–21; Su Jing 蘇精, "Wang Tao de Jidujiao xili 王韜的基督教洗禮" [The baptism of Wang Tao], in *Malixun yu Zhongwen yinshua chuban* 馬禮遜與中文印刷出版 [Robert Morrison and printing and publishing in China] (Taibei: Xuesheng shuju, 2000), pp. 243–258.

61 He deleted the paragraph in his diary which recorded his baptism. Cf., Zhang Hailin 張海林, *Wang Tao pingzhuan* 王韜評傳 [A critical biography of Wang Tao] (Nanjing: Nanjing daxue chubanshe, 1993), pp. 62–63.

62 Wang Tao, "Taoyuan laomin zizhuan," p. 40.

63 Wang Tao, *Wang Tao riji*, pp. 92–93.

64 Ibid., p. 67; Wang Tao, *Taoyuan chidu*, p. 24.

him from taking up this job.)[65] This was extremely painful for Wang Tao, a traditional man-of-letters who happened to take up translation jobs in the 1860s. Without doubt, this kind of pains and pressure came from the traditional Chinese concept that Westerners were barbarians.[66]

Of course, as we have repeatedly stated, Wang Tao was a traditional kind of man-of-letters who happened to have the opportunity to work with the Westerners at the newly-opened treaty ports. When he first acted as an assistant translator for the Westerners, China had opened to the West for just a brief period, and it is understandable that most people still bore the same traditional thinking of Westerners as barbarians. But what about a lapse of 30 years, after the emergence of a new generation of intellectuals who had in fact received "new education" at the new schools set up as part of the programmes for the Self-strengthening Movement? Yan Fu 嚴復 (1854–1921) has generally been considered as the greatest translator of the late Qing, for his famous translation of Thomas Henry Huxley's (1825–1895) *Evolution and Ethics*, as well as other works like John Stewart Mills' (1806–1873) *On Liberty*.[67] He started to learn English at the age of 17 at the Fuzhou Navy Yard School and was sent to study at the Royal Naval College in Greenwich, Britain. No doubt, he was one of those who could claim to have a thorough understanding of Western culture. But how disheartening it is to read the following poetic lines he wrote in 1892:

> What a mistake that I learned a foreign language;
> The whole world now takes me as a barbarian.[68]

65 Wang Tao, *Taoyuan chidu*, pp. 5, 24.

66 For a thorough analysis of the dilemma of Wang Tao, as a traditional man-of-letters and a translation assistant to the Westerners, cf., Wang Hongzhi, "Maishen shiyi de Wang Tao: Dang chuantong wenshi dangshangle yizhe 賣身侍夷的王韜：當傳統文士當上了譯者" [Wang Tao selling himself to the barbarians: When a traditional man-of-letters became a translator], *Fudan xuebao* 復旦學報 [Fudan University Journal], no. 2 (March 2011), pp. 25–40.

67 Max Ko-wu Huang, *The Meaning of Freedom: Yan Fu and the Origins of Chinese Liberalism* (Hong Kong: The Chinese University Press, 2008).

68 Yan Fu, "Song Chen Tonglu gui Min 送陳彤卣歸閩" [Farewell to Chen Tonglu on his way back to Fujian], in *Yan Fu ji* 嚴復集 [Works of Yan Fu], ed. Wang Chi 王栻, vol. 2 (Beijing: Zhonghua shuju, 1986), p. 361.

Bibliography

Biggestaff, Knight. "The T'ung-wen Kuan." In *The Earliest Modern Government Schools in China*. Ithaca: Cornell University Press, 1961, pp. 94–153.

Bingham, Elliot J. *Narrative of the Expedition to China, from the Commencement of the War to Its Termination in 1842*. 2nd ed. Vol. 2. London: Henry Colburn, 1843.

Broomhall, Marshall. *Robert Morrison: A Master-Builder*. London: Church Missionary Society, 1924.

Cohen, Paul A. *Between Tradition and Modernity: Wang T'ao and Reform in Ch'ing China*. Cambridge, MA: Harvard University Press, 1974.

Cranmer-Byng, J. L. "Lord Macartney's Embassy to Peking in 1793: From Official Chinese Documents." In vol. 7 of *Britain and the China Trade 1635–1842*, selected by Patrick Tuck. London and New York: Routledge, 2000, pp. 118–183.

Cumming, Gordon C. F. *Wanderings in China*. Vol. 2. Edinburgh and London: William Blackwood and Sons, 1886.

Fairbank, John K., ed. *The Chinese World Order: Traditional China's Foreign Relations*. Cambridge, MA: Harvard University Press, 1968.

———. *Trade and Diplomacy on the China Coast: The Opening of the Treaty Ports, 1842–1854*. Stanford: Stanford University Press, 1969.

Gallagher, Louis J., SJ, trans. *China in the Sixteenth Century: The Journals of Matthew Ricci: 1583–1610*. New York: Random House, 1953.

Hanan, Patrick. "Chinese Christian Literature: The Writing Process." In *Treasures of the Yenching: Seventy-fifth Anniversary of the Harvard-Yenching Library*, edited by Patrick Hanan. Cambridge, MA: Harvard-Yenching Library, 2003, pp. 261–283.

Hsu, Immanuel C. Y. *The Rise of Modern China*. Hong Kong: Oxford University Press, 1975.

Huang, Max Ko-wu. *The Meaning of Freedom: Yan Fu and the Origins of Chinese Liberalism*. Hong Kong: The Chinese University Press, 2008.

Hunter, William C. *Bits of Old China*. London: Kegan Paul, Trench, & Co., 1855.

———. *The "Fan Kwae" at Canton before the Treaty Days, 1825–1844*. London: Kegan Paul, Trench, & Co., 1882.

Liang, Jiabin 梁嘉彬. *Guangdong shisanhang kao* 廣東十三行考 [A study of the Thirteen Hongs in Guangdong]. Shanghai: Guoli bianyiguan, 1937.

Liang, Tingnan 梁廷枏. *Yue haiguan zhi* 粵海關志 [Records of the Guangdong customs]. Shaoguan: Guangdong renmin chubanshe, 2002.

Liu, Kwang-ching. "Politics, Intellectual Outlook and Reform: The T'ung-wen Kuan Controversy of 1867." In *Reform in Nineteenth-century China*, edited by Paul A. Cohen and John E. Schrecker. Cambridge, MA: Harvard University Press, 1976, pp. 87–100.

Liu, Lydia H. *The Clash of Empires: The Invention of China in Modern World Making*. Cambridge, MA and London: Harvard University Press, 2004.

Martin, W. A. P. *A Cycle of Cathay, or China, South and North with Personal Reminiscences*. New York, Chicago, and Toronto: Fleming H. Revell Co., 1900.

Morrison, Eliza A. Appendix to "Narrative of an Affair between a Watering Party of Seamen, from the *Topaz*, an English Frigate, and the Chinese Inhabitants of Lin-tin Island, Situated above Macao, in the Passage from the Sea to the Anchorage at Whampoa, Interspersed with Remarks on the Current Affairs of Canton, 1821–2." In vol. 2 of *Memoirs of the Life and Labours of Robert Morrison, DD*. London: Longman, Orme, Brown, Green and Longmans, 1839, pp. 10–32.

Morrison, John Robert. *Chinese Commercial Guide, Consisting of a Collection of Details Respecting Foreign Trade in China*. Canton: Albion Press, 1834.

Morrison, Robert. *A Dictionary of the Chinese Language*. Vol. 1. Macao: East India Company Press, 1815.

Morse, H. B. *The Chronicles of the East India Company Trading to China, 1635–1834*. 5 vols. London: Oxford University Press, 1926.

Peyrefitte, Alain. *The Collision of Two Civilizations: The British Expedition to China in 1792–4*. Translated by Jon Rothschile. London: Harvill, 1993.

Qi, Rushan 齊如山. *Qi Rushan huiyilu* 齊如山回憶錄 [Recollections of Qi Rushan]. Taibei: Zhongyang wenwu gongyingshe, 1956.

Qianlong 乾隆. "Daqing huangdi gei yingjili guowang chiyu 大清皇帝給英吉利國王勅諭" [The imperial edict from the Emperor of Great Qing to the King of England]. In *Yingshi Majia'erni fanghua dang'an shiliao huibian* 英使馬戛爾尼訪華檔案史料匯編 [A collection of historical materials on the Macartney Embassy to China], edited by The First Archive of Chinese History. Beijing: Guoji wenhua chuban gongshi, 1996, pp. 165–166.

Rennie, D. F. *Peking and the Pekingese during the First Year of the British Embassy at Peking*. Vol. 1. London: John Murray, 1865.

Su, Jing 蘇精. "Wang Tao de Jidujiao xili 王韜的基督教洗禮" [The baptism of Wang Tao]. In *Malixun yu Zhongwen yinshua chuban* 馬禮遜與中文印刷出版 [Robert Morrison and printing and publishing in China]. Taibei: Taiwan xuesheng shuju, 2000, pp. 243–258.

"Treaty of Tientsin" (1858). In vol. 1 of *Treaties, Conventions, etc., between China and Foreign States*. Shanghai: Inspector General of Customs, 1917. Reprint, New York: AMS Press, 1973, pp. 404–421.

Van Dyke, Paul A. *The Canton Trade: Life and Enterprise on the China Coast, 1700–1845*. Hong Kong: Hong Kong University Press, 2005.

Waley, Arthur. *The Opium War through Chinese Eyes*. London: George Allen & Unwin, 1958.

Wang, Hongzhi 王宏志 (Lawrence Wang-chi Wong). "Majia'erni shihua de fanyi wenti 馬戛爾尼使華的翻譯問題" [Translation in the Macartney Embassy to China]. *Zhongyang yanjiuyuan jindaishi yanjiusuo jikan* 中央研究院近代史研究所集刊 [Bulletin of the Institute of Modern History, Academia Sinica], no. 63 (March 2009), pp. 97–145.

———. "Maishen shiyi de Wang Tao: Dang chuantong wenshi dangshangle yizhe 賣身侍夷的王韜：當傳統文士當上了譯者" [Wang Tao selling himself to the barbarians: When a traditional man-of-letters became a translator]. *Fudan xuebao* 復旦學報 [Fudan University Journal], no. 2 (March 2011), pp. 25–40.

Wang, Tao 王韜. *Taoyuan chidu* 弢園尺牘 [The letters of Wang Tao]. Beijing: Zhonghua shuju, 1959.

———. *Wang Tao riji* 王韜日記 [Diaries of Wang Tao]. Edited by Fang Xing 方行 and Tang Zhijun 湯志鈞. Beijing: Zhonghua shuju, 1987.

———. "Taoyuan laomin zizhuan 弢園老民自傳" [An autobiography of the old man Wang Tao]. In *Taoyuan wenlu waibian* 弢園文錄外編 [Additional essays of Wang Tao]. Shanghai: Shanghai shudian chubanshe, 2002, pp. 269–272.

"Wo Ren zouzhe 倭仁奏折" [Memorial of Wo Ren]. In vol. 2 of *Yangwu yundong* 洋務運動 [Self-strengthening Movement], edited by Zhongguo shixue hui 中國史學會. Shanghai: Shanghai renmin chubanshe, 2000, pp. 30–31.

Wong, Lawrence Wang-chi. "Barbarians or Not Barbarians: Translating *Yi* in the Context of Sino-British Relations in the Eighteenth and Nineteenth Centuries." In vol. 3 of *Towards a History of Translating: In Commemoration of the 40th Anniversary of the Research Centre for Translation, CUHK*, edited by Lawrence Wang-chi Wong. Hong Kong: Research Centre for Translation, The Chinese University of Hong Kong, 2013, pp. 293–387.

"Xingbu zouzhe 刑部奏折" [Memorial from the Board of Punishments]. In *Yapian zhanzheng* 鴉片戰爭. Vol. 3 of *Zhongguo jindaishi ziliao congkan* 中國近代史資料叢刊 [Corpus of materials on Chinese modern history], edited by Qi Sihe 齊思和 et al. Shanghai: Shanghai renmin chubanshe, 1955, pp. 380–282.

Xiong, Yuezhi 熊月之. *Xixue dongjian yu wan Qing shehui* 西學東漸與晚清社會 [The dissemination of Western learning and the late Qing society]. Shanghai: Shanghai renmin chubanshe, 1994.

Yan, Fu 嚴復. "Song Chen Tonglu gui Min 送陳彤卣歸閩" [Farewell to Chen Tonglu on his way back to Fujian]. In vol. 2 of *Yan Fu ji* 嚴復集 [Works of Yan Fu], edited by Wang Chi 王栻. Beijing: Zhonghua shuju, 1986, p. 361.

Yi, Xin 奕訢 et al. "Tongchou yangwu quanju zhuoni zhangcheng liutiao 通籌洋務全局酌擬章程六條" [A draft scheme of six items for the overall management of foreign affairs]. In vol. 5 of *Di'erci Yapian Zhanzheng* 第二次鴉片戰爭 [The Second Opium War], edited by Qi Sihe 齊思和 et al. Shanghai: Shanghai renmin chubanshe, 1978, pp. 340–346.

Zhang, Hailin 張海林. *Wang Tao pingzhuan* 王韜評傳 [A critical biography of Wang Tao]. Nanjing: Nanjing daxue chubanshe, 1993.

Cultural Divergence and Assimilation through Translation

"What's in a Name?"
North Korean Literary Translators and the Appropriation of Foreign Culture from the Late 1940s to the Mid-1960s, the Case of Im Hak-Su

Theresa HYUN

Introduction[1]

This paper is part of a larger research project to publish a book-length study focusing on the reception and translation of foreign (particularly Western European) literature in North Korea from the founding of the Democratic People's Republic of Korea (DPRK) in the late 1940s through the 1960s when *Chuch'e Sasang*[2] (Self-reliance Thought) was being established.[3] During this period the North Koreans emphasized the importance of literary translation both as a means of communication with other cultures and as a step in the development of their national language and literature. An examination of the North Korean literary world offers a unique opportunity to study the role of translation in the formation of national identity, as well

---

1 The research for this paper was supported by a York University Faculty of Arts Research Grant. I would also like to express my appreciation to Prof. Yoo Im-Ha, Prof. Jeon Young Sun, Prof. Kim Jae-Yong, Prof. Yi Sang-Kyong, Prof. Yi Sang-Suk and Choi Jini of Imjingang Publishing Co., for their guidance and support, and Prof. Cho Mina and Dr Rhee Jooyeon for their advice in preparing this paper.

2 Except in cases where a previously accepted form of romanization exists, I have followed the McCune-Reishauer system of romanizing Korean.

3 *Chuch'e Sasang* is the predominant ideology in North Korea, and it is fundamental to all social spheres. In North Korea Self-reliance Thought is regarded as a new human-centred philosophical approach according to which humans are responsible for all aspects of their development. See Yi Myong-Jae, *Pukhan Munhak Sajon* [Dictionary of North Korean literature] (Seoul: Kukhak Charyowon, 2007), p. 975.

as to explore an agent-oriented approach.[4]

During this period there were at least three major stages in the development of literary translation in North Korea. The first stage was the late 1940s through the Korean War period of the early 1950s when the socialist regime was being established and Soviet models were followed in literature and culture.[5] At this time there was a focus on translating works from Russia and other socialist countries.[6] Second, during the mid to late 1950s various groups were competing for influence in the literary world, as well as in politics. The relatively high degree of openness facilitated the publication of articles on translation policy and foreign literary trends. And third, the mid-1960s saw the publication of some volumes of *Segye Munhak Sonchip* (Anthology of world literature). This ambitious project aimed to publish translations of literary works from each region of the world. Although the project was never completed, the heightened interest in literary translation was reflected in the periodicals of the time.

This paper focuses on the reception of foreign literature and culture in North Korea giving particular emphasis to the work of Im Hak-Su, a translator and scholar of English literature.[7] First, I comment on the role of the Soviet Koreans in introducing Soviet literature, and I provide an overview of the situation of literary translation in North Korea. Next, I

4 Helene Buzelin comments on the trend to go beyond the depersonalized aspects of polysystems theory towards a focus on the activities of translators throughout history. See Helene Buzelin, "Unexpected Allies, How Latour's Network Theory Could Complement Bourdieusian Analyses in Translation Studies," *The Translator* 11, no. 2 (2005), pp. 202–205.

5 However, Charles Armstrong maintains that the Soviet occupation in the late 1940s aimed at establishing a friendly regime in North Korea, rather than controlling all levels of North Korean society. See Charles K. Armstrong, *The North Korean Revolution 1945–1950* (Ithaca, New York: Cornell University Press, 2003), p. 54.

6 Shin Hyong-Ki and O Song-Ho comment on the trend among North Korean intellectuals in the late 1940s to view Soviet-style democracy as a step beyond outmoded Western democracy. They praised the Soviet victory over fascism as enabling a free and peaceful life for the people. See Shin Hyong-Ki and O Song-Ho, *Pukhan Munhaksa* [North Korean literary history] (Seoul: P'yongminsa, 2000), p. 105.

7 Throughout this paper I have used the South Korean spelling, "Im Hak-Su," rather than the North Korean version, "Lim Hak-Su."

examine the work of Im Hak-Su in the 1930s and 1940s, as well as his career in North Korea. Finally, I consider the significance of this material within the context of the larger project.

Background of the Reception of Foreign Literatre and Culture in North Korea

Soviet Koreans and the Reception of Soviet Literature

During the Japanese colonial period (1910–1945) many Koreans immigrated north to Siberia and a Korean town developed in Vladivostok. By 1937 around 500,000 Koreans had immigrated to Central Asia. There were Korean periodicals and other publications distributed in the Soviet Union. After the Second World War some of these people came to North Korea and took part in formulating literary and artistic policy. Before the establishment of the North Korean government in 1948 many Soviets occupied high positions, and Soviet Korean writers and intellectuals were included among them. These Soviet Korean writers influenced the development of North Korean literature in the following ways.

First, as soon as Kim Il Sung gained power the North Koreans emphasized the production of literature which followed the tenets of Marxist-Leninism. Socialist literature had been known in Korea since the 1920s and 1930s when the Korean Artists' Proletarian Federation was active. The Soviet influence, which was strongest in the late 1940s and early 1950s, was lessened due to the political purges following the anti-Kim Il Sung movement in the 1950s and the establishment of Self-reliance Thought in the 1960s.

Second, the Soviet Koreans were accustomed to propagandistic Marxist literature and they transmitted these norms to the North Korean literary world. We can say that ideological concerns took precedence over aesthetic ones. Cho Myong-Hui, who was an active member of the proletarian literature movement during the Japanese colonial period, defected to Russia in order to pursue his interest in Soviet literature. Cho was one of the Soviet Korean writers who contributed to the production of North Korean works focusing on socialist themes.

Third, Kim Il Sung was considered as similar to Lenin and Stalin, and qualities of the Soviets were transferred to the North Korean leader. In the late 1940s poems eulogizing Kim Il Sung began to appear. While in the Soviet Union eulogistic literature was downplayed after the death of Stalin, the movement to oust Kim Il Sung from the centre of party politics provided his supporters the opportunity to strengthen his power, and literature praising the Great Leader became more prominent.

In his article on the influence of Soviet literature on North Korean literature Yi Myong-Jae summarizes the role of the Soviet Koreans in the formation of North Korean literature in the following way. North Korean literature differs from the works of the Japanese colonial period proletarian movement, as well as from South Korean literature, which takes some inspiration from European and American trends. North Korean literature has been influenced by Marxist-Leninism and tends to produce propagandistic works. The North Korean literary world still reflects the image-building tendencies of the 1950s which equated Lenin, Stalin, and Kim Il Sung.[8]

Overview of the Situation of Literary Translation in North Korea

This information is based on a review of the following prominent literary periodicals: 1) *Choson Munhak/Munhak Yesul* (Choson literature/Literature and art) September 1947 to May 1966, 2) *Munhak Shinmun* (Literary newspaper) January 1966 to December 1967, 3) *Ch'ollima* (Flying horse) February 1964 to December 1969.[9] This project is at a preliminary stage, and the material selected above represents a sample to indicate the direction the research will take.

8 Yi Myong-Jae, "Pukhan Munhak e Kkich'in Soryon Munhak ui Yonghyang" [The influence of Soviet literature on North Korean literature], *Omunhak* [Language and literary research] 116 (December 2002), pp. 181–183.

9 Jeon Young Sun emphasizes the importance of the official North Korean government periodicals as the way for writers to gain recognition. See Jeon Young Sun, *Pukhan ui Munhak Yesul Unyong Ch'ekye wa Munye Iron* [The North Korean literary and artistic administrative system and literary and artistic theory] (Seoul: Toso Ch'ulp'an Yokrak, 2002), p. 45.

I have identified a number of different genres in my first attempt at a survey of literary translation in North Korea such as: criticism, poetry, fiction works, plays, memoirs, essays, songs, and fables. In *Choson Literature* the greatest number of translations are from the Soviet Union, followed by China, Germany, India, and a variety of European and Asian countries. In terms of genre, the most frequently appearing forms are poetry, criticism and fiction. In 1966 and 1967 the *Literary Newspaper* focused mainly on fiction and poetry from South American, Asian and African countries. During the period from 1964 to 1969 *Flying Horse* featured poems and memoirs from various Asian and African nations.

Based on this preliminary overview of literary translation in North Korea from the late 1940s through the 1960s we can identify certain trends. In *Choson Literature* while works from the Soviet Union are by far the most numerous, the numbers peaked in the mid-1950s and had fallen off sharply by the early 1960s. Interest in works from China, which trailed behind the Soviet Union, also peaked in the mid-1950s and waned by the late 1950s and early 1960s.[10] In comparison with translations of works from the Soviet Union, China, and third world countries, translations of works from North America or Western Europe are relatively few in number.

The Translation of Im Hak-Su

Im Hak-Su's Early Works during the 1930s and 1940s

Im Hak-Su was born in 1911 in the southern part of the Korean peninsula, and he died in 1982 in North Korea. After obtaining a degree in English

10 Kim Il Sung stressed the importance of Soviet and Chinese literature in a 1951 speech: "In our literature and art the Soviet Union, the stronghold of world peace, and the Soviet people, the eternal friends of our people, have not been depicted enough; neither have the great Chinese People's Volunteers, who are fighting heroically at the side of the Korean People's Army, nor have the peoples of the democratic countries giving our masses international support and encouragement." Quoted in Brian Myers, *Han Sorya and North Korean Literature, The Failure of Socialist Realism in the DPRK* (Ithaca, New York: Cornell East Asia Series, 1994), p. 77.

from Kyongsong Imperial University (Kyongsong Chedae) he taught at the secondary-school level during the 1930s. After the Second World War he taught at Seoul Women's University and Koryo University. He went to North Korea during the Korean War in 1951.

Original Works

Im began to publish his own poetry in the early 1930s, and in the late 1930s several volumes of his poetry appeared: *Sokryu* (Pomegranate, 1937), *P'aldo P'ungmul Sijip* (Folk customs of the eight provinces, 1938), *Hujo* (Migratory birds, 1939), and *Chonson Sijip* (The front line poetry volume, 1939). In 1948 another volume of his poetry appeared, *P'ilbu ui Norae* (Songs of the common people). Im's poems sing, on the one hand of the anguish of living in the dark circumstances of Japanese colonial domination, and on the other of the longing for freedom and liberation.[11]

Im's first volume of poetry, *Pomegranate*, includes descriptions of the night world, stars, and shellfish which all relate to a distant world. The star appearing in the quiet night sky, the rose, and the golden shellfish combine the botanical and mineral beauty of a far-away land. This utopian view rejects the modern urban lifestyle in favour of a pastoral existence, and is also a rejection of the literary trends of imagism and modernism which were prevalent in Korea at the time. Most of the poems in *Pomegranate* focus on individual emotions rather than aspects of contemporary society. The nostalgic tone of the works in *Folk Customs of the Eight Provinces* and the images of promenades and voyages in *Migratory Birds* continue this trend of escaping the conflicts of war and the harshness of colonial rule. Im also wrote stories "Kamagui" (Crow, 1934), "Kumhonsik" (Golden wedding anniversary, 1937), and works of literary criticism including "Hyondae Yongsi ui Tonghyang" (Tendencies of contemporary English poetry, 1936).[12]

Im's poems of the 1930s display some similarities with the English

11 Yi Myong-Jae, *Pukhan Munhak Sajon*, pp. 406–407.

12 Kwon Yong-Min, *Hanguk Munhak Taesajon* [Comprehensive dictionary of Korean literature] (Seoul: Souldae Ch'ulp'anbu, 2004), p. 807.

works with which he was familiar as a scholar. Much like Kim Sowol and other Korean poets of the time, there is a correlation between the vocabulary and forms of his original works and translations of foreign works. A few examples include images of birds, wind, and golden and silver hues. The poems in Im's 1939 volume *Hujo* derive some inspiration from Keats' "Ode to a Nightingale," which Im translated as "Yaaeng ege" (1938). Some of the works in *Sokryu* (1937) depict windy scenes in ways which can be related to Shelley's "Ode to the West Wind."[13] There are similar descriptions of silver and golden hues in Im's poem "Chokun Saengmyong" (Small life, from *Pomegranate*) and his translation of Yeats' "He Wishes for the Cloths of Heaven" ("Pidan hanul," 1949). These few brief examples indicate that a much more in-depth examination of Im's original poetry and translations will prove fruitful.

During the 1930s and early 1940s Im used poetic language to indirectly express the anguish of the colonial subject. In contrast, in the late 1940s after the end of Japanese rule Im's poetry deals more openly with the political and social conditions prevailing in Korea. This is partially related to Im's imprisonment for leftist activities in 1947. The poems in *Songs of the Common People* (1948) display an awareness of the need to find solutions to social problems, which indicates that Im enjoyed more freedom of expression after the liberation from Japanese domination. The pastoral images of the earlier poetry are replaced by indications of the troubling aspects of the ideological division of North and South Korea. "Demok'urassi" (Democracy) decries social injustices: "*Uri tulun ajikdo yesnal gwa tarum opnun/Ch'aejjik gwa paekop'um e shinum hago issdapnida*" (Like in old times we are still groaning from the whip and hunger).[14] The poetic speaker in "Pyolli" (Separation) is trying to escape from the confusion and oppression of the present situation where he/she is wandering in darkness.[15] However, even escape proves difficult, and the people are left to

13 Percy Bysshe Shelley, "Sojjok Param ege" [Ode to the west wind], trans. Im Hak-Su, *Siin* [Poet] 2, no. 1 (March 1948), pp. 26–28.

14 Ch'ae Su-Yong, "Cholmang ui Chongshin Chiri" [The spiritual geography of despair], *Pip'ypong Munhak* [Literary criticism] 4 (October 1990), pp. 76–77.

15 Ibid., pp. 77–78.

cope with their struggles. Although Koreans are freed from the oppression of Japanese colonial rule, they must deal with the ideological divisions of the North and the South, power struggles and political confusion. "Ssaum" (Battle) gives expression to the will of the common people who strive to overcome feelings of defeat in their everyday lives.[16]

Translations

During the late 1930s Im began to publish translations of foreign literature, and the following is a sample of his works. In March 1938 Im's translation of Keats' "Ode to a Nightingale" appeared. And in the same year he published a translation of Yeats' short play *The Words upon the Window Pane* (*Ch'angsal e Namun Sigu*) and added some background comments. In order to overcome the hardships of their historical situation the Irish people developed a yearning for the world of the spirits. Im gives a brief account of Yeats' artistic activities, including the award of the Nobel Prize for literature in 1923. Yeats' interest in mysticism led him to undertake research into the Theosophical movement. The translator praises the play for its zest and use of modern techniques. March 1948 saw the publication of Im's translation of Shelley's "Ode to the West Wind." Im published translations of 10 Sappho poems in November 1948 under the title "Sappho's Lyric Poetry" ("Ssap'o ui Sojong Si"). Im again turned his attention to Yeats in 1949 with his article "The Reburial of the Poet Yeats" ("Siin Yeich'u ui Ijang") which included translations of "The Lake Isle of Innisfree" ("Inisup'uri ro") and "He Wishes for the Cloths of Heaven," as well as some commentary in which the translator praised Yeats as the best poet of Ireland and gave details of the author's death and reburial in Sligo.

Based on a preliminary examination of Im's translations of the period we can identify some characteristics of his work. First, Im tended to employ many Chinese character-based expressions in his Korean translations. Since for many centuries Chinese characters had been used for official writing in Korea, during the 1930s and 1940s writing in the native Korean script *hangul* was still being standardized. Therefore, some

16 Ch'ae Su-Yong, "Cholmang ui Chongshin Chiri," p. 78.

intellectuals mixed many Chinese characters with their Korean writing. Im's tendency to use Chinese characters changed after he went to North Korea in the 1950s.

Second, in terms of the selection of texts, Im favoured works of writers such as Keats, Shelley, and Yeats. Many of these works were popular in Japan at the time, and it is possible that Im had access to Japanese translations. Third, Im preferred a target-oriented approach and when translating works which deal with European culture and religion he tended to employ everyday language that would appeal to Korean readers. Thus we can say that one of his aims was acceptability with the Korean audience.[17] Fourth, Im's works display the modern narrative verbal endings which had been employed by Kim Ok in his translations of foreign poetry, especially that of the Indian poet Tagore. These stylistic features were widely adopted by Korean writers in the 1920s and 1930s.[18] Finally, Im tended to downplay the lofty significance in works like Shelley's "Ode to the West Wind."

Example One:

> Thine azure sister of the spring ...[19]
> *Kohi kkumin ne nui pombaram ...*[20]

The more formal "Thine" of the original is replaced by the informal Korean pronoun "*ne*" (your). This tendency to transform exalted or religious terms intensified after Im went to North Korea.

---

17 As Theo Hermans has pointed out, it is not simply a matter of polar alternatives ("acceptable" vs. "adequate"), but rather a multiplicity of factors which determine choices made by translators. See Theo Hermans, *Translation in Systems: Descriptive and System-oriented Approaches Explained* (Manchester: St. Jerome's Publishing, 1999), p. 77.

18 Kim Jae-Hong examines similarities in style, structure, and poetic methods in Korean translations of foreign literary works and original Korean poetic works of the Japanese colonial period. He focuses on poet/translator Kim Ok's Tagore translations and the original works of Han Yong-Un. See Kim Jae-Hong, *Han Yong-Un Munhak Yongu* [The literary works of Han Yong-Un] (Seoul: Iljisa, 1982), pp. 212–232.

19 Percy Bysshe Shelley, "Ode to the West Wind," in *The Norton Anthology of English Literature*, ed. M. H. Abrams (New York: W. W. Norton and Company, 1979), p. 704.

20 Shelley, "Sojjok Param ege," p. 26.

Im Hak-Su's Career in North Korea

In the late 1940s Im Hak-Su, along with other leftist writers (Im Hwa, Kim Nam-Ch'on, Yo Won-Ji), was a member of the League of Choson Cultural Organizations.[21] From his arrival in North Korea in 1951 after the outbreak of the Korean War until his death in 1982, Im taught at the university level and continued to translate foreign literature.[22] Although in the late 1940s and 1950s literary translation in North Korea focused on the Soviet Union, China, and Eastern Europe, Im had been recognized as a translator in the 1930s and 1940s, and his skill in English was valued.[23] In 1955 Im was relieved of his position at Kim Il Sung University, but he escaped the purges of writers in the mid-1950s and established himself as one of the leading translators of English literature in North Korea.[24]

Im Hak-Su's Essays on Foreign Literature

During the 1950s and 1960s Im Hak-Su wrote a number of articles on foreign literature which appeared in *Choson Literature* (*Choson Munhak*). An examination of a few of these articles gives an indication of the reception of foreign literature in North Korea at the time. In "The Work of Howard Fast" ("Hawodu P'asut'u ui Munhak"), which appeared in *Choson Literature* in April 1954, Im writes that Howard Fast is a "progressive writer and eminent champion of peace." He describes how Howard Fast, American author of the 1951 novel *Sparticus*, had the honour of receiving

---

21 Ch'ae Su-Yong, "Cholmang ui Chongshin Chiri," p. 54.

22 Yi Myong-Jae, *Pukhan Munhak Sajon*, pp. 407–408.

23 Kim Jae-Yong points out that Korean writers who had been prominent during the Japanese colonial period played a fundamental role in organizing the North Korean literary world starting in the late 1940s. See Kim Jae-Yong, *Pundan Kujo wa Pukhan Munhak* [The structure of the partition of the Korean peninsula and North Korean literature] (Seoul: Somyong Ch'ulp'an, 2003), p. 32.

24 Andrei Lankov recounts that during the purges of the 1950s many writers were subject to political criticism and accused of ideological mistakes. See Andrei Lankov, *Crisis in North Korea, The Failure of De-Stalinization, 1956* (Honolulu: University of Hawai'i Press, 2005), pp. 34–35.

the International Stalin Prize which "promotes the stability of peace among the people of all nations."[25] In an October 1954 article entitled "Henry Fielding's Realism" ("Henri P'ilding ui Sasilchuui") Im reports that the World Peace Committee organized an international festival in honour of the 200th anniversary of the death of Henry Fielding who is a distinguished representative of world culture. Im criticizes the feudalistic aristocratic society and emphasizes the universal literary value of Fielding's works. While the English novelist Richardson wrote hypocritical and sentimental works supporting bourgeois morality, Fielding's novels are among the masterpieces of eighteenth-century English literature. In his novel *Joseph Andrews* Fielding criticizes the injustices of the bourgeois society and creates protagonists based on the lives of the common people. Im has high praise for *Tom Jones* which displays Fielding's humanism and realistic portrayal of the main characters. The works of Shakespeare and Fielding have universal appeal because they deal with the movements of societies. Im goes on to explain that in the eighteenth century England was expanding its territorial control over India and America as part of the imperialistic competition between European countries. Politics was controlled by the aristocrats and landlords, while common people endured hardship, poverty, and abuse.[26]

In his November 1954 article "Shakespeare and Humanism" ("Syeiksup'io wa Hyumonijum") Im points out that it was not until a few centuries after Shakespeare's death that his works began to be appreciated in Europe by French romantics, and by Marx and Engels. Im comments on several of Shakespeare's works beginning with *Hamlet*, which he claims follows a typical dramatic pattern of conflict: presentation, worsening, peak, and resolution. Shakespeare's humanism can be seen in the way he develops conflicts between characters. As a ruthless money-worshipper, Shylock of *The Merchant of Venice* provides a model for the imperialistic plunderers of the twentieth century. The scene in which Macbeth kills Macduff's wife

25 Im Hak-Su, "Hawodu P'asut'u ui Munhak" [The work of Howard Fast], *Choson Munhak* 2, no. 4 (April 1954), pp. 143–148.

26 Im Hak-Su, "Henri P'ilding ui Sasilchuui" [Henry Fielding's realism], *Choson Munhak* 2, no. 10 (October 1954), pp. 94–103.

and helpless children demonstrates how Macbeth's cruelty goes to extremes, and how he personifies power as king. *Romeo and Juliet* criticizes feudalistic class consciousness. The tragedy occurs because Juliet's conservative parents are compelling her to marry the nobleman Paris. A victim of feudalistic pressure, Juliet's resistance is a cry for freedom and equality between men and women. Im analyses the characters of *Othello* and is particularly critical of the wickedness of Iago who represents the most difficult type of person in any society. While he is seemingly loyal, inwardly he is full of discontent, cunning, ruses and plots to exploit the nation and betray the people. *Coriolanus* displays the power of the people to oust an unjust ruler.

Im explains that in England the sixteenth century marked a cultural renaissance which replaced medieval feudalism with enlightened humanism. Shakespeare allows the audience and the readers to draw the conclusions from his realistic descriptions of the lives of the aristocrats and the people. In his historical plays Shakespeare emphasizes that unless they have the support of the people monarchies can be overthrown. Shakespeare's works paint a broad picture of the lives of all social classes from royalty and aristocrats to the bourgeoisie and the common people, and underlying individual conflicts there are always social forces at work. His plays combine lofty moral views and refined aestheticism with realistic descriptive methods. The bourgeois critics who praise *The Tempest* as one of Shakespeare's best works because of its imaginative and artistic qualities are engaging in formalistic nonsense. As a realistic writer Shakespeare's art is always focused on life's profound problems, and therefore progressive writers consider him their mentor and evaluate his works among the world's literary masterpieces.[27]

Translations

The following are among Im Hak-Su's translations in North Korea: *Hoyong ui Sijang* (Thackeray's *Vanity Fair*, reprinted in 1994), *Pairon Sison* (Selected poems of Byron, reprinted in 1991), *Kundae Yongguk Sison* (Anthology of modern English poetry, reprinted in 1991), *Syeiksup'io Hikokson* (Selected

27 Im Hak-Su, "Syeiksup'io wa Hyumonijum" [Shakespeare and humanism], *Choson Munhak* 2, no. 11 (November 1954), pp. 122–134.

plays of Shakespeare, 1963), *Wolt'u Hwit'uman Sison* (Selected poems of Walt Whitman, 1956). My initial attempt to examine Im Hak-Su's work as a translator in North Korea reveals the following traits. First, as is the case with his translations of the 1930s and 1940s, Im aims for acceptability with the target audience. In many cases where the source text deals with abstract concepts or aspects of European culture, Im's translations employ simple everyday language to appeal to the imagination of a wide range of Korean readers. Second, some of Im's translations display the types of honorific terms and verbal endings which started to come into wide use among Korean writers after Kim Ok's translations of foreign poets in the 1920s, indicating that Im was continuing these trends.

Example Two:

> One pang, my girl, and all is over[28]
> *Nimiyo, han bon ttonamyon kkuti nanuna*[29]

Example Three:

> O Captain! My Captain! Our fearful trip is done[30]
> *O Sonjang iyo! Na ui sonjang iyo! Uri tul ui Musoun Hanghae nun kkutnassnaida*[31]

Example Four:

> A people starved and stabbed in the untilled field,—[32]
> *Paeksong tulun kulmjurogo issora, ssurojigo issora*[33]

28 George Gordon Byron, "To Emma," in *The Complete Poetical Works of Byron*, ed. Paul Elmer More (Cambridge, MA: The Riverside Press, 1933), p. 89.

29 George Gordon Byron, "Emma ege" [To Emma], trans. Im Hak-Su, in *Pairon Sison* [Selected poems of Byron] (Pyongyang: Munye Ch'ulp'ansa, 1991), p. 433.

30 Walt Whitman, "O Captain! My Captain!" in *Walt Whitman Leaves of Grass*, ed. Sculley Bradley and Harold W. Blodgett (New York: W. W. Norton and Company Inc., 1973), p. 337.

31 Walt Whitman, "O Songjang iyo! Na ui Songjang iyo!" [O captain! My captain!], trans. Im Hak-Su, in *Wolt'u Hwit'uman Sison* [Selected poems of Walt Whitman] (Pyongyang: Kukrip Ch'ulp'ansa, 1956), p. 216.

32 Percy Bysshe Shelley, "England in 1819," in *The Poems of Percy Bysshe Shelley*, ed. C. D. Locock (London: Methuen and Co. Ltd., 1911), p. 191.

33 Percy Bysshe Shelley, "Ssonet'u–1819 Nyon ui Yongguk" [Sonnet–England in 1819],

Example two shows that Im translates "my girl" with "*Nimiyo*" a way of addressing a beloved person that indicates both respect and affection. In example three Im's rendering of the line from the Whitman poem employs a type of honorific verbal ending, "*kkutnassnaida*," which was frequently used in the 1920s. On the other hand, the fourth example shows translator Chu Chong-Gil using the more traditional verbal ending "*issora*." Such divergent techniques among North Korean translators will be explored further as the research progresses.

Third, compared to Im's translations of the 1930s and 1940s, we see a decreased use of Chinese character-based expressions in his North Korean works. This fits with the general trend of North Korean literary translation to use simple language for the common people.

Example Five:

> Of <u>physiology</u> from top to toe I sing[34]
> *Mori eso palkkus kkaji <u>momttungi</u> rul noraehanda*[35]

Example Six:

> Not <u>charioted</u> by Bacchus and his pards[36]
> *Pak'osu ui P'yopom <u>talguji</u> rul anit'ago ttwiokari*[37]

In example five for "physiology" Im uses the pure Korean word "*momttungi*" instead of the Chinese character-based expression "*yukshin*." Chang Ch'ong-Hyon's choice (example six) of the pure Korean term "*talguji*" rather than the Chinese phrase "*saryunch'a*" is an indication that Im was not alone in his attempt to appeal to the common people by emphasizing the resources of the Korean language.

---

trans. Chu Chong-Gil, in *Kundae Yongguk Sison* [Anthology of modern English poetry] (Pyongyang: Munye Ch'ulp'ansa, 1991), p. 159.

34 Walt Whitman, "One's-Self I Sing," in *Walt Whitman Leaves of Grass*, p. 1.

35 Walt Whitman, "Kaesong ul Na nun Noraehanda" [One's-self I sing], trans. Im Hak-Su, in *Wolt'u Hwit'uman Sison*, p. 9.

36 John Keats, "Ode to a Nightingale," in *The Poetical Works of John Keats*, ed. H. W. Garrod (Oxford: The Clarendon Press, 1939), p. 258.

37 John Keats, "Pamkkoekkori ege" [Ode to a nightingale], trans. Chang Ch'ong-Hyon, in *Kundae Yongguk Sison*, p. 218.

Fourth, in line with the attempt to conform to everyday usage, Im endeavours to employ indigenous Korean terms. The need to overcome the limits of Korean as a vehicle for the translation of foreign literature was a concern of North Korean translators at the time. In some of his translations Im uses folkloristic terms to display the richness of the Korean language and to evoke an emotional response in his readers.[38]

Example Seven:

> … they make me a pet besides[39]
> … *ku tulun na rul toryongnim uro yoginda*[40]

Example Eight:

> Good Kosciusko, thy great name alone[41]
> *Hyonmyonghan Kkosutchyusyukkoyo, aeoraji kudae ui widaehan irum mani*.[42]

In example seven Im Hak-Su uses the folkloric term "*toryongnim*" which was a traditional way of referring to a son of an aristocrat, while in example eight Chang employs the rather archaic phrase "*aeoraji*." These expressions would have had a resonance with the readers and demonstrated the resources of the Korean language.

Finally, as we've seen, Im's earlier translations of the works of English poets such as Shelley tended to replace lofty expressions with informal

38 The use of colloquial Korean writing style to translate foreign literature can be compared to the techniques employed by Japanese translators. "Due to linguistic differences, Japanese Shakespeareans have seldom sought to imitate Shakespeare's language in the manner of the mimetic approach theorized by Holmes. Instead they have enjoyed considerable freedom to rewrite Shakespeare's dramatic poetry in modern literary Japanese." See Daniel Gallimore, "Measuring Distance, Tsubouchi Shoyo and the Myth of Shakespeare Translation in Modern Japan," in *Translating Others*, ed. Theo Hermans, vol. 2 (Manchester: St. Jerome Publishing, 2006), p. 489.

39 Walt Whitman, "The Sleepers," in *Walt Whitman Leaves of Grass*, p. 426.

40 Walt Whitman, "Chamchanun Saram tul" [The sleepers], trans. Im Hak-Su, in *Wolt'u Hwit'uman Sison*, p. 141.

41 John Keats, "To Kosciusko," in *The Poetical Works of John Keats*, p. 50.

42 John Keats, "Kkosutchyusyukko ege Pach'inora" [To Kosciusko], trans. Chang Ch'ong-Hyon, in *Kundae Yongguk Sison*, p. 209.

ones. This trend intensified in Im's North Korean translations in which religious images were transformed into mundane ones.

Example Nine:

> Cheerful, for freest action form'd under the laws divine[43]
> *Kosanghan popryul mit eso orukhaejin hankkot chayuroun haengdong ul chulginun saeng ul*[44]

Example Ten:

> Religion Christless, Godless—a book sealed[45]
> *Chonggyo nun sinui opsnun uison gwa kasik—ch'aek un milbong tanghaessko*[46]

Since worship of a transcendent being was not deemed appropriate in socialist North Korea, Im Hak-Su transforms "the laws divine" of Whitman's poem into "refined/elegant law" ("*Kosanghan popryul*"). Similarly, Chu Chong-Gil renders the line from the Shelley poem as "Religion insincere hypocrisy and pretence" ("*Chonggyo nun sinui opsnun uison gwa kasik*") de-emphasizing the Christian element.

Conclusion

This paper has touched on two of the streams of influence during the formative phase of North Korean literature and culture: one coming in by way of the Soviet Koreans, the other from Korean scholars specializing in European literature. The focus has been on the development of Im Hak-Su's work from his early years in the South writing and translating poetry in the 1930s to his mature career as a scholar and translator of English literature in North Korea. We have considered some examples which indicate that while Im continued to use some of the stylistic features which came into use in the 1920s and 1930s, his North Korean

43 Whitman, "One's-Self I Sing," p. 1.

44 Whitman, "Kaesong ul Na nun Noraehanda," p. 9.

45 Shelley, "England in 1819," p. 192.

46 Shelley, "Ssonet'u–1819 Nyon ui Yongguk," p. 159.

translations employ indigenous Korean terms and emphasize the resources of the Korean language in line with the socialist aim of educating the common people.

While the predominance of Soviet influence on North Korean society at this time is recognized, not much attention has been paid to the role of European literature. Much more detailed work is needed, and as the research progresses I'll be attempting to answer questions concerning: 1) models followed by translators, 2) distinctive characteristics of women translators, 3) working conditions of translators, 4) the contributions of translators during the formative phase of North Korean socialist culture. North Korea is undergoing many changes, and I hope that this research will contribute to a better understanding of this complex society, as well as to greater insight into the ways in which constraints and enabling factors may affect the work of translators.[47]

47 André Lefevere and his collaborators comment that while most translators work within the boundaries of social and political structures: "The relatively rare translators who break with the norms of their society do so because they are able to make use of delegated power, because they are able to exploit their insertion between contradictory forces and because their forms of multiple employment sometimes allow them more social authority than is usually accorded them." See André Lefevere et al., "Translators and the Reins of Power," in *Translators through History*, ed. Jean Delisle and Judith Woodsworth (Philadelphia: John Benjamins Publishing Co., 1995), p. 153.

Bibliography

Armstrong, Charles K. *The North Korean Revolution 1945–1950.* Ithaca, New York: Cornell University Press, 2003.

Buzelin, Helene. "Unexpected Allies, How Latour's Network Theory Could Complement Bourdieusian Analyses in Translation Studies." *The Translator* 11, no. 2 (2005), pp. 193–218.

Byron, George Gordon. "To Emma." In *The Complete Poetical Works of Byron*, edited by Paul Elmer More. Cambridge, MA: The Riverside Press, 1933, p. 89.

———. "Emma ege" [To Emma]. Translated by Im Hak-Su. In *Pairon Sison* [Selected poems of Byron]. Pyongyang: Munye Ch'ulp'ansa, 1991, p. 433.

Ch'ae, Su-Yong. "Cholmang ui Chongshin Chiri" [The spiritual geography of despair]. *Pip'ypong Munhak* [Literary criticism] 4 (October 1990), pp. 51–82.

Gallimore, Daniel. "Measuring Distance, Tsubouchi Shoyo and the Myth of Shakespeare Translation in Modern Japan." In vol. 2 of *Translating Others*, edited by Theo Hermans. Manchester: St. Jerome Publishing, 2006, pp. 483–492.

Hermans, Theo. *Translation in Systems: Descriptive and System-oriented Approaches Explained.* Manchester: St. Jerome's Publishing, 1999.

Im, Ch'ae-Mun. "Na ui Aboji Im Hak-Su" [My father Im Hak-Su]. *Munye Undong* [Literary movement], September 2005, pp. 27–86.

Im, Hak-Su. *Chonson Sijip* [The front line poetry volume]. Seoul: Inmunsa, 1939.

———. "Hawodu P'asut'u ui Munhak" [The work of Howard Fast]. *Choson Munhak* [Choson literature] 2, no. 4 (April 1954), pp. 143–148.

———. "Henri P'ilding ui Sasilchuui" [Henry Fielding's realism]. *Choson Munhak* [Choson literature] 2, no. 10 (October 1954), pp. 94–103.

———. "Syeiksup'io wa Hyumonijum" [Shakespeare and humanism]. *Choson Munhak* [Choson literature] 2, no. 11 (November 1954), pp. 122–134.

Jeon, Young Sun. *Pukhan ui Munhak Yesul Unyong Ch'ekye wa Munye Iron* [The North Korean literary and artistic administrative system and literary and artistic theory]. Seoul: Toso Ch'ulp'an Yokrak, 2002.

Keats, John. "Yaaeng ege" [Ode to a nightingale]. Translated by Im Hak-Su. *Choson Ilbo* [Choson daily], 12 March 1938.

———. "To Kosciusko." In *The Poetical Works of John Keats*, edited by H. W. Garrod. Oxford: The Clarendon Press, 1939, p. 50.

———. "Ode to a Nightingale." In *The Poetical Works of John Keats*, edited by H. W. Garrod. Oxford: The Clarendon Press, 1939, pp. 257–260.

———. "Kkosutchyusyukko ege Pach'inora" [To Kosciusko]. Translated by Chang Ch'ong-Hyon. In *Kundae Yongguk Sison* [Anthology of modern English poetry]. Pyongyang: Munye Ch'ulp'ansa, 1991, p. 209.

———. "Pamkkoekkori ege" [Ode to a nightingale]. Translated by Chang Ch'ong-Hyon. In *Kundae Yongguk Sison* [Anthology of modern English poetry]. Pyongyang: Munye Ch'ulp'ansa, 1991, p. 218.

Kim, Jae-Hong. *Han Yong-Un Munhak Yongu* [The literary works of Han Yong-Un]. Seoul: Iljisa, 1982.

Kim, Jae-Yong. *Pundan Kujo wa Pukhan Munhak* [The structure of the partition of the Korean peninsula and North Korean literature]. Seoul: Somyong Ch'ulp'an, 2003.

Kwon, Yong-Min. *Hanguk Munhak Taesajon* [Comprehensive dictionary of Korean literature]. Seoul: Souldae Ch'ulp'anbu, 2004.

Lankov, Andrei. *Crisis in North Korea, The Failure of De-Stalinization, 1956.* Honolulu: University of Hawai'i Press, 2005.

Lefevere, André et al. "Translators and the Reins of Power." In *Translators through History*, edited by Jean Delisle and Judtih Woodsworth. Philadelphia: John Benjamins Publishing Co., 1995, pp. 131–155.

Myers, Brian. *Han Sorya and North Korean Literature, The Failure of Socialist Realism in the DPRK.* Ithaca, New York: Cornell East Asia Series, 1994.

Sappho. *The Songs of Sappho: In English Translation by Many Poets.* Mount Vernon, New York: The Peter Pauper Press, 1942.

———. "Ssap'o ui Sojong Si" [Sappho's lyric poetry]. Translated by Im Hak-Su. *Hakp'ung* [Academic traditions], November 1948, pp. 100–103.

Shelley, Percy Bysshe. "England in 1819." In *The Poems of Percy Bysshe Shelley*, edited by C. D. Locock. London: Methuen and Co. Ltd., 1911, pp. 191–192.

———. "Sojjok Param ege" [Ode to the west wind]. Translated by Im Hak-Su. *Siin* [Poet] 2, no. 1 (March 1948), pp. 26–28.

———. "Ode to the West Wind." In *The Norton Anthology of English Literature*, edited by M. H. Abrams. New York: W. W. Norton and Company, 1979, pp. 704–706.

———. "Ssonet'u–1819 Nyon ui Yongguk" [Sonnet–England in 1819]. Translated by Chu Chong-Gil. In *Kundae Yongguk Sison* [Anthology of modern English poetry]. Pyongyang: Munye Ch'ulp'ansa, 1991, pp. 158–159.

Shin, Hyong-Ki, and O Song-Ho. *Pukhan Munhaksa* [North Korean literary history]. Seoul: P'yongminsa, 2000.

Whitman, Walt. "Chamchanun Saram tul" [The sleepers]. Translated by Im Hak-Su. In *Wolt'u Hwit'uman Sison* [Selected poems of Walt Whitman]. Pyongyang: Kukrip Ch'ulp'ansa, 1956, pp. 137–156.

———. "Kaesong ul Na nun Noraehanda" [One's-self I sing]. Translated by Im Hak-Su. In *Wolt'u Hwit'uman Sison* [Selected poems of Walt Whitman]. Pyongyang: Kukrip Ch'ulp'ansa, 1956, p. 9.

———. "O Songjang iyo! Na ui Songjang iyo!" [O captain! My captain!]. Translated by Im Hak-Su. In *Wolt'u Hwit'uman Sison* [Selected poems of Walt Whitman]. Pyongyang: Kukrip Ch'ulp'ansa, 1956, pp. 216–218.

———. "O Captain! My Captain!" In *Walt Whitman Leaves of Grass*, edited by Sculley Bradley and Harold W. Blodgett. New York: W. W. Norton and Company Inc., 1973, pp. 337–338.

———. "One's-Self I Sing." In *Walt Whitman Leaves of Grass*, edited by Sculley Bradley and Harold W. Blodgett. New York: W. W. Norton and Company Inc., 1973, p. 1.

———. "The Sleepers." In *Walt Whitman Leaves of Grass*, edited by Sculley Bradley and Harold W. Blodgett. New York: W. W. Norton and Company Inc., 1973, pp. 424–433.

Yeats, William Butler. *Ch'angsal e Namun Sigu* [The words upon the window pane]. Translated by Im Hak-Su. *Munchang*, September 1938, pp. 92–109.

———. "Inisup'uri ro" [The Lake Isle of Innisfree]. Translated by Im Hak-Su. In "Siin Yeich'u ui Ijang" [The reburial of the poet Yeats]. *Minsong* 5, no. 6 (January 1949), pp. 53–54.

———. "Pidan Hanul" [He wishes for the cloths of heaven]. Translated by Im Hak-Su. In "Siin Yeich'u ui Ijang" [The reburial of the poet Yeats]. *Minsong* 5, no. 6 (January 1949), pp. 53–54.

Yi, Myong-Jae. "Pukhan Munhak e Kkich'in Soryon Munhak ui Yonghyang" [The influence of Soviet literature on North Korean literature]. *Omunhak* [Language and literary research] 116 (December 2002), pp. 159–186.

———. *Pukhan Munhak Sajon* [Dictionary of North Korean literature]. Seoul: Kukhak Charyowon, 2007.

Tinio Translating: *May Katwiran Ba?*[1]

Corazon D. VILLAREAL

Introduction

This paper explores the aesthetics of Rolando S. Tinio's translations. The term "aesthetics" (1790) could have originated from the German word *ästhetisch* (Alexander Baumgarten, *c.*1750)[2] or the French *esthétique*, but both are derived from the Greek word *aisthetikos*, meaning to perceive/feel/sense. The term "aesthetics" refers then to the pleasure arising from sensation and feeling. But to Kant, such sensory pleasure must also engage our potentials for reflective contemplation. The aesthetics of Tinio's translations would thus involve the sensory, the emotional, and the intellectual.

The project is both daunting and presumptuous because Tinio's body of works is monumental. But we could deal mainly with the intellectual aspect or the vision that drove him to translate plays (approximately 50). This is articulated in the philosophy and objectives of the Teatro Pilipino,

---

1 This paper was developed from shorter papers read at a forum on Aesthetics of Philippine Theatre sponsored by the Philippines's National Commission on Culture and the Arts (NCCA) in February 2010 and another paper read at The Asian Translation Traditions 4, an international conference held at The Chinese University of Hong Kong from 15–17 December 2010. The researcher would like to acknowledge support from NCCA. In Filipino, "*katwiran*" means literally "reason" or "argument." The question "*May katwiran ba*?" may be translated into English as: "Was there reason for Tinio to translate?" The use of "*katwiran*" also resonates with an original play by Tinio, entitled: *May Katwiran ba ang Katwiran*? [Does reason have its reason?]. All English gloss unless otherwise stated are provided by the author.

2 Alexander Gottlieb Baumgarten, *Asthetik*, ed. and trans. Dagmer Mirbach (Hamburg: Meiner, 2007).

the drama group which he founded in 1975 and the main vehicle for producing the plays he translated. Teatro Pilipino:

1. believes in the ability of the national language to convey to Filipinos the essential truths of human existence which the heritage of the world classics offers,
2. aims to enrich the national language through translations of drama masterpieces, and
3. is committed to the production of Pilipino plays that adhere to the rigorous standards of theatre expertise.

The above objectives show that a central concern of Tinio the translator is language: to demonstrate the capability of Pilipino[3] to express and embody a wide range of concepts and experience previously thought impossible in a language considered both common and provincial. He would write: "It is not a question of understanding the syntax and vocabulary of an acquired language. It is a question of being able to feel in that language, to be able to relate its inner rhythms in the deepest portions of one's life and soul."[4] A study of his plays should thus begin with the linguistic aspect or the encoded text: how his translations prove the richness of Pilipino and, simultaneously, how they challenge and enrich the language.

Translation, as Walter Benjamin wrote, is concerned with a source text's "afterlife." This is a touchstone, I think, of Tinio's translation aesthetics (and as well, of my interest in translation studies). Benjamin draws us away from the concept of a superior originary text to the infinite possibilities of its translations. This is key to viewing the translated text as equal to the original, which is of particular importance to a discussion of Tinio, translator into Filipino of "classic" texts (Western texts, actually);

3 Pilipino is based mainly on Tagalog, the main language spoken in Metro Manila and surrounding provinces. Pilipino was the name given to the national language of the Philippines from 1959 up until 1987, when the new Constitution renamed it to Filipino. Filipino is supposed to develop not just from Tagalog but from the various regional and ethnic languages of the country.

4 Pepe Nieva, "Adios Amerika! Or How a Poet, Playwright, Director and Professor Is Bringing Back Art to the 'Masa,'" *Sunburst* 3 (October 1975), pp. 52–55.

and to believing that to read, interpret, translate a text, and translate it again by performing it, is a way to define and redefine our social aesthetics.

Rolando Tinio: A Prodigious Talent

Tinio was a poet, teacher, columnist, playwright, scriptwriter for television and the movies, director, costume designer, singer, essayist, actor—and translator (the dream he had which somehow he was unable to realize was to be a dancer!). Even to Bienvenido Lumbera, his good friend from their days at the University of Santo Tomas in Manila and later, like Tinio, also National Artist for Literature (2006), it was difficult to mine Tinio's achievement:

> *Bagaman pamilyar naman ako sa buhay at karera ni Rolando ... kailangan ko pa ring saliksikin ang mga yugto ng kanyang pag-unlad bilang manlilikha. Sa panahong ginugol ko sa pananaliksik, saka pa lamang natiim sa aking kamalayan na ang yumao kong kaibigan ay, walang kadudadudang isang berdaderong henyo.*[5]
>
> Although I am familiar with the life and career of Rolando ... I still need to research on his development as an artist. I spent a lot of time researching on this, but it is only now that I can fully comprehend that my late friend was, without doubt, a true genius.

But for Lumbera, it was in translations that Tinio made the most mark.

> *Marahil ang pinakamatibay na monumentong dadakila kay Rolando bilang Artista ng bayan ay ang kanyang natipong mga salin ng mga dula mula sa iba-ibang panahon ng teatro sa kanluran, ang mga akdang kanyang isinaTagalog, dinirihe, dinesenyo at inihanap ng mga kabataang manonood.*[6]
>
> Perhaps, the most enduring monument to Rolando as National Artist is his collection of translations of plays from various times and places in the West—the works he translated into Tagalog, directed, and designed—and for which he looked for a young audience.

5 Bienvenido Lumbera, "Introduksyon," in *May Katwiran ang Katwiran at Iba Pang Dula*, by Rolando S. Tinio (Quezon City: University of the Philippines Press, 2001), p. vii.

6 Ibid., p. xii.

Archiving Tinio (Translations of Plays)

Note: The years indicate the year of performance in pre-Teatro Pilipino days (before 1975), by Teatro Pilipino (founded in 1975), and by Dulaang UP, the oldest Theatre Arts Company of the University of the Philippines (founded in 1976).

1. *Pahimakas sa Isang Ahente*, 1966, 1999 (*Death of a Salesman* by Arthur Miller)
2. *Ang Pagpaslang sa Katedral*, 1966 (*Murder in the Cathedral* by T. S. Eliot)
3. *Bernardo Alba*, 1967 (*Bernarda Alba* by Federico Garcia Lorca)
4. *Kaaway ng Bayan*, 1969, 1994 (*An Enemy of the People* by Henrik Ibsen)
5. *Ang Masayahing Biyuda*, 1969 (*The Merry Widow* by Franz Lehar)
6. *Para Akong Kamera*, 1977 (*I Am a Camera* by John van Druten)
7. *Ang Abaniko*, 1975 (*The Fan* by Carlo Goldoni)
8. *Salising Landas*, 1975 (*Cross Purpose* by Albert Camus)
9. *Tiyo Vanya*, 1976 (*Uncle Vanya* by Anton Chekhov)
10. *Kawawang Marat*, 1976 (*My Poor Marat* by Alexei Arbuzov)
11. *La Traviata*, 1976, 1990 (*La Traviata* by Giuseppe Verdi); sung in Filipino and Italian
12. *Santa Juana*, 1977 (*Saint Joan* by George Bernard Shaw)
13. *Hedda Gabler*, 1977 (*Hedda Gabler* by Henrik Ibsen)
14. *Ang Negosyante ng Venecia*, 1977 (*The Merchant of Venice* by William Shakespeare)
15. *Ang Kuripot*, 1978 (*The Miser* by Molière)
16. *Camille*, 1978 (*Camille* by Alexander Dumas)
17. *Ang Laruang Kristal*, 1979 (*The Glass Menagerie* by Tennessee Williams)
18. *Hamlet*, 1979, 2006 (*Hamlet* by William Shakespeare)
19. *Ang Tagak*, 1979 (*The Sea-gull* by Anton Chekhov)
20. *Ang Kambal*, 1979 (*The Brothers Menaechmus* by Plautus)
21. *Binibining Julie*, 1979 (*Miss Julie* by August Strindberg)
22. *Ang Malakas*, 1979 (*The Stronger* by August Strindberg)
23. *Pangarap sa isang Gabing Gitnang Tag-araw*, 1980 (*A Midsummer Night's Dream* by William Shakespeare)
24. *Armas at Ang Lalaki*, 1980 (*Arms and the Man* by George Bernard Shaw)
25. *Tartuffe*, 1980 (*Tartuffe* by Molière)

26. *Caligula*, 1981 (*Caligula* by Albert Camus)
27. *Pamamanhikan*, 1981 (*The Proposal* by Anton Chekhov)
28. *Ang Bastos*, 1981 (*The Boor* by Anton Chekhov)
29. *Ang Heredera*, 1981 (*The Heiress* by August and Ruth Goetz)
30. *Ang Mga Tagahabi*, 1981 (*The Weavers* by Gerhart Hauptmann)
31. *Romeo at Julieta*, 1981(*Romeo and Juliet* by William Shakespeare)
32. *Ang Barbero ng Seville*, 1982 (*The Barber of Seville* by Pierre Beaumarchais)
33. *Antigone*, 1982 (*Antigone* by Jean Anouilh)
34. *Ang Halaga ng Pagiging Masigasig*, 1982 (*The Importance of Being Earnest* by Oscar Wilde)
35. *Ang Reyna at ang Rebelde*, 1982 (*The Queen and the Rebel* by Ugo Betti)
36. *Ang Mabuting Tao ng Setzuan*, 1983 (*The Good Woman of Setzuan* by Bertolt Brecht)
37. *Ang Paghihintay kay Godo/Pagputi ng Uwak*, 1967, 1984 (*Waiting for Godot* by Samuel Beckett)
38. *Ang Senyora ng Hotel*, 1984 (*The Mistress of the Inn* by Carlo Goldoni)
39. *Ang Kuwentong Katawatawa*, 1985 (*When the Music Stops* by Armand Salacrou)
40. *Ang Multo*, 1985 (*Ghosts* by Henrik Ibsen)
41. *Ang Tenor*, 1987 (*The Tenor* by Frank Wedekind)
42. *Ang Sopranong Kalbo*, 1987 (*The Bald Soprano* by Ionesco)
43. *Medea*, 1988 (*Medea* by Euripedes)
44. *Makbet*, 1989, 1995 (*Macbeth* by William Shakespeare)
45. *Ikalabindalawang Gabi*, 1988, 1992 (*Twelfth Night* by William Shakespeare)
46. *La Boheme*, 1992 (*La Bohème* by Giacomo Puccini); sung in Filipino
47. *Salome*, 1993 (*Salome* by Oscar Wilde)
48. *Haring Edipo*, 2002 (*Oedipus Rex* by Sophocles)
49. *Paano Man Ang Umibig*, 2008 (*As You Like It* by William Shakespeare)

Tinio's World: Dissonances and Counterpoints

Rolando Santos Tinio was born in Gagalangin, Tondo, Manila, on 5 March 1937 and lived up to 1997, also the year when he was awarded posthumously the title of National Artist for Literature. In 1955, he graduated with a bachelor's degree in philosophy from the University of Santo Tomas, the oldest university in the Philippines (founded by the Dominican Order in 1611). He received his MFA in Creative Writing from Iowa State University in 1958, and completed a non-degree course in theatre in UK through a British Council scholarship. He taught at the Ateneo de Manila University of the Jesuit Order from 1958–1975 where he headed the Department of English and later, the Department of Filipino. His adult years were marked by creative frenzy and prodigious energy.

To understand the world of Tinio's translations, or, to answer the question "*May katwiran ba*?" we should site Tinio within the issues and concerns of the theatre of his time. His translations were first performed, and in rapid succession, in 1966 with *Ang Laruang Kristal* (*The Glass Menagerie*), *Pahimakas sa Isang Ahente* (*Death of a Salesman*), *Binibining Julie* (*Miss Julie*), *Pagputi ng Uwak* (*Waiting for Godot*). Beginning 1975, all were performed by the Teatro Pilipino which was the resident company of the Cultural Centre of the Philippines (CCP). There was a steady stream of Tinio translations and these were staged up until 1986. With the downfall of the Marcos regime in 1987, Tinio lost Teatro's biggest sponsor, Imelda Marcos. Teatro, however, continued until its farewell performance of *Ikalabindalawang Gabi* (*Twelfth Night*) in February 1992. Tinio decided to close Teatro with the death of his wife and lead actress, Ella Luansing, in 1991.

The period when Tinio was at his most prolific especially in translating and staging Western plays into Pilipino was also a time of literary experimentation and nationalistic ferment in the Philippines. Lumbera would write:

> … there are now at least 24 authors who have had at least two plays performed in the years between 1972 and 1979.[7] More than half of this number are below 30 which means that … [their] best writing years are still ahead of them … [they are] products of the nationalistic ferment of the previous decade, and thus reflect the questioning stance of the time when everything about the established order was subjected to scrutiny.[8]

7 The Marcos dictatorship (1972–1987) was fertile ground for the creation of protest literature, especially protest plays.

8 Doreen G. Fernandez, *Palabas* (Quezon City: Ateneo de Manila University Press, 1996), pp. 123–124.

Five years later, Lumbera wrote:

> Nationalist consciousness implanted among writers by the mass movement of the late 1960s has found a way of asserting itself through approved trends. Nativist nationalism encourages artists to look back to the country's past to retrieve forgotten folkloric material, a neglected traditional form, or a historical moment of interest to the present.[9]

He was referring, for instance, to the social realist plays of the young playwrights who wrote and translated for the Philippine Educational Theatre Association (PETA).[10] Or to laboratory theatre groups such as Ateneo's Dulaang Sibol ("Dulaang" is a term for "Drama Group") and the Dulaang UP.[11] Or to those who wrote/improvised proletarian street theatre, as well as drama groups with specific advocacies such as the Dulaang Babaylan and the Teatro Kabataan (Youth's Theatre) and many other theatre groups.

The Dulaang Sibol was founded at the Ateneo by Onofre Pagsanhan (*c.*the 1960s), while the Dulaang Babaylan in 1973 was organized by drama notables from various schools. The latter's motto was: "*Ang hindi marunong maglingon sa pinanggalingan di makakarating sa paroroonan.*" (A popular Philippine proverb, which means: "He who cannot look back to where he came from cannot reach his destination.") Philippine theatre can come home only thru its history, and with this vision, Babaylan aimed to document and study traditional Philippine drama thru the re-stagings of traditional plays such as the *duplo*, *komedya*, *sinakulo*, and *sarsuela*,

9 Bienvenido Lumbera, "The Nationalist Literary Tradition," in *Revaluation. Essays on Philippine Literature, Cinema, and Popular Culture* (Manila: Index Press, 1984), pp. 138–139.

10 Manuel Pambid, "Paano nga ba ang Peta Play (O Ano nga ba ang play na Petang-Peta?)" [What makes a play a PETA play?] (Paper read at the Forum on Aesthetics of Philippine Theatre sponsored by National Commission on Culture and the Arts held in Intramuros, Manila, February 2010).

11 Please see Alexander Cortez, "Dulaang UP (University of the Philippines): A Laboratory for Future Artists" (Paper read at the Forum on Aesthetics of Philippine Theatre sponsored by National Commission on Culture and the Arts held in Intramuros, Manila, February 2010).

mixed imaginatively with world theatre. Works of new playwrights in the vernacular were also presented.[12] Daroy noted this experimentation cum revival, the mix of the traditional and the modern, for example, in Al Santos' *Si Tatang atbp. Mga Tauhan ng Aming Dula* (My father, etc. The cast of our play), a *sinakulo*[13] based on the *Watawat ng Lahi* (literally The emblem of a race, which refers to a millenarian group) and the life of its founder, Valentin de los Santos; in Nonilon Queano's *Alipato* (Flying ember) and in Manuel Pambid's *Batilyos*.[14] Daroy's reading was that "the consciousness of those in theater—directors, writers, actors, stage crews, etc.—has assimilated the whole history of the theatrical tradition in the country."[15]

In this context, the spectacle of Filipino actors and actresses clothed in Western costumes but speaking in Filipino did not sit well with certain sectors, for example, with those whom Tinio called by various names such as the "naïve super-nationalists of the UP (University of the Philippines) school."

Some counterpoints between Tinio's Teatro Pilipino and the other theatre groups such as PETA and Dulaang UP are obvious: the concept of theatre as education, the inclusion of translations (of both foreign and local plays) in the repertoires, the cultivation of the community as audience. But Tinio was always a controversial figure. Why this drive to translating Western plays when such creative energy could be turned towards writing original plays in Pilipino? Nicanor Tiongson, a noted theatre scholar and playwright, asserts that in the 1960s and the early 1970s, directors could claim that there were not enough legitimate plays written in Pilipino that could be staged. But by the mid-seventies:

---

12 This capsule history of theatre from the sixties to the seventies was provided by Doreen Fernandez in Fernandez, *Palabas*, pp. 107–109.

13 A *sinakulo* is a play on Christ's Passion and Death. This was a nativized form of the *cenaculo* which was introduced by the Spaniards in the Spanish colonial era (1565–1898), along with other dramatic forms like the *comedia* and the *zarzuela*. The popularity of these drama forms waned during the American colonial period (1899–1948) and in the post-colonial period.

14 *Batilyos* refers to those hired to carry heavy loads in seaports, constructions sites, etc.

15 Petronilo Bn. Daroy, "Drama: New Methods, New Directions," *Expressweek*, 3 June 1976, p. 51.

> *Ang pagmamatigas na isalin pa rin ang mga "klasikong" dula, lalo na ang mga walang kinalaman sa ating sariling kalagayan at nagpapalaganap ng isang kaisipan salungat sa diwa ng paglaban para sa katarungan, ay katigasan na lamang ng ulo at dekadenteng pagpapasasa sa ating pagkahumaling sa dulang kanluranin.*[16]
>
> The insistence to translate "classic" theatre, especially those that have nothing to do with our social situation and that spread a frame of mind counter to the impulse to fight against injustice, is plain stubbornness and a decadent wallowing in Western theatre.

Why persist, moreover, in the incongruity of a Hamlet or an Amanda or a Tiyo Vanya speaking in Pilipino? And why stage the plays in the elitist halls of the Cultural Centre of the Philippines under the patronage of Imelda Marcos during the Marcos dictatorship?

It should be noted that most of the plays Tinio translated are relay translations, that is, translations into Filipino of English translations of works by non-English playwrights from Europe. On the other hand, the new playwrights that Lumbera and Tiongson referred to utilized traditional forms such as the *koridos*, the *komedya*, the *sinakulo*, the *sarsuela*, as mentioned earlier.[17] These were initially translations into the vernaculars of European works, and therefore as Western as the plays Tinio translated. Later though, they became so indigenized by Filipino writers and performers, they were considered as traditional Filipino plays. The revivals of these traditional forms in the 1970s and the 1980s at the height of the curtailment of freedom and unrelieved social injustices were particularly timely because through the creativity of the playwrights and the directors, social and political themes were highlighted. This social bent was not new for even in the Spanish period these traditional plays were avenues for anti-Spanish sentiments. Such tradition of resistance

16 Nicanor Tiongson, "Pagsasali'y di Biro," *Sagisag* 2, no. 5 (May 1976), p. 54.

17 See, for instance, Vicente Rafael, *The Promise of the Foreign, Nationalism and the Technics of Translation in the Spanish Philippines* (Pasig: Anvil, 2006; North Carolina: Duke University Press, 2005).

was firmed up even more with the seditious dramas in major Philippine languages in the early American period. The "new" plays during the Marcos dictatorship had this critical edge but it was deemed absent in Tinio's translations.

It was difficult to then understand why Tinio continued on translating and presenting Western plays at a time when many felt a subversive wind needed to blow. The plays he first translated came from contemporary American theatre. The first was Tennessee Williams' *The Glass Menagerie*, followed by Arthur Miller's *Death of a Salesman* (both in 1966). The latter, which was translated as *Pahimakas sa Isang Ahente*, was considered a milestone in theatre history.[18] However, an initial blessing came from an icon in Philippine literature. Citing the review of *Pahimakas* by Quijano de Manila (Nick Joaquin) of the *Philippine Free Press*,[19] Lumbera writes: "*ang lengguaheng ginamit ni Rolando bilang katumbas ng Ingles ng mga taga- Bronx sa New York ay nagpatunay na 'ang wika ng kanto' ay siyang buhay na wika na kailangan ng teatro sa Filipinas upang ito ay makaugnay sa mga manonood na Filipino.*"[20] (The language Tinio used for the English spoken in Bronx in New York proves that street language is the living language Filipino theatre needs, to connect with its audience.)

It appears then that for Tinio, as well as for Joaquin and Lumbera, it did not matter if the plays performed were translations of Western plays, as long as the translations could connect with the audience. Yet, while Doreen Fernandez hails the founding of the Teatro Pilipino as the beginning of the return to the vernacular and credits him for making a body of Western classics available in Filipino translation, it "was not that successful at building an audience."[21]

In light of Fernandez's remarks, Tinio's insistence—that the translator must include only what is meaningful to the Filipino audience and "throw

18 Lumbera, "Introduksyon, " p. xi.

19 Joaquin's article is included in Quijano de Manila's *Manila: Sin City? and Other Chronicles*. Quijano de Manila is the pen name of Nick Joaquin, also National Artist for Literature. I am grateful to Dennis Marasigan for showing me a copy of this article.

20 Lumbera, "Introduksyon," p. xi.

21 Fernandez, *Palabas*, p. 124.

out" those meaningful only to the people using the original language—may have run aground. Works are translated, he says:

> ... entirely within the sensibility of the translator which, if he is a good translator, coincides with the sensibility of the community for which he is translating. In other words, we translate Shakespeare and Shaw and van Druten not because we want to see what is English in us, but because we want to see what is Filipino or Pilipino in the things they have written.[22]

His theory of translating plays was tied up closely with his vision of what theatre should aim for. A play is successful, he would say, not because of technical and formal advantages but because it embodies a value system the audience upholds. The translation of a foreign play places it within the value system of the target culture and is structured by the language and history of that culture.

Yet, if an audience was so elusive, where did Tinio and his audience meet?

At this point, we could line up the following as the components of Tinio's aesthetics of translating plays (what he considers appealing sensually, imaginatively, and intellectually):

1. Developing Pilipino to its fullest potentials;
2. Dovetailing the value systems of the translation and those of the audience;
3. Translating processes of thinking and modes of experience that can come to us only through foreign models;
4. Viewing tradition as "products of a particular phase in our history; it's something to grow from."[23]

Like Tinio, Tiongson believes that translations of foreign plays into Tagalog allow the Filipino audience access to the dramatic experience, but Tiongson thinks that language alone is not enough to elicit "gut" reaction from the audience. It is the substance or content that matters. To quote

22 Rolando Tinio, "National Meaning in Our Theater," *Metro Manila* 1, no. 20 (June 1977), p. 19.

23 Rolando Tinio, "The Folly of Cultural Chauvinism," *Metro Manila* 2, nos. 5–6 (November 1977), p. 55.

Tiongson: "*Una at pinakamahalaga, dapat itanong kung ang kalamnan ng dula ay maaring matanggap at maunawaan ng karaniwang Pilipino, batay sa kanyang karanasan at pananaw-mundo.*"[24] (First and foremost, it must be asked whether the ordinary Filipino can accept and understand the substance of the play, based on his/her experience and world-view.)

Tinio and Tiongson agree that the play must appeal to the audience's value system/world-view, but the problem is that they differ in their perception of what that value system is. Tiongson, for instance, points out the difficulty of a Filipino to identify with the sustained rage and vengeance depicted in Friedrich Durenmatt's *The Visit*. Moreover, he thinks the translated play must bring changes and innovations in Philippine drama: "*Bakit nating pag-aaksayahan ng panahon ang mga dulang wala namang maidudulot na pagbabago sa ating dulaan?*"[25] (Why waste our time on plays that will not introduce any changes in our theatre?) The translated play must also be socially transformative: "*kung may maidudulot itong pagkamulat sa kanya hinggil sa sarili niyang lipunan sa kasalukuyan.*"[26] (If the play can contribute to awakening the audience to the social realities of the time.)

Rody Vera—stage actor, translator, and playwright—would continue to ask:

> *... bakit nga ba salin lang ng salin si Tinio nung panahon ng mga banyaga.... Sa tingin ko, ang hindi pagkakaintindihan tulad ng Babaylan ng PETA sa estetika ni Tinio, ang tanong ay bakit nililimita ni Tinio ang pagsasalin? Bakit hindi puedeng pagsabayin? Puede namang magsulat ng orihinal na dula.*[27]
>
> ... so why did Tinio keep on translating the plays of the colonizers.... In my opinion, this conflict in aesthetics, such as that between the Babaylan group of PETA and Tinio's, the question is why did Tinio limit himself to translating? Why didn't he write and translate? He could have written original plays.

24 Tiongson, "Pagsasali'y di Biro," p. 54.

25 Ibid.

26 Ibid.

27 Rody Vera, Q and A Session at the Second Forum on Aesthetics of Philippine Theatre sponsored by the National Commission on Culture and the Arts held in Intramuros, Manila, October 2009.

Tinio did write original plays in Pilipino (*May Katwiran ang Katwiran*) and movie scripts in Pilipino, besides. He directed an original play in English. This was Virginia Moreno's *The Onyx Wolf*, which was the inaugural presentation of the Little Theatre of the Cultural Centre of the Philippines in 1971. However, he likewise directed both traditional and modern plays in Pilipino, among them: the *sarswela*, *Paglipas ng Dilim* (After darkness) by Precioso Palma; *Ang Gintong Salakot* (The golden hat) which was the inaugural presentation of the Cultural Centre of the Philippines in 1969; the *komedya*, *Prinsipe Baldovino* (1971); and the *sarswela*, *Ang Kiri* (The flirt) (1974). He also published three collections of poetry in Pilipino. Still, translating from English into Pilipino was his main preoccupation.

Was this a matter of Tinio's limitations, or a reflection of an ideological divide? Tinio said at one time: "I am not an activist. I let history take care of itself. I am interested in life, not in ideology. Ideology is artificially induced."[28] It should be noted though that in the Dulaang UP archive of plays performed,[29] out of about 86 plays presented between its inception in 1976 up to 1992 when Tinio closed down Teatro Pilipino, 37 were foreign plays translated into Filipino. The PETA archive yields a predominance of plays of varied themes and styles written and performed in Pilipino, but it includes translations and adaptations from Western plays and stories[30] performed between the seventies and the mid-eighties. They ran in a parallel period as the Tinio productions (except for *Ang Operang Tatlong Pera*, Rody Vera's translation of Brecht's *The Three-penny Opera* which was staged in 1998).

Two Plays: Looking for a Theatre Aesthetics

To return to Benjamin's thoughts, we could say that a foreign play assumes an afterlife in the translations—in the text and in each and every performance

28 Nieva, "Adios Amerika!" p. 55.

29 Cortez, "Dulaang UP."

30 Ibid.

of the play. Since the afterlife is potentially endless, the master-slave metaphor of translation in which the source is the master and the translation its slave is denied.[31] The translator can thus be a manipulator of meaning and the translation process never neutral. The *Hamlet* of Shakespeare or the *Death of a Salesman* by Miller are not equal or the same as the *Hamlet* and the *Pahimakas* of Tinio. Being filtered through the vision of the translator, his language, and his culture, the translation is not necessarily its Western source but Tinio's reading of that source. A study of Tinio's translations must address a number of questions: Do these show the aesthetics he has enunciated in his essays and interviews? Do his critics prove themselves right? Finally, what can these dialogues/ confrontations suggest for an aesthetics of drama translations in the Philippines? To see is to believe.

The conclusions will necessarily be partial since the essay will focus only on two translations, but the aim is for specificity and not comprehensiveness. These are *Pahimakas sa Isang Ahente* (*Death of a Salesman* by Arthur Miller), said to be his first translation, staged and directed by Tinio himself at the Manila Girl Scouts Auditorium in September 1966, and then again by Tinio at the Cultural Centre of the Philippines in 1979. *Pahimakas* was staged 33 years after its first performance under the direction of Amiel Leonardia for the Dulaang UP in its 24th season (1999–2000) with Ray Ventura in the lead role for the Pilipino translation. Tinio produced and directed *Hamlet* for Teatro Pilipino on 22–24, 30 June and 1–2 July 1979 (with movie actor Ernie Garcia as Hamlet). It was presented again 28 years later as *Hamlet Redux*[32] under the direction of Antonio Mabesa for Dulaang UP in its 31st season in 2006–2007 with Arnold Reyes in the lead role for the Pilipino translation. *Hamlet* is the only published translation by Tinio.[33]

31 Susan Bassnett-McGuire, *Translation Studies*, rev. ed. (London and New York: Routledge, 1996), p. xv.

32 *Hamlet Redux*, Souvenir Program, Dulaang UP, 2006.

33 Rolando Tinio, trans., *Ang Trahedya ni Hamlet, Prinsipe ng Dinamarka* [Hamlet] (Quezon City: University of the Philippines Press, 1991).

Pahimakas: Pinoy ang Dating?[34]

Tinio's translation is what Jacobson classifies as interlingual translation: the interpretation of verbal signs by means of some other language.[35] Interlingual translation is a wide spectrum but it is generally of two types: translation (*salin*) or adaptation (*halaw*). Tinio's work is a translation. In the following juxtaposition of the opening scene in Miller's play and Tinio's translation, a close correspondence of the lines in the two versions is noticeable (please see Appendix A for evidence). The text of *Pahimakas* is not an adaptation (or *halaw*). It remains to be seen if Tinio the director would take liberties with setting, characters, language—the way, for instance, that Onofre Pagsanhan did when he staged *Doon Po sa Amin* in place of Wilder's *Our Town*.

While there is correspondence, there is no equivalence. There are differences, for instance, in specificity. In the two lines below, the first segment comes from Williams' play, the second is from Tinio's translation, and the third is the literal translation into English of the Filipino translation.

> Did something happen?/*Nadisgrasya ka ba?* (Did you meet an accident?)
> Did you smash the car?/*Binangga mo ba ang kotse?* (Did you hit the car?)

The difference in specificity derives sometimes from idiomatic expressions peculiar to English and to Filipino.

> Don't you feel well?/*Masama ba'ng katawan mo?* (Does your body ache?)
> What?/*Ha?*
> There's such an undercurrent in him./*Nasa loob ang kulo ng anak mo.* (Your son boils inside.)

---

34 "*Pinoy*" is the diminutive for Filipino; it is an informal, in-group term that Filipinos use to refer to themselves. "*Dating*" is an expression which means "overall effect," or "mark."

35 Roman Jacobson, "On Linguistic Aspects of Translation," in *The Translation Studies Reader*, ed. Lawrence Venuti (London and New York: Routledge, 2000), pp. 113–118.

Or, to differences in physical terrain: in the Philippines many roads do not have shoulders; so, we don't normally refer to roads with shoulders.

> The car kept going off the shoulder./*Kumakabig sa kanan.* (Tends to turn right.)

Of particular importance is the way Tinio translates expletives or intensives to express strong emotions such as surprise or amazement, or anger, e.g., in the excerpt that follows:

> These goddam arch supports are killing me./*Pinapahirapan ako ng putang'nang kalsong iyan.* (Son of a bitch, this arch's giving me a hard time.)

"*Puta*" (literally, "whore") is the first "vulgar" expression found in the text, but we can surmise from Nick Joaquin's review that Tinio exercised directorial liberties with his own translated text and added expressions in the actual performance. His "*ahente*" (salesperson), according to Nick Joaquin, "tentatively starts with curse words like *puneta* and from there moves on to graver locutions: *'tang 'na* and *'dot mo* and so forth," as translations of tamer English expressions like, "Gee" and "Gee whiz." Joaquin raves about Tinio's success in proving both in the Tagalog text and the performance that "contemporary, colloquial, vulgar and even obscene Tagalog" can be used as medium for great drama.

The use of the street Tagalog in the translations comes from Tinio's reading of the characters: these are "*machos*" (men having a strong sense of masculine pride) both asserting their masculinity and camouflaging their insecurities through vulgar expletives. As Joaquin writes: "Miller's men not only swear in masculine terms but need the taboo terms for ordinary syntax—and Tinio has given their Billingsgate some resounding Philippine equivalents."

In the translation, premium is given therefore to what is naturally spoken. One critic of Miller's *Death*[36] remarks how dialogue sometimes slips into "a fanciness that is slightly ludicrous," as when he hears Linda

36 Stanley Kauffmann, "Death of a Salesman," in *Persons of the Drama* (New York: Harper and Row, 1976), p. 20.

say of Biff "He was crestfallen." This is unheard of in Brooklyn Jewish speech which, as Kauffmann implies, is the English variety spoken by the characters in the English play. There is no such slippage in *Pahimakas*. For Tinio, this simply translates into the common Tagalog expression: "*Masamang-masama ang loob*." These lines are easy to pronounce and so the actors were likely understood by the audience who watched the play in the three nights it was first presented in 1966 at the Girl Scouts Auditorium in Manila. The profile of the audience, from Nick Joaquin's account, "was mostly of the polite, the prim and the pious: ladies and gents, sisters and reverends, not to mention all those convent-school girls who earnestly come to an evening of culture."[37] Joaquin implies so much of the theatre aesthetics of the time: theatre was of and for the cultured, performed in closed spaces and delivered in formal language. The staging of *Pahimakas* was definitely a "revolution" of sorts and Tinio was "prepared to have people walk out on us."[38]

Other than the obscene expressions, *Pahimakas* also uses Spanish-derived words—characteristic, it seems, of colloquial language in 1966: "*nadisgrasya*," "*katre*," "*koche*," "*kabisado*," "*sumisenta*," "*pihado*," "*andar ng andar*" (as in the opening scene). Today, about 45 years after, these are considered anachronistic and thus, if Tinio's translation would be printed as is, the language would ring false. Tinio's idea that the translation must connect with the audience would falter. For instance, when Willy says these lines about his son Biff: "*Panginoon ko! Natatandaan mo ba nung high school siya, ang daming susunod sunod sa kanya?*" (Oh, God! Do you remember in high school how girls would follow him wherever he went?) These may have sounded colloquial in 1966, but today, people would likely say: "*Diyos ko!*" Biff and Happy refer to the girls they have a good time with as "*ebobot*," but nobody uses it anymore; perhaps, GRO (Guest Relations Officer) would be apt. This is the reason why we speak of the translation as an afterlife of the original, especially of the dramatic text that would have to be performed to a different audience by a different cast at different times. *Pahimakas*

---

37 Joaquin, *Manila: Sin City? and Other Chronicles*, p. 144.

38 Ibid., p. 143.

would be different in each of the three nights of its initial performance, would be different in 1979, and again in 1999.

But some elements of translation such as rhythm and tone are harder to pinpoint. Even so, a reader of *Pahimakas* might wish to feel if the translation has captured the "staccato" rhythm of the original manifesting the distress and unrest in the characters such as Willy Lohman and Biff. Or, the tone of quiet sadness as Linda bids a very private farewell to her husband. With the masterly use of Pilipino and the unabashed use of street language, the translator invests *Pahimakas* with playability.

Performing *Pahimakas*

Efforts to track video documentations on stagings of *Pahimakas* have yielded negative results, but some reviews can be accessed. Doreen Fernandez, for instance, described the performance as having had an "electrifying effect on the audience."[39] Nick Joaquin had this to say:

> The intricate staging has been deftly handled by Tinio. His economical set never looks cramped; the transitions in time, the shifts in scene have movie fluidity. The slightest fumble here and the audience would have lost its way. But the actors don't stumble as they shuttle from present to past and back again to the present. However, the Willy in the memory scenes should have had a different set of gestures, more confident ones, than the older Willy who remembers.... The acting has ensemble smoothness, no one in the major roles standing out from the others.... The two floozies in the restaurant and the whore in the hotel room seem rather "stagey."[40]

The actors in *Pahimakas*, e.g., Teddy Yabut (Willy) and Barbara Paredes Quirino (Linda) were used to speak in English, but they segued successfully into Pilipino, even as the former remarked there were so many words he "couldn't understand or even pronounce." But to Joaquin, the "real star of the play is the language." His conclusion to his review of *Pahimakas* reveals a theatre aesthetics dovetailing with Tinio's:

39 Fernandez, *Palabas*, p. 106.

40 Joaquin, *Manila: Sin City? and Other Chronicles*, pp. 153–154.

> If we are to have a great theatre, a great literature, we must use the language we actually speak, the live tongue of street and market, not the Pilipino of the academies. We don't recognize ourselves in anything written in Pilipino: but in Pahimakas, though an American play about Americans, we heard, with shock and rapture, ourselves speaking.[41]

Amiel Leonardia's directing style in the 1999 production appears to differ from that of Tinio. His main actors for the Filipino translation were Ray Ventura as Willy, Ana Quiambao as Linda, Mario Magalona as Biff, and Neil Sese as Happy. He recalls he set the general plan: sets, lighting, costumes, blocking which included the pacing, rhythm, loudness, the way characters would relate to each other. The actors were then pretty much on their own in the interpretations of their roles. Leonardia, however, observes the ease with which the actors could speak the lines in Tinio's *Pahimakas*. These were spoken with smoothness and naturalness and with hardly any change in the translated script. Pilipino was easier on the actors ... "*madaling sabihin*" (lines flow smoothly). He also notes that in the Tagalog translation, the emphasis changes. For instance, in the hotel room scene with Biff and the woman, the lines are "*mas masakit*" (hitting one harder) than in the English text where emotions are filtered through a language foreign to the performers. There is no need thus for expletives, as was noted of the Tinio productions.

Obviously, the excerpts are too short and quite removed from context, so no less than a reading of the translation and the source from end to end is in order for the longer paper. But the questions raised could provide the key to the larger question: "*Pinoy ba ang dating ng Pahimakas?*" (Does *Pahimakas* convey the feel and the sounds of the Filipino?) Interestingly, while Tinio tried to prove that foreign plays embodied the Filipino value system and sensibility, it was not to say that these were unique: the "classics," he said, are "useful because they embody a process of thinking from which both artist and audience can learn how to investigate their *common life*."[42] The translation thus expresses what is "*Pinoy*" as much as

41 Joaquin, *Manila: Sin City? and Other Chronicles*, p. 154.

42 Tinio, "The Folly of Cultural Chauvinism," p. 55. Tanghalang Pilipinio staged Tinio's

what the "*Pinoy*" has in common with the source text and culture—through a language that grows as it articulates both difference and similarity. Rody Vera points to this mediating task of the translator in the following remarks:

> *Ang tanda ng husay ng mansasalin, ay hindi lamang ipakita kung ano ang Filipino, kundi importanteng linawain sa Filipinong manonood at mambabasa kung ano ang sinasabi ng orihinal na may akda*—what is the objective? To bring the gap of consciousness and philosophical understanding between the two cultures involved—*ang maihatid sa lalong madaling panahon ang mga ideyang nasa kabilang mundo, para lumiit ang mundo, para itanghal ang humanidad.*[43]
>
> The mark of a good translation is not just to show what is Filipino. It is important to make clear to the Filipino audience what the playwright of the original wanted to say—what is the objective? To bring the gap of consciousness and philosophical understanding between the two cultures involved—to convey in the shortest time possible the ideas from the other world, so the world is made smaller, to celebrate humanity.

Hamlet: The Aesthetics of Its Translations

The challenges of translating Shakespeare from English to Pilipino are complex for various reasons. The translation is first of all a particular reading of *Hamlet*. Tinio could do this task ably because of his solid grounding in English literature from his days at the University of Santo Tomas Manila, at the University of Iowa where he was on fellowship, and later, in England where he had a grant to train under a known theatre expert. To Leonardia, this English education was his edge over other translators equally competent in Pilipino.

Shakespeare's plays were written and first performed in the sixteenth and the seventeenth centuries in Renaissance England in the English register and the performance styles of that time. Thus contemporary

---

Pahimakas in September–October 2014 when this book was in its final stages of production.

43 Vera, Q and A Session at the Second Forum on Aesthetics of Philippine Theatre.

editions published from the Folger Shakespeare Library come with copious notes explaining words, phrases, and allusions. Some are words we no longer use, e.g., *soft*, *perchance*, and *parle*. In the first line below, Tinio renders "soft" as "*hintay*" (in Filipino, this means "to wait"), although this meaning may vary depending on the context as in the second line below where "soft" is translated as "*manahimik*" (keep quiet). Kindly see Appendix B for the portions from *Hamlet* (both the English version and Tinio's translation) where the succeeding excerpts are taken.

> But soft, behold! Lo, where it comes again!/*Nguni't, hintay! Masdan niyo! Muling lumitaw!*
> Soft you now. Fair Ophelia./*Manahimik muna. Marikit na Ofelia.*

Even more problematic are the words extant today, but no longer meaning the same as in Shakespeare's England, e.g., "extravagant" and "sensible" which at that time meant "wandering" and "confirmed by the senses."[44]

Repetition of words or phrases may be part of a linguistic pattern to convey meaning. For instance, in the opening scene of the play, a mythological world is implicit in a network of local references, such as "the Dane," a "buried Denmark," Elsinore and Hercules, Hyperion and Niobe.[45] Tinio takes these into account in his translation, these "trials of the foreign," among them the retrieval of "underlying networks of signification."[46] In *Hamlet*'s soliloquy in Act II, Scene 1 (excerpted below), the beginning line "To be or not to be—that is the question" can be rendered with a literal translation: "*Ang maging o ang hindi maging* . . ." but this doesn't make sense in Pilipino. It was necessary for Tinio to get to the rest of the soliloquy to understand its meaning and thus translate the line into "*Mabuhay ba o hindi, iyan ang katanungan*" (literally, this means "To live or not to live, that is the question").

---

44 William Shakespeare, *Hamlet*, ed. Barbara Mowat and Paul Werstine (New York: Washington Square Press, 1992), p. xv.

45 Ibid.

46 Antoine Berman, "Translation and the Trials of the Foreign," in Venuti, *The Translation Studies Reader*, pp. 284–297.

A major concern of Tinio in translating *Hamlet* (as in *Pahimakas* and other plays) is playability: "*Isinalin ito upang maitanghal sa dulaan kaya't kailangan malinawan agad ng artista at manonood and lahat ng pangungusap.*"[47] (This is translated so it can be performed for an audience, that's why the artists and the audience must understand immediately the sentences.) In this regard, simplicity of language was an imperative: "*Sa saling ito, nagiging mas payak ang lengguahe kaysa sa orihinal dahil isinasalin ang kahulugan ng Isabelino at barokong Ingles ni Shakespeare na wala ng nakauunawa nang hindi tinutulungan ng mga tala.*"[48] (In this translation, the language is made simple because no one understands any more the Elizabethan English of Shakespeare without the help of footnotes.) Appended to the published translation of *Hamlet* is a short section on *Tala* (Endnotes) for each act which is introduced by a very short synopsis. On the whole, however, the translation is meant to stand by itself, accessible not just to the readers, but to the players.

But his overriding concern appeared to be to preserve the poetry of Shakespeare in the translation: "*Higit sa lahat, itinuturing kong kinakailangan na maparating sa bumabasa ang tindi ng pagkamatulain ni Shakespeare na, sa palagay ko, hindi maaring masumpungan lamang sa mga kadiwarian ng ika-labing anim, ikalabingpitong siglo niyang pangungusap.*"[49] (Most of all, I consider it most important to convey to the audience the poetry of Shakespeare's language which I think cannot just be found in the language of centuries past.)

In short, simplicity, playability, and poetry were primary considerations for the aesthetics of Tinio's translations. These are difficult to achieve, since poetry in English, particularly Shakespeare's, is generally distant from everyday speech of the Filipino. A translator would need not just to consider differences in time, culture, and language register, but also poetic conventions. For example, Shakespeare wrote in blank verse where

47 Rolando S. Tinio, "Pauna ng Hamlet" [Foreword], in *Ang Trahedya ni Hamlet, Prinsipe ng Dinamarka*, trans. Rolando S. Tinio (Quezon City: University of the Philippines Press, 1991), p. vii.

48 Ibid.

49 Ibid.

the lines had meter, usually in iambic pentameter, but no rhyme. He would sometimes combine these poetic features with enjambments where a syntactic unit—phrase, clause, or sentence—is broken at the end of the line to continue on to the next line. Or, he would employ end-stopping where each linguistic unit corresponds with a single line, or a caesura where the linguistic unit ends at mid-line. Shakespeare exploited these features to make his poetry serve the purposes of everyday speech. In the following line-by-line juxtaposition, Tinio preserves such features, but adds some rhyming lines and internal rhyme, as a way to connect to the Filipino. In traditional Tagalog poetry, the meter ranged from 4 to 16 lines with a caesura in the middle; in contrast, however, to blank verse, poets kept their rhymes, as in:

Twelve-syllable lines:

Sumikat na Ina // sa sinisilangan
Ang araw ng poot // ng Katagalugan,
Tatlong daang taong // aming iningatan
Sa dagat ng dusa // ang karalitaan.

Andres Bonifacio, "Katapusang Hibik ng Pilipinas"
(Final appeal of the Philippines), 1896

In the above poem, each half of the line consists of six syllables.

Sixteen-syllable lines:

Bawa't palo ng martilyo // sa bakal mong pinapanday,
Alipatong nagtilamsik // alitaptap sa karimlan;
Mga apoy ng pawis mong // sa bakal ay kumikinang,
Tandang ikaw ay may-gawa // nitong buong Santinakpan.

Jose Corazon de Jesus, "Manggagawa" (The laborer), 1929

In the above poem, each half of the line consists of eight syllables.

In the following excerpt from Tinio's *Hamlet*, the caesuras break the lines in the middle both to segment the ideas and provide breaks in speech. There are enjambments (lines 3–4, 6–7) and some rhyming lines. Such poetic features have been harnessed to approximate everyday speech, or keep the poetic simple and playable.

Mabuhay ba, o hindi, // iyan ang katanungan:
Kung higit na marangal // isipin ang gawang magtiis
Sa mga palaso ng // karumal-dumal na kapalaran
Upang matapos ang lahat. // Ang mamatay-paghimbing—
Wala na; at sa paghimbing // na yaon, magwawakas
Ang mga kapaitan at // ang libu-libong sindak
Na pamana sa laman. // Isang kaganapan 'yong
Mahihiling nang lubusan. // Mamatay—humimbing,

Other than these features, Tinio found ways to translate line by line and word for word when possible, as one sees in the excerpt below. He edits though some redundancies in the English lines, while retaining some clichés ("sea of troubles"/"*dagat ng dusa*").

Or to take arms against a sea of troubles And, by opposing, end them. To die, to sleep—	O ang lumabang tahasan sa dagat ng dusa Upang matapos ang lahat. Ang mamatay-paghimbing—

Tinio uses concrete, specific and fresh words in his translation, compared to the English equivalents (some of which sound overused at this time):

For who would bear the whips and scorns of time,	Dahil sino'ng susuong sa dagok at haplit ng panahon

Or, the following lines:

And makes us rather bear those ills we have	At nagtutulak sa 'ting manatili sa dusang dinaranas
Than fly to others that we know not of?	Kaysa naman sumagupa sa hindi pa natin nawawawaan?
Thus conscience does make cowards (of us all),	Kung kaya't naduduwag tayo sa banta ng budhi,
And thus the native hue of resolution	At namumutla sa pagpusyaw na lilim ng pagmumuni
Is (sicklied) o'er with the pale cast of thought,	Ang likas na kulay

Tinio also clarifies and simplifies what listeners and actors would not otherwise understand without research as in:

With a bare bodkin? What fardels bear	Sa tulong ng isang punyal? Sinong magtitiis

Performing *Hamlet*

Dulaang UP does not have a video production of *Hamlet Redux* (2006);[50] neither does the Cultural Centre of the Philippines's video collection. Available on YouTube, however, is a video of Ron Capinding delivering the soliloquy cited above.[51] One can watch it and listen to it to see how Tinio's Pilipino translation works on stage. In addition, reviews are available.

Hamlet Redux was reviewed by Mars Cavestany, an actor for Tinio's Teatro Pilipino, and Walter Ang. Cavestany recalls the Teatro Pilipino days in the 1970s through the 1980s when a coterie of actors—he and Mabesa included—were "coached diligently in the rhythmic elegance of Filipino language and idiom into which the world's greatest dramatic masterpieces were mined and translated by the trailblazing" Tinio. He salutes Mabesa for his out-of-the-box production, and his efforts to include multimedia devices and contemporary drama through the Broadway chorus girls. However, he notes how the cast did not do justice to both the English and Pilipino texts:

> If not for the charming looks and arresting energy of the puerile cast, it would have been torturous as torture can be. Indeed it was punishing to contend with almost everyone's occasional parapraxis (e.g., slip-slop tone and pattern of speaking), speech blunders such as mispronunciation and

50 Antonio Mabesa, esteemed Filipino stage director who directed the play, notes that *Hamlet* would ordinarily take four hours to stage; the title *Hamlet Redux* is used to refer to the two-hour production.

51 Ron Capinding, "Hamlet's 'To be or not to be,'" http://www.youtube.com/watch?v=g2_oHJQk0YA.

> slip of the tongue apart from memory lapse, and slipshod blocking, plus tentative movement and usual amateur slip-ups.[52]

Like Cavestany, Ang notes the efforts to bring *Hamlet* close to a contemporary audience's taste: the use of modern dress, pop culture references, and set design using video montages. Both, however, note the "melodramatic acting" of the actors. Cavestany thinks acting was overdone;[53] Ang notes that the Tagalog cast, "led by Arnold Reyes, as Filipinos are wont to do, wear their emotions on their sleeves. Reyes takes *Hamlet* on a more frenzied path...."[54] He observes that Tinio had actually meant some scenes and the poetry to be funny, but the melodrama makes the audience "smirk."

Conclusions

Philippine vernacular literature had a brief flowering in the early twentieth century soon after the end of the Spanish colonial period but this was short-lived because of the implementation of English as a medium of instruction. Except for the interlude of the Japanese occupation, English was the language of culture in the Philippines for most of the twentieth century; it also was the language of literature and drama. However, with Tinio's translations and with the young playwrights writing in Filipino from the sixties and the seventies, there was a sharp shift from the use of English into Filipino as medium for the stage. The shift, according to Doreen Fernandez, reflected a return to the vernaculars.

Tinio's translations also came at a time when linguists were speaking of the need to "intellectualize Pilipino," or to make it suitable for culture and the sciences. Thus, it was very timely for Teatro Pilipino to prove

52 Here, we must note that Dulaang UP is an in-house training vehicle for theatre majors at the University of the Philippines; most of the cast are students but professionals are usually asked to join them to attract an audience.

53 Mars Cavestany, "Mabesa's 'Hamlet' the Quintessence of Campus Theatre," *Manila Times*, 11 December 2006.

54 Walter Ang, "Distilling 'Hamlet,'" *Philippine Daily Inquirer*, 27 November 2006.

Pilipino as a language suitable for the world's masterpieces. But since there was not just one *Pahimakas* nor one *Trahedya ni Hamlet*, Tinio's translations of plays (both in script and performance) participate in the "afterlife" of the text; they are "informed by the history of their reception." This implies an audience whose aesthetics—not just what pleases sensually and emotionally but what values it upholds—changes through time. This likewise implies locating the translation within a "polysystem" of a country's literature.[55] As configurations within that system vary, so does the placement of translations as central or peripheral. Joaquin and Fernandez could rave about *Pahimakas* in 1966 as original and innovative. But with the distance of Tinio's translations from the social imperatives during the Marcos era, his translations and stagings of Western plays in this period were perceived by some sectors as lacking in critical edge. Yet, Tinio's translations continue to be performed today and transformed thru each performance.

Tinio translating: *May katwiran ba?*

Postscript

A note on the afterlife of Tinio's translations: As of the time of the writing of this paper in July 2011, a play entitled *Sintang Dalisay* (Pure love) is being performed at the Rizal Mini-Theatre of the Ateneo de Manila University. It is based on two translations of Shakespeare's *Romeo and Juliet*: Tinio's Tagalog translation (1981) and a translation in the traditional Filipino metrical romance, published in 1901. *Sintang* transcends boundaries of time and space. The setting is not in Europe but in a Muslim community in Mindanao, south of the Philippines; gestures, music and dance are based on the *Igal*, the traditional dance of the Sama tribe in the islands of Tawi-Tawi, at the southernmost tip of the country.

55 Itamar Even-Zohar, "The Position of Translated Literature within the Literary Polysystem," in Venuti, *The Translation Studies Reader*, pp. 192–197.

Bibliography

Ang, Walter. "Distilling 'Hamlet.'" *Philippine Daily Inquirer*, 27 November 2006.

Bassnett-McGuire, Susan. *Translation Studies*. Rev. ed. London and New York: Routledge, 1996.

Baumgarten, Alexander Gottlieb. *Asthetik*. Translated and edited by Dagmer Mirbach. Hamburg: Meiner, 2007.

Benjamin, Walter. "The Task of the Translator." In *The Translation Studies Reader*, edited by Lawrence Venuti. London: Routledge, 2000, pp. 15–23.

Berman, Antoine. "Translation and the Trials of the Foreign." In *The Translation Studies Reader*, edited by Lawrence Venuti. London: Routledge, 2000, pp. 284–297.

Capinding, Ron. "Hamlet's 'To be or not to be.'" http://www.youtube.com/watch?v=g2_oHJQk0YA.

Cavestany, Mars. "Mabesa's 'Hamlet' the Quintessence of Campus Theatre." *Manila Times*, 11 December 2006.

Cortez, Alexander. "Dulaang UP (University of the Philippines): A Laboratory for Future Artists." Paper read at the Forum on Aesthetics of Philippine Theatre sponsored by National Commission on Culture and the Arts held in Intramuros, Manila, February 2010.

Daroy, Petronilo Bn. "Drama: New Methods, New Directions." *Expressweek*, 3 June 1976, pp. 50–51.

Even-Zohar, Itamar. "The Position of Translated Literature within the Literary Polysystem." In *The Translation Studies Reader*, edited by Lawrence Venuti. London: Routledge, 2000, pp. 192–197.

Fernandez, Doreen G. *Palabas*. Quezon City: Ateneo de Manila University Press, 1996.

Gulle, Ramil Digal. "The Song of Rolando: Creative Genius." In *The National Artists of the Philippines*, edited by Nestor Jardin et al. Manila: CCP, NCCA, Anvil Publishing, 1998.

Hamlet Redux. Souvenir Program, Dulaang UP, 2006.

Jacobson, Roman. "On Linguistic Aspects of Translation." In *The Translation Studies Reader*, edited by Lawrence Venuti. London and New York: Routledge, 2000, pp. 113–118.

Joaquin, Nick. *Manila: Sin City? and Other Chronicles*. Manila: National Bookstore, 1980.

Kauffmann, Stanley. "Death of a Salesman." In *Persons of the Drama*. New York: Harper and Row, 1976, pp. 31–33.

Leonardia, Amiel. Interview by Corazon D. Villareal on the Dulaang UP production of *Pahimakas sa Isang Ahente*. 1 December 2009. Vargas Museum Café, University of the Philippines, Diliman.

Lumbera, Bienvenido. "The Nationalist Literary Tradition." In *Revaluation. Essays on Philippine Literature, Cinema, and Popular Culture*. Manila: Index Press, 1984, pp. 70–83.

———. *Tagalog Poetry*. Quezon City: Ateneo de Manila University Press, 1986.

———. "Introduksyon." In *May Katwiran ang Katwiran at Iba Pang Dula*, by Rolando S. Tinio. Quezon City: University of the Philippines Press, 2001, pp. vii–xiii.

Nieva, Pepe. "Adios Amerika! Or How a Poet, Playwright, Director and Professor Is Bringing Back Art to the 'Masa.'" *Sunburst* 3 (October 1975), pp. 52–55.

Pambid, Manuel. "Paano nga ba ang Peta Play (O Ano nga ba ang play na Petang-Peta?)" [What makes a play a PETA play?]. Paper read at the Forum on Aesthetics of Philippine Theatre sponsored by National Commission on Culture and the Arts held in Intramuros, Manila, February 2010.

Rafael, Vicente L. *The Promise of the Foreign, Nationalism and the Technics of Translation in the Spanish Philippines*. Pasig: Anvil, 2006; North Carolina: Duke University Press, 2005.

Shakespeare, William. *Hamlet*. Edited by Barbara Mowat and Paul Werstine. New York: Washington Square Press, 1992.

"Teatro Pilipino Philosophy and Objectives. Program Notes of *Paghihintay kay Godot* [Waiting for Godot]", 12th season of the Teatro Pilipino 1984–1985.

Tinio, Rolando S. "National Meaning in Our Theater." *Metro Manila* 1, no. 20 (1–15 June 1977), pp. 20–21.

———. "The Folly of Cultural Chauvinism." *Metro Manila* 2, nos. 5–6 (November 1977), p. 55.

———, trans. *Ang Trahedya ni Hamlet, Prinsipe ng Dinamarka* [Hamlet]. Quezon City: University of the Philippines Press, 1991.

———, trans. *Pahimakas sa Isang Ahente* [Death of a salesman]. Manuscript from the University of the Philippines Main Library Collection, n.d.

Tiongson, Nicanor. "Pagsasali'y di Biro." *Sagisag* 2, no. 5 (May 1976), pp. 53–54.

Venuti, Lawrence, ed. *The Translation Studies Reader*. London: Routledge, 2000.

Vera, Rody. Q and A Session at the Second Forum on Aesthetics of Philippine Theatre sponsored by the National Commission on Culture and the Arts held in Intramuros, Manila, October 2009.

Appendix A

From the opening scene of *Death of a Salesman* (*Mula sa pambungad na eksena ng Pahimakas sa Isang Ahente*):

LINDA, *hearing WILLY outside the bedroom, calls with some trepidation*: Willy!	LINDA, *Pagkarinig kay WILLY sa labas ng silid-tulugan, kakabakabang tatawag*: Willy!
WILLY: It's all right. I came back.	WILLY: Ako nga. Umuwi na 'ko.
LINDA: Why? What happened? *Slight pause*. Did something happen, Willy?	LINDA: Bakit? Ano'ng nangyari? *Titigil sandali*. Nadisgrasya ka ba. Willy?
WILLY: No, nothing happened.	WILLY: Hindi.
LINDA: You didn't smash the car, did you?	LINDA: Ibinangga mo ba'ng koche?
WILLY, *with casual irritation*: I said nothing happened. Didn't you hear me?	WILLY, *Naiinis ng kaunti*: Sinabing hindi. Di mo ba 'ko narinig?
LINDA: Don't you feel well?	LINDA: Masama ba'ng katawan mo?
WILLY: I'm tired to death. *The flute has faded away. He sits on the bed beside her, a little numb*. I couldn't make it. I just couldn't make it, Linda.	WILLY: Mamatay ako sa pagod. *Nakalayo na ang plawta. Uupo siya sa tabi ni LINDA sa katre,*[56] *parang namamanhid*. Hindi ako puede. Hindi ako puede, Linda.
LINDA, *very carefully, delicately*: Where were you all day? You look terrible.	LINDA, *Maingat na maingat*: Saan ka nakarating maghapon? Ang sama ng ichura mo?
WILLY: I got as far as a little above Yonkers. I stopped for a cup of coffee. Maybe it was the coffee.	WILLY: Umabot na 'ko lampas ng Yonkers. Bumaba ako para magkape. Baka 'yong kapeng nakadiperensiya sa akin.
LINDA: What?	LINDA: Ha?
WILLY, *after a pause*: I suddenly couldn't drive anymore. The car kept going off the shoulder, y'know?	WILLY, *Pagkatapos matigilan sandal*: Bigla lang, hindi ko makaya'ng koche. Kumakabig sa kanan.
LINDA, *helpfully*: Oh, maybe it was the steering again. I don't think Angelo knows the Studebaker.	LINDA, *Nagpipilit makagaang sa loob ng asawa*: Oh, baka 'yon na naming manibela. Sa palagay ko, hindi kabisado ni Angel 'ng Studebaker.

56 The underlined words are Filipino words derived from Spanish.

WILLY: No, it's me, it's me. Suddenly I realize I'm going sixty miles an hour and I don't remember the last five minutes. I'm—I can't seem to—keep my mind to it.	WILLY: Ako'ng me diperensiya. Biglang-bigla, sumisisenta 'ko. Hindi ko naman matandaan kung ano'ng nangyari nung nakaraang singko minutes. Parang—hindi—ang isip ko sa pagmamaneho.
LINDA: Maybe it's your glasses. You never went for your new glasses.	LINDA: Baka 'yang salamin mo. Hindi mo pa kasi papalitan.
WILLY: No, I see everything, I came back ten miles an hour. It took me nearly four hours from Yonkers.	WILLY: Hindi, ang linaw-linaw na tingin ko. Pabalik, diyes lang ang takbo. Inapat na oras ako mula sa Yonkers.
LINDA, *resigned*: Well, you'll just have to take a rest. Willy, you can't continue this way.	LINDA, *Wala nang magawa*: Kailangan kang magbakasyon, Willy. Hindi na puedeng ganyan ka ng ganyan.
WILLY: I just got back from Florida.	WILLY: Kababakasyon ko lang sa Florida.
LINDA: But you didn't rest your mind. Your mind is overactive, and the mind is what counts, dear.	LINDA: Pero hindi mapahinga'ng isip mo. Andar ng andar ang isip mo. Ang isip mo dear, ang dapat magpahinga.
WILLY: I'll start out in the morning. Maybe I'll feel better in the morning. *She is taking off his shoes.* These goddam arch supports are killing me.	WILLY: Bukas nang maaga na 'ko lalakad uli. Pihadong bubuti na bukas ang katawan ko. *Huhubaran siya ni Linda ng sapatos.* Pinapahirapan ako ng putang'nang kalsong iyan.

Another excerpt later in Act 1:

WILLY, *worried and angered*: There's such an undercurrent in him. He became a moody man. Did he apologize when I left this morning?	WILLY, *Nababahala't nagagalit*: Nasa loob ang kulo ng anak mo. Nagiging sumpungin. Humingi bang deskargo pagkaalis ko kaninang 'maga?
LINDA: He was crestfallen, Willy. You know how he admires you. I think if he finds himself, then you'll both be happier and not fight any more.	LINDA: Masamang-masama ang loob, Willy. Alam mo namang tinitingala ka no'n. Pag pumanatag na'ng loob no'n, hindi na kayo mahihirapang magkasundo, hindi na kayo ganyang alitan ng alitan.

Appendix B

Hamlet, Act II, Scene 1, lines 62–96, pp. 127–128 (*Ham*, Yugto II, Eksena 1, Linya 62–96, pah. 55–56).

HAMLET: To be or not to be—that is the question;	HAM: Mabuhay ba, o hindi, iyan ang katanungan:
Whether 'tis nobler in the mind to suffer	Kung higit na marangal isipin ang gawang magtiis
the slings and arrows of outrageous fortune,	Sa mga palaso ng karumal-dumal na kapalaran
Or to take arms against a sea of troubles	O ang lumabang tahasan sa dagat ng dusa
And, by opposing, end them. To die, to sleep—	Upang matapos ang lahat. Ang mamatay-paghimbing—
No more—and by a sleep to say we end	Wala na; at sa paghimbing na yaon, magwawakas
The heartache and the thousand natural shocks	Ang mga kapaitan at ang libu-libong sindak
That flesh is heir to—'tis a consummation	Na pamana sa laman. Isang kaganapan 'yong
Devoutly to be wished. To die, to sleep—	Mahihiling nang lubusan. Mamatay—humimbing,
To sleep, perchance to dream. Ay, there's the rub,	Humimbing—baka managinip; ay, 'yon ang salabit!
For in that sleep of death what dreams may come,	Dahil sa himbing ng kamatayan, ang baka mapanaginip
When we have shuffled off this mortal coil,	Pagkatapos mahubad ang pinapasang katawan,
Must give us pause. There's the respect	Kailangan ding pangambahan. Masasabi ngang
That makes calamity of so long life.	Malaking kapahamakan kapag humaba ang buhay.
For who would bear the whips and scorns of time,	Dahil sino'ng susuong sa dagok at haplit ng panahon,
Th'oppressor's wrong, the proud man's contumely,	Sa lupit ng maniniil, pagdusta sa marangal,
The pangs of despised love, the law's delay,	Kirot ng sinawing pag-ibig, kupad ng batas,

The insolence of office, and the spurns	Kaimbian ng nanunungkulan, at mga pagtatakwil
that patient merit of th' unworthy takes,	Na mapakumbabang binabata nang hindi dapat,
When he himself might his quietus make	Samantalang kaya naman niyang makalaya sa lahat
With a bare bodkin? What fardels bear,	Sa tulong ng isang punyal? Sinong magtitiis,
To grunt and sweat under a weary life,	Magpapakahirap sa patang-pata ng buhay
But that the dread of something after death,	Kung hindi lang takot sa kung ano sa ibayo ng kamatayan—
The undiscovered country from whose bourn	Ang di-unawang bayan, na hindi napanggagalingan
No traveller returns, puzzles the will	Ng sinumang manlalakbay—na lumilito sa kalooban,
And makes us rather bear those ills we have	At nagtutulak sa 'ting manatili sa dusang dinaranas
Than fly to others that we know not of?	Kaysa naman sumagupa sa hindi pa natin nawawawaan?
Thus conscience does make cowards (of us all),	Kung kaya't naduduwag tayo sa banta ng budhi,
And thus the native hue of resolution	At namumutla sa pagpusyaw na lilim ng pagmumuni
Is (sicklied) o'er with the pale cast of thought,	Ang likas na kulay sa pisngi ng nabuo nang isip,
And enterprises of great pitch and moment	At kahit pagbabalak ng mga dakilang hangarin,
With this regard their currents turn awry	Dahil sa kahuhunos-dili, natutungo sa iba
And lose the name of action.—Soft you now, The fair Ophelia.—Nymph, in thy orisons	At nawawalang-katuparan,—Manahimik muna! Ang marikit na si Ofelia!—Nimpa, sa iyong mga dalangin,
Be all my sins remembered.	Alalahanin ang lahat ng kasalanan ko.
OPHELIA: Good my lord,	OFE: Poon ko,
How does your Honor for this many a day?	Kumusta'ng lagay mo nitong mga nagdaang araw?
HAMLET: I humbly thank you, well.	HAM: Salamat sa 'yo; mabuti, mabuti.

OPHELIA: My Lord, I have remembrances of yours	OFE: May mga alaalang galling sa "yo
That I have longed long to redeliver.	Na kay tagal ko nang ibig maisauli.
I pray you now receive them.	Utang na loob, tanggapin mo ngayon.
HAMLET: No, not I. I never gave you aught.	HAM: Ayoko! Wala akong ibinigay sa 'yo.

Hamlet, Act 1, Scene 2, lines 63–89 (*Ham*, Unang Yugto, Tagpo 2, linya 68–87).

KING: Take thy fair hour, Laertes. Time be thine,	HARI: Samantalahin, Laertes, ang iyong kabataan,
And thy best graces spend it at thy will.—	Bagaman kailnagang maghari ang 'yong kabaitan.—
But now, my cousin Hamlet and my son—	Nguini't ngayon, pamangkin at anak na Hamlet—
HAMLET, *aside*: A little more than kin and less than kind.	HAM, *Aparte*: Higit ngang kamag-anak hindi ko man kamag-isip.
KING: How is it that the clouds still hang on you?	HARI: Ano't nagdidilim pa ang iyong mukha?
HAMLET: Not so, my lord: I am too much in the sun.	HAM: Hindi, panginoon. Lagi akong nasa araw.
QUEEN: Good Hamlet, cast thy knighted color off,	REYNA: Butihing Hamlet, iwaksi ang gabi ng loob,
And let thine eye look like a friend on Denmark.	At ituring na kaibigan ang bagong Hari ng Dinamarka,
Do not forever with thy veiled lids	Huwag nang magpatuloy sa pagpapako ng mata sa lupa
Seek for thy noble father in the dust.	Upang hanapin pa ang ama sa alabok.
Thou know'st 'tis common: all that lives must die,	Karaniwa naming namamatay ang buhay,
Passing through nature to eternity.	Nauuwing lahat sa kawalang-hannggan.
HAMLET: Ay madam, it is common.	HAM: Oo, senyora, karaniwan nga.
QUEEN: If it be,	REYNA: Kung gayon,
Why seems it so particular with thee?	Ano't parang ikaw lang ang naulila?
HAMLET: "Seems," madam? Nay, it is. I know not "seems."	HAM: "Parang," senyora" Aba'y hindi ko kilala ang "parang."

'Tis not alone my inky cloak, (good) mother,	Hindi lang ang kappa kong itim, butihing ina,
Nor customary suits of solemn black,	O ang nakaugaliang pagluluksa,
Nor windy suspiration of forced breath,	O ang maingay na paghugot ng buntong-hininga,
No, nor the fruitful river in the eye,	Ni hindi ang pagbabatis ng luha sa pisngi,
Nor the dejected havior of the visage,	O ang dilim bumabalot sa "king anyo,
Together with all forms, moods, [shapes] of grief,	Klakip ng lahat ng hubog at hugis ng lungkot,
That can (denote) me truly. These indeed "seem,"	Ang naghahayag sa tunay kong loob. Lahat-lahat 'yan,
For they are actions that a man might play;	Para ngang kalungkutang maa'ring panggapin ng sinuman;
But I have that within which passes show,	Ngunit ang nasa loob ko, hindi mapalitaw—
These but the trappings and the suits of woe.	Ang namamasdan ni'yo, mga bihis at pakita lamang.

Translating the Foreign into the Local:
The Cultural Production and Canonization of Buddhist Texts in Imperial Tibet

Georgios T. HALKIAS

The Buddha's Doctrine in Tibetan Translation

After Buddha Śākyamuni's demise, his lay and monastic followers in the Indian subcontinent and throughout Asia laboured to propagate his teachings in oral vernaculars and written scripts. Major collections of the Buddha's doctrines formed canonical compilations extant in Pāli, Tibetan, Chinese, Mongol, and Manchu, while Buddhist scriptures and their commentaries abound in much greater numbers of Asian translations in various writing systems including Gāndhāri, Khotanese, Tokharian, Sogdian, Japanese, Korean, old Javanese, Vietnamese, Lao, Thai, Cambodian, and Burmese among others. The translation of Buddhist texts in Asia took place at different times and often in both or several directions (i.e., from Tibetan to Khotanese and the reverse). The enormous geographical range of their occasion across South, East and Central Asia bears witness to transnational networks of production, reproduction and distribution of religious knowledge and reveals processes of cultural appropriation in localized and context-specific settings that admitted regional variations of Buddhist institutions and state-supported practices.

During one of the most impressive translation events in the history of mankind, thousands of Buddhist scriptures, in different languages and scripts, were systematically imported in imperial Tibet. They were then translated, edited, and catalogued in Tibetan with the aid of local translators and Buddhist scholars from regions as far afield as Sri Lanka,

India, Nepal, Central Asia, and China. These translated texts reflect nearly a millennium of Indian Buddhist doctrinal and ritual developments. For the most part Tibetans continue to organize their historical memory in terms of the introduction and spread of Buddhism in Tibet in two major periods. The first period coincides with an early translation of Buddhist doctrines (Tibetan *bstan-pa snga-dar*) under the auspices of three "Buddhist monarchs" (Sanskrit *dharmarāja*), the emperors (Tibetan *btsan-po*) Songtsen Gampo (Srong btsan sgam po), Tri Songdetsen (Khri srong lde btsan) and Tri Tsukdetsen (Khri gtsug lde btsan). The second dissemination and translation of Buddhist texts (Tibetan *bstan-pa phyi-dar*) gave rise to Tibetan monastic schools differentiated on the basis of Indian lineages, texts and teachings, sometime from the eleventh century onwards. In this study we will revisit some indigenized factors and internal conditions that contributed to the creation of an extensive network of Buddhist texts and related vocations in imperial Tibet (seventh to ninth centuries) and to the earliest-known state-endorsed ecclesiastical arrangements for the regulation and canonization of religious knowledge across the empire.

The early spread of Buddhism in Tibet is traditionally attributed to the first Buddhist ruler (Sanskrit *dharmarāja*; Tibetan *chos-rgyal*) Songtsen Gampo (*c.*617–649/650), a shrewd statesman who consolidated Tibet into a great Central Asian empire that dominated for 200 years the trading networks of the ancient Silk Routes, parts of western China, and much of Inner and Central Asia. The *Tang Annals* 舊唐書 report that he sent tribute with imperial envoys to the Chinese emperor petitioning for a matrimonial alliance. In 641 he received the Chinese Princess Wencheng 文成公主 along with an entourage of Chinese scholars, scribes and bureaucrats in his court. Allegedly, the princess brought with her Chinese books on medicine, astrology, divination, and Buddhism and took an active part in Sino-Tibetan translations in partnership with the Chinese scholar Ācārya Hashang Mahādeva and Lhalung Dorjé Pal.[1] The *Annals* state that seven years

1 Muge Samten, *A History of Traditional Fields of Learning: A Concise History of Dissemination of Traditional Fields of Learning in Tibet* (Dharamsala: Library of Tibetan Works and Archives, 2005), p. 7.

after her arrival, Songtsen Gampo invited skilled men from China to manufacture paper and ink for use in the administration of his state. His request was granted by the Chinese emperor serving as proof that Tibetan writing was practised during his reign.[2]

The official instigation of a writing system and the availability of paper paved the way for a gradual increase in the translation of Buddhist scriptures in palaces and monasteries across Tibet. Emperor Songtsen Gampo was said to have invited Indian, Kashmiri, Nepalese and Chinese Buddhist scholars to his cosmopolitan court comprising members of the aristocracy, government officials, visiting scholars, artists, and the Tibetan literati that had developed a taste and thirst for literary culture.[3] The demand for the acquisition and translation of religious texts, with the exotic mystique that all foreign importations usually beget, practically followed the establishment of paper communication in the civil and military Tibetan administration.[4] The official introduction of writing presents the most compelling evidence for an early and formative connection forged between institutionalized forms of Buddhism and the Tibetan imperial machine.

During the reign of Songtsen Gampo, Buddhism had been well-rooted in Tibet's neighbouring polities and societies, and there was no shortage

---

2 Berthold Laufer, "Origins of Tibetan Writing," *Journal of the American Oriental Society* 38 (1918), pp. 34–35. The Tibetans also requested silkworm eggs, stone crushers, presses for making wine and paper, and ink makers—all of which was granted by the Chinese emperor together with the almanac; for the Chinese sources, see Woodville Rockhill, "Tibet: A Geographical, Ethnographical, and Historical Sketch, Derived from Chinese Sources," *Journal of the Royal Asiatic Society of Great Britain and Ireland* 23, no. 2 (April 1891), p. 191; Stephen Wootton Bushell, "The Early History of Tibet from Chinese Sources," *Journal of the Royal Asiatic Society of Great Britain and Ireland* 12, no. 4 (1880), p. 446.

3 Muge Samten, *A History of Traditional Fields of Learning*, p. 7, writes that Tönmi Sambhoṭa and his disciples Dharmakosha, Aloka, Yeshe Pel, and others, assisted with the visits of foreign scholars from India, Kashmir, Nepal, and China, and served as translators.

4 Helga Uebach, "From Red Tally to Yellow Paper: The Official Introduction of Paper in Tibetan Administration in 744–745," in "Tibetan Studies in Honour of Samten Karmay: Part I—Historical, Cultural and Linguistic Studies," ed. Françoise Pommaret and Jean-Luc Achard, special issue, *Revue d'Etudes Tibétaines* 14 (2008), p. 65.

of Buddhist scholars, teachers and monks from India, Nepal, China, and Central Asia looking for new markets and friendly courts. Buddhism had much to offer. It boasted efficient monastic institutions that coordinated many activities, including schools for the study of languages, literature, grammar, medicine, astrology, music, crafts, and the arts. Buddhist monasteries were invariably linked with religious and secular establishments forming a large and powerful network of routes and mid-way stations commonly situated along or near major commercial courses and hubs. Monasteries were often constructed as forts to withstand a siege—hence, they were ideal places for storing valuable commodities (i.e., texts, records, gold, grain, weapons), for providing administrative resources (i.e., literate personnel, financial assistance, etc), and if need be male population to be mobilized in war and defence.[5]

The backing that Buddhism received from the Tibetan imperium had much to do with the cosmopolitan yet humble character of Buddhism and its international prestige. It also had to do with the currency of its symbolic capital among the privileged classes and various guilds, and its egalitarian soteriological mission that reached towards the wider population at large. It is understandable that some Buddhist clergy may have actively propagandized a ritual system that elevated kings and other monarchs into the status of *cakravartin*, a wheel-turning king legitimized by the church to yield spiritual and secular authority over his subjects. Should his majesty convert to the truth of the Buddha's teachings, he would accumulate merit, like a wheel-turning king, by erecting Buddhist edifices, temples, and monasteries, seeing to the sustenance of the monastic communities, and sponsoring the scriptural translation and distribution of the Buddha's words into local vernaculars.

While the *Tang Annals* make no reference to the origins of the Tibetan script and remain silent about the admission of Buddhism at the Tibetan court, most Tibetan post-dynastic histories relate that Songtsen Gampo dispatched to India one of his ministers, Tönmi Sambhoṭa (Ton mi

5 Michael Walter, *Buddhism and Empire: The Political and Religious Culture of Early Tibet* (Leiden: Brill, 2009), p. 4.

sambhoṭa), to study Buddhism and Indic languages, from which he devised with the assistance of Indian scholars, the Tibetan script comprising twenty-six consonants (that existed in Sanskrit) and four vowels. Tönmi Sambhoṭa is also credited for composing eight Tibetan grammatical treatises according to the polymath Butön Rinchen Drup (Bu ston rin chen grub, 1290–1364).[6] While Tönmi's role and contributions may have been exaggerated by later traditions, there is no doubt that the imperial patronage of Buddhist monastic cultures caused significant changes in Tibet's socio-economic fabric and fostered an intellectual environment that witnessed a sharp increase in literacy.[7] The labour of hundreds of Tibetan and foreign scholars who translated a great number of texts from Sanskrit, Chinese, Khotanese, and the language of Zahor is attested in the colophons of many surviving works that were incorporated in the Tibetan Buddhist canon, the *Kangyur* (bKa'.'gyur; literal translation of "the words of the Buddha") and *Tengyur* (bsTan.'gyur; literal translation of "the commentaries") featuring over 4,500 texts and more than 300 volumes.

Translation Studies at the Tibetan Monastery Samye

The earliest edict to mention the state adaptation of Buddhism in Tibet is found at Samye (bSam yas) where Tibet's first monastic complex was completed in 779 during the reign of the second religious Emperor Tri

6 Peter Skilling, "From bKa' bstan bcos to bKa' 'gyur and bsTan 'gyur," in *Transmission of the Tibetan Canon*, ed. Helmut Eimer (Wien: Österreichische Akademie Der Wissenschaften, 1997), pp. 87–89. Until the time of Songtsen Gampo, Tibetan was a spoken language without a standardized writing system. It is said that when the gifted minister returned to Lhasa he formed two Tibetan alphabets, one "with heads" (Tibetan *dbu-can*) said to have been derived from the Lāñcā script, and another "headless" (Tibetan *dbu-med*) fashioned out of the Wartula characters.

7 The Kadampa master Chomden Reldri (1227–1305) lists approximately 1,094 titles of texts translated during the early spread of Buddhism to Tibet; see Kurtis Schaeffer and Leonard van der Kuijp, *An Early Tibetan Survey of Buddhist Literature: The Bstan Pa Rgyas Pa Rgyan Gyi Nyi 'Od of Bcom Ldan Ral Gri* (Cambridge, MA: Harvard University Press, 2009), p. 62.

Songdetsen (742–*c*.800).[8] According to a contemporary study in Tibetan by Tri Samten, the *Skad gnyis smra ba'i rin chen bang mdzod* (Jewel treasury of translations), after the completion of the monastic compound at Samye an imperial academy for translators was established, which was called "Translation Department," or Dragyur Ling (Sgra bsgyur gling). Songdetsen, who was in charge, assigned the renowned Indian scholars Śāntarakṣita and Padmasambhava as the leading teachers, while Vairocana, Kawa Paltseg (Ska ba dpal brtsegs), and Chogro Lui Gyaltsen (Cog ro klu'i rgyal mtshan) served among the assistant mentors. At that time, an auspicious number of 108 intelligent and diligent young boys and men were selected to begin their training in translation studies. Translators were selected from any region in the Tibetan empire provided that they were between eight and eighteen years old, in good health, without any physical disabilities and visible illnesses, clever and eager to learn, and of a kind disposition. Those candidates who met the conditions were further screened by the emperor as to their abilities to memorize words, understand their meaning, answer questions, and analyze statements. If the emperor was satisfied with the results he would ask the parents for their permission to recruit their sons as translators, rewarding them and further supporting families in places with limited resources by granting tax breaks. Those who were sent to train as translators abroad were provided by the emperor with medicine, money for fees, and supplies for the arduous journey to the subcontinent in gold, gifts, and introduction letters to the kings of Nepal and India. Translators were handsomely rewarded for their work with *solthang* (*gsol-thang*), a compensation package given to generals and ministers.

8 The edict reads as follows: "The Buddha-images set up in the temples of Ra-sa, of the Red Crag (Brag-dmar) and elsewhere, as well as the practice of the Buddhist religion, are never to be abandoned. The religious items provided are not to be diminished or neglected. From now on in every generation the king and his heir shall make a vow to this effect. That this oath may never be transgressed or changed, the celestial divinities, the gods of this world and non-human beings, all are called to witness that the king and the heir and all ministers have made this solemn oath"; David Snellgrove, *Indo-Tibetan Buddhism* (London: Serindia, 1987), p. 409.

It amounted to a third of the ratio of food (grain, butter, tea, oil, meat, fruits, and so forth) that the emperor consumed daily. The same *solthang* was given to ministers whose food supply was a third of that received by the emperor and it was equivalent to the resources given to 100 guards. Hence, translators earned supplies worth that of 33 guards combined.[9] Their professional tasks were divided according to their skills and they were classified either as: a) "chief editors" (*zhu-chen*), senior members responsible for proofreading and editing the final translations of texts; b) "editorial revisers" (*zhu-chung*), overseeing the first edition of the rough translations produced by the copyists; or c) "scribes" (*yi-ge-pa*).

The Registration and Classification of Tibetan Buddhist Translations

Three state-sponsored catalogues (Tibetan *dkar-chag*) of Tibetan translations and some native compositions of Buddhist scriptures testify to the quantity and variety of Buddhist texts that were available in Central Tibet in the ninth century. In agreement with a prevailing system of reckoning, the oldest of the three is the *Denkarma Catalogue* compiled during the second reign of Emperor Tri Desongtsen (*c.*802–815).[10] In

9 The following information has been extracted from Tri Samten, *Skad gnyis smra ba'i rin chen bang mdzod* [Jewel treasury of translations] (Lanzhou: Gansu Nationalities Publishing House, 2005), p. 82–83.

10 The chronological sequence of the three catalogues followed is in agreement with Butön Rinchen Drup (1290–1364), who may have been indebted to Chomden Reldri and testimonies preserved in several Tibetan histories; see Bu-ston, *Bu ston chos 'byung* [Butön's religious history] (Krung-go: Shes rig dpe skrun khang, 1988), p. 314; and Georgios T. Halkias, "Tibetan Buddhism Registered: An Imperial Catalogue from the Palace Temple of 'Phang-thang," *The Eastern Buddhist* 36, nos. 1–2 (2004), pp. 46–105. Situ Paṇchen advocates an alternative Tibetan tradition that places the catalogue from Pangtang first among the three Tibetan catalogues; see Schaeffer and van der Kuijp, *An Early Tibetan Survey of Buddhist Literature*, p. 55. Herrmann-Pfandt argues for the tradition followed by Situ Paṇchen. See Adelheid Herrmann-Pfandt, *Die lHan kar ma: Ein früher Katalog der ins Tibetische übersetzten buddhistischen Texte. Kritische Neuausgabe mit Einleitung und Materialien* [The lHan kar ma: An earlier catalogue of translated Tibetan Buddhist texts] (Wien: Verlag der Österreichischen Akademie der Wissenschaften, 2008).

his palace at Denkar resided the well-known imperial translators Kawa Paltsek, Khön Lü Wanpo (Khon klu'i dbang po), Namkha Nyingpo (Nam mkha'i snying po) and others, who verified the titles of works that have been translated in Tibetan and compiled the *Denkarma Catalogue*—the only imperial catalogue of proto-canonical scriptures preserved in the Tibetan Buddhist canon.[11] A second official catalogue is mentioned in several Tibetan historical sources, but the so-called *Samye Chimpuma* has not been seen to date. Chronologically, the last of the three is the *Pangtangma Catalogue* that was composed and kept at the royal palace of Pangtang in upper Yarlung valley. The translators Kawa Paltsek, Chökyi Nyingpo (Chos kyi snying po), Devendra, and Pelgyi Lhünpo (Dpal gyi lhun po) are credited as its compilers and there are references to other inventories consulted for its compilation.[12]

These early canonical compilations, in the form of inventories, were kept at the royal repositories of Denkar and Pangtang and they contained authorized translations of Buddhist texts listed by their Tibetan titles and often their length measured in units of *bam-po* and *śloka*. They were grouped in categories that divided them according to their Chinese or Indian origins, the orientation to which they belong (Hīnayāna or Mahāyāna), their length (short/long), genre (*sūtra, dhāraṇī, śāstra*), and subject-matter (i.e., Vinaya, Madhyamaka). Most Tibetan translations were allocated in the *sūtra* and *śāstra* sections with a dozen or so Sino-Tibetan translations of *sūtras* and commentaries (Sanskrit *śāstra*) listed under separate headings.[13] A fair number of scriptural divisions and

11 The *Denkarma Catalogue* is located in the *Tengyur* (Derge, no. 4364) canonical collection with the Tibetan title *Pho brang stod thang ldan dkar gyi chos kyi 'gyur ro cog gi dkar chag.*

12 An extant version of the *Pangtangma Catalogue* was published in China in 2003. According to the estimation of its editor, this catalogue was the last of the three and continued to be used and augmented during the second spread of the teachings to Tibet; see Halkias, "Tibetan Buddhism Registered," pp. 46–105.

13 Most Tibetan translations occupy the *sūtra* and *śāstra* sections with only a dozen or so scriptures listed in different categories as translations from Chinese. During the reign of Tri Tsukdetsen, the Buddhist Council took up the question of the suitability of the tantras as a teaching fit for the Tibetans. The translation of certain types of

hundreds of texts included in the early catalogues found their way in what constitutes the Tibetan Buddhist canon, or Tripiṭaka.[14]

The colophons of Tibetan *sūtras* inform us that small teams of Tibetan translators (Tibetan *lo-tsā-ba*) worked together with Buddhist scholars (Sanskrit *paṇḍita*) primarily from India but also from China, Uḍḍiyāna (present-day Swat), Gilgit (Tibetan 'Bru-źa), Khotan, and Nepal.[15] They solicited the assistance of many scribes to sort through a substantial corpus of imported scriptures perhaps with duplicate and triplicate versions of the same texts written in Sanskrit, Central Asian languages, and/or Chinese. This enormous enterprise (nearly one thousand translations listed in the third catalogue that remained open) would have required considerable physical resources. As we will see, the production of imperial catalogues coincided with a literary revision movement instigated across the Tibetan-speaking world. On a practical level, an operation of this scale suggests royal funds and a high degree of centralized organization and

---

texts, particularly the Mother Tantras, was forbidden; see Snellgrove, *Indo-Tibetan Buddhism*, p. 456.

14 Andrew I. Vostrikov, *Tibetan Historical Literature* (Calcutta: R. D. Press, 1970), p. 205, was the first historian to ascertain the value of the Tibetan catalogues as historical documents for their obvious importance as summaries of the kinds of Buddhism that were adopted in Tibet. The Tibetan Buddhist master Chomden Reldri and the polymath librarian Butön consulted them to create their own inventories of Tibetan Buddhist scriptures. Herrmann-Pfandt states that out of the 735 texts included in the *Denkarma Catalogue*, the first 445 texts were later put into the *Kangyur*, and the rest, "so far as they have survived," were mostly to become texts included in the *Tengyur*. See Herrmann-Pfandt, "The Lhan kar ma as a Source for the History of Tantric Buddhism," in *The Many Canons of Tibetan Buddhism*, ed. Helmut Eimer and David Germano (Leiden: Brill, 2002), p. 135.

15 Walter, *Buddhism and Empire*, p. 16, notes that Newari artisans and teachers served the Tibetan kings and may have been a dominant foreign influence in the Tibetan court. There were also scholars from Khotan, and a few of their works are included in the Tibetan Buddhist canon; see Laufer, "Origins of Tibetan Writing," p. 46. For the contributions of Nepalese scholars in Tibet, see Erberto Lo Bue, "The Role of Newar Scholars in Transmitting the Indian Buddhist Heritage to Tibet," in *Les habitants du Toit du monde: Études recueilles en hommage à Alexander W. Macdonald* [The inhabitants of the roof of the world: Studies in honour of Alexander W. Macdonald], ed. Samten Karmay et al. (Nanterre: Société d'ethnologie, 1997), pp. 629–658.

international cooperation among qualified experts. Inventories of Sanskrit manuscripts kept in monasteries at Kashmir and Khotan may have been consulted, while experts would have been invited from China where Buddhist texts had a long history of translation, revision and classification by Chinese-speaking and foreign scholars.[16]

These inventories are not meant to be exhaustive but indicative of the challenging ways translators and scholars had to deal with issues of excluding or including Buddhist texts from the catalogues and from those works sectioned for translation. The bulk of recorded texts are Indo-Tibetan translations, a fact that reflects an active market and demand for Sanskrit scholarship and a traditional Tibetan preference for Indic Buddhist scriptures. Naturally, competence in Sanskrit language was essential to this extensive translation activity and Tibetan translators pursued the study of various aspects of Sanskrit lexicography, grammar, poetics and metrics. Indian techniques for studying Sanskrit were in time also applied to the study of the Tibetans' own language.[17]

---

16 The compilation of catalogues providing listings of scriptural translations and indigenous works appears to have been a "quintessentially" Chinese phenomenon. Kyoko Tokuno writes: "The compilation of catalogues began during the nascency of Chinese Buddhism and continued throughout its history. According to one set of statistics, a total of seventy-six catalogues, including both extant and nonextant compilations, was compiled through the eighteenth century, the majority of which (some fifty-nine catalogues, or 78 percent of the total) fate from the T'ang dynasty or earlier." See Kyoko Tokuno, "The Evaluation of Indigenous Scriptures in Chinese Buddhist Bibliographical Catalogues," in *Chinese Buddhist Apocrypha*, ed. Robert Buswell (Honolulu: Hawai'i University Press, 1990), p. 31.

17 Traditionally in Tibet, the study of lexicography was regarded as one of the minor sciences ancillary to the major science of grammar, forming an integral part of the complete cultural equipment of an educated person. In other words, together with the other secular sciences lexicography and grammar were intimately linked with the adaptation and cultivation of Buddhist thought and civilization in Tibet. Pieter C. Verhagen explains: "The creation of this translation-literature, consisting of several thousands of translations generally of high quality, reliable and consistent in terminology, demanded that the Tibetan translators be thoroughly competent in and acquainted with the intricacies of Sanskrit language and literature. This in turn led to the development of a tradition of Sanskrit linguistic studies within the Tibetan monastic curriculum. Sanskrit studies covered such diverse topics as grammar,

Official Edicts and Requisite Compendia

Bilingual dictionaries/glossaries and compendia for special terms are requisite tools for any translation work. In ninth-century Tibet, three such compendia were compiled by the best translator-scholar teams of the time. Their publication was endorsed by a series of imperial decrees (Tibetan *bkas-bcad*) that laid out normative standards, instructions and guidelines for all translations across the empire. In all probability, these compendia were compiled before the so-called "Great Revision" of Tibetan literature initiated by Emperor Tri Tsukdetsen (817–841), the third religious emperor who sponsored the Tashi Gephel Temple (bKra shis dge 'phel gyi gtsug lag khang) at Ushangdo (u shang rdo) palace as residence for *paṇḍitas* and translators entrusted with the task of reviewing all previously translated texts and revising them according to a uniform religious terminology and translation techniques fixed for the new language of translations (Tibetan *skad-gsar-bcad*). The "Great Revision" was the outcome of three imperial injunctions related to the codification of religious language that occurred prior to Tri Tsukdetsen's reign, in 763, 783, and 814 respectively.[18] The guidelines in the *Vyutpatti* compendia were laid out by the Buddhist Council (Tibetan *mdun-sa*) that was established under the tutelage of the devout Buddhist Emperor Tri Songdetsen. The *Vyutpatti* enumerated authoritative rules for word-by-word translation, exact equivalences for Sanskrit-Tibetan

---

poetics, metrics and lexicography. A high level of proficiency in these disciplines was attained in the Tibetan tradition." See Pieter C. Verhagen, *A History of Sanskrit Grammatical Literature in Tibet*, vol. 1 (Leiden: Brill, 1994), p. 2.

18 Christina Scherrer-Schaub explains that "in 783–795 the ecclesiastic chancery followed an established hierarchical procedure: the colleges of translating and explaining Buddhist texts had to refer proposed terminology for approval to the high ecclesiastic representative and the college of translators attached to the palace ... The canonical and Dunhuang versions, possibly reflecting the 814 situation, bear evidence to a flourishing ecclesiastic bureaucracy." See Christina Scherrer-Schaub, "Enacting Words: A Diplomatic Analysis of the Imperial Decrees and Their Application in the Sgra sbyor bam po gñis pa Tradition," *Journal of the International Association of Buddhist Studies* 25, nos. 1–2 (2002), p. 288. Tibetan tradition maintains that three revisions took place by royal decree.

terms, and provided practical advice on grammar and clarification of doctrine.

Three *Vyutpatti* compendia are recorded in Tibetan literature: the *Mahāvyutpatti* (Tibetan *Bye brag tu rtogs byed chen po*); the *Madhyavyutpatti* (Tibetan *Bye brag tu rtogs byed 'bring po*), commonly known as the *Drajor Bampo Nyipa* (Tibetan *Sgra sbyor bam po gnyis pa*); and the **Alpavyutpatti/*Svalpavyutpatti/*Kṣudravyutpatti* (Tibetan *Bye brag tu rtogs byed chung ngu*), which was either lost or subsumed in the *Mahāvyutpati*.[19] The *Mahāvyutpatti*, or *Great Repertory* (of terms and expressions), is a large bilingual dictionary comprising Sanskrit terms and expressions and their standardized Tibetan equivalents. The terms are not arranged alphabetically but onomasiologically in clusters (Sanskrit *varga*; Tibetan *sde-tshan*) according to subject-categories, 283 in number covering a total of 9,565 entries.[20]

The second compendium, the *Madhyavyutpatti* (Middle repertory), known in Tibetan as the *Drajor Bampo Nyipa*, or (Treatise on) the formation of words in two volumes, was completed in the early ninth century. It includes historical information about a royal edict issued by Emperor Tri Desongtsen and the circumstances of its composition. The relevant passage reads:

19 Géza Uray, "Contributions to the Date of the Vyutpatti-treatises," *Acta Orientalia Academiae Scientiarum Hungaricae* 43, no. 1 (1989), p. 3. Verhagen, *A History of Sanskrit Grammatical Literature in Tibet*, pp. 12–13, lists three Tibetan grammatical treatises from the time, said to have been composed by the Tibetan translator Chekhyi Druk: the *Gnas brgyad chen po'i rtsa ba*; its commentary, the *Gnas brgyad kyi 'grel pa*; and a linguistic treatise of unlisted authorship, the *Sgra'i rnam par dbye btsan pa*.

20 David Seyfort Ruegg, "Sanskrit-Tibetan and Tibetan-Sanskrit Dictionaries and Some Problems in Indo-Tibetan Philosophical Lexicography," in *Lexicography in the Indian and Buddhist Cultural Field: Proceedings of a Conference at the University of Strasbourg, 25 to 27 April 1996*, ed. Boris L. Oguibénine (München: Kommission für Zentralasiatische Studien, Bayerische Akad. der Wiss, 1998), p. 116. On the dating of the *Vyutpatti* treatises see Uray, "Contributions to the Date of the Vyutpatti-treatises," pp. 3–21. The *Dharmasaṃgraha*, a much smaller, but otherwise comparable lexicon of Buddhist terms in Sanskrit divided in 140 subject rubrics was translated into Chinese *c.*1000 CE (Taishō 764); see Ruegg, "Sanskrit-Tibetan and Tibetan-Sanskrit Dictionaries," p. 117.

> In the horse year the Emperor Tri Desongtsen dwelt in the Öncangdo palace in Kyi. The old armies of east and west had been rotated and the brigands quelled. The messenger(s) of the Karluk offered homage. The Great Ministers ... and others brought much tribute from the territories, and offered camels, horses and cattle to His Majesty. As a follow-up to the awards that he granted to each according to rank from Zhanglön on down, he gave his command that ... those who had become master translators ... should write a catalogue of the Tibetan translations and coinages deriving from the Sanskrit of the Greater and Lesser Vehicles.[21]

In consultation with the emperor, a congress of senior monk scholars and others reached an agreement upon the methods of translation of Buddhist scriptures and the use of established terminology. The same work enunciates some general translation principles and furnishes important grammatical and etymological explanations of Sanskrit terms and their Tibetan equivalents for 414 entries listed also in the *Mahāvyutpatti*. Along with the *Great Repertory*, the *Drajor Bampo Nyipa* played a crucial role in the development of Tibet's Buddhist literary heritage. A millennium later, the same repertories were consulted and their guidelines applied in the creation of a definitive version of the Mongolian *Tengyur* produced in the eighteenth century under the direction of Changkya Rölpa Dorjé (Lcang skya rol pa'i rdo rje, 1717–1786).

The Fidelity of Indo-Tibetan Translations: Topics and Challenges

The Tibetan lexicographical traditions incorporated thousands of new terms for the purpose of representing the rich language of Sanskrit, for the Tibetans did not have the vocabulary necessary to supply a different word for each of the technical terms, synonyms, and nuances utilized in the Sanskrit texts. Refraining from an indiscriminate adoption of Sanskrit loan words, the Tibetan translator-teams opted for the creation of a new range of Buddhist vocabulary by compounding existing Tibetan

21 Matthew T. Kapstein, *The Tibetan Assimilation of Buddhism: Conversion, Contestation, and Memory* (Oxford: Oxford University Press, 2000), p. 52.

words together to convey technical terminology, and by adding suffixes and affixes to verbs to represent various Sanskrit tenses. In the ninth century, the process of creating new Tibetan terms was strictly regulated and no one was encouraged to introduce new words of translation when existing ones were to be found in the authorized glossaries. The *Drajor Bampo Nyipa* states: "no one should translate apart from this tradition and devise new equivalents on his own. If any educational institution or translation department of a monastery needs to develop new terms, this process should be done in conformity with grammar only after the careful examination of the context of the scripture." Furthermore, all new terms should be submitted to the "Committee for the Translation of Dharma Texts" at the palace where senior translators may have them revised and if need be established.[22]

The *Drajor Bampo Nyipa* contains additional guidelines and instructions including explanations of Sanskrit terms, etymological paraphrases, and discussions on technical issues of grammar. For example, when a word in the source language is polysemic, and if no word in the target language is available that covers all its possible meanings, then according to the guidelines the word of the source language should be retained rather than translated into the target language. The name "Gautama" is a case cited in the compendium that cannot be readily translated into Tibetan. This is because the Sanskrit root *gau/go* has several meanings (word, direction, earth, light, *vajra*, bull, etc.) that can't be conveyed by any single translation equivalent.[23]

The stipulation that Sanskrit words requiring interpretation may be translated in the way that best suits the context is justified in those instances where there is no regular and unique one-to-one correspondence between terms in the source and target languages. There are a number of inconsistent cases with variations in the rendering of technical words and expressions of philosophical import. For example, while translators

22 Muge Samten, *A History of Traditional Fields of Learning*, p. 25.

23 Ruegg discusses this and other conventions stipulated in the lexicographical works in "Sanskrit-Tibetan and Tibetan-Sanskrit Dictionaries," p. 123.

unanimously translated the polysemic Sanskrit term *dharma* simply as *chos* in Tibetan, this is not the case with the philosophically pertinent term *svabhāva*, which has been translated as *rang-bzhin* and sometimes as *ngo-bo-nyid*, where it is not possible to pinpoint a clear distinction in usage between these two frequently occurring Tibetan equivalents.[24]

The formal investigation of language and the various etymological, grammatical and syntactic ways in which the intended meaning is interpreted are necessary and in use in the actual works of translation. The expert teams responsible for endorsing translation guidelines were in favour of actual principles limiting the Indian grammatical tradition and seeking the best interpretation on the basis of eliciting meaning from the contents of the original and authoritative Buddhist texts. The following two passages from *Drajor Bampo Nyipa* illustrate the resolutions of their predilections "with regard to the method of translating the Good *Dharma*."

> [A]s long as there is no contradiction to the meaning, then translate to the full advantage of Tibetan. When in translating into Tibetan language without deviating from the arrangement of the Sanskrit [that is to say without deviating from the Sanskrit syntax], [thereby making] the connexion between expression and meaning well-adapted [to Tibetan], then translate without deviating from [the arrangement of words in Sanskrit]. If good [Tibetan] and intelligibility occur only by changing [the Sanskrit syntax], in the case of a stanza of four or six verses, then change [the order] within the limits of a single stanza, and translate to the full advantage [of Tibetan] and [having in view] both the expression and the meaning.[25]

In another passage from the same compendium Sanskrit terms are preferred when equivalents cannot be ascertained:

---

24 Ruegg, "Sanskrit-Tibetan and Tibetan-Sanskrit Dictionaries," p. 124.

25 Translation by Scherrer-Schaub, in Christina Scherrer-Schaub, "Translation, Transmission, Tradition: Suggestions from Ninth-Century Tibet," *Journal of Indian Philosophy* 27 (1999), p. 72.

> When in translating the names of regions, sentient beings, flowers, fruits, etc., [the translator] hesitates about the exact meaning or whether the corresponding [Tibetan] expression is inadequate [to that meaning] and even if, generally speaking, the possibility of translating [it] exists, but [the translator] does not know whether the meaning [of the supposed term] is adequate or not, [it is better] in this case to leave the Sanskrit expression and add at the head, as an appellative, the suitable [common noun in Tibetan], such as "*yul*," "*me tog*."[26]

On the whole, Tibetan translations of Buddhist scriptures show remarkable precision and fidelity for the original work—a presumption which has led some Buddhist scholars to attempt "back translating" Tibetan texts into Sanskrit. This is because Tibetan translators adhered to a rather strict policy of following prescribed translation-equivalents set out in the *Mahāvyutpatti* and its companion work the *Drajor Bampo Nyipa* that instigated rules for Sanskrit syntax, including (in so far as possible) verbal prefixes, synonyms, and word order. However, as noted by Wedemayer, this claim to conformity fails to take cognisance of the fact that the *seeming* uniformity of Tibetan translations is not exclusively attributable to the translators themselves nor to the guidelines set forth by the imperial compendia, but to "historical developments in canon and its associated technology (in particular the influence of xylography) which resulted in the disappearance of variant translations." The uniformity in Tibetan translations is the result of the standardization of the texts selected for inclusion in the canonical collections of the *Kangyur* and *Tengyur*. Therefore, the fidelity of the Tibetan translations of Sanskrit Buddhist texts is not as usually maintained exclusively the result only of widespread standards in translation, but it is "an epiphenomenon of factors which have led to there only *being* one canonical translation."[27]

---

26 Scherrer-Schaub, "Translation, Transmission, Tradition," pp. 72–73.

27 Christian Wedemeyer, "Tantalizing Traces of the Labours of the Lotsāwas: Alternative Translations of Sanskrit Sources in the Writing of Rje Tsong Kha pa," in *Tibetan Buddhist Literature and Praxis: Studies in Its Formative Period, 900–1400*, ed. Ronald M. Davidson and Christian K. Wedemeyer (Leiden: Brill, 2006), pp. 152–154.

Indo-Tibetan and Indo-Chinese Translations: Networks of Cultural Production and Distribution in Comparative Perspectives

Even though India had a profound effect on the development of Tibetan civilization, the salient contributions of China in the cultural sphere of Tibetan translations should not be overlooked. The Chinese bordered directly on the eastern parts of the Tibetan empire and were responsible for a number of imported social and cultural models. The state chancellery of the Tibetan emperors was patterned after the Chinese model, and the use of paper and the technique of block printing, as well as a great number of elements in Tibetan culture, art, and iconography were clearly of Chinese inspiration. In China, by order of Emperor Taizu of Song 宋太祖 the first woodblock print of the entire Buddhist canon was completed in 971 CE, that is, several centuries before the first printing of the Tibetan Tripiṭaka at Narthang. The influence of Chinese Buddhist traditions (e.g., *chan*) with regard to the development of Tibetan Buddhism in the earliest periods should not be underestimated.[28] There are many recorded cases of intra-religious interactions and exchanges between Chinese and Tibetan Buddhists such as, the scholar Sangshi who allegedly brought from China one thousand volumes of religious books, but had to bury them in a cave at Chimpu near Samye monastery in fear that he might be persecuted by his anti-Buddhist maternal uncle.[29] Tri Songdetsen erected Buddhist temples both at the "centre and borders" (Tibetan *dbung-mthar*) of his Central Asian empire. Many of those built at the borders of his dominion, in multi-cultural places like Dunhuang, are

28 See Kenneth K. Tanaka and Raymond Robertson, "A Ch'an Text from Tun-huang: Implications for Ch'an Influence on Tibetan Buddhism," in *Tibetan Buddhism: Reason and Revelation*, ed. Steven Goodman et al. (New York: State University of New York Press, 1992), pp. 57–78; and Carmen Meinert, "Chinese Chan and Tibetan Rdzogs Chen: Preliminary Remarks on Two Dunhuang Manuscripts," in *Religion and Secular Culture in Tibet*, ed. Henk Blezer (Leiden: Brill, 2002), pp. 289–308.

29 Muge Samten, *A History of Traditional Fields of Learning*, p. 14.

listed by name.[30] The religiously, commercially and politically entangled interactions between Chinese and Tibetans in Dunhuang betray, *inter alia*, the confluence of two translation currents of Indic Buddhism taking place outside the subcontinent. A reciprocal fascination for each other's traditions and divergent soteriological interpretations of Indian Buddhism fuelled Indo-Sinitic philosophical debates said to have been held at Samye monastery, and incited collaborations as testified by Sino-Tibetan manuscripts of Buddhist scriptures (*sūtra, śāstra, vinaya*), library inventories, names of temples and copyists, lists of doctrinal terminology, *dhāraṇī*, and *mantra*, discovered in Dunhuang.[31] It appears that Chinese Buddhist temples kept Chinese and Tibetan manuscripts in their libraries and lodged Tibetan monastics, officials and pilgrims visiting Dunhuang during summer festivals. The granting of donations for the meritorious reproduction of Buddhist scriptures were often jointly made by the Chinese and Tibetan *saṅgha* including the Chinese families Yin, Li, Pei, Shi, Song, Zhang, Wang, Cao and so forth, and the Tibetan families from the divisions' Nyingchom (Snying choms), Tongsar (Stong sar) and Gösar (Rgod sar).[32] The colophons of many *sūtras* attest

30 William F. Thomas, *Tibetan Literary Texts and Documents Concerning Chinese Turkestan*, vol. 2, *Documents* (London: The Royal Asiatic Society, 1951), pp. 88–91. The dates of the Tibetan occupation of Dunhuang are in dispute; see Jacob Dalton, Tom Davis, and Sam van Schaik, "Beyond Anonymity: Paleographic Analyses of the Dunhuang Manuscripts," *Journal of the International Association of Tibetan Studies* 3 (2007), p. 18, n29. In the Chinese sources, Li Jifu 李吉甫 reports that the Tibetans conquered Dunhuang in the second year of the Jianzhong reign (781) under the Tang Emperor Dezong 唐德宗. *Yue Shi* 樂史 dates the Tibetan conquest near the end of the Tianbao reign (742–756) and records that the Tang court reclaimed its sovereignty over Dunhuang in 851, a date on which the two standard histories of the Tang dynasty agree. One Dunhuang manuscript shows the year to be 848; see Y. Edmund Lien, "Dunhuang Gazetteers of the Tang Period," *T'ang Studies* 27 (2009), p. 21.

31 Henrik H. Sørensen, "Perspectives on Buddhism in Dunhuang during the Tang and Five Dynasties Period," in *The Silk Roads: Highways of Culture and Commerce*, ed. Vadime Elisseef (Paris: Unesco, 1998), p. 37.

32 Ibid., pp. 38–39. Apparently, the Tibetan councillors ordered the *Prajñāpāramitā* to be copied in Tibetan in eight sections and in six hundred chapters in Chinese; see Thomas, *Tibetan Literary Texts and Documents Concerning Chinese Turkestan*, pp. 75–78.

to Chinese professional scribes at Dunhuang making a living by copying Tibetan texts.[33]

Political, social and commercial networks facilitated pilgrimage and religious exchanges across Asia. Elsewhere I have shown that "the importation, reproduction, and exportation of Buddhist manuscripts in Central Eurasia was invariably linked to literate members of the sangha, patrons, pilgrims, and traders operating across local and translocal networks of distribution."[34] The acquisition and translation of Buddhist scriptures in a variety of languages points to the emergence of new markets of religious knowledge and technical expertise and to the circulation of funds through profitable exchanges in silk and precious merchandise and through lay and royal donations for the collection of religious merit.

> Buddhist monasticism and trade supported each other in intricate ways, since the profit gained through business could be converted into symbolic capital (religious merit) by sponsoring Buddhist establishments and monks and supporting merit-earning activities, such as commissioning temples, murals, and so on. As we have seen, the demand for religious merit was readily met through the reproduction of Buddhist sutras.[35]

Manuscript *Pelliot tibétain* 999 bears witness to joint Pure Land ventures between Chinese and Tibetan families in Dunhuang.

33 Dalton, Davis, and van Schaik, "Beyond Anonymity," p. 11. Thomas, *Tibetan Literary Texts and Documents Concerning Chinese Turkestan*, p. 77, refers to a Dunhuang document that lists 80 scribes *(yi-ge-pa)* and 20 editorial revisers (*zhu-chen*). Apropos, Snellgrove, *Indo-Tibetan Buddhism*, p. 445, writes concerning the Great Revision, "[B]y the ninth century high standards of competence in this most difficult of translating work was achieved. In this respect, the best known figure must be the Chinese scholar Fa-ch'eng, known in Tibetan as Chos-grub with the equivalent meaning 'Perfect in Religion.' Active in Dun-huang from the early ninth century onward, he received from the Tibetan administration the title of 'Great Translator-Reviser of the Kingdom of Great Tibet' [Bod chen-po'i chab-srid-kyi zhu-chen gyi lo-tsa-ba], producing translations of Buddhist works subject to the sympathetic interest of a Tibetan district commissioner who was himself a fervent Buddhist."

34 Georgios T. Halkias, *Luminous Bliss: A Religious History of Pure Land Literature in Tibet* (Honolulu: University of Hawai'i Press, 2013), p. 50.

35 Ibid., p. 50.

Buddhist scriptures are commonly considered "sacred objects" and "objects of worship." Hence, religious merit could be acquired by anyone involved in the preservation and reproduction of sacred texts and in related activities such as, sponsorship, production, procurement, and translation. State-initiated regulatory mechanisms gave rise to authoritative catalogues of translated Buddhist works (Tibetan *dkar-chag*; Chinese *jinglu*), bilingual lexica, and related compendia-edicts that overshadowed the transnational origins of Buddhist texts and highlighted their regional and social conditions of adaptation in local vernaculars. As in Tibet, the Chinese translation of Buddhist scriptures introduced thousands of new words into the Chinese language, including new verse styles and the use of Chinese characters as phonetic signs to denote the sounds of Indian letters. Many of the specific tasks and translation methods of the Chinese translation committees involved checking, correcting and amending Chinese texts since the *lingua franca* of the translation teams was Chinese.[36] In the case of Tibet, we cannot be certain of a dominant language used by Indian and Chinese scholars who collaborated with Tibetan translators. Cases are known of foreign scholars producing Tibetan translations independently and even composing original philosophical treatises in Tibetan. We may assume that at least some Indian and Chinese scholars mastered Tibetan sufficiently to be able to communicate in Tibetan that was the *lingua franca* in the empire and its colonies. On the other side, many Tibetan translators are known to have travelled in India to study with local masters and thus communicate fluently in Indian languages.

Approximate dates assigned to translated works often provide us with a *terminus ante quem* for the Indian originals and for their stage of development at that date, while philological comparisons between Chinese and Tibetan translations of the same Sanskrit text reveal much about the chronological progression, and the reception and impact of

36 For an informative discussion of translation theories employed in the translation of Chinese Buddhist texts, see Chu Chi Yu, "Translation Theory in Chinese Translations of Buddhist Texts," in *Investigating Translation: Selected Papers from the 4th International Congress on Translation*, ed. Allison Beeby et al. (The Netherlands: John Benjamins B. V., 2000), pp. 43–53.

Indian Mahāyāna scriptures in regional and transregional settings. While there are still many questions to be asked concerning the cultural production and canonization of Buddhist translations in Tibetan and Chinese political, social and economic contexts, future comparative and interdisciplinary studies on Asian traditions of religious translation will undoubtedly shed light on how privileged interpretations, material reproductions of religious knowledge, and the inflation of symbolic capital reinforced the fabrication and accretion of maritime and overland commercial and religious networks across Asia.

Bibliography

Bushell, Stephen Wootton. "The Early History of Tibet from Chinese Sources." *Journal of the Royal Asiatic Society of Great Britain and Ireland* 12, no. 4 (1880), pp. 435–541.

Bu-ston. *Bu ston chos 'byung* [Butön's religious history]. Krung-go: Shes rig dpe skrun khang, 1988.

Chu, Chi Yu. "Translation Theory in Chinese Translations of Buddhist Texts." In *Investigating Translation: Selected Papers from the 4th International Congress on Translation*, edited by Allison Beeby et al. The Netherlands: John Benjamins B. V., 2000, pp. 43–53.

Dalton, Jacob, Tom Davis, and Sam van Schaik. "Beyond Anonymity: Paleographic Analyses of the Dunhuang Manuscripts." *Journal of the International Association of Tibetan Studies* 3 (2007), pp. 1–23.

Halkias, Georgios T. "Tibetan Buddhism Registered: An Imperial Catalogue from the Palace Temple of 'Phang-thang." *The Eastern Buddhist* 36, nos. 1–2 (2004), pp. 46–105.

———. *Luminous Bliss: A Religious History of Pure Land Literature in Tibet.* Honolulu: University of Hawai'i Press, 2013.

Herrmann-Pfandt, Adelheid. "The Lhan kar ma as a Source for the History of Tantric Buddhism." In *The Many Canons of Tibetan Buddhism*, edited by Helmut Eimer and David Germano. Leiden: Brill, 2002, pp. 129–149.

———. *Die lHan kar ma: Ein früher Katalog der ins Tibetische übersetzten buddhistischen Texte. Kritische Neuausgabe mit Einleitung und Materialien* [The lHan kar ma: An earlier catalogue of translated Tibetan Buddhist texts]. Wien: Verlag der Österreichischen Akademie der Wissenschaften, 2008.

Kapstein, Matthew T. *The Tibetan Assimilation of Buddhism: Conversion, Contestation, and Memory.* Oxford: Oxford University Press, 2000.

Laufer, Berthold. "Origins of Tibetan Writing." *Journal of the American Oriental Society* 38 (1918), pp. 34–46.

Lien, Y. Edmund. "Dunhuang Gazetteers of the Tang Period." *T'ang Studies* 27 (2009), pp. 19–39.

Lo Bue, Erberto. "The Role of Newar Scholars in Transmitting the Indian Buddhist Heritage to Tibet." In *Les habitants du Toit de monde: Études recueilles en hommage à Alexander W. Macdonald* [The inhabitants of the roof of the world: Studies in honour of Alexander W. Macdonald], edited by Samten Karmay et al. Nanterre: Société d'ethnologie, 1997, pp. 629–658.

Meinert, Carmen. "Chinese Chan and Tibetan Rdzogs Chen: Preliminary Remarks on Two Dunhuang Manuscripts." In *Religion and Secular Culture in Tibet*, edited by Henk Blezer. Leiden: Brill, 2002, pp. 289–308.

Rockhill, Woodville. "Tibet: A Geographical, Ethnographical, and Historical Sketch, Derived from Chinese Sources." *Journal of the Royal Asiatic Society of Great Britain and Ireland* 23, no. 2 (April 1891), pp. 186–291.

Ruegg, David Seyfort. "Sanskrit-Tibetan and Tibetan-Sanskrit Dictionaries and Some Problems in Indo-Tibetan Philosophical Lexicography." In *Lexicography in the Indian and Buddhist Cultural Field: Proceedings of a Conference at the University of Strasbourg, 25 to 27 April 1996*, edited by Boris L. Oguibénine. München: Kommission für Zentralasiatische Studien, Bayerische Akad. der Wiss, 1998, pp. 115–142.

Samten, Muge. *A History of Traditional Fields of Learning: A Concise History of Dissemination of Traditional Fields of Learning in Tibet.* Dharamsala: Library of Tibetan Works and Archives, 2005.

Samten, Tri. *Skad gnyis smra ba'i rin chen bang mdzod* [Jewel treasury of translations]. Lanzhou: Gansu Nationalities Publishing House, 2005.

Schaeffer, Kurtis, and Leonard van der Kuijp. *An Early Tibetan Survey of Buddhist Literature: The Bstan Pa Rgyas Pa Rgyan Gyi Nyi 'Od of Bcom Ldan Ral Gri.* Cambridge, MA: Harvard University Press, 2009.

Scherrer-Schaub, Christina. "Translation, Transmission, Tradition: Suggestions from Ninth-Century Tibet." *Journal of Indian Philosophy* 27 (1999), pp. 67–77.

———. "Enacting Words: A Diplomatic Analysis of the Imperial Decrees and Their Application in the Sgra sbyor bam po gñis pa Tradition." *Journal of the International Association of Buddhist Studies* 25, nos. 1–2 (2002), pp. 263–340.

Skilling, Peter. "From bKa' bstan bcos to bKa' 'gyur and bsTan 'gyur." In *Transmission of the Tibetan Canon*, edited by Helmut Eimer. Wien: Österreichische Akademie Der Wissenschaften, 1997, pp. 87–111.

Snellgrove, David. *Indo-Tibetan Buddhism*. London: Serindia, 1987.

Sørensen, Henrik H. "Perspectives on Buddhism in Dunhuang during the Tang and Five Dynasties Period." In *The Silk Roads: Highways of Culture and Commerce*, edited by Vadime Elisseef. Paris: Unesco, 1998, pp. 27–48.

Tanaka, Kenneth K., and Raymond Robertson. "A Ch'an Text from Tun-huang: Implications for Ch'an Influence on Tibetan Buddhism." In *Tibetan Buddhism:*

Reason and Revelation, edited by Steven Goodman et al. New York: State University of New York Press, 1992.

Thomas, William F. *Tibetan Literary Texts and Documents Concerning Chinese Turkestan*. Vol. 2, *Documents*. London: The Royal Asiatic Society, 1951.

Tokuno, Kyoko. "The Evaluation of Indigenous Scriptures in Chinese Buddhist Bibliographical Catalogues." In *Chinese Buddhist Apocrypha*, edited by Robert Buswell. Honolulu: Hawai'i University Press, 1990, pp. 31–74.

Uebach, Helga. "From Red Tally to Yellow Paper: The Official Introduction of Paper in Tibetan Administration in 744–745." In "Tibetan Studies in Honour of Samten Karmay: Part I—Historical, Cultural and Linguistic Studies," edited by Françoise Pommaret and Jean-Luc Achard. Special issue, *Revue d'Etudes Tibétaines* 14 (2008), pp. 57–70.

Uray, Géza. "Contributions to the Date of the Vyutpatti-treatises." *Acta Orientalia Academiae Scientiarum Hungaricae* 43, no. 1 (1989), pp. 3–21.

Verhagen, Pieter C. *A History of Sanskrit Grammatical Literature in Tibet*. Vol. 1. Leiden: Brill, 1994.

Vostrikov, Andrew I. *Tibetan Historical Literature*. Calcutta: R. D. Press, 1970.

Walter, Michael. *Buddhism and Empire: The Political and Religious Culture of Early Tibet*. Leiden: Brill, 2009.

Wedemeyer, Christian. "Tantalizing Traces of the Labours of the Lotsāwas: Alternative Translations of Sanskrit Sources in the Writing of Rje Tsong Kha pa." In *Tibetan Buddhist Literature and Praxis: Studies in Its Formative Period, 900–1400*, edited by Ronald M. Davidson and Christian K. Wedemeyer. Leiden: Brill, 2006, pp. 149–182.

Navigating and Negotiating Cultural Space through Literary Translation

Habitations of Resistance:
The Role of Translation in the Creation of a Literary Public Sphere in Kerala

E. V. RAMAKRISHNAN

Introduction

The present paper examines a critical moment of transformation in the literary sensibility of modern Indian literatures in general and Malayalam literature in particular from the larger perspective of the role of translation in radicalizing the literary discourse in society. The period between the 1930s and the 1950s in India witnessed momentous events in the political field as part of the nationalist freedom struggle and they impacted the cultural productions from theatre to painting and literature. As Priyamvada Gopal notes, "The years from about 1936 to 1954 were the heyday of a hugely influential radical cultural movement that spanned several regions and languages across India (as well as the region that became Pakistan)."[1] The writers responded to the massive socio-political changes that swept across India in the wake of anti-imperialist resistance movements by radicalizing the role of literature in society and interrogating prevalent modes of representation. Translation played a significant part in this process of radicalization of literary sensibility.

The 1930s and 1940s of the twentieth century were marked by socio-political upheavals across the world as evidenced by the economic depression in America, rise of fascism in Europe, and intensification of struggle against imperialism in Asia and Africa. It was against this backdrop that a group

---

1 Priyamvada Gopal, *Literary Radicalism in India: Gender, Nation and the Transition to Independence* (London and New York: Routledge, 2005), p. 1.

of writers from 15 countries met in Paris in the spring of 1935 under the banner, "International Writers for Defence of Culture." Among the writers who participated in the conference were Andre Gide, Andre Malraux, Andre Breton, Tristan Tzara, Aldous Huxley, E. M. Forster, Boris Pasternak, Isaac Babel, Bertolt Brecht, Julien Benda, Heinrich Mann, and Gustav Regler. The conference had set "the guarding of our civil liberties, the organization of writers to safeguard their own economic interests and to render help to the writers exiled by fascism" as its larger goals.[2] Mulk Raj Anand and Sajjad Zahir, both young writers from India, participated in the conference and felt the need to disseminate the radical ideas highlighted in the conference in India. Sajjad Zahir had already edited a volume of Urdu short stories, *Angare* (Live coals) in 1932 that had caught the attention of young readership. The influence of the European avant-garde of the 1930s is apparent in these stories. This volume raised a storm in the Urdu-speaking Muslim community as most of the stories were highly critical of "the middle-class Muslim mores and practices of the period" and later the book came to be banned by the United Provinces Legislature.[3] Sajjad Zahir was forced to leave India as a result of the controversy surrounding *Angare*. He went to London for studies and there, along with Mulk Raj Anand, formed an organization called the Progressive Writers Association. The Association drafted a manifesto which appeared in English in *Left Review* in February 1936 and in the Hindi journal *Hans*, edited by Premchand, an eminent Hindi novelist, in October 1935.

Progressive Literary Movement—Contexts and Issues

Mulk Raj Anand and Zahir were instrumental in organizing the 1936 Lucknow Conference presided over by Premchand. Zahir mobilized support for the Progressive Literary Association by forming local chapters of the association at several places like Allahabad, Lahore, Hyderabad, and

2 Gopal, *Literary Radicalism in India*, p. 24.

3 Carlo Coppalo, "Premchand's Address to the First Meeting of the All India Progressive Literary Association: Some Speculations," *Journal of South Asian Literature* 21, no. 2 (1986), p. 21.

Aligarh. The Conference of the All India Progressive Literary Association was planned at Lucknow in early April 1936 because a national convention of the Congress Party was scheduled there at the same time. The organizers hoped to rope in Jawaharlal Nehru to preside over the All India Progressive Literary Association. But eventually it was Premchand, the most eminent Hindi writer of his generation, who presided over the conference that was attended by writers from all over India, including Kerala. The founding of Progressive Literary Association of Indian Writers in the Lucknow Conference galvanized the undercurrent of popular anguish against the oppressive apparatus of colonialism, exploitative regime of feudalism, and the regimentation of society along the lines of caste, class and gender. The manifesto that was prepared to commemorate the 1936 conference spelt out the social role of writers explicitly:

> We believe that the new literature of India must deal with the basic problems of our existence today: the problems of hunger and poverty, *social backwardness and political subjection*. All that drags us down to passivity, *inaction and un-reason* we reject as reactionary. All that arouses in us *the critical spirit*, which examines institutions and customs *in the light of reason* which helps us to act, to organize ourselves, to transform, we accept as progressive.[4] [Emphases by author]

The above statement identifies the social backwardness of India as the main reason for its political subjection. The writer as activist is also a rationalist, interrogating tradition and orthodoxy. The critical spirit enables the transformation of literature. In the presidential address given by Premchand, some of these ideas were reiterated. He declared that a writer is by nature progressive, and "the greater the intensity of his pain the more powerful his writings and the more realistic his portrayal."[5] He added: "Progress, to me, is that situation which generates in us the

4 Mulk Raj Anand, "On the Progressive Writers Movement," in *Marxist Cultural Movement in India*, ed. S. Pradhan, vol. 1 (Calcutta [Kolkata]: National Book Agency, 1979), pp. 20–21.

5 Jasbir Jain, *The Writer as Critic: Essays in Literature, History and Culture* (Jaipur and Delhi: Rawat Publications, 2010), p. 123.

resolution and the will to act, which makes us aware of our pain, which helps us identify the various internal and external reasons that have led to this condition of desolation and decline, and which impels us to try and overcome them."[6] He wanted writers to redefine their ideas of beauty in the context of changing society and inculcate in them openness to new knowledge. He concluded his speech with these words:

> But we do not consider literature as a means of enjoyment and luxury alone. Real literature for us is one which consists of high philosophy, a desire for independence, the essence of beauty, the instinct for creativity, and which is illuminated by the realities of life—one which can generate a momentum in our lives, make us restless and generate in us the will to fight; it should not put us to sleep, for to sleep any more now is a sign of death.[7]

The credo of social realism, thus, becomes a mode of embodying the social ferment and gathering its potential for intervention in the direction of a radical poetic. Most of the literatures in India came under the spell of this radical poetic during the period from the mid-thirties to the late fifties. Sisir Kumar Das in his history of Indian literature has said that the impact of Progressive Movement was felt in all major literatures of India:

> The most positive impact of the (All India Progressive) Association was on the growth of literature which can be loosely described as "socialist" so far as its themes and moods are concerned. There was hardly any growing literature in India now which did not respond to the growing and expanding socialist ideas.[8]

The case of Malayalam literature will be taken up here for detailed study as it will illustrate the nature of contestations that defined the trajectory of this transformative poetic that emerged during this phase of literary development.

---

6 Jain, *The Writer as Critic*, p. 124.

7 Ibid., p. 131.

8 Sisir Kumar Das, *A History of Indian Literature 1911–1956: Struggle for Freedom: Triumph and Tragedy* (New Delhi: Sahitya Akademi, 1995), p. 88.

"*Jeeval Sahityam*" in Malayalam Sets a New Social Agenda

Translation has played an enabling role in the development of Malayalam fiction even before the arrival of Progressive Literary Movement on the scene. In 1925 the appearance of the translation of Victor Hugo's *Les Misérables* into Malayalam brought about a shift in the prevailing literary sensibility. Hugo may be better known as a romantic poet in France but for the readers of Malayalam, his *Les Misérables* opened up possibilities of imagining alternative models of reality. Malayalam novel after the pioneering efforts of social reformist writers like O. Chandu Menon in the late nineteenth century had become stereotyped in their approach to reality. While Malayalam poetry had responded to the anti-colonial nationalist movement in the 1920s with a new poetic, the novel in Malayalam merely reproduced formulaic plots. Against such a backdrop, the translation of Hugo's novel based on its English version, by Nalappat Narayana Menon, proved a creative intervention. Menon employed the foreignizing mode of translation which had the effect of defamiliarizing the very syntax of Malayalam. Many of his literal translations have become part of everyday idiom in the language. This translation provided a new set of subtexts that could render into tangible narrative the unfocussed disquiet of a period that was yet to find expression. *Les Misérables* problematized the conflict between law and justice, suffering and survival, dehumanizing repression and the redemptive epiphany of human dignity against the turbulent period of a revolutionary France where people rose in mass revolt. This translation revamped the apparatus of fictional representation by making available to the reader a new discourse about being human. This amounted making visible the inner contradictions of a stratified society divided along caste, class, and gender.

A meeting of Progressive Literary Association was held at Thrissur in Kerala on 20 April 1937 under the leadership of K. Damodaran who had attended the 1936 Lucknow meeting, and a few political activists and writers like P. Keshav Dev, K. A. Damodara Menon, E. M. S. Nambuthiripad, C. Narayana Pillai, K. K. Variyar, P. Narayanan Nair, and A. Madhavan. It is significant to note that E. M. S. Nambuthiripad and K. A. Damodara Menon became well-known politicians later. During the proceedings of the meeting, contemporary Malayalam literature was criticized severely for its elitist bias and lack of social concern. The "Progressive Literary Association" was rechristened as "Jeeval Sahitya Samgham" in Malayalam to signify its close affinity with life ("*jeeva*" suggests "life") and "*jeeval sahityam*" (literature of life, literally) was defined as the "new literature that will promote equality of opportunity opposing the present exploitative system in favour of a realistic representation of man's struggles against nature as well as his circumstances."[9] In an article published in the Malayalam daily, *Mathrubhumi*, on 25 May 1937, the following objectives of the "*Jeeval Sahitya*" Movement were spelt out: "to publish literature of the progressive kind, to forge unity among progressive writers, to translate 'progressive literature' from other languages and oppose reactionary forces in culture and fight for the freedom of expression."[10] The model provided by Victor Hugo received further legitimation from the endorsement of social realist mode by progressive writers. As shown by the example of *Angare* in Urdu, the critical examination of existing social mores was the new role Progressive Movement had envisaged for writers. The social realist mode functioned as an oppositional discourse interrogating the existing attitudes to culture and contemporary social thought.

The trajectory of Jeeval Sahitya Samgham which held a series of meetings across Kerala in the next decade is one of bitter controversies and acrimonious dialogues between those who considered freedom of expression sacrosanct and those who wanted to use literature as a vehicle of social change. In the 1949 meeting held at Thrissur the eminent critic M. P. Paul who presided over it spoke against the main resolution that sought to ensure the allegiance of the writers to the political ideology of the Communist movement. The Progressive Movement soon lost its sense of direction and purpose, but by

---

9 E. Sardarkutty, *Purogamana Sahitya Niroopanam* [A critical history of progressive literature] (Thiruvananthapuram: State Institute of Languages, Kerala, 1993), p. 49.

10 Ibid., p. 52.

this time it had succeeded in putting on the social agenda of writers in Malayalam issues related to the writer's commitment to political ideology, the relation between form and content and the irreconcilable dichotomies of aesthetics and politics in contemporary literature. In effect, the writings that appeared in the wake of the Progressive Literary Movement problematized the very idea of "the literary" and its relation with the socio-political.

A. Balakrishna Pillai and the European Avant-Garde

The radicalization of literary discourse during this phase of Malayalam literature was largely achieved through the agency of translation. Here we will briefly examine the critical role of the writer A. Balakrishna Pillai who through his interventions as editor, translator, literary critic and social commentator shaped a secular, progressive and analytical language to speak of literature and its relation to life. Though A. Balakrishna Pillai was never part of the Progressive Literary Movement, he supported its radical agenda, articulating its core ideas through commentaries and review articles in his periodicals and prologues to contemporary works. He was arrested thrice by the Travancore government for inciting "rebellion." His periodicals *Prabodhakan* and *Kesari* in the 1930s, proscribed later by the authorities, published a wide variety of translations from European avant-garde literature. A. Balakrishna Pillai, by combining the role of political activist, literary critic and social thinker, redefined the relation between literature and the public sphere in Kerala society. In the pages of the periodical *Kesari*, A. Balakrishna Pillai published translations of major European authors who had experimented with new language and style. He encouraged writers like Thakazhi Sivasankara Pillai to translate social realist fiction from European languages. Among the writers A. Balakrishna Pillai translated and published were Flaubert, Mauppasant, Balazac, Stendhal, and Ibsen. In his editorials he dealt with literary subjects along with social and political topics which mounted scathing attacks on the king and his diwan of Travancore. In an editorial written on 21 January 1931, titled

"The Turbulent Malayalam Literature," A. Balakrishna Pillai argued that free thinking and "desecration of the idols" (*vigraha dhwamsanam* in Malayalam) is essential for literature to develop. The epic as a form, he said, was in decline all over the world. Quoting the Italian critic Croce, he argued that there was no essential difference between prose and verse. His essays contained translations from European thinkers and writers, translations clearing a space and breaching the closed world of prevailing literary culture.

What these translations of avant-garde authors from Europe and America belonging to different schools of writing collectively did was to create a literary public sphere where the discourses of literature were seen as part of socio-political discourses. The critical role of literature, particularly the novel, in democratizing society can be discerned in these comments taken from his essay, "The Pitiable State of Malayalam Prose":

> When Malayalam writers produce novels portraying the reality of Kerala society, they will have to be critical of Kerala society. When they do so, the government, the Universities and then text-book committees will withdraw their patronage though they would not send them to jail as Mussolini did in Italy. Real novels can appear only when this state of affairs changes. And the public will have to work very hard to change it.[11]

His book, *Novel Prasthanangal* documents the new trends in European novel elaborately through examples. The essays in this book carry translations of long passages from European novels to illustrate the narrative styles and techniques of writers such as Marcel Proust, Thomas Mann, Andre Gide, John Dos Passos, D. H. Lawrence, and Faulkner. The psychological breakthrough achieved in the treatment of sexuality by Western writers is highlighted in another long section. A. Balakrishna Pillai's interest in European avant-garde was prompted by the need to critique the Malayalam literary field. Central to his project was the creation of a new social imaginary which enables writers to critique the practices of a society

11 A. Balakrishna Pillai, *Novel Prasthanangal* [Movements in the history of the novel] (Kottayam: D. C. Books, 1991), p. 11.

and create a modern secular literary discourse. A. Balakrishna Pillai also wrote extensively on the new trends in European art illustrating with examples the characteristics of movements such as Impressionism, Post-Impressionism, Cubism, Futurism, Expressionism, Surrealism, and the Abstract Art. He has entire essays on Van Gogh, Cezanne, Picasso, and other masters of European art. What this accent on the European avant-garde achieved in the 1930s and 1940s in Malayalam was the creation of a new consciousness about the role of art and literature in society. This enabled a new generation of writers to question the existing poetic, and through it, the prevailing prestige styles of literature and its canons. *The Scavenger's Son* and *Two Measures of Rice* by Thakazhi Sivasankara Pillai, *The Voices* by Vaikkom Muhammad Basheer, and stories such as "The Goddess of Revenge" and "Admission of Guilt" by Lalitambika Antarjanam partake of the new social imaginary as a metaphorical space that maps the fault-lines and fissures of a fractured society and polity. Nation becomes a contested space where the false consensus of elitist narratives is critiqued from the margins. Most of the writers of this period such as Thakazhi Sivasankara Pillai, Keshav Dev, and Ponkunnam Varkey were also translators. The domain of fiction externalizes the oppositional content through the marginalized voices which became available for representation through the enabling role provided by translation.

Translation as Refraction/Rewriting

The concept of translation has to be understood in wider perspective in the context of this article. Andre Lefevere has argued that literature is a system "embedded in the environment of a culture or society"[12] and that "the degree to which the foreign writer is accepted in the native system will be determined by the need that native system has of him in a certain phase of its evolution."[13] It is the inner dynamics of the native literary

12 Lawrence Venuti, ed., *The Translation Studies Reader* (London and New York: Routledge, 2000), p. 235.

13 Ibid., p. 237.

system that decides the "acceptability" of the translated works. Lefevere also argues that we need to expand the very concept of translation to include various forms of receptions of foreign authors. He uses the word "refractions" or "rewriting" to suggest:

> Refractions are to be found in the obvious form of translation, or in the less obvious form of criticism (the wholesale allegorization of the literature of the Antiquity by the Church Fathers, e.g.), commentary, historiography (of the plot summary of famous works cum evaluation type, in which the evaluation is unabashedly based on the current concept of what "good" literature should be), teaching, the collection of works in anthologies, the production of plays.[14]

New writing styles and themes come to be validated through the patronage extended to the translations, thus facilitating a transformation in the very structure of the sensibility. The patterns of contestations of the prevailing "prestige styles," initiated by the A. Balakrishna Pillai's critical articles, became an organized form of revolt with the arrival of Progressive Literary Movement in Malayalam. The debates on the relative merits of the old and the new, the role of the artist in society, and the relation between literature and politics soon defined the direction taken by the literature in the next two decades.

To illustrate the nature of these debates we may briefly look at the arguments of those who opposed the Progressive Literary Movement. Kuttikrishna Marar, an eminent critic, was outspoken in his contempt for the group of writers who supported "*jeeval sahityam*." He agreed that all literature has a social function of imparting moral instruction. However, for him, the literary form was primary and not the content. It is the formal perfection that enables art to influence society and not the mere fact of its content. A. Balakrishna Pillai had argued that a poet or a novelist is only a skilled worker and he cannot claim any greater status than other skilled workers in society. Kuttikrishna Marar countered that readers have to make efforts to reach the sublime levels attained by the aesthetic beauty of

14 Venuti, *The Translation Studies Reader*, p. 235.

the artist. He or she has to cultivate taste through education and reflection since the artist will always remain above and beyond the reader.[15] The key words of the debate that continued through the thirties and the forties were life, society, reality, commitment, art for art's sake, art for life's sake, proletarian literature vs. "prestige" literature, form and content, and the public role of the artist. In his history of Malayalam literature, N. Krishna Pillai lists more than 40 European and American novelists who were translated into Malayalam during the three decades from the mid-thirties.[16]

The social energy generated by these translations and debates democratized literature and widened the literary public sphere. The new fiction could effectively channelize this social energy into narratives of resistance which began appearing in Malayalam from the late 1930s onwards. Thakazhi's *Thyagathinte Pratiphalam* (The reward for the sacrifice, 1939) tells the life of a woman forced into prostitution. P. Keshav Dev's *Otayilninnu* (From the gutter, 1948) narrates the struggles of a rickshaw-puller to lead a life of dignity. Thakazhi's *Thottiyude Makan* (The scavenger's son, 1948) narrates the life of the depressed classes who are condemned to work as scavengers, *Rantidangazhi* (Two measures of rice, 1949) the life of the Dalit farmers from Kuttanad. Vaikkom Muhammad Basheer's *Balyakalasakhi* (Childhood friend, 1944) tells a tragic love story against the background of poverty and suffering set in Muslim community, while his *Sabdangal* (The voices, 1947) projects the traumatic memories of an ex-soldier haunted by war and violence. Previously unknown communities now became visible through fictional narratives. Indian society that had been immobilized by colonial power structures and the stratified caste system resulting in the alienation of large section of Indian society found its articulation through these oppositional narratives.

15 Kuttikrishna Marar, *Theranjedutha Prabandhangal* [Selected essays] (Trichur [Thrissur]: Kerala Sahitya Akademi, 1990), pp. 354–359.

16 N. Krishna Pillai, *Kairaliyude Katha* [A history of Malayalam literature] (Kottayam: SPCS, 1998), p. 375.

Conclusion

To conclude, it was the agency of translation in all its various forms of "refraction"/"rewriting" that mediated the creation of a literary "public sphere" by legitimating new modes of expression and mapping new contours of experience. Translation negotiates between two literary sensibilities, pluralizing centres of authorities and opening up possibilities when a literary system is in a state of ferment. Editorials in the periodicals, manifestoes of the literary associations, commentaries on new books and authors, descriptions of new artistic and literary movements, debates on the comparative merits of two approaches to art and aesthetics, introductions to anthologies and new historiography have to be studied in consonance with translations to understand how the literary system in Malayalam and other Indian languages during the Progressive phase developed a new habitus and a new poetic that reflected as well as engaged the contradictions of a transitional period and formulated a new equation between the literary and the political by incorporating the marginalized into the literary public sphere.

Bibliography

Anand, Mulk Raj. "On the Progressive Writers Movement." In vol. 1 of *Marxist Cultural Movement in India*, edited by S. Pradhan. Calcutta [Kolkata]: National Book Agency, 1979, pp. 20–21.

Chandrasekharan, M. R. *Keralathile Purogamana Sahityathinte Charitram* [A history of progressive literature in Kerala]. Kottayam: D. C. Books, 2010.

Coppalo, Carlo. "Premchand's Address to the First Meeting of the All India Progressive Literary Association: Some Speculations." *Journal of South Asian Literature* 21, no. 2 (1986), pp. 21–39.

Das, Sisir Kumar. *A History of Indian Literature 1911–1956: Struggle for Freedom: Triumph and Tragedy*. New Delhi: Sahitya Akademi, 1995.

Gopal, Priyamvada. *Literary Radicalism in India: Gender, Nation and the Transition to Independence*. London and New York: Routledge, 2005.

Jain, Jasbir. *The Writer as Critic: Essays in Literature, History and Culture*. Jaipur and Delhi: Rawat Publications, 2010.

Marar, Kuttikrishna. *Theranjedutha Prabandhangal* [Selected essays]. Trichur [Thrissur]: Kerala Sahitya Akademi, 1990.

Pillai, A. Balakrishna. *Kesariyude Lokangal* [Selected prose of Kesari Balakrishna Pillai]. Tellicherry: Kesari Krithikalude Prasidheekarana Samithi, 1989.

———. *Naveena Chitrakala* [Essays on art]. Thrissur [Trichur]: Lalita Kala Akademi, 1990.

———. *Novel Prasthanangal* [Movements in the history of the novel]. Kottayam: D. C. Books, 1991.

———. *Kesariyude Mukhaprasangangal* [The editorials from Kesari]. Kottayam: D. C. Books, 2010.

Pillai, N. Krishna. *Kairaliyude Katha* [A history of Malayalam literature]. Kottayam: SPCS, 1998.

Sankaran, Thayattu. *Theranjedutha Prabadhangal* [Selected essays]. Thrissur: Kerala Sahitya Akademi, 2007.

Sardarkutty, E. *Purogamana Sahitya Niroopanam* [A critical history of progressive literature]. Thiruvananthapuram: State Institute of Languages, Kerala, 1993.

Singh, K. P. "Premchand's Ideology." *Social Scientist* 5, no. 3 (October 1976), pp. 69–76.

Venuti, Lawrence, ed. *The Translation Studies Reader*. London and New York: Routledge, 2000.

Russian Literature in Marathi[1] Polysystem:
In the Colonial and Neocolonial Context

Megha PANSARE

Introduction

The modern approach to translation does not treat literature as an autonomous and independent domain. It is seen in a much broader social and cultural framework. Literature is understood, from this perspective, in relation with other social institutions. Modern translation theory examines the complex interconnections between poetics, politics, metaphysics, economics, and history. It is closely allied to the discipline of cultural studies and is keenly interested in the historical and political dimensions of literature.[2]

---

1 Marathi is an Indo-Aryan language of the larger Indo-European family. Evolving from Sanskrit through Prakrit and Apabhransha, it is believed to be 1,300 years old. The oldest document found in Marathi dates back to 700 CE. Marathi is written in the Devanagari script. It is spoken mainly by the Marathi or Maharashtrians living in the state of Maharashtra. It is also spoken in some other regions of India, in Mauritius and Israel. Emigrant Maharashtrians worldwide, especially in the US and Europe, also speak Marathi. Spoken by 90 million speakers, 70 million native and 20 million second-language speakers, it is considered to be the fourth most spoken language in India and fifteenth in the world. Today, standard Marathi is the official language of the State of Maharashtra.

2 "It is necessary to include translated literature in the polysystem. This is rarely done, but no observer of the history of any literature can avoid recognizing as an important fact the impact of translations and their role in the synchrony and diachrony of a certain literature." Itamar Even-Zohar, *Papers in Historical Poetics*, Papers on Poetics and Semiotics 8, ed. Benjamin Hrushovsky and Itamar Even-Zohar (Tel Aviv: University Publishing Projects, 1978), p. 15. Quoted from Edwin Gentzler, *Contemporary Translation Theories* (London and New York: Routledge, 1993), p. 116.

Itamar Even-Zohar, in his *Polysystem Theory*, emphasizes that translated literature operates as a system in two ways:

1. in the way the Target Language (TL) selects works for translation;
2. in the way translation norms, behaviour and policies are influenced by other co-systems.

Thus, for the polysystem theory, the system of translated literature does not work in isolation. It fully participates in the history of literary polysystem, as an integral part of it, and is related with all other co-systems. The polysystem approach, therefore, endeavours to arrive at a historical and social understanding of the way translated works function collectively, as a subsystem within the target polysystem.

Gideon Toury (1985), working on similar lines, emphasizes that translations are facts of one system alone: the target system and it is the target or recipient culture or a certain section of it which serves as the initiator of the decision to translate; and consequently translators operate first and foremost in the interest of the culture into which they are translating.

We can study the tradition of translation from Russian into Marathi in view of the polysystem approach. It is hoped that the polysystem approach can be quite productive in translation studies. That is why the present paper seeks to analyse the broad historical and socio-political context in which Russian literature entered the Marathi polysystem and the resultant mechanisms operating in this interface. The paper attempts to present its analysis in two parts:

1. An overview of the Russo-Indian contact, which served as a background for the cultural interface that facilitated the entry of Russian literature into Marathi; and
2. The making of the Marathi polysystem, wherein we examine the evolution of translation culture during the colonial and neocolonial periods, creating a space for Russian literature.

The Russo-Indian Contact

The cultural contacts between central Asian countries including India and Russia existed from ancient times.[3] Buddhist missionaries and traders from India had established religious and commercial links with Russian people. But there is no written record about these pioneers and adventurers. Afanasy Nikitin, a Russian trader, was the first Russian to record his unique experiences in India in the fifteenth century.

India has a long history of cultural contact with other countries. The Western countries' interest in India was motivated mainly by the concerns of their colonial policies. Most of the Western writers glorified the "mission" of the Europeans to "civilize" India.[4] Russo-Indian relations in the nineteenth and twentieth centuries were determined in terms of the general international situation of the time and political and socio-economic factors operative in the Russian Empire, in Great Britain, and in colonial India.

At the beginning of the nineteenth century there were some 2,000 miles separating British India and the outlying regions of Tsarist Russia. Much of the land in between was unmapped. The expansion of imperial Russia threatened to destroy the so-called *jewel in the crown* of the British Empire, India. "The Great Game" was the term used to describe the rivalry and strategic conflict between the British Empire and the Tsarist Russian Empire for supremacy in central Asia.[5] The colonial enslavement of India disrupted her long economic and cultural links with other countries,

---

3 Great Indian scholar Rahul Sanskrutyayan (1893–1963) in his book *Volga se Ganga* (1944) traces this contact back to 8,000 years ago (6000 BCE).

4 "The languages of Western Europe civilized Russia. I cannot doubt that they will do for the Hindoo what they have done for the Tartar." Thomos Macaulay, "Minute by the Hon'ble T. B. Macaulay, Dated 2 February 1835," in *Selections from Educational Records, Part I (1781–1839)*, ed. Henry Sharp (Calcutta: Superintendent, Government Printing, 1920; repr., Delhi: National Archives of India, 1965), pp. 107–117.

5 In Russia the term was known as the *Tournaments of Shadows* (*Турниры теней*). The classic Great Game period is generally regarded as running from approximately 1813 to the Anglo-Russian Convention in 1907. The Bolshevik Revolution of 1917 nullified existing treaties and a second phase of the Great Game began. In May 1921, Afghanistan and the Russian Soviet Republic signed a Treaty of Friendship.

including those with Russia. Very little information on Russia reached India at the end of the eighteenth and the beginning of the nineteenth century. The British denied Indians access to accurate information about Russia and the life of the people there. Although the Russian Consulate was established in Mumbai in British India under the Trade and Commerce Treaty in 1859, the British-Indian authorities were extremely suspicious of the Russians and all staff-members of the Consulate were under permanent and vigilant police surveillance. The Consulate of Russia in Bombay helped, to some extent, in organizing the visits of Russian scientists, engineers, and cultural workers to Maharashtra. Yet the British government tried to keep Indians in dark about the revolutionary movements in Russia.[6]

In spite of the reluctance of the British administration some humanitarian exchanges between the two countries had started as early as the mid-nineteenth century. Some Russian literature found its way through English translations. However, major interest in Russian literature developed only in the twentieth century. The development of the national liberation movement in India and the upsurge of the revolutionary struggle in Russia gave a new meaning and dimension to Russo-Indian links. An exchange of emancipatory ideas in the two countries began in the early twentieth century. Vladimir Lenin himself noted the political significance of the agitation launched by the Bombay Mill Workers in protest against Lokmanya Tilak's arrest. This shows that there must have been some indirect interactions between the two societies. These further developed into more organized contacts. Many Indian patriots were inspired by the mass revolutionary movement in Russia. They realized the need for intensifying organized mass struggle against colonial oppression and spreading socialist ideas in India. The Indian revolutionaries were in close contact with political émigrés from Russia.[7]

6 While speaking at the Indian Legislative Assembly, great freedom fighter Mr Motilal Nehru had asked the British in 1929: "Can you erect barbed wire entanglements and artificial barriers to keep ideas out of India?" See Shriniwas Sardesai, *India and the Russian Revolution* (New Delhi: Communist Party Publications, 1967), p. 77.

7 Evgeni Chelyshev and Alexei Litman, *Traditions of Great Friendship* (USSR: Raduga Publishers, 1985).

The October Revolution (1917) in Russia had an enormous impact on the rise of the National Liberation Movement in India. It opened new prospects for the Indian people in their struggle against the colonial and social oppression. Indian patriots and leaders welcomed the victory of the Bolshevik socialist revolution. In February 1922, following the violence in Chauri-Chaura, the National Congress withdrew the Civil Disobedience campaign at the suggestion of Mahatma Gandhi, which resulted in the frustration among a number of young activists. This was the time when the Communist movement started taking a concrete shape in India. In 1920s, the October Revolution and the Socialist experiment in Russia inspired publication of books and journals, which appeared mostly underground.[8] The authorities persecuted those who published Communist literature. The organizers of the magazine *The Socialist* were arrested and charged of hatching a conspiracy to overthrow the British regime. This came to be known as the "Kanpur Bolshevik Conspiracy." The persons involved were tried and sentenced to lengthy terms in prison. In December 1925, the Communist Party of India was founded. The authorities invariably hounded members of the Communist Party and trade unions. Many of their leaders were arrested and put on trial. The Kanpur Bolshevik Conspiracy[9] case (1924) and the Meerut Conspiracy trial[10] (1929–1932)

8 They include *Gandhi vs. Lenin* (1921) written by Shripad Amrit Dange, and the journals *The Socialist* (1924), *The Worker* (1925), *Revolution* (1926) published by the Communists.

9 Manavendra Nath Roy, Dange and others were charged, in what was called the Cawnpore (now spelt Kanpur) Bolshevik Conspiracy case. The specific charge was that they as Communists were seeking "to deprive the King Emperor of his sovereignty of British India, by complete separation of India from imperialistic Britain by a violent revolution."

10 Several trade unionists, including three Englishmen, were arrested for organizing Indian-rail strike in March 1929. The main charges were that in 1921 Dange, Shaukat Usmani, and Muzaffar Ahmad entered into a conspiracy to establish a branch of Comintern in India and they were helped by various persons sent to India by the Communist International. The aim of the accused persons, according to the charges raised against them, was under section 121–A of the Indian Penal Code (Act 45 of 1860) to deprive the King Emperor of the sovereignty of British India, and for such purpose to use the methods and carry out the programme and plan of campaign

ultimately helped to spread the ideas of Communism. A number of accused in the Meerut trial were from Maharashtra. The Communist movement, although seriously suppressed, revived in 1933. But again in 1934, the authorities declared the Communist Party illegal, and it was again forced to go underground. This greatly hampered its operations. In spite of the police censorship, vicious slander, and misinformation about the Russian Revolution in the bourgeois newspapers, many Indians from the National Liberation Movement, writers and journalists grasped the significance of the revolution. Indians with a progressive outlook were influenced by the doctrines of Karl Marx and Vladimir Lenin. Reading of Marxian literature and the Russian Revolution encouraged not only a spirit of freedom amongst the subject people, but also the revolutionary class concept of political and social change.

The October Socialist Revolution in Russia and the emergence of Communist movement in Maharashtra created favourable condition for dissemination of Russian political literature. This politically charged atmosphere of the time facilitated the entry of Russian literature into the Marathi polysystem.

During the World War II, many Indian writers and poets glorified the feats of the Soviet army fighting against the Nazi aggressors. The heroic resistance of the Soviet people and their victory in the war created a wave of admiration among the Indians. It gave a new spirit to the struggle of the oppressed in the world. The democratization of literature became the first item on the agenda of cultural resurgence. Indian writers experienced a need to link themselves with the progressive trends in world literature, especially Russian literature.

It was against this background that the literature about Russia started emerging and being translated in India. It included articles, essays, feature stories, memoirs, poetry, prose, drama, research papers on various political, socio-cultural aspects of Soviet life, literary criticism of books by

---

outlined and ordained by the Communist International. In the trial the accused were all labelled as Bolsheviks. During the trial of four and a half years, the defendants turned the courtroom into a public platform to espouse their cause.

Soviet authors, and studies of Russian language. Books and articles on the October Revolution and Lenin, ideas of Marx and Engels, and literature on socialism were now being published regularly in the country.

Within the Marathi Polysystem

As has been noted, literature is an organic part of the social, cultural, and historical framework. It is organically embedded in a particular social ethos in which various systems of cultural production operate within the context of certain conventions. Translation too is not merely a linguistic activity but a cross-cultural, communicative phenomenon. Hence, it cannot be separated from society and culture, in fact from the social and historical formation in which it is generated. It therefore becomes essential to examine, from a historical perspective, the conditions in the socio-cultural ethos of Maharashtra in which Marathi translators turned towards Russian literature. It is interesting to see what relationship developed between the Russian and Marathi cultures, and more specifically, between Russian literature and the Marathi literary polysystem.

Earlier we put forth a proposition that the tradition of Russian literature in Marathi emerged as a part of cultural change that took place in the nineteenth- and twentieth-century Maharashtra in the prominently colonial background. Russian fiction appeared in Marathi in 1932, during the British colonial period. Historians often refer to the nineteenth- and twentieth-century period as the renaissance period in Marathi. The basis of this renaissance was the contact between the East and the West. In the beginning of the nineteenth century, viz. in 1818, the Peshwa rule in Maharashtra came to an end. The Peshwa rule was characterized by the domination and exploitation by the Brahmin caste of the rest of the community. Education, mostly of religious practices, was a prerogative of the Brahmins. Both the educational as well as cultural life was dominated by this caste. The common people led a hard life. Religion and caste were the most dominant, self-perpetuating and self-sufficient systems organizing social life. The Brahmins considered Marathi as a vulgar language and the Vedic language Sanskrit was held in high esteem. This, of course, was to deprive the masses of any recourse to intellectual activity. Marathi had not developed as a medium of education or a means of intellectual discourse.

The entry of the British power in India, and specifically in Maharashtra, created a new dynamism in the socio-cultural life of the native people. New values of democracy, equality, rationality, and individualism started making inroads in social life. Five important influences that led the society to the renaissance were: the rise of British-India commerce and trade, the introduction of English education, British Orientalism, Christianity, and perhaps most importantly, the way intellectuals themselves responded to these influences. The native intellectuals unconditionally surrendered to the colonial strategies of domination initially because they were the first beneficiaries of new education and could visualize great opportunities in future. They became the agency in the strategies of the rulers. The initial response of the common people to this new regime was favourable. They welcomed the new rule, as they found it comparatively just and kind.

Marathi Literary Tradition

The foundations of Marathi prose were laid mainly by the Mahanubhavas[11] in the thirteenth century. There was a strong tradition of oral literary culture, which had achieved its own richness. But there was no sustained tradition of prose writing, especially for educational and intellectual interaction. Marathi was reconstructed through translations on the models of English and Sanskrit in the colonial period. Translation became

11 A religious sect founded by Shri Chakradhar Swami in 1267 which rejected the traditional ritualistic religion. People were accepted in the sect irrespective of their castes. Shri Chakradhar Swami regarded Marathi as the language of Religion in order to propagate the philosophy of his sect. His biography *Leela Charitra*, written by his disciple Mahimbhatta, is the first known prose text in Marathi. It is a significant historical reference work in socio-cultural studies of the society in the thirteenth-century Maharashtra.

the chief point of textual and cultural contact between the colonial rulers and the colonized people. Translation culture acquired a crucial position in the newly developing Marathi literary polysystem.[12]

Marathi had its own indigenous tradition of translations from Sanskrit.[13] All through the Middle Ages, Sanskrit classics like the epics and *puranas* continued to be retold, adapted, subverted, and "translated" into Marathi. However, a review of translation culture in Maharashtra in the nineteenth century shows us the evolution of Marathi literary polysystem and the role of translation in this process. We find a whole stratified subsystem of translated literature developed in Marathi literary culture. It includes:

1. translations of Bible done by various missionaries with an aim of proselytization;
2. translations of educational texts carried out in order to introduce a new educational system;
3. translations of popular literary works catering to the needs of ordinary readers.

Similar to the history in Europe and Britain, the translation culture developed and played a great role in materially realizing renaissance of ideas, language and literature in Maharashtra too. The old order collapsed,

12 Still under the involvement of European officials like James Molesworth and Thomas Candy a lot of work was done in the vocabulary and grammar in Marathi. The British compiled works on Marathi grammar and lexicography. William Carey (arrived in Calcutta 1793, died 1831) published in 1805 *A Grammar of the Mharatta Language* and *Saint Matthewche Shubhawartaman*, the first two printed books in Marathi. In 1810, came the *Marathi-English Kosh* [Marathi-English dictionary] in the Modi script with some 10,000 entries, the first modern Marathi-English dictionary. In 1831 Molesworth, assisted by George Candy and Thomas Candy, published the monumental *Marathi-English Dictionary*, a classic reference work even today.

13 *Bhavarthdeepika* or *Dnyaneshwari* written by Dnyaneshwar in 1290 is the best example of this tradition. It was a great work of interpreting the *Bhagwadgeeta* in the language of the people and bringing the spiritual solace within the reach of the common man. The activity of rewriting the Sanskrit texts into the regional languages ranged from commentaries "*teeka*," "*bhashya*" to more faithful renderings.

the new socio-political order was initiated and the literary polysystem developed. The language developed, particularly through the translations made during this period. One can thus consider the Indian renaissance to be essentially a function of the colonial situation. The British intentionally developed the polysystem of Marathi in their colonial interests and gave impetus to the translation culture in Maharashtra.

Many scholars in Marathi tried to relate the state of the language with the state of the country. In their view translation was a means to develop their own language. This era saw a vibrant debate on the relationship between readers and writers, emergence of translation criticism, discussions on the problems in the translation process, relationship between translation and independent literature, criteria for evaluation of translation and their relation with literary criticism. A debate developed between the two methods of translation, i.e. faithful translation and adaptation. For some scholars[14] translation was the most important means of enriching Marathi. While some others[15] looked at translation as an instrument of social change, a weapon in the hands of the reformers who aimed at cultural and political reorganization of society.

Vishwanath Kashinath Rajwade (1863–1926), a renowned Marathi historian, strongly protested against the established translation culture. He tried to redefine the role of the translator. In his view, the function of the translator was to make readers conscious of the terrible fate that had befallen on the people as a result of exploitation—social, religious, economic and political. He rejected the trend of adaptations and equated the faithful translation to a nationalistic consciousness. Indeed, the importance he attached to translation is evident from the fact that he started a journal called *Bhashanta* (Translation) in 1894. The Marathi literary polysystem was dominated at the turn of the century by the populist writings of popular novels in England. Rajwade made an attempt

14 Vishnushastri Chiplunkar (1850–1882) completed the translations of *Russell* as begun by his father.

15 Gopal Ganesh Agarkar (1856–1895) translated *Hamlet* with the title *Vikar-Vilasit*, which has a long preface on the problems of translation and the state of the Marathi language.

to free the translation culture from the clutches of populism whereby writers had translated or adapted only the popular and substandard writers like Henry Wood, Lord Litton, and Reynolds, etc. for the newly educated middle-class readers who wanted something to read that could entertain them. Rajwade stated that there is a vast difference in the quality of writings of English authors and that of French or other European writers. English writers do not go beyond "the individual." He argued that the novels with social and national spirit flourished only in France and Russia. There was a lack of independent literary creations in England. According to Rajwade the main reason for this was the imperialist policy and accumulation of wealth in England through exploitation of India and consequently its ignorance of education and arts. He felt that literature played an important role in the socio-political developments in any nation.[16]

> Thanks to the absolutist state power of the Tsar, there is no freedom of press in Russia and people cannot express their thoughts through a proper channel. As a result, Russian authors had to express their nationalistic feelings through novels since 1840, i.e. from the time when Gogol's first novel was published. *The Cossacks, Guerreet Paix, Anna Karenina*, etc. are the well-known novels of writers like Gogol, Goncharov, Pisensky, Dostoevsky, Turgenev, and Tolstoy. The thinking of the young generation in Russia is shaped by reading these novels.[17] (Translated from Marathi by author)

This erudite scholar urged translators to encompass the works not of the substandard *English* writers, but those of the great masters of the *European* tradition like Zola, Balzac, Dumas, Hugo, and Tolstoy. He rejected the tradition of the contemporary English romance writers and acclaimed the tradition of realistic novels in European culture. He criticized the tendency in the translators to adapt the source texts to cater to the populist taste.

16 Vishwanath Kashinath Rajwade, "Kadambari" [The novel], in *Nivadak Sahitya Sameeksha* [A criticism of selected literature], ed. Gopal Maruti Pawar and Madhukar Dattatraya Hatkananglekar (New Delhi: Sahitya Akademi, 1999), p. 28.

17 Rajwade, "Kadambari," p. 31.

He felt that the function of translators was to mould the public taste as well. He analysed the role of translators during the renaissance of English literature and argued that it was the translations which had brought to the people "knowledge" relevant for building the nation. Thus Rajwade talks about creating an alternative path for the development of the nation through translations.[18] He talks about creating an alternative translation culture which translators of Russian literature later on actualized.

Many times translation is treated by the contemporary intellectuals as a noble task of bridging the gap between peoples, as a *humanistic* endeavour. Translation is seen as performing the task of providing the people with the knowledge about *unknown* people. However, translations of non-English literatures by the Marathi literary polysystem during the growth and expansion of colonialism have great socio-political implication. It can be seen as a process of negating the established colonial English culture as well as accepting new views and ideological values through translations of other cultures. Here, as it becomes evident, the intense disillusionment of a section of intellectual strata gave rise to establishing new contacts with world literature, including Russian literature.

In the nineteenth century, Marathi prose was in the process of development and was acquiring a new form based on the English model. The traditions of indigenous prose writing were totally forgotten under the influence of English. The form of fiction emerged in Marathi literary system mainly through translations and imitations of the English novel. However, gradually we see the beginnings of a realistic tradition in Marathi fiction. Absorbing Western literary and cultural influences, the novels depicted the harsh socio-cultural reality of that time. Rajwade categorically gives a new direction to an understanding of the creative writers in Marathi:

> So, every novelist must consider it his primary duty to depict the status of the downtrodden in the society. The novelists from nations, which have become blind in opulence, may find it shameful. Let it be. But the

18 Maya Narkar, "A Linguistic Study of the Nineteenth Century Marathi Translations" (Ph.D. dissertation, Shivaji University, Kolhapur, 1990).

> novelists from India, from Maharashtra, should not think that way. Who else will take cause of the ordinary masses in this country tormented by poverty, troubled by diseases and lacking education, if not the novelists, the concrete embodiments of kindness? There is no other means except a novel to realistically impress the status of people on their own minds. A great responsibility has befallen on the novelists in Maharashtra to make proper and full use of this means.[19] (Translated from Marathi by author)

Going through this tradition, Marathi literature in the twentieth century underwent a radical change in form and content and turned decisively towards realism.

After the death of Lokmanya Tilak, a leader of the Indian freedom movement, in 1920, the impact of Mahatma Gandhi's Satyagraha movement was felt in Maharashtra at the beginning of 1930s. The trade-union movement gathered much strength in the twenties, and was largely controlled by the Communists. Communism had a limited following in Maharashtra, yet the youth welcomed the leftist literature, creative as well as theoretical, enthusiastically. The left thought strongly impacted both Marathi prose and poetry. Anant Kanekar, a renowned Marathi author, writes:

> So, when there emerged a wave of progressive literature in Indian writers around 1935, and when Marathi newspapers were producing editorials on Marxism in Marathi literature, Maxim Gorky from Russia and Upton Sinclair from America had become our Gods; and their novels and their short stories had become our scriptures.[20] (Translated from Marathi by author)

Earlier, the Western influence meant only English influence. But the situation changed gradually and radically. The English influence waned as the Indian youth responded to the volatile international situation with great vigour. Now there was a great international awareness among the youth, as it followed the developments in other countries of Europe. Now

19 Rajwade, "Kadambari," p. 34.

20 Anant Kanekar, "Upton Sinclair," in *Nilya Thinagya* [Blue sparks] (Nagpur: Saroj Prakashan, 1972), pp. 47–48.

the West was no more confined to England. In the literary scene, many of the Victorian models were displaced and even thrown away by the new writers. The German and Soviet novelists, who resisted the Nazis, provided stimulation to them.

> As entertaining novels were being written in Marathi in large numbers, the readers did not feel any need to read novels from foreign languages for entertainment. The people started looking at literature in foreign languages to understand complexities of human mind, and further enrich their literary experience. We turned to Russian literature at around 1935. The main force behind this was the Russian Revolution. The Marathi mind developed an inclination towards Russian literature thanks to the influence of socialist thought.[21] (Translated from Marathi by author)

The most important and far-reaching impact made by the Socialist Revolution and renaissance was in the field of Marathi journalism. It brought into existence a new genre, the literary essay. The newspapers extended the mental horizons of their readers far beyond their usual narrow vision. The periodicals awakened the curiosity of the newly educated classes about the events in the world and their impact on India. They introduced the revolutionary philosophical ideas of the Western world, particularly those of the British Left. The educated middle-class youth started publishing newspapers, periodicals, and books with an aim to create a new awareness among the people. In Maharashtra, the newspapers became a means of enlightenment of the neo-literate masses. But the British tried to suppress the new liberal thought by imposing the Press Act (1879). A movement started against this policy of the government generating a demand to stop the suppression of the writing-printing-publishing rights of the people. Resolutions were passed in various Marathi Literary Conferences (*Sahitya Sammelans*) held in 1921, 1926, 1927, 1934, and 1936 against the restrictions on freedom of thought and printing literature. There was a ban

21 Chandrakant Bandiwadekar, *Marathi Kadambaricha Itihas (1920–1947)* [A history of Marathi novel (1920–1947)] (1989; repr., Pune: Mehta Publishing House, 1996), p. 154.

on Russian literature, too.[22] A large section of intelligentsia used to read the underground literature on Communist movement through English. Many books were translated and distributed among Marathi readers.[23] Social and socialist realism also emerged as a force in the post-war Marathi literature. We find the reflection of Marxist ideology in poetry, travelogues, and essays. A summarized form of Marx's *The Capital* was also published. There was a raging controversy, in the forties and fifties, in Marathi literary circles around the concept of the function of art. The entire literary community was divided along two axes: "Art for Art's sake" and "Art for Life's sake." Marxist critics naturally propounded the concept of "Art for Life's sake." For them, art was a product of the socio-economic conditions under which it was produced, and the artist had a responsibility to the society. In this context, the word "progressive" acquired a positive meaning. Thus the entire intellectual milieu was engulfed by "progressive" ideas. During 1935–1945, much was written and discussed on democracy, nationalism, dictatorship, Communism, fascism and war in the print media. This includes books and articles on Socialism, materialism, Marxian Dialectics, Imperialism, the history of Communism, the Communist State, the Russian social system, the changing status of Russia after the Bolshevik Revolution, whether there was real Communism in Russia, and so on.[24]

---

22 The Communist literature occupied a definite space in the society and the imperialist state was not in a position to accept it. A list of 144 books banned and seized by the government was published by *Kesari*, which includes books on the history of Russian revolution, trade union, Communist ideology, and biography of Lenin. See Govind Malhar Kulkarni and Vasant Digambar Kulkarni, *Marathi Vangmayacha Itihas—1920–1950* [A history of Marathi literature, 1920–1950], vol. 6 (Pune: Maharashtra Sahitya Parishad, 1991), part 2, pp. 412–417.

23 Anna Bhau Sathe (1920–1969), a well-known Marathi writer, mentions in his travelogue *My Journey to Russia*: "I had gone through many books banned in this country around 1934. Books like *The History of Russian Revolution, The Biography of Lenin* had made great impression on my mind." (Translated from Marathi by author.) See Anna Bhau Sathe, *Maza Rushiyacha Pravas* [My journey to Russia], 6th ed. (Pune: Suresh Agency, 2005), p. 2.

24 Yashwant Gopal Joshi published 12 books on these themes in Marathi. The books were written by Pandurang Vaman Gadgil, Kamal Narayan Phadake, Narayan Ganesh Gore, and Lakshmanshastri Joshi. In a series of articles *Tirangi Navmatwad* [Tricoloured

The Progressive Writers' Association (PWA, 1936) and Indian People's Theatre Association (IPTA, 1942) started advocating socialist realism and played a catalytic role in the development of modern literature. This movement brought forth significant changes in the attitudes of writers and artists. The latter became more aware of international problems. They took sides on world issues. Their horizons were broadened. They became conscious of a continuous war against exploitation, poverty, ignorance, superstition, casteism, and communalism.

The Russian Connection

A review of the history of Russo-Indian contact and of the developments in Marathi translation culture during the colonial period reveals the complex interconnections between poetics, politics, metaphysics, economics, and history. We see how the subsystem of translated literature has been an integral part of the progress of Marathi language and culture. It shows how the system of translated literature fully participates in the history of the literary polysystem. The review makes clear how the British developed the translation culture in Marathi for their colonial interests and how, reacting to it, the Marathi intelligentsia turned, among other literatures, towards Russian literature and a space for translations from Russian into Marathi was created at a particular phase of the political history in Maharashtra.

During the colonial period the Marathi intelligentsia used to read Russian literature in English, mostly political literature. However, there were attempts at fiction translations as well. The first novel translated from Russian into Marathi was published in 1932. It was a part of Maxim Gorky's *Mother* (1906), and was translated through English and was published by an association set up for dissemination of workers' literature, Mumbai.

---

new thinking], Narasinha Chintamani Kelkar introduced the political, social, and economic aspects of Communism. Taking *Navmatwad* as Communism, Kelkar wrote 12 articles in the newspaper *Kesari* [Saffron]. Narasinha Chintamani Kelkar, *Samagra Kelkar Vangmaya* [The complete works of Kelkar], vol. 3, *Kesari* (Pune: Manohar Mahadev Kelkar, 1938), pp. 815–956.

It would be interesting to look at the translations of Russian literature, as facts of the target system, i.e. Marathi. On the lines of Toury, we argue that it is the Marathi culture or a certain section of it, which has served as the initiator of the decision to translate. The translators have worked in the interest of the recipient culture. The selection of the literary works for translation is made taking into consideration the socio-political condition of the time and the need of the target culture. A few observations of the Russian fiction translated into Marathi support this proposition. Maksim Gorky and Leo Tolstoy are two major Russian authors, whose literature has been translated in great numbers in Marathi. Sixteen Russian novels entered Marathi literary polysystem during the period 1932 to 1947. They mainly include ten works of Soviet authors Gorky, Kuprin, Grossman, Sholokhov and six novels of pre-Soviet Russian authors Tolstoy and Turgenev. Three versions of Gorky's *Mother*, *Foma Gordeev*, and his two autobiographical works make a major part of this number. The major themes which the Marathi literary polysystem took interest in are classics by well-known writers, novels, and stories on October Revolution, the socialist system, history, civil war, World War II, and children's literature. An important observation regarding the translators reveals that except a few, no major mainstream Marathi writer has made an attempt to translate Russian literature. Lack of source-language knowledge may be one reason behind this, but there has been no attempt from their side to translate through English either. Most of the translators have taken up the translation activity through their ideological affinity towards Socialism and Soviet Russia. The contextual analysis reveals the facts about the intention/purpose of the translation activity, the choice of literary work, and the translation process in para-textual tools such as preface, introduction, translator's/publisher's note, blurb of books. They include factors such as the aesthetic value of literary works and its impact, ideology of the translator/publisher, relevance and functional value in the target culture, an urge to introduce classic literature to target readers, enrichment and development of the target language and literature, etc. A few examples of Marathi translations of Russian literature may prove to be self-explanatory here.

The first Marathi translation of Gorky's *Mother* (Part I, 1932) was published by Mumbai Association set up for the dissemination of workers' literature. There is no mention of the translator in the book. The preface speaks about the relevance of this novel to India. A note on the translation process makes it clear that the translation is literal and the reader has to be careful about a possible semantic loss. It mentions that there was a common trend in translating novels from other languages into Marathi, especially from the European ones. It consisted of transforming the original text, changing the location, culture, and time in the target text, that is, "rupantar" (adaptation). But the given translation did not follow the existing trend in the target language culture. This speaks of a clear stand on the part of the translator. The then contemporary reader was accustomed to adaptations of works from foreign languages, rather than their faithful translations. But in that case the translator was ready to reject the established model and use a new approach. This reminds us of the circumstances identified by Even-Zohar. The literary vacuum in Marathi for a work with a clear ideological stand made it possible for the translator to stick to his guns. However, the 1941 version of Marathi translation of *Mother* was an adaptation, a totally Indianized form of the novel.

We can compare the contextual information of the 1945 and 1958 versions of the same novel, which reveals the functional value of the target text. In a brief note "Two Words," which precedes the preface, the translator of the earlier version says:

> Gorky, through his novel, has shown an ideal to the writers in slave countries how to depict through literature realistically the human life and its problems in capitalist era....
>
> Gorky's *Mother* is a mother of peasants and workers. This *Mother* should be read in every room of workers' chawls and peasants' slums. It should be spread in millions of copies and hands.[25] (Translated from Marathi by author)

---

25 Maxim Gorky, "Preface," in *Aai* [Mother], trans. Vinayak Mahadev Bhuskute (Pune: Deshmukh ani Company, 1945).

The latest edition of the 1958 version of *Mother* in Marathi is available in market for the readers. The following statement by a well-known progressive Marathi poet is highlighted in the advertisement of the novel, thus expressing its functional role in the contemporary Marathi polysystem. On the occasion of the first centenary of the publication of novel *Mother* in Russian, the poet says:

> The day *Mother* waited for has not come yet. The struggle for its arrival, too, has not ended. It is possible that we need to fight for it incessantly; and will have to prepare ourselves for a long drawn struggle. We all, and the next generations to come, will have to read *Mother* again and again.[26] (Translated from Marathi by author)

Another example is of a blurb of the 1991 Marathi translation of the novella *Family Happiness* (1859). It describes the work as a tender love story of Tolstoy, written on his own experience, which seems fresh even today, just like it was then and also quite contemporary.

One of the Marathi translators of Russian literature in her book published in 2004 describes herself as a person having love for language and literature and says that she has selected only those stories, which are less descriptive and have more dialogues. She explains that she does not follow any political ideology and therefore none of the stories have the influence of political atmosphere or an awareness of the contemporary economic system. Hence, the most of these stories depict universal human concerns like family, love, human relations, etc.[27]

It is important to note that though Marathi polysystem created a space for Russian literature out of some specific political choice at a particular historical period, it has not confined its interest to only specific political literature. It has accepted the pre-Soviet, Soviet as well as dissident Russian literature. Russian literature did serve the primary function of building an interface between Russian and Marathi cultures. It has certainly enriched the

26 Satish Kalasekar, advertisement of *Aai* [Mother], *Apale Vangmaya Vritta* [News on our literature] (Mumbai), October 2007, p. 3.

27 Suniti Deshpande, *Antar-Parva* [Inter-epoch] (Pune: Mehta Publishing House, 2004).

target language and culture, introducing Marathi readers to a new language system as well as a new outlook, new values, and new trends in thought.

Translation Culture in Marathi in the Neocolonial Context

The collapse of the Soviet Union in 1991 and the setback to Communist ideology in East Europe made a deep impact on the minds of intellectuals and literary figures in Maharashtra. This was followed by the new economic policies adopted by the government and a phase of globalization. There appeared an ideological vacuum, which affected the various progressive socio-political movements in Maharashtra. The concept of *End of Ideology* was being put forward through the bourgeois mass media. Anti-establishment movements such as the Little Magazine Movement, the Dalit Movement, and the Feminist Movement received a setback and they became weak. All this was reflected in Marathi literature at the end of the twentieth century.

The translation culture in Maharashtra has seen great changes in recent years, especially in the first decade of the twenty-first century. These changes become visible in the framework of changing socio-economic conditions in India in the context of globalization, free market economy and the effects of consumerism. The translation activity has flourished today with increasing number of translated works being published day by day. There has been a constant inflow of literature meant for mere entertainment. There have been translations of popular literature from different world languages. All this may be interpreted as an aspect of decadence of literary culture in Maharashtra. The role of publishing companies has changed, thus making the translation activity an industry, selling the most profitable product. The selection of the texts for translation is done by the publishers, not by translators themselves any more. The publishing of best-sellers has acquired a boom. This has influenced the reading habits of the people. We see more investment in translation into the regional languages in the era of globalization. However, there is not much translation activity in the reverse direction, i.e. from

Marathi into English. We observe that the processes of globalization are threatening the local languages and cultures. A realization and a resistance to this trend have led to the ideology of *Nativism* in Marathi culture. It propagates the urge to return to native roots.

A well-known Marathi writer and exponent of the idea of nativism, Bhalchandra Nemade, reminds us of the line of Rajwade and highlights the common link between Russian and Marathi literature:

> If we compare the literatures of different countries, we can say that Russian literature is closer to us, because Russian writers do not consider poverty worth hiding. They see people's worth even in poverty. Like us, the Russian writers, too, consider that there is some dignity even in poverty. So, there must be something common in such authors in Russia and those amongst us.[28] (Translated from Marathi by author)

In such a situation, there exists a lot more space for Russian literature in the Marathi literary system within the subsystem of translated literature. In the twenty-first century we find translations of Russian novels of Tolstoy, Dostoevsky, Pasternak, Aitmatov, Panova, and short story books of Tolstoy, Chekhov, Bunin, as well as collections of representative Russian stories starting from Pushkin to Soviet and dissident authors. The recent publications indicate that the Marathi literary system still turns to Russian classics and the tradition of nineteenth-century Russian writers like Tolstoy, Dostoevsky, and Chekhov. In the context of the collapse of the Soviet system, there seems to be no more attraction for the Soviet novels, which depicted the Soviet life in socialist realistic style. However, there is a space for those Soviet or dissident novels, which are considered as Russian classics. They include authors like Gorky, Pasternak, etc. The tradition of translating serious literature goes parallel with the translations of popular and utility literature. And the tradition of translating Russian literature links itself to the long tradition of social realism in Marathi literature as was anticipated by Rajwade.

---

28 Bhalchandra Nemade, *Teekaswayamwar* [Critical self-choice] (Aurangabad: Saket Prakashan, 1990), pp. 293–294.

Bibliography

Adhikari, Gangadhar, ed. *Documents of the History of Communist Party of India*. Vol. 1, *1917–1922*. New Delhi: Peoples' Publishing House, 1971.

———. *Documents of the History of Communist Party of India*. Vol. 2, *1923–1935*. New Delhi: Peoples' Publishing House, 1974.

Bandiwadekar, Chandrakant. *Marathi Kadambaricha Itihas (1920–1947)* [A history of Marathi novel (1920–1947)]. 1989. Reprint, Pune: Mehta Publishing House, 1996.

Chelyshev, Evgeni, and Alexei Litman. *Traditions of Great Friendship*. USSR: Raduga Publishers, 1985.

Coppola, Carlo, ed. *Marxist Influences and South Asian Literature*. 1974. Reprint, Delhi: Chanakya Publications, 1988.

Deshpande, Suniti. *Antar-Parva* [Inter-epoch]. Pune: Mehta Publishing House, 2004.

Even-Zohar, Itamar. *Papers in Historical Poetics*. Papers on Poetics and Semiotics 8, edited by Benjamin Hrushovsky and Itamar Even-Zohar. Tel Aviv: University Publishing Projects, 1978.

Gentzler, Edwin. *Contemporary Translation Theories*. London and New York: Routledge, 1993.

Gopal, Sarvepalli. *British Policy in India*. Translated by Saroj Deshpande. Pune: Diamond Publications, 2006.

Gorky, Maxim. "Preface." In *Aai* [Mother], translated by Vinayak Mahadev Bhuskute. Pune: Deshmukh ani Company, 1945.

Kadakin, Alexander M. "100 Years of Russian Consulate." *New Delhi*, 17 November 2000. Accessed 2 November 2007, http://www.indiaonestop.com/russianconsulate.htm.

Kalasekar, Satish. Advertisement of *Aai* [Mother]. *Apale Vangmaya Vritta* [News on our literature] (Mumbai), October 2007, p. 3.

Kanekar, Anant. "Upton Sinclair." In *Nilya Thinagya* [Blue sparks]. Nagpur: Saroj Prakashan, 1972, pp. 47–48.

Kelkar, Narasinha Chintamani. *Samagra Kelkar Vangmaya* [The complete works of Kelkar]. Vol. 3, *Kesari*. Pune: Manohar Mahadev Kelkar, 1938, pp. 815–956.

Kulkarni, Govind Malhar, and Vasant Digambar Kulkarni. *Marathi Vangmayacha Itihas—1920–1950* [A history of Marathi literature, 1920–1950]. Vol. 6, part 2. Pune: Maharashtra Sahitya Parishad, 1991.

Macaulay, Thomos. "Minute by the Hon'ble T. B. Macaulay, Dated 2 February 1835." In *Selections from Educational Records, Part I (1781–1839)*, edited by Henry Sharp. Calcutta: Superintendent, Government Printing, 1920. Reprint, Delhi: National Archives of India, 1965, pp. 107–117.

Munday, Jeremy. *Introducing Translation Studies: Theories and Applications*. London and New York: Routledge, 2001.

Narkar, Maya. "A Linguistic Study of the Nineteenth Century Marathi Translations." Ph.D. dissertation, Shivaji University, Kolhapur, 1990.

Nemade, Bhalchandra. *Teekaswayamwar* [Critical self-choice]. Aurangabad: Saket Prakashan, 1990.

Niranjana, Tejaswini. *Siting Translation: History, Post-Structuralism and the Colonial Context*. Hyderabad: Orient Longman, 1992.

Rajwade, Vishwanath Kashinath. "Kadambari" [The novel]. In *Nivadak Sahitya Sameeksha* [A criticism of selected literature], edited by Gopal Maruti Pawar and Madhukar Dattatraya Hatkananglekar. New Delhi: Sahitya Akademi, 1999, p. 23–38.

Roy, Purabi et al., eds. *Russo-Indian Relations in the Nineteenth Century: A Selection of Documents: English Translation*. Calcutta: The Asiatic Society, 1999.

Sardesai, Shriniwas Ganesh. *India and the Russian Revolution*. New Delhi: Communist Party Publications, 1967.

Sathe, Anna Bhau. *Maza Rushiyacha Pravas* [My journey to Russia]. 6th ed. Pune: Suresh Agency, 2005.

Tolstoy, Leo. Blurb to *Gruhasaukhya* [Family happiness]. Translated by Shankar Sarada. Pune: Vimal Prakashan, 1991.

The Emerging Literariness:
Translation, Dynamic Canonicity and the Problematic Verisimilitude in Early Thai Prose Fictions[1]

Phrae CHITTIPHALANGSRI

Introduction

The encounters between Siam and the West in the age of imperialism have long been an attractive topic for historians, literary and cultural studies scholars alike given that Siam, unlike its neighbouring Southeast Asian countries, was never officially colonized, and therefore stands as a great challenge to the predominant post-colonial scholarship which caters mainly for the study of Western powers' ex-colonies. Nevertheless, recent scholarship on Thai studies has demonstrated that Siam, recognized as "unique" in the absence of its colonial past, did not, in fact, escape the impact of imperialism and colonization, and has suffered a great deal from the "mythology" of its own uniqueness. In the recently published *The Ambiguous Allure of the West: Traces of the Colonial in Thailand*, Rachel Harrison recounts how the discourse of nationalism, which started to gain firm ground during the reign of King Vajiravudh or Rama VI (1910–1925) and has ever since been reinforced by local scholars, has prevented the study of Thai history, literature, and culture from coming into contact with Western scholarship, especially the application of critical theories originating in the West.[2]

---

1 This article is made possible by the research funded by the Ratchadaphiseksomphot Endowment Fund for Young Researchers 2010.

2 Rachel Harrison, "Introduction: The Allure of Ambiguity: The 'West' and the Making of Thai Identities," in *The Ambiguous Allure of the West: Traces of the Colonial in Thailand*, ed. Rachel Harrison and Peter Jackson (Hong Kong: Hong Kong University Press, 2010), pp. 4–7.

This discourse of nationalism has also had a visible impact on the study of translation as an intercultural phenomenon. Thai literary scholars generally acknowledge early translated prose fiction from English (1900–1929) as a significant transitional period in Thai literary history, noting their importance in introducing literature in prosaic form to the Thai readership and their influence on local prose fictions.[3] However, these studies mostly focus on the making of "authentic" Thai novels which involve Thai characters, Thai settings and Thai values, and thus tend to bypass translated fictions for more detailed studies of what are agreed to be the first real and authentic Thai novels: three novels published in 1929. They are M. C. Akatdamkoeng Raphiphat's *Lakorn haeng chiwit* (The circus of life), M. L. Buppha Nimmanhemin's *Satru kong chao lon* (Her enemy), and Kulab Saipradit's *Luk phuchai* (The real man). In his article "Making New Space in the Thai Literary Canon," Thak Chaloemtiarana argues that the scholarship on the Thai literary canon follows Wibha Senanan's and Suphannee Warathorn's lead as we can see in subsequent reiterations of these three works as the first authentic Thai novels.[4]

In the same article, Thak Chaloemtiarana also calls for a reconsideration of those novels written prior to 1929 and for them to be given a place in the Thai literary canon as they also demonstrate an achievement in literature despite their statuses as translation, parody or even a "pretend" translation.[5]

---

3 See Wibha Senanan, *The Genesis of the Novel in Thailand* (Bangkok: Thai Watana Panich, 1975); Wibha Senanan Kongkanan, *Kamnerd nawaniyay nai prathet thai* กำเนิดนวนิยายในประเทศไทย [The genesis of the novel in Thailand] (Bangkok: Dokya, 1997); Suphannee Warathorn, *Prawat karnpraphan nawaniyay thai tangtae samai rermraek chon theung phutthasakkarat 2475* ประวัติการประพันธ์นวนิยายไทยตั้งแต่สมัยเริ่มแรกจนถึง พ.ศ. ๒๔๗๕ [History of Thai prose fictions from the beginning to 1932] (Bangkok: Social Sciences and Humanities Text Books Foundation, 1976).

4 Thak Chaloemtiarana, "Making New Space in the Thai Literary Canon," *Journal of Southeast Asian Studies* 40, no. 1 (2009), pp. 90–91. The three works Thak Chaloemtiarana referred to are: Mattani Mojdara Rutnin, *Modern Thai Literature: The Process of Modernization and the Transformation of Values* (Bangkok: Thammasat University Press, 1988); Marcel Barang, *The 20 Best Novels of Thailand* (Bangkok: TMC, 1994); and David Smyth, "Towards the Canonizing of the Thai Novel," in *The Canon in Southeast Asian Literatures*, ed. David Smyth (Surrey: Curzon Press, 2000).

5 Chaloemtiarana, "Making New Space in the Thai Literary Canon," p. 101.

The three works to which Thak Chaloemtiarana refers are *Khwam phayabat* (1902), a novel translated from Marie Corelli's *Vendetta: Or the Story of One Forgotten* (1886) by Mae Wan (a pseudonym of Nokyung Wisetkul or Phraya Surintracha, a high-ranking civil service officer); *Khwam mai phayabat* (1915), or "The non-vendetta," written as a "parody" in response to Mae Wan's *Khwam phayabat* by "Khru Liam" or Liam Winthuphramanakul under the pseudonym Nai Samran (Mr Happy); and *Nang neramid* (1916), literally "Created nymphs," also written by Khru Liam as a story that reads as if it was translated from European adventure fiction. Started in 2007, Thak initiated a "revisionist project,"[6] which comprises three seminal works on the reinterpretation of these early novels against the traditional literary history scholarship. This project manages to reconstruct the genealogy of early Thai novels that have long been kept distanced from the discussion of the Thai modern literary canon. It brings Thailand into dialogue with colonial studies as seen in Thak's analysis of Western modernity's impact on Thai social values and literary conventions. By applying a post-colonial translation approach such as Vicente Rafael's concept of colonial agency in *Contracting Colonialism* (1993) as a critical framework, Thak argues that "translation was a way to cushion the impact of Western domination"[7] and hence directs our attention to the connection between Thai literature and the influence of Western power.

---

6 The 2009 article "Making New Space in the Thai Literary Canon" is based on Thak Chaloemtiarana's previous three seminal works on these early novels: "Khru Liam's *Nang neramid*: Siamese Fantasy, Rider Haggard's *She*, and the Divine Egyptian Nymphs," *South East Asia Research* 15, no. 1 (2007), pp. 29–52; "*Khwam mai phayabat* khong khru liam lae khwam than samai khong thai thi pen panha ความไม่พยาบาทของครูเหลี้ยมและความทันสมัยของไทยที่เป็นปัญหา" [Khru Liam's *Khwam mai phayabat* and the problematics of Thai modernity], *Rathasatsan* รัฐศาสตร์สาร [Political sciences journal] 28, no. 2 (2007), pp. 63–112; "*Nang neramid*: Theptida Egypt, ruang phet lae khwam phoefan khong phuchai nai nawaniyay thai yuk raek นางเนรมิต: เทพธิดาอียิปต์ เรื่องเพศ และความเพ้อฝันของผู้ชายในนวนิยายไทยยุคแรก" [*Nang neramid*: Egyptian nymphs, sex, and the male fantasy in an early Thai novel], *Rathasatsan* รัฐศาสตร์สาร [Political sciences journal] 29, no. 1 (2008), pp. 1–37. These articles form a significant revision on the traditional scholarship of early Thai literary history.

7 Chaloemtiarana, "Making New Space in the Thai Literary Canon," p. 95.

Moreover, Thak Chaloemtiarana foregrounds literary translation and adaptation as a medium through which the negotiation of power is subtly displayed through semantic reconstruction of characters, settings, dialogues, and narratives. In particular, Thak's project venturesomely raises the status of translation and other "derivative" formats to the canonical level—an assertion that hugely challenges traditional Thai literary scholarship. In this article, I join Thak's argument that early prose fictions manifest significant literary achievements that should not be overlooked simply because they belong to derivative formats and therefore unauthentic. However, at many points Thak's anxiety about the inferior status of translation (including parody and imitation) seems to manifest itself when he urges us to see these novels as "original." He writes, for example, that "[*Khwam phayabat*] is an original Thai appropriation of the English novel that is representative of a genre of literature that educated the Siamese public about the West,"[8] or that "Khru Liam's *Khwam mai phayabat* is far from being a copy or a plagiarized version of Western original novels, it is in fact an example of Thai excellence,"[9] and "*Nang neramid* is nevertheless a genuine Thai novel about a group of English, Egyptian, Arab and Negro characters in Egypt."[10] Thak also believes that the formats, be it translation, parody or "pretend" translation, may be closely related to Western literary conventions, but the contents inserted into these Western formats are what really make the novels Thai.[11] While I find Thak's analyses of these novels extremely convincing, his anxiety about the "originality in the form of translation" (and other derivative forms) seems to shift the focus away from translation, and instead place more importance on the quality of being original. Apart from this, before trying to simply include these three novels in the canon, I think it is also

---

8 Chaloemtiarana, "Making New Space in the Thai Literary Canon," p. 106.

9 The Thai original reads:

> ความไม่พยาบาทของ "ครูเหลี่ยม" นั้น ห่างไกลจากการลักขโมยหรือฉกฉวยต้นฉบับของนวนิยายตะวันตก หากทว่าเป็นตัวอย่างอันยอดเยี่ยมของความเป็นไทย

Chaloemtiarana, "*Khwam mai phayabat*," p. 112.

10 Chaloemtiarana, "Khru Liam's *Nang neramid*," p. 39.

11 Chaloemtiarana, "Making New Space in the Thai Literary Canon," p. 110.

necessary to probe the very function of canonization rather than asserting a new ideology in order to easily accommodate "original translated fictions."

Inspired by Thak Chaloemtiarana's initiation, I intend to reinvestigate the case of this early Thai "derivative" fiction by trying to identify its literary contribution to the Thai literary repertoire. In doing so, I will use Itamar Even-Zohar's concept of *dynamic canonicity* to help explain the importation of Western literary genre as a challenge to static (conservative) Thai canonicity. The underlying significance of this model is that it aims to identify what local readership looks for in the new literary genre that the conservative one cannot offer. This notion of canon as a dynamic system allows us to see literary achievement as a constantly changing process rather than accepting canonized items as a static, unchanging end product. I will argue that these early prose fictions bring to the Thai literary canon a new kind of literariness that gradually changes the way Thai readership aestheticizes literature. This "emerging" literariness lies in the novel's *verisimilitude*, or the realistic quality, a *vraisemblance* of narrative fiction, which begins to gain more presence compared to the predominant poetic forms of traditional Thai versification. I will analyse how the translator/author deals with verisimilitude, a rather new literary mode for Thai readership that comes with the importation of prose fictions through translation, adaptation, and imitation.

Translated Fictions and Dynamic Canonicity

For a translated work to enter the national literary canon, it normally requires a substantial degree of consecration from the literary authorities. Its entrance into the canon is also generally associated with a particular trend in literary history. For example, when Sir William Jones translated *Śakuntalā* from Sanskrit in 1789, his translation became an immediate success; to use Romilar Thapar's words—"[it] took Europe by storm."[12] Jones's *Śakuntalā* was retranslated into many other European languages such as the 1791

12 Romilar Thapar, *Śakuntalā: Texts, Readings, Histories* (New Delhi: Kali for Women, 1999), p. 206.

German translation by Georg Forster and the 1803 French version by André Bruguière. In the nineteenth century alone, there were 49 unique translations of *Śakuntalā* in 10 European languages, including Icelandic and Bohemian.[13] Goethe read Forster's translation and was so enamoured by this Indian drama that he composed a poem in dedication to *Śakuntalā*, which became one of the most celebrated plays among German Romanticists such as Friedrich and August Wilhelm von Schlegel as well as Novalis.[14] Such a phenomenon was apparently boosted by the strong currents of Orientalism and Romanticism. *Śakuntalā* allowed Romanticism to experience a new sentiment that existing European literature could not offer. It is in this particular context that a translated work, such as *Śakuntalā*, was so well-received by the European readership. It remained in the canon for many years, during which time it was adapted into a number of performances, such as a successful ballet pantomime by Théophile Gautier in 1858.

Similarly, early translated fiction in Siam was met with enthusiastic reception among European-educated Siamese elites. However, Thai literary historians tend to downplay this event to a "transitional period" which paved the way for subsequent "authentic" Thai novels.[15] This "progressive" approach is geared towards establishing a linear construction of authentic Thai literary history. With such an approach, that is, when literary history is written to serve the purpose of establishing a genealogy of a national literature, it is impossible to find a place for investigating how translated and derivative fictions enter the Thai literary canon. To solve this problem, we need a new ground of inquiry.

To date, the only theory that is tailor-made for the question of translation and literary canonicity is Itamar Even-Zohar's "Polysystem Theory" which describes the positions of literary forms, genres, and modes as pertaining to a dynamic system in which the centre proves to be the

13 Montgomery Schuyler Jr, "The Editions and Translations of *Çakuntala*," *Journal of the American Oriental Society* 22 (1901), pp. 237–248.

14 Thapar, *Śakuntalā*, p. 211.

15 See Wibha Senanan, *The Genesis of the Novel in Thailand*, p. 64; Wibha Senanan Kongkanan, *Kamnerd nawaniyay nai prathet thai*, pp. 243–244; Warathorn, *Prawat karnpraphan nawaniyay thai*, pp. 54–57.

most prestigious repertoire and therefore determines the canonicity of the repertoire.[16] Even-Zohar views translation as a kind of literary form that can enter the system should the historical context allow. This includes the importation from abroad of new literary modes (e.g. novel, spoken drama), or new audience-oriented genres (e.g. crime fictions, children literature). Even-Zohar identifies three possible scenarios in which literary translation can occupy the canonized position: a) when a literature is still young and undergoing the process of crystallization, b) when a literature is either peripheral or weak, and c) when a literature is at a turning point, or there is a "literary vacuum" in a literature.[17]

Nevertheless, it is impossible to accept these three scenarios as universal conditions for translated works to enter literary canons, despite the fact that they may prove convincing for some literary situations, as in Israel where Even-Zohar is based.[18] It is doubtful, for example, whether there actually exists a "literary vacuum" in a literature. Not to mention how a literature can be qualified as young or weak.[19] Nevertheless, despite the "crude" classification attributed to polysystem studies, I found Even-Zohar's concept of dynamic and static canonicity helpful in analysing the relationship between translation and the process of canonization. Therefore, this study will focus mainly on the question of dynamic canonicity which aims to highlight a particular literary moment in order to better understand the function of translated prose fictions. It by no means intends to launch a full-scale polysystem study, which is beyond the scope of this article.

According to Even-Zohar, canonicity not only refers to a finished

16 Itamar Even-Zohar, "Polysystem Theory," *Poetics Today* 11, no. 1 (1990), p. 17.

17 Itamar Even-Zohar, "The Position of Translated Literature within the Literary Polysystem," *Poetics Today* 11, no. 1 (1990), p. 47.

18 In "The Position of Translated Literature within the Literary Polysystem," Even-Zohar explains that the centre of Hebrew literary repertoire between the two world wars was occupied by literatures translated from Russian whereas those translated from English, German, Polish, and other languages obviously took peripheral positions. See Even-Zohar, "The Position of Translated Literature," p. 49.

19 Theo Hermans, *Translation in Systems* (Manchester: St. Jerome, 1999), p. 109.

product that enjoys a high-level consecration and widespread celebration, it is also used to describe the process through which new literary forms challenge and negotiate existing traditions and in turn make themselves part of the prestigious centre. These two types of canonicity are called "static" and "dynamic" respectively, as Even-Zohar explains:

> In the first case, which may be called static canonicity, a certain text is accepted as a finalized product and inserted into a set of sanctified texts literature (culture) wants to preserve. In the second case, which may be called dynamic canonicity, a certain literary model manages to establish itself as a productive principle in the system through the latter's repertoire.[20]

Even-Zohar goes on to say that dynamic canonicity is the most crucial part for constantly changing characteristic of the system since it is a kind of canonization that "generates the canon."[21] While static canonicity is characterized as a primary condition for a distinct and autonomous system that is presented in the form of finalized products, i.e. established literary works, dynamic canonicity is a process through which literary forms undergo negotiations between the established and the emerging conventions. In this way, dynamic canonicity involves literary models that struggle for the centre position—they may be accepted into, rejected from or even "recycled" into the canon. Even-Zohar refers to the case of Leo Tolstoy whose position in the canon was well established, enabling the famous author to introduce new literary models several times as a reaction to the public rejection of his previous models.[22] This shows dynamic movements within the canon that can be shaped and reshaped by changing literary preferences and historical contexts.

The concept of dynamic canonicity therefore, to a large extent, provides an answer to Thak Chaloemtiarana's question on the Thai literary canon. The importation of prose fictions into the Thai literary scene marks a crucial landmark in Thai literary history. It changes the face

20 Even-Zohar, "Polysystem Theory," p. 19.

21 Ibid.

22 Ibid., p. 20.

of Thai literature to the extent that Thai readers would feel the need to reconfigure the way they appreciate and aestheticize literary works, which had long been dominated by verse forms. That is why literary works in derivative formats such as translation, adaptation, and imitation should be considered part of the canon since they introduce new literary models that later become established, or "static" to use Even-Zohar's term. Nevertheless it is true that these works were not fortunate enough to be recognized as innovatory by many literary scholars due to the lack of interest in, and the prejudice against, their derivative forms. Dynamic canonicity allows us to reconsider the role of translated fictions (including adaptation and imitation) by looking at how the translators and authors introduce new models and negotiate with established ones. By analysing *Khwam phayabat*, *Khwam mai phayabat*, and *Nang neramid*, I found that one of the crucial elements these books brought to the Thai literary canon is the subtle attempt to assimilate "verisimilitude" in prose fiction into Thai literary aesthetics. Verisimilitude of the prosaic form gradually began to be taken as an "emerging literariness" that yields a sense of literary aesthetics among Thais, whose taste had long been associated with the art of versification.

Verisimilitude: The Aesthetics of Fictional Reality

Verisimilitude in literature is closely related to *vraisemblance*, or the quality of being close to truth or reality. Fiction is thought of as "verisimilar" in the sense that it depicts the real world in a lifelike manner. In the West, the concept of verisimilitude is linked with realist writings, especially the *œuvres* of prominent French realist authors, namely Balzac, Stendhal, Flaubert, and Sartre. However, verisimilitude has a long presence in Western literary history and does not subscribe solely to realism as a mode of literary expression, nor is it limited to a certain literary form. Rather, its particularities change according to when and where it is applied.[23] Verisimilitude, therefore, is not exclusive to realism, a genre that tends to be attached to a certain period and

23 Lawrence R. Schehr, *Subversions of Verisimilitude: Reading Narrative from Balzac to Sartre* (New York: Fordham University Press, 2009), p. 1.

aesthetic (e.g. nineteenth-century French literature, socialist realism in Soviet Russia).

Such a convenient association may result from a conception of verisimilitude as a literary school or style of composition. Lawrence R. Schehr suggests that viewing verisimilitude in a wider perspective would reveal the term as "praxis"—an approach that realism utilizes in the construction of narratives.[24] Verisimilitude is in this sense construed as a *practice* by which fictional reality is made believable, not just a faithful description of the physical world in made-up stories. The arguments on verisimilitude have largely been focused on whether its power lies in its *persuasive* function or the ability to invoke a sense of *probability*. According to Ewlyn F. Sterling's study of the theory of verisimilitude in the French novel before 1830, there were at least two significant conceptualizations of verisimilitude that were discussed from the mid-seventeenth century to 1830. The first one centred around the relationship between the reader, the text, and the author. Verisimilitude in this conceptualization focused on the reader's willing suspension of disbelief which leads to the acceptance of the text as convincing and believable. As early French novels were mostly didactic in nature, novelists tended to distort elements of the novel in order to "buy" readers' credulity, and hence focused on separate fragments rather than the novel as a whole.[25] In this way, this kind of verisimilitude depends, to a great extent, on the narrative's persuasiveness and the readers' *a priori* collaboration in believing the story to be true—a condition external to the novel itself.

The second concept of verisimilitude was largely formed by French theorists who, after 1830s, thought of verisimilitude as constructed from the novel's internal logic. Instead of relying on external factors such as readers' collaboration, this kind of verisimilitude, as Pierre Nicolas Desmolets suggested, aimed at preserving the "illusion" of *vraisemblance* by using techniques intrinsic to the novel, such as "a wider social spectrum

24 Schehr, *Subversion of Verisimilitude*, p. 2.

25 Ewlyn F. Sterling, "The Theory of Verisimilitude in the French Novel Prior to 1830," *The French Review* 40, no. 5 (1967), p. 614.

of characters, [...] fidelity and consistency in characterization, [...] rapidity of action" and so forth.[26] This emphasis on the novel's internal logic was geared towards *roman total* or the *total novel* with verisimilitude coextensive to itself rather than remaining external and separated.[27] In this way, verisimilitude in *roman total* bears close affinity to the idea of "representational truth" derived from Aristotle's *mimesis*. In Greek drama, tragedy is an imitation of truth, expressed through dramatic elements, namely plots, characters, diction, thought, spectacle, and melody. It aims to "show" rather than "tell" in order to excite the audience's pity and fear, which leads to the purification of the soul or *katharsis*, once the audience recognizes the truth represented in the dramatic art of imitation.[28] The fact that tragedy does not try to establish an explicit link with the audience makes the idea of dramatic representational truth very similar to verisimilitude in the total novel which relies on its internal rather than external logic. The tradition of mimesis, therefore, brings verisimilitude closer to the law of probability in which fictional elements are combined to create a sense of contingency, a condition suggesting that the fictionalized events in the narrative could happen in reality.

While the arguments on the persuasiveness and probability of verisimilitude seem to depart in different directions, I do not view them as in complete conflict with one another. Rather, the persuasive and the probable stand on different ends of a continuum. A narrative may show an explicit complicity with the readers in order to gain their credulity while presenting the probable world predicated on various literary strategies and tropes. The situation can also occur vice versa. To determine whether the verisimilitude in a narrative is considered more persuasive or probable, we need to pay attention to why the author or the translator chooses to lean towards a particular direction. In the case of translation and Thai prose writings, the translator and author negotiate with the tension

26 Sterling, "The Theory of Verisimilitude in the French Novel Prior to 1830," p. 617.

27 Ibid., p. 616.

28 Leon Golden, "Aristotle," in *The Johns Hopkins Guide to Literary Theory and Criticism*, ed. Michael Groden, Martin Kreiswirth, and Imre Szeman (Baltimore and London: The Johns Hopkins University Press, 1994), pp. 68–69.

between these two poles to differing degrees, due to changes in literary consumption in the early period of prose fictions.

Thai Realism: From Verse to Prose Writings

Before the term *wannakadee* was coined in 1914 to account for the Western concept of literature, Siamese were familiar with oral literature which abounded in the forms of folk plays, dances or storytellings (*kap sebha*). These forms of oral literature were very popular among Siamese who were mostly illiterate. The orality of Siamese Thai court and folk literatures is evidence of Siamese eminent taste in poetry, which exhibits a high level of rhyming patterns and musicality. Prior to the arrival of prose fiction, poetry dominates Siam's literary scene, while prose was meant for informative writings and official matters such as royal decrees, public announcements, laws, historical records, letters, and business transactions.[29] At that time, to imagine prose writings as a form of fiction or literary works was unconceivable. The idea of literature was rather solidly formed in the mind of Siamese people as an embellished, stylized poetry of idiosyncratic rhyme schemes. In his doctoral thesis on Thai books of versification and literary conventions, Dhanate Vespada writes that, since the Ayutthaya period (1351–1767), court poets and learned men paid scrupulous attention to the structure, sound, rhyme, and musicality of poems, as we can see in the endless lists of versification rules in books such as *Alankarashastra*, *Phra kamphee suphotharangara*, *Kamphee wuttotai*, all of which show a strong influence of Sanskrit versification.[30] Subsequent books of versification by local pundits also conformed to this literary tradition.[31] It is therefore not an overstatement to affirm that the concept of literature in the mind of the Siamese is necessarily poetical, as described by Prince Bidyalankarana, a prominent Thai elite writer:

29 Mojdara Rutnin, *Modern Thai Literature*, p. 11.

30 See the detailed lists of Sanskrit-influenced Thai versification in Dhanate Vespada, "Thai Texts on Poetics: Concept and Relation to Thai Literary Convention" (Ph.D. dissertation, Chulalongkorn University, 2000), pp. 9–106.

31 Ibid., p. 106.

"The Siamese people are a poetically minded people … there is a natural aptitude for poetry which is general not only among the intellectual classes, but among the unlettered peasants themselves."[32] Poetic quality therefore became a literariness that Siamese people aestheticized as literary art. This kind of literariness is well established with numerous endorsements from poets and learned gentlemen, and can be said to lay a solid ground for the Thai literary canon to the point that it becomes "static" according to Even-Zohar's concept of canonicity.

The verse form in Thai literature also designates literature as a story to entertain, not an account of real events. In the Ayutthaya period, local residents enjoyed literary works, all of them written in various recognized verse forms, with a tacit awareness that these stories were made up and meant for entertainment. Coupled with other "unreal" elements, literature in verse recounts stories that exist in their own universes, detached from the reality of the actual world. For example, local oral folk tales, transmitted through poetical recitation, normally concern imaginary characters who are princes and princesses; they are deceived by the "bad characters," usually the stepmothers or corrupted courtiers, and thus the princes and princesses undergo hardship, until the bad characters are punished and order is restored; the heroes and heroines live happily ever after. Similarly, Sanskrit-influenced literary works carry on the tradition of idealized stock characters. For example, in *Ramakien*, or the Thai version of the Hindu verse epic *Rāmāyana*, the characters Rama and Sita are not meant to be real. They are meant to exemplify different types of virtues; for example, Rama is a hero who represents the dharma (duties) of his *kṣatriyā* (king, warrior) caste, whereas Sita represents an ideal wife who never wavered in her faithfulness to Rama. Unlike the Aristotelian tradition of *mimesis*, these characters are iconic idealism rather than an imitation of human beings who cannot escape their fates.

Nevertheless, it cannot be concluded that Thais had never experienced realism in the works of fiction. An oral folk tale such as *Khun Chang Khun Phaen*, with its "lifelike" depiction of the folk way of living, is

32 This quotation is cited in Mojdara Rutnin, *Modern Thai Literature*, p. 10.

praised as displaying an early form of humanistic realism.[33] The tale was compiled and transcribed into written manuscripts in the verse form of *kap sebha* by the royal court in the early Rattanakosindra period (*c.*1782–1868). Unlike other folk tales, *Khun Chang Khun Phaen* depicts the lives of ordinary townsmen; this adventure-packed story recounts the love triangle between two men and a woman who were believed to have actually existed around 1600. *Khun Chang Khun Phaen*, despite its penchant for black magic, violence, obscenity, and male chauvinism, tackles human desire in a straightforward manner—love, lust, vengeance, and anger are generally not euphemized or masked by literary decorum.

The realistic narrative in the verse form of *Khun Chang Khun Phaen* provides an interesting case of verisimilitude in Thai literature. Readers or listeners to the story would find the events relatable to them because the characters—Khun Phaen, Khun Chang, and Nang Phim—were ordinary folks living in towns that truly exist (e.g. Suphanburi, Kanchanaburi, Ayutthaya), not just some made-up kingdoms abundantly found in most oral folk tales. Yet the verse form, as well as supernatural elements in many scenes, remind readers and listeners that the story is fictional. I view the verse form as a crucial element in maintaining the story's verisimilitude. Readers and listeners enter the contract with the understanding that a story told in this form, no matter how realistic, is by all means make-believe. Realism in verse form is also associated with the rise of literary humanism. The historian Nidhi Eoseewong argues that realism in Thai literature saw a significant development in the early Rattanakosindra period as seen in the increasingly perceptible forms of human realism in poetry. Although Nidhi notes the significant role translated prose fictions play in expanding reading culture, he does not elaborate on its contribution to realism.[34] Verse forms were still to Thai literary consumers

33 See the preface to the translation of *Khun Chang Khun Phaen*, Chris Baker and Pasuk Phongpaichit, trans., *The Tale of Khun Chang Khun Phaen* (Chiang Mai: Silkworm Books, 2010), p. ix.

34 Ibid., pp. 238–239.

a predominant literary aesthetic. Verse was indicative of fiction, of an imaginary world separated from daily life, whereas prose served to record factual statements. To combine fiction with prose would run the risk of stripping fiction of its safe, sterile and embellished form of poetry. Rid of its protective, poeticized shell, fiction is laid bare with hardly anything to appreciate, to aestheticize about. Its only virtue is its power to incite readers' imagination and its suggestion that there can be truth in fiction; it may not be factual but it could yet happen in reality. This power is verisimilitude.

Unlike Western literary tradition, verisimilitude in this transitional period of Thai literature depends, crucially, more on literary forms, i.e. verse and prose, than on tropes, characters, and settings. Unless verisimilitude in prose fiction was considered "literary," it would be difficult for prose fiction to enter the Thai literary canon since that would require a complex process of negotiation. The problem with prose is that it requires readers to possess a new kind of aesthetics that allows them to appreciate prose writings as literature, not as a mundane means of communication. It therefore took prose fiction quite some time to find a way into Thai literary scene, and much longer into the literary canon.

The rise of prose fiction coincides with developments in publishing and journalism. The first Thai press was set up in Bangkok in 1836 by the American missionary Dr D. B. Bradley. A number of journals began to circulate and gradually the Thai readership grew, generating a growth in related professions and intellectuals such as writers, editors, and publishers. The well-known early journals that were influential in the birth of prose fiction are *Darunowat* (Lesson for young men), published between 1874 and 1875, and *Wachirayanwiset* (1884–1894). Both contained news, announcements, advertisements, historical anecdotes, and moral lessons in verse. Apart from the usual staples, they also published "fables" or *nithan*, considered an early form of prose fiction before the public learned of Western short stories and novels. The existence of *nithan* in these journals is crucial because it gave readers a sense of the nature and characteristics of prose fiction. *Nithans* belonged to an oral genre, well-established before the printing era, that began, with the printing press in Siam, to be written in the new form of prose. Nevertheless, there remained a tacit understanding that *nithans* did not pertain to any "truth" or "reality" but were composed to give readers pleasure or a moral lesson, just as Mom Anuwongworawat, an elite writer, described in an issue of *Wachirayanwiset*:

> I believe that *nithans* are indispensable [for this journal] ("*nithan*," as we understood, has to be a made up story, not a true story, or pretending to be a true story. We cannot think of it as real, otherwise it is not considered "*nithan*"). Even though it does not give us any moral lesson, or any harmful thought, that *nithan* is still beneficial because it lacks vices. What is its benefit, then? An entertainment that is a feast to the readers' hearts, of course.[35] (Author's own translation)

Didacticism, amusement, and alienation from reality are important characteristics of *nithan*. To a large extent, they are the reasons why most Thai readers in that period could not understand or conceptualize prose fiction (the short story and the novel) without recourse to the imperativeness of moral lesson and entertainment. *Nithans* published in the early journals were either *nithan boran*, a fable involving historical events or Aesop-style stories, or *nithan pratyuban*, an anecdote depicting current issues through fictionalized characters. Both kinds of *nithan* were meant for the improvement of readers' spiritual imports, as Prince Kasemsant Sobhakya, the editor of *Darunowat*, noted in an editorial:

> … and [we publish] poems, verses—that is, poetry and drama. They can be old or newly written. [We also welcome] stories, old and new *nithans*—

35 The original Thai reads:

> เรื่องนิทานต่างๆนั้น ข้าพเจ้าเห็นจำเป็นต้องมีเปนแท้ ตามที่เข้าใจกันต้องเปนเรื่องแต่ง
> (คำว่านิทานนี้ไม่ใช่เรื่องจริงหรือที่แอบอ้างว่าเปนเรื่องจริง แต่เห็นว่าจะเปนจริงไปไม่ได้นั้น
> เรื่องเหล่านี้นับว่าเปนนิทานถึงโดยเรื่องนั้นจะไม่เปนคำสั่งสอนก็ดี แต่ไม่ให้โทษแก่ผู้ใด ก็ต้องนับว่า
> เรื่องนั้นมีคุณเพราะปราศจากโทษ คุณคืออันใดเล่า คือเปนเรื่องสนุกสำหรับบำรุงใจให้ผู้อ่านหรือผู้ฟังเบิกบาน

Phittaya Wongkul, *Anyamanee haeng Wannakam Thai* อัญมณีแห่งวรรณกรรมไทย [The gems of Thai literature] (Bangkok: Dok Mali, 1990), p. 71.

> that is, fable, which will guide our readers towards an enlightened path.[36] (Author's own translation)

The strong sense of didacticism that came with *nithan*, together with the amusement purpose, became a kind of literariness associated with prose fiction in the early period. Prose fiction that did not intend to deliver a moral message or simply to entertain would fail to be qualified as *nithan* and would be perceived as a threat that would destroy the fictional quality of the prose, especially when it tried to discuss real events. The 1874 "anecdote" entitled "The Conversation of Nai Chit and Nai Chai," published in *Darunowat*, was perhaps the first prose writing that broke the "rules." Written in a form of conversation, it tells the story through two fictional characters, Nai Chit (Mr Chit) and Nai Chai (Mr Chai), who worked as secretaries for two of King Chulalongkorn's (Rama V) councillors. One of the councillors, Chaophraya[37] Mahintarasakthamrong, felt he was insulted by the anecdote and appealed to King Chulalongkorn. The king intervened and made the writer, Chaophraya Bhasakornwong, accept his "wrongdoing." The announcement regarding the case was published in the *Royal Gazette* on 17 December 1874, detailing the verbal punishment of an unnamed officer, who could be no one but the writer of "The Conversation of Nai Chit and Nai Chai."[38] The incident partly led to the discontinuation of *Darunowat*, and subsequent prose fiction was strictly limited to *nithan*.[39] It was not until 1886 that another attempt at non-*nithan* prose fiction took place, this time with the journal *Wachirayanwiset*. Prince Phichitpreechakorn, the editor of *Wachirayanwiset*, wrote a story called "*Sanuknuek*" (Fun-filled thoughts) about four monks of Wat Bawornniwes discussing what they would do after leaving monkhood. The story infuriated

---

36 The quotation in original Thai is:

> แลเรื่องนิยายนิทานเก่า, ของโบราณบ้าง ของใหม่บ้าง, พาคยฉันท์ คือ โปยตริแอนด์ดรัมมา
> แลหนังสือบทกลอนกาพย์โคลง ... ที่เปนคติชักจูงปัญญาของคนให้ฉลาดขึ้น, คือ เฟเบลอ, ใหม่

Wongkul, *Anyamanee haeng Wannakam Thai*, p. 152.

37 Chaophraya is an officer's rank roughly equivalent to "Lord."

38 Wongkul, *Anyamanee haeng Wannakam Thai*, p. 172.

39 Sumalee Weerawong, *Roykaew naew mai khong thai phutthasakkarat 2417 theung 2453* ร้อยแก้วแนวใหม่ของไทย พ.ศ. ๒๔๑๗-๒๔๕๓ [Thai prose fictions from 1874 to 1910] (Bangkok: Siam publishing house, 2004), p. 8.

the abbot. Again, King Chulalongkorn needed to intervene. In his letter to the abbot, the King stated that "[Prince Phichitpreechakorn] was taking example from *farang*[40] novels. There exist thousands of them already. They are just made up stories that are meant for pleasure reading."[41] (Author's own translation.)

These two cases epitomize the puzzlement of early readers who found it problematic to appreciate a form of "reality" presented through fiction. They might learn from the didactic message implied or explicitly stated in the story but all of these relied on the conditions that the characters, settings, dialogues and other elements were not an immediate daily reality. Moreover, the highly stylized versification that dominates the composition augments the sense of poetical embellishment, which takes the audience away from the realm of reality. Prince Damrongrachanuphap, the celebrated "father of Thai history," recalled the "*Sanuknuek*" incident and remarked that:

> When the story was published, those who knew *farang* languages or had read *farang* novels would not feel estranged. They only praised Prince Phichit that he was very keen in weaving Thai stories into a novel like those by *farangs*. His style was also pleasant to read. However, there were more senior people who did not know *farang* and had never read novels. They thought Prince Phichit wrote about the real events in order to condemn [the monks of Bawornniwes temple].[42] (Author's own translation)

Most Thai scholars agree that the "realistic quality" is one of the most important criteria that distinguishes modern short stories from *nithans*. Both

---

40 *Farang* is a term possibly derived from a Persian word *farangi*, meaning "foreigner." Thais use *farang* to refer to white Europeans or Caucasians.

41 The original Thai reads:

ทำอย่างหนังสือโนเวลฝรั่ง ที่เขาแต่งกันนับพันนับหมื่นเรื่อง เปนเรื่องคิดผูกพันอ่านเล่นพอสนุก

Wongkul, *Anyamanee haeng Wannakam Thai*, p. 100.

42 The original Thai reads:

ในเวลาที่พิมพ์เรื่องนี้ ผู้ที่รู้ภาษาฝรั่งอ่านนอเวลฝรั่งก็ไม่เห็นเป็นสิ่งสำคัญอันใด เป็นแต่ชมว่ากรมหลวงพิชิตฯ
ช่างทรงเทียบเคียงประดิษฐ์คิดผูกเรื่องในเมืองไทยให้เป็นนอเวลอย่างฝรั่ง และแต่งสำนวนน่าอ่าน
แต่ในสมัยนั้นชั้นผู้ใหญ่ที่ไม่รู้ภาษาฝรั่งและไม่เคยอ่านนอเวลมีมากกว่า สำคัญว่ากรมพิชิตฯ เอาเรื่องจริงมาประจาน

Wongkul, *Anyamanee haeng Wannakam Thai*, p. 103.

Sudarat Seriwat (1979) and Phittaya Wongkul (1990) give long explanations of which story should be considered Thailand's first modern short story. Although their decisions differ, their choices reflect the emphasis on the departure from *nithan chak chak wong wong* (stories of princes and princesses in the made-up or far-away kingdoms) to short stories which make use of realistic settings and realistic characters.[43] However, they did not explore further the topic of realistic quality as an emerging literariness, especially as a result of the importation of Western literary genres. In fact, early Thai prose fiction writers tried to come to terms with this new aesthetics since this new genre was still in its infancy. Chaophraya Thammasakmontree (Sanan Devahastin na Ayutthaya), writer and education minister (1916–1926), wrote in 1900 in the postscript of the journal *Lakwitthaya* (literally, to steal knowledge; to plagiarize) under the pseudonym "Chingcho" (literally, kangaroo) about what should be considered a good style of writing for *ruang an len* (story for pleasure reading), which was the term used to describe short stories in that period. He suggested that *ruang an len* should not be overlooked because of its lack of decisiveness; in fact, it addressed serious issues through its realistic depiction of humans and nature. He explained that just as paintings were considered good because they were life-like, and just as the *khon* (masked dance drama) performers who took the role of monkey warriors could dance exactly like monkeys, so writing short stories was:

> … in the same way. If the writer wants to express meanings through characters, he needs to make them real and identifiable. Even if one closes one's eyes, one should be able to sense the characters as if one has met them in real life. If meanings are expressed through settings, readers should be able to sense them as if they were there even with their eyes closed. If writers only gave account of the events, say, having breakfast, going there, doing this, then making up funny circumstances such as

---

43 See Sudarat Seriwat, *Wiwatthanakan khong ruangsan nai muang thai tangtae raek jon theung phutthasakkarat 2475* วิวัฒนาการเรื่องสั้นในเมืองไทยตั้งแต่แรกจนถึง พ.ศ. ๒๔๗๕ [The evolution of short stories in Thailand from the beginning to 1932] (Bangkok: Ministry of Education, 1979), p. 20 and Wongkul, *Anyamanee haeng Wannakam Thai*, p. 154.

> someone fell, showed his teeth, did dumb things, how could these be considered enjoyable?[44] (Author's own translation)

Chaophraya Thammasakmontree's remarks were perhaps the first time in Thai history that literary realism was properly conceptualized. Being able to convey realistic quality was an important criterion for good prose fiction. But Chaophraya Thammasakmontree did not limit this quality to only realistic description of characters and settings, he also called attention to another form of "reality" that went beyond the descriptive level—the idea that prose fiction tried to convey a heightened form of reality. He explained that there were two ways of writing prose fiction; one was a plot-oriented writing (*ruang taeng pai tam Khwam*), and the other was theme-oriented (*ruang phuk Khwam*). The first style was popular and easier to follow, whereas the second style involved more complex layers of story and intended to present the vicious and virtuous natures of human being.[45] Chaophraya Thammasakmontree's theme-oriented writing style was not only a major development in the aestheticization of realistic quality; it took realistic quality to another level, the level of "representational truth," which is a kind of truth that can only be represented through fiction. I read these two levels of realistic quality as a form of "verisimilitude."

By translating, adapting or imitating foreign prose fiction, it is perhaps inevitable that early Thai translators and authors found a way to make verisimilitude an accessible literary aesthetic for those who were not familiar with prose fiction. The translation *Khwam phayabat*, the novel *Khwam mai phayabat* and the pseudotranslation *Nang neramid* all show a great amount of difficulty negotiating with verisimilitude, despite the

44 The quotation in Thai reads:

> การแต่งหนังสือก็ดุจกัน ถ้าจะแสดงด้วยคนก็ต้องให้ซึมจับอกจับใจ ผู้อ่านว่าคนๆนั้นเป็นอย่างนั้น เมื่อหลับตาดู ก็ให้แลเห็นได้เท่ากับเคยพบเคยเห็นกันมาแล้ว ถ้าแสดงด้วยสถานที่ ก็ให้ผู้อ่านหลับตาเห็นได้เท่ากับเคยได้ไปมาเหมือนกัน อันจะพูดถึงแต่ว่าได้รับปทานเข้าเช้าเวลานั้นๆ ไปถึงที่นั่น แล้วติดตลกไปว่าหกคเมน ไปยิงฟัน ไปขยายขี้เท่อ ดังนี้จะขันอย่างไร แลจะเอาสนุกที่ไหนมา

See Sanan Devahastin na Ayutthaya [Chaophraya Thammasakmontree], "Maihed bedtaled หมายเหตุเบ็ดเตล็ด" [Miscellaneous postscripts], *Lakwitthaya* ลักวิทยา [Stealing knowledge journal] 1, no. 8 (1900), pp. 656–657.

45 Ibid., pp. 658–659.

development in literary realism in poetry in the early Rattanakosindra period. Their pioneering effort in dealing with prosaic verisimilitude introduces this literariness to the Thai literary canon and generates a vital literary dynamicity that dramatically changes the face of Thai literature.

Khwam phayabat: Translation and the Negotiation of Vrisimilitude

Mae Wan translated *Khwam phayabat* from an English novel set in Italy—*Vendetta: Or the Story of One Forgotten* (1886), written by Marie Corelli, a Scottish writer whose real name was Mary Mackay. The translation was serialized in the journal *Lakwitthaya* in 1900 and published as a complete book in 1902. A "lowbrow" novel, it tells the story of Fabio Romani, a rich noble man of Naples, who is cheated by his wife Nina and her lover who is also his friend, Guido Ferrari. During the cholera epidemic in Naples, Romani is thought to have died from the disease and thus buried. However, it turns out that he is still alive and manages to escape the tomb, only to find himself betrayed by his wife and Ferrari. Romani vows revenge. He takes the new name of Cesare Oliva and, so disguised, succeeding in seducing Nina and defeating Ferrari in a duel. On the eve of Oliva's marriage to Nina, he tells her the truth. Nina goes mad, and is then crushed to death by a falling stone in the crypt. Romani leaves Italy and never returns.

Mae Wan's *Khwam phayabat* became a huge success. It was the first time a novel was "translated" rather than adapted or imitated as in earlier short stories published in *Wachirayanwiset*. Even so, Mae Wan's translation was far from faithful and was not even a complete translation. A number of pages were omitted in Mae Wan's version; quotations in French or songs in Italian were skipped. This reflects the translator's shortcoming in multilingual capacity and relevant background knowledge. This is not strange for such an attempt at literary translation in that period.

The deletion and alteration of the original also indicate the translator's attempt to convey the verisimilitude of the original English novel, especially in avoiding the readers' suspension of disbelief. Mae Wan carefully excluded the scenes deemed inappropriate or too risky for Thai readers at the turn of the century, such as the one where Romani visits the convent where Nina is staying and is told by a nun of the "lesbian" unions among girls in the convent. The scene where Romani takes Nina to a lurid play, which makes fun of a loose woman and her cuckolded husband, was also omitted in Mae Wan's translation.[46] The censorship is understandable; otherwise the novel would risk being condemned for its explicit description of clearly immoral behaviours. The external condition, in this case the persuasiveness, is prioritized at the cost of the faithful rendition of the original novel.

Mae Wan also skipped a number of pages that involved the historical figure, King Umberto I of Italy. Corelli describes in great detail a scene in which the king visits the cholera-infected crowd, depicting his deep sorrow on seeing the doomed fate of his people.[47] The translator's choice to omit historical references reflects the downplaying of real events. This decision, on the one hand, may be interpreted as a disruption of verisimilitude; on the other hand, it reflects the translator's attempt to maintain the illusion of credibility, since a detailed description of real events might deviate the readers from believing the story as fictions. It is highly probable that Mae Wan had learned from the previous incidents concerning "The Conversation of Nai Chit and Nai Chai" and "*Sanuknuek*" and thus decided to keep the illusion of fiction consistent throughout.

Mae Wan's intervention was apparently meant to ensure the novel's accessibility for Thai readers. Such an act was not unusual especially when the reader's credulity was not *a priori* to the novel, and therefore requires interventions on the translator's or the author's part. Marie Corelli herself had to explain for her English readers of the Victorian period in the preface that Romani's taking revenge on his wife was not too implausible because, unlike English law, Italian law did not provide fair compensation for dishonoured husbands, and therefore such extreme revenge was not

46 See the introduction to the 2003 Thai translation of *Vendetta: Or the Story of One Forgotten*, W. Winichaikul, trans., *Khwam phayabat* ความพยาบาท [Vendetta: Or the story of one forgotten], by Marie Corelli, 3rd ed. (Bangkok: Pheundee, 2003), pp. 12–14.

47 Ibid., pp. 7–8.

unusual.[48] The author even had Romani address the English readers directly in the novel:

> Of course I married her. We Neapolitans lose no time in such matters. We are not prudent. Unlike the calm blood of Englishmen, ours rushes swiftly through our veins—it is warm as wine and sunlight, and needs no fictitious stimulant. We love, we desire, we possess; and then? We tire, you say? These southern races are so fickle! All wrong—we are less tired than you deem. And do not Englishmen tire? Have they no secret ennui at times when sitting in the chimney nook of "home, sweet home," with their fat wives and ever-spreading families? Truly, yes! But they are too cautious to say so.[49]

This mediation by Corelli through Romani can be seen as an attempt to justify Romani's quick decision to marry Nina by alluding to the well-known stereotype of the Italians as a passionate, spontaneous people. Mae Wan omitted this section. Apparently, having an Italian character address English readers in Thai would lead to the readers' disbelief. Mae Wan rather chose to maintain the "credible" dialogue between the narrator (Romani) and the Thai readers by inserting a part in which Romani compares Christian burial custom to Thai funeral custom of cremation:

> Cremation is the best and only way. It is not dirty and also safe. Why didn't we take after the Thais? It is better to purify the body of the one whom we love (or pretend to love) with fire than to pile it up with others' or store it in the cold and wet *hong suey*.[50] (Author's own translation)[51]

---

48 See Marie Corelli, preface to *Vendetta: Or the Story of One Forgotten* (1886; Project Gutenberg, 2003), http://www.gutenberg.org/ebooks/4360.

49 Ibid.

50 *Hong suey* is a Chinese (Teochew dialect) term for tomb. At that time, the concept of burial place was not common in Thailand. The closest possible was the term *hong suey* borrowed from Chinese immigrants who were predominantly Teochew speakers.

51 The English original of this part is as follows:
Cremation is the best way—the only way, and SAFE. Why should there be any prejudice against it? Surely it is better to give the remains of what we loved (or pretend to love) to cleansing fire and pure air than to lay them in a cold vault of stone, or down, down in the wet and clinging earth.

Mae Wan also changed the ending of the story. Instead of taking a ship to South America, Romani sails to Bangkok, the capital of Siam, far from Naples, the scene of tragedy. Furthermore, in the scene where Romani, disguised as Oliva, takes Nina to the family crypt to reveal the truth, Mae Wan added that Nina's tragic death in the crypt was caused by her own bad karma, a fitting Buddhist explanation for a Thai audience.[52] Thak Chaloemtiarana sees the addition and alteration that allude to Thai customs, beliefs and the city of Bangkok as Mae Wan's attempt to "[place] Siam on par with the other great cities in the world."[53] Translation, in this sense, is far from faithful. In fact, most Thais did not see themselves as technicians of languages, but rather, as creative artists, and the alterations, additions, and omissions of the original text were meant to "cushion the impact of Western domination." Thus, Mae Wan found himself in the position that could not escape the strong current of globalization, and decided to downplay the outlandish, peculiar, and perplexing Western customs of the novel by injecting more familiar elements into his translation.

The verisimilitude in this novel was also a result of globalization. Mae Wan showed a full awareness that Thai readers were not ready to experience full-scale novel in its Western form, so he could not but adapt the text to make it more palatable to the Thai readers. Verisimilitude, in this case, relies heavily on an external factor, the readers, rather than on its own internal logic. It is illogical to have Romani, a nineteenth-century Neapolitan nobleman, show a familiarity and affinity to Thai customs and manners but this was done for the sake of the audience whose credulity needed to be maintained. Despite his rather crude approach to verisimilitude, Mae Wan left a legacy for later translators and authors, that is, making prose fiction more accessible to Thai readers through compromising strategies. Mae Wan's *Khwam phayabat* paved the way for later translations and adaptations that dominated the Thai literary scene

---

For the Thai translation, see Mae Wan, trans., *Khwam phayabat* ความพยาบาท [Vendetta: Or the story of one forgotten], by Marie Corelli, 2nd ed. (Bangkok: Ongkarnkha Khong Khurusabha, 1975), p. 4.

52 Chaloemtiarana, "Making New Space in the Thai Literary Canon," p. 99.

53 Ibid.

for almost three decades. Western novels in translation were very popular to the point where it was difficult for indigenous Thai novels to penetrate the literary market. In this way, *Khwam phayabat* brought to the Thai literary canon a new, dynamic negotiation of verisimilitude that, unlike the "realism" of "*Sanuknuek*," makes prose fiction accessible and enjoyable. Gradually, readers were tuned to this new "literariness" that proved to be as aesthetical as poetical forms.

Khwam mai phayabat: A Tragedy of an Untimely *Roman Total*

The success of Mae Wan's *Khwam phayabat* did not automatically give rise to indigenous Thai novels. On the contrary, Thailand's first novel suffered from a lack of recognition. In 1915, Khru Liam (Liam Winthuphramanakul) was commissioned by a publishing house owner to write a novel similar to Mae Wan's *Khwam phayabat*,[54] but the novel was not to be a *farang* story—it could be Thai or *Khaek*.[55] It took Khru Liam 22 days to complete a two-volume novel which became *Khwam mai phayabat*, "The non-vendetta." The story, as suggested by the title, was a parody of *Vendetta* or *Khwam phayabat* since it advocated an opposite morale. Instead of plotting revenge against his unfaithful wife, Jian, a civil officer, tried hard to overcome his grudge over his wife Prung, a country beauty who was corrupted by Bangkok's growing urban modernity and seduced by a rich Bangkokian. In the end, Jian forgave Prung and took her back. Together with Jian's loyal second wife, Praphai, they lived happily ever after.

Khwam mai phayabat was published in late 1915 only to be shunned by the Thai readership. Few copies sold, and it barely registered in the public memory. In fact, before 1997, when it was incidentally found in a writer's private library, no Thai literary scholar had ever even seen the novel in

54 See the postscript in Liam Winthuphramanakul, *Khwam mai phayabat* ความไม่พยาบาท [The non-vendetta] (Bangkok: Rong Phim Thai Na Saphan Yotse, 1915), p. 720.

55 *Khaek* is a colloquial term used to refer to Arab, Indian or Malay peoples. Here it probably means stories derived from Sanskrit, which is the classical language of India.

print, but only knew of its existence from an advertisement in other books from the same period.[56]

As mentioned above, after the translation of *Vendetta*, translated fictions from the West—mostly low to middlebrow literature,[57] romance, adventure, and detective novels—flooded the Thai literary market; for example, H. Rider Haggard's *She* and *King Solomon's Mines* (translated by Khru Liam), Marie Corelli's *Thelma*, and the popular *Sherlock Holmes* and *Arsène Lupin*. Rachel Harrison observes that the dominance of romance and adventure fiction in the Southeast Asian literary scene reflects the tastes of local audiences who were drawn to "the action of Western fiction more than to its in-depth portrayal of individuals or its extensive treatment of their personal motivations."[58] Thus, Thai readers became even more familiar with prose fiction, but with a tacit awareness that these novels, with their exotic Western settings, did not recount real events.

The reception failure of *Khwam mai phayabat* was, to a large extent, caused by the change in the Thai literary repertoire which was transformed by the increasing volume of prose fiction. This change was geared towards the demand for prose fiction to maintain readers' suspension of disbelief. Therefore, this prose fiction did not promise or try to account for an abstract reality, or a "representational truth" that did not have a discernible root in Thai literary tradition. Otherwise, it would lose the illusion of fiction, of the story that was meant to entertain rather than refer to "truth" at a level other than mundane reality. However, unlike the prevailing translated prose fiction, Khru Liam's *Khwam mai phayabat* was not written to entertain readers with exotic settings or exciting plots. On the contrary, it criticized the corrupt modern Thai society, in which innocent country women such as Prung could fall victim to the

56 Warathorn, *Prawat karnpraphan nawaniyay thai*, p. 57.

57 Winita Ditheeyont, *Pakkai wannakam* ปากไก่วรรณกรรม [Feather pen of literature] (Bangkok: Dokya, 1994), p. 16–17.

58 Rachel Harrison, "'Elementary, My Dear Wat': Influence and Imitation in the Early Crime Fiction of 'Late Victorian' Siam," in *Chewing over the West: Occidental Narratives in Non-Western Readings*, ed. Doris Jedamski (Amsterdam: Rodopi, 2009), p. 324.

encroaching Western influences. While Mae Wan deletes "inappropriate" parts to protect the sensibilities of his audience, Khru Liam shows the sordidness of modern Thai men in explicit, lurid scenes, such as how prostitutes were called in to "service" men at the party,[59] or indeed, the orgy, held in honour of Jian's promotion. In fact, Thak Chaloemtiarana argues that Khru Liam's novel was the first to present the impact of modernity on Thai culture; it was realistic and did not shy away from telling unpleasant truths.

To use Chaophraya Thammasakmontree's word, *Khwam mai phayabat* could be considered a "theme-based" fiction. The novel exposed the corrupt behaviour of modern Thai men, and the triumph of a hero who could overcome his betrayal. In terms of verisimilitude, Khru Liam apparently paid more attention to crafting the story's consistent internal logic, than to accommodating readers by adapting the text and making it more accessible. In this sense, *Khwam mai phayabat* clearly moved towards a *roman total* or a "total novel" which treats verisimilitude in terms of a complete fictional illusion, a probability that can be experienced in the real world. This argument can be supported by Khru Liam's telling comment in the novel's postscript: "[I was asked to] compose a novel about adultery. An impressive one. It would be composed as a tragedy, a drama-like story."[60] (Author's own translation.) The fact that Khru Liam wrote *Khwam mai phayabat* with the genre of "tragedy" in mind recalls the tradition of mimesis. While in Mae Wan's *Khwam phayabat*, verisimilitude was compromised to make the text accessible to the Thai audience, Khru Liam painstakingly wrote about Jian's struggle to defeat his own antagonism. In the seven hundred pages, Khru Liam does not compromise his straightforward depiction of modern Thai characters and an urbanized Bangkok. The complete fictional illusion is maintained throughout, with no intervention by the author. However, because of the massive

---

59 Winthuphramanakul, *Khwam mai phayabat*, pp. 253–261.

60 The original Thai reads:

> ... มาวานให้ข้าพเจ้าแต่งเรื่องการมีชู้ ซึ่งเปนเรื่องจับอกจับใจ เปนชนิดเรื่องแทรจิดี้ให้แต่งเปนสำเนาดราม่า

Winthuphramanakul, *Khwam mai phayabat*, p. 729.

number of *ruang an len* translated from low to middlebrow Western fiction that dominated the literary market, it was not until much later that indigenous Thai novels that were written as a *roman total* received proper recognition. Khru Liam's *Khwam mai phayabat* was, therefore, a novel before its time that failed to cause a stir,[61] and was yet to succeed in bringing the concepts of verisimilitude and representational truth to Thai literature.

Nang neramid as a Pseudotranslation

Khwam mai phayabat's failure to make an impact on the literary repertoire points to the popularity at the time of translated novels, which were dominant enough to be considered a separated genre that was beginning to replace *nithans* as readers grew used to consuming prose fiction that recounted the stories of exotic lands. Yet it is ironic that readers still preferred stories of foreign characters and settings so far removed from their day-to-day reality, just as earlier readers had enjoyed the *nithans* that recounted stories of princes and princesses in made-up kingdoms. Readers' credulity at that time was somehow tied to the belief that stories written in prose were believable and enjoyable as long as they did not emphasize the immediate reality that was so mundane to most readers. Prose fiction, thus, should be exotic, and the description must be believable; otherwise readers would lose interest as well as credulity.

After the financial failure of his first novel, Khru Liam published another novel called *Nang neramid* (Created nymphs) in 1916 about a young English man, James Bilford, who travels to Egypt and becomes involved in several adventures. The subtitle of the novel, "An extraordinary story set in Egypt to entertain the world,"[62] clearly signals an exotic,

61 Chaloemtiarana, "*Khwam mai phayabat,*" p. 111.

62 The original was written as follows:

นางเนระมิตร เปนเรื่องประโลมโลกยล้ำลึก ณ ประเทศอียิปต์

The term เรื่องประโลมโลกย (*ruang pralomlok*) is literally "the story to entertain the world" or "the story to console the world."

action-packed, promisingly enjoyable story. Indeed, James falls in love with Vivian, an English woman, and together they explore the pyramids, discovering a trove of female mummies, who turn out to be not only still alive, but beautiful and physically alluring. Whoever touches them becomes filled with a sexual desire, so strong that he cannot resist making love to them. The sex scenes in this novel are very explicit, including the one where the war between British and Muslim soldiers turns into an orgy as the soldiers are captivated by the nymph-like mummies. The penultimate scene involves the major characters, including James, blindly making love to the nymphs in the cave.

The real surprise, however, is yet to come. In the postscript to the novel, Khru Liam wrote: "The original *farang* of this story is difficult to find. If I told you there wasn't any original in any *farang* language, we could say that's why it is difficult to find one, because there wasn't any."[63] (Author's own translation.) At this point, readers discover that they have been tricked into believing that what they had just read was not a translation, but an original novel! Khru Liam goes on to explain that because his last book (*Khwam mai phayabat*) was such a flop, he needed to write a new one that could make him some more money. Hence the thrilling story of *Nang neramid*.

Under the nationalist approach discussed at the beginning of this paper, *Nang neramid* can hardly be considered a "Thai" novel. Yet, Thak Chaloemtiarana argues that, if Marie Corelli, an English author, could write about Italy in *Vendetta*, and the English H. Rider Haggard wrote comfortably about Egypt in *She*, "[w]hy then should Khru Liam, a Thai, not write about the English in Egypt in his novel *Nang neramid*?"[64] However, I would call *Nang neramid* a "pseudotranslation," even though the translator did not keep its real status a secret throughout, unlike most

63 The original Thai reads:

> ต้นฉบับฝรั่งเรื่องนี้หายากมาก ถ้าข้าพเจ้าบอกโดยตรงว่าเรื่องนี้ไม่มีในภาษาฝรั่งที่ไหนเลยในโลกนี้
> เพราะฉะนั้นจึงจะเห็นได้ว่าต้นฉบับเรื่องนี้ในฝรั่งเปนหายากที่สุด เพราะมันไม่มีในภาษาฝรั่งที่ไหนเลย

See the postscript in Winthuphramanakul, *Nang neramid* นางเนระมิตร [Created nymphs] (Bangkok, 1916), p. 402.

64 Chaloemtiarana, "Khru Liam's *Nang neramid*," p. 39.

cases of pseudotranslation.[65] Yet, despite the final revelation, it is clear that Khru Liam intended to make use of the pseudotranslation status in order to, not only attract a large readership and hence a good turnover, but also voice his cynicism towards Thai readers who shunned his first novel, which was not written as a lowbrow fiction, as he stated, "we cannot change people's belief that Thais cannot write a good and fun story because they do not have talent. I decided to write this *farang* story, *Nang neramid*, and other *farang* stories. They were written by me. They were not translation."[66] (Author's own translation.)

The case of *Nang neramid* is strong evidence that translation played an important role in the evolution of the Thai literary repertoire. From a time when writing "true" accounts in prose was strongly condemned, to a time when translated fiction was so popular that an indigenous Thai novel could not challenge their dominance, and it was only under the guise of pseudotranslation that a novel could enjoy the same popularity, translated prose fiction created a literary dynamism by introducing a way to appreciate verisimilitude as the literariness of prosaic form.

---

65 James Macpherson never revealed that his collection of Ossian poems were in fact the Gaelic translations of his own English poems. Many Italian translators in the eighteenth century also pretended that their own novels were translated from English and French. They even went so far as producing fake letters or writing prefaces endorsing the status of their novels as translations. This was because professional writing, i.e. "writing novels for money," was not accepted in Italy, therefore if novels were translated from English and French, they would easily be accepted. Italian writers then found pseudotranslation a way to "mask" their creation so that it could be accepted in the literary market. Undoubtedly, they would keep the real status under cover in order that their novels would enjoy the status of a translation. See Douglas Robinson, "Pseudotranslation," in *Routledge Encyclopedia of Translation Studies*, ed. Mona Baker (London and New York: Routledge, 2001), pp. 183–185.

66 The original Thai reads:

> เราไม่มี [illegible due to termite damage]
> โยกถอนความเชื่อของบุคคลที่ยึดถือมั่นว่าไทยแต่งเรื่องไม่ดีไม่
> เพราะไม่สนุกไม่มีฝีมือเสียแล้ว ข้าพเจ้าจึงแต่งเรื่องฝรั่งเรื่องนางเนรมิตนี้
> แลเรื่องฝรั่งอื่นๆซึ่งแต่งเองทั้งนั้นมากกว่าเรื่องที่ได้แปลโดยมาก

See the postscript in Winthuphramanakul, *Nang neramid*, p. 403.

Conclusion

Translation changed the Thai literary repertoire. For a new literary model to enter the repertoire, it requires a complex process of negotiation, as we can see in the cases of "The Conversation of Nai Chit and Nai Chai" and "*Sanuknuek*" in which prose fiction was rejected outright, whereas later works of literary translation enjoy increasing acceptance. Although humanistic realism began to gain a presence in Thai poetry, translation introduced verisimilitude as a new literary aesthetic that did not need verse forms to ensure readers' acceptance. Mae Wan devised a way to deal with the fictional illusion of *Khwam phayabat* in order to maintain readers' willing suspension of disbelief. He decisively deleted those parts of the translation which might evoke the readers' doubt, and inserted more description in order to make the story more palatable for Thai readers. The "adaptive" translation strategy was widely used among translators at that time. Translated fictions were also so popular that a local novel such as *Khwam mai phayabat* could not break into the circle. *Khwam mai phayabat* aimed at another level of reality—a representational truth—that comes with verisimilitude in the form of *roman total.* Sophisticated as it was, the first Thai novel did not manage to challenge the "static" perception of prose fiction as an exotic story written to give pleasure. The resort to pseudotranslation in *Nang neramid* is testimony to this.

As an answer to Thak Chaloemtiarana's proposal to include these three novels in the Thai literary canon, I believe that, considering their roles in negotiating with the "static" canonicity, these three works exhibit complex struggles to make the canon more dynamic. They made available the aesthetics that had barely been elaborated in traditional Thai literary conventions. Even though their models might not be considered "static" or stable in their time, these models were taken up by later translators and authors who benefited from these pioneering works. In this way, *Khwam phayabat*, *Khwam mai phayabat*, and *Nang neramid* deserve a place in the Thai literary canon for generating literary dynamism that endows Thai literature with more diversity.

Bibliography

Baker, Chris, and Pasuk Phongpaichit, trans. *The Tale of Khun Chang Khun Phaen*. Chiang Mai: Silkworm Books, 2010.

Barang, Marcel. *The 20 Best Novels of Thailand*. Bangkok: TMC, 1994.

Chaloemtiarana, Thak. "Khru Liam's *Nang neramid*: Siamese Fantasy, Rider Haggard's *She*, and the Divine Egyptian Nymphs." *South East Asia Research* 15, no. 1 (2007), pp. 29–52.

———. "*Khwam mai phayabat* khong khru liam lae khwam than samai khong thai thi pen panha ความไม่พยาบาทของครูเหลียมและความทันสมัยของไทยที่เป็นปัญหา" [Khru Liam's *Khwam mai phayabat* and the problematics of Thai modernity]. *Rathasatsan* รัฐศาสตร์สาร [Political sciences journal] 28, no. 2 (2007), pp. 63–112.

———. "*Nang neramid*: Theptida Egypt, ruang phet lae khwam phoefan khong phuchai nai nawaniyay thai yuk raek นางเนรมิต: เทพธิดาอียิปต์ เรื่องเพศและความเพ้อฝันของผู้ชายไทยในนวนิยายไทยยุคแรก" [*Nang neramid*: Egyptian nymphs, sex, and the male fantasy in an early Thai novel]. *Rathasatsan* รัฐศาสตร์สาร [Political sciences journal] 29, no. 1 (2008), pp. 1–37.

———. "Making New Space in the Thai Literary Canon." *Journal of Southeast Asian Studies* 40, no. 1 (2009), pp. 87–110.

Corelli, Marie. *Vendetta: Or the Story of One Forgotten*. 1886. Project Gutenberg, 2003. http://www.gutenberg.org/ebooks/4360.

Devahastin na Ayutthaya, Sanan [Chaophraya Thammasakmontree]. "Maihed bedtaled หมายเหตุเบ็ดเตล็ด" [Miscellaneous postscripts]. *Lakwitthaya* ลักวิทยา [Stealing knowledge journal] 1, no. 8 (1900), pp. 654–661.

Ditheeyont, Winita. *Pakkai wannakam* ปากไก่วรรณกรรม [Feather pen of literature]. Bangkok: Dokya, 1994.

Eoseewong, Nidhi. *Pakkai lae bairua* ปากไก่และใบเรือ: ว่าด้วยการศึกษาประวัติศาสตร์วรรณกรรมต้นรัตนโกสินทร์ [Pen and sail: Literature and history in early Bangkok]. Bangkok: Praew Samnakphim, 2000.

Even-Zohar, Itamar. "Polysystem Theory." *Poetics Today* 11, no. 1 (1990), pp. 9–26.

———. "The Position of Translated Literature within the Literary Polysystem." *Poetics Today* 11, no. 1 (1990), pp. 45–51.

Golden, Leon. "Aristotle." In *The Johns Hopkins Guide to Literary Theory and Criticism*, edited by Michael Groden, Martin Kreiswirth, and Imre Szeman. Baltimore and London: The Johns Hopkins University Press, 1994, pp. 67–71.

Harrison, Rachel. "'Elementary, My Dear Wat'—Influence and Imitation in the Early Crime Fiction of 'Late Victorian' Siam." In *Chewing over the West: Occidental Narratives in Non-Western Readings*, edited by Doris Jedamski. Amsterdam: Rodopi, 2009, pp. 303–348.

———. "Introduction: The Allure of Ambiguity: The 'West' and the Making of Thai Identities." In *The Ambiguous Allure of the West: Traces of the Colonial in Thailand*, edited by Rachel Harrison and Peter Jackson. Hong Kong: Hong Kong University Press, 2010, pp. 1–36.

Hermans, Theo. *Translation in Systems*. Manchester: St. Jerome, 1999.

Herzfeld, Michael. "The Conceptual Allure of the West: Dilemmas and Ambiguities of Crypto-Colonialism in Thailand." In *The Ambiguous Allure of the West: Traces of the Colonial in Thailand*, edited by Rachel Harrison and Peter Jackson. Hong Kong: Hong Kong University Press, 2010, pp. 173–186.

Limapichart, Thanapol. "The Prescription of Good Books: The Formation of the Discourse and Cultural Authority of Literature in Modern Thailand (1860s–1950s)." Ph.D. dissertation, University of Wisconsin-Madison, 2008.

Loos, Tamara. *Subject Siam: Family, Law, and Colonial Modernity in Thailand*. Chiang Mai: Silkworm Books, 2006.

Mae Wan [pseud.], trans. *Khwam phayabat* ความพยาบาท [Vendetta: Or the story of one forgotten]. By Marie Corelli. 2nd ed. Bangkok: Ongkarnkha Khong Khurusabha, 1975.

Mojdara Rutnin, Mattani. *Modern Thai Literature: The Process of Modernization and the Transformation of Values*. Bangkok: Thammasat University Press, 1988.

Nuttall, A. D. *A New Mimesis: Shakespeare and the Representation of Reality*. New Haven and London: Yale University Press, 2007.

Rambelli, Paolo. "Pseudotranslations, Authorship and Novelists in Eighteenth-Century Italy." In vol. 1 of *Translating Others*, edited by Theo Hermans. Manchester: St. Jerome, 2006, pp. 181–194.

Robinson, Douglas. "Pseudotranslation." In *Routledge Encyclopedia of Translation Studies*, edited by Mona Baker. London and New York: Routledge, 2001, pp. 183–185.

Schehr, Lawrence R. *Subversions of Verisimilitude: Reading Narrative from Balzac to Sartre*. New York: Fordham University Press, 2009.

Schuyler Jr, Montgomery. "The Editions and Translations of *Çakuntala*." *Journal of the American Oriental Society* 22 (1901), pp. 237–248.

Senanan Kongkanan, Wibha. *Kamnerd nawaniyay nai prathet thai* กำเนิดนวนิยายในประเทศไทย [The genesis of the novel in Thailand]. Bangkok: Dokya, 1997.

Senanan, Wibha. *The Genesis of the Novel in Thailand*. Bangkok: Thai Watana Panich, 1975.

Seriwat, Sudarat. *Wiwatthanakan khong ruangsan nai muang thai tangtae raek jon theung phutthasakkarat 2475* วิวัฒนาการเรื่องสั้นในเมืองไทยตั้งแต่แรกจนถึง พ.ศ. ๒๔๗๕ [The evolution of short stories in Thailand from the beginning to 1932]. Bangkok: Ministry of Education, 1979.

Smyth, David. "Towards the Canonizing of the Thai Novel." In *The Canon in Southeast Asian Literatures*, edited by David Smyth. Surrey: Curzon Press, 2000, pp. 171–181.

Sterling, Ewlyn F. "The Theory of Verisimilitude in the French Novel Prior to 1830." *The French Review* 40, no. 5 (1967), pp. 613–619.

Thapar, Romilar. *Śakuntalā*: *Texts, Readings, Histories*. New Delhi: Kali for Women, 1999.

Vespada, Dhanate. "Thai Texts on Poetics: Concept and Relation to Thai Literary Convention." Ph.D. dissertation, Chulalongkorn University, 2000.

W. Winichaikul [pseud.], trans. *Khwam phayabat* ความพยาบาท [Vendetta: Or the story of one forgotten]. By Marie Corelli. 3rd ed. Bangkok: Pheundee, 2003.

Warathorn, Suphannee. *Prawat karnpraphan nawaniyay thai tangtae samai rermraek chon theung phutthasakkarat 2475* ประวัติการประพันธ์นวนิยายไทยตั้งแต่สมัยเริ่มแรกจนถึง พ.ศ. ๒๔๗๕ [History of Thai prose fictions from the beginning to 1932]. Bangkok: Social Sciences and Humanities Text Books Foundation, 1976.

Weerawong, Sumalee. *Roykaew naew mai khong thai phutthasakkarat 2417 theung 2453* ร้อยแก้วแนวใหม่ของไทย พ.ศ. ๒๔๑๗-๒๔๕๓ [Thai prose fictions from 1874 to 1910]. Bangkok: Siam publishing house, 2004.

Winthuphramanakul, Liam. *Khwam mai phayabat* ความไม่พยาบาท [The non-vendetta]. Bangkok: Rong Phim Thai Na Saphan Yotse, 1915.

———. *Nang neramid* นางเนรมิตร [Created nymphs]. Bangkok, 1916.

Wongkul, Phittaya. *Anyamanee haeng Wannakam Thai* อัญมณีแห่งวรรณกรรมไทย [The gems of Thai literature]. Bangkok: Dok Mali, 1990.

(De)Colonialization and Elite Collusion

“Incest Performed”: The Neocolonial Perversion of Translation in Malaysia

Nazry BAHRAWI

Introduction

As a decolonial strategy, translation scholars have argued that the act of appropriating source texts is a liberating enterprise for translators.[1] Yet, if the practice of translation in post-independence Malaysia were to be factored, this sense of empowerment assumes an ominous tone in serving to maintain the dominance of an elite class to the detriment of minority groups. Indeed, translation is never an “innocent, transparent activity” but one embroiled in issues of power relations, argues translation theorist Susan Bassnett.[2] Another theorist André Lefevere accords the translator a more prominent role than the author when he portrays translation as “a rewriting of an original text.”[3] With post-colonial translation, Bassnett and Trivedi speak of “the Empire translating back” where translations performed by the formerly colonized are imbued with the spirit of unshackling hegemony and empowering themselves.[4] Here, Bassnett points to a vividly visual metaphor that has

1 See, for instance, Shantha Ramakrishna, “Cultural Transmission through Translation: An Indian Perspective,” in *Changing the Terms: Translating in the Postcolonial Era*, ed. Sherry Simon and Peter St-Pierre (Ottawa, Canada: University of Ottawa Press, 2000), pp. 87–100. In this essay, Ramakrishna argues that India’s “counter-translation” projects by translators like Ganesh Shankar Vidyarthi is aimed at diminishing the legacy of British colonialism.

2 Susan Bassnett, *Comparative Literature: A Critical Introduction* (Oxford: Blackwell, 1993), p. 2.

3 André Lefevere, *Translation, Rewriting, and the Manipulation of Literary Fame* (London: Routledge, 1992), p. xi.

4 Susan Bassnett and Harish Trivedi, “Of Colonies, Cannibals and Vernaculars,” in

come to define this phenomenon—that of cannibalism. She cites the Brazilian poet Oswald de Andrade who argues that "only by devouring Europe could the colonized break away from what was imposed upon them."[5] Despite this being a formidable parable, the idea of translating for decolonization is not quite as straightforward. It begs the question: Could these rewritings subjugate as much as, or even more than, they liberate?

This paper argues that such is the case if one examines translation practices in twentieth-century Malaysia. I arrive at this position through an analysis of the Malay translation of *The Myth of the Lazy Native*, a sociological treatise first penned in English in 1977 by the Malaysian intellectual Syed Hussein Alatas that challenges the European imperialists' construction of the Malays, Javanese and Filipinos in Southeast Asia as indigenous people averse to hard work, thereby justifying colonization as a necessary civilizing force to instill "progress" in these societies. I argue that if *Myth* was intended to liberate oppressed groups when it was first penned, its Malay translation signifies a sinister turn in subjugating the nation's ethnic minorities[6] to a racialized ideology known as "*ketuanan Melayu*," or Malay supremacy.

My analysis will be primarily couched in André Lefevere's concept of patronage as playing a central role in determining the kinds of texts that get translated into a literary system. Lefevere posits that patronage can be invested in persons, institutions or political parties, and that it comprises three components: ideology, the economic imperative, and status.[7] Though a system may have multiple patrons that conform to different components,

---

Postcolonial Translation Theory: Theory and Practice, ed. Susan Bassnett and Harish Trivedi (London: Routledge, 1999), p. 8.

5 Bassnett and Trivedi, "Of Colonies, Cannibals and Vernaculars," pp. 4–5.

6 Malays are demographically figured as the majority, at about 50.1 percent of the population. The Chinese form about 22.6 percent, and the Indians about 6.7 percent. Indigenous non-Malays make up about 11 percent of the population. These figures are taken from the CIA World Factbook website, accessed 29 August 2014, https://www.cia.gov/library/publications/the-world-factbook/geos/my.html.

7 Lefevere, *Translation, Rewriting, and the Manipulation*, pp. 15–16.

this paper explores how and why all three components in our case study can be traced back to the same patron—the United Malays National Organization, or UMNO for short, which is the dominant political party in Malaysia's ruling coalition.[8] Politically, UMNO's appeal hinges on its stature as advocates of "*ketuanan Melayu*," an ideology that accords special privileges to the majority Malays by virtue of their official status as the "natives" of Malaysia. This paper will also explore the ways in which patronage in Malaysia is complicated by the figure of Mahathir Mohamad, Malaysia's prime minister and the leader of UMNO at the time the Malay adaptation of *Myth* was published. Finally, I will outline the wider implications of this case study in reframing the discourse of neocolonialism and the metaphoric of post-colonial translation.

The Text and Its Context

I begin by situating Alatas' *Myth* in Malaysia's socio-political climate. First published in English in 1977, *Myth* was translated into the Indonesian language in 1988 and then into Malay just a year after in 1989. Although focused on the Malay translation, this paper will refer to the Indonesian translation of *Myth* as a foil for comparison to highlight the discrepancies in the Malay version. This is plausible because both languages share similar syntactical structure and semantics, though some differences exist in spelling and vocabulary. For ease of reference, I shall henceforth refer to the two target texts such: the Malay translation will be coined TTM to signify "target text Malay" and the Indonesian version as TTI as an abbreviation for "target text Indonesian."

A work of international significance, *Myth* has been cited by at least 478 subsequent academic works, chiefly in the field of post-colonial studies.[9] Most

8 At the time this paper was written, Malaysia's ruling coalition known as Barisan Nasional, or National Front still forms the majority in parliament. Formed in 1973, this coalition is made up primarily of ethnic-based political parties that include the Malaysian Chinese Association (MCA) and the Malaysian Indian Congress (MIC) besides UMNO.

9 This figure refers to the 1977 edition of *The Myth of the Lazy Native* as indicated on

notably, the key post-colonial thinker Edward Said has referred to the book twice, first in *Covering Islam* where he calls it a "penetrating study"[10] and later in *Culture and Imperialism*.[11] Given its influence on Said, one can argue that *Myth* is a seminal work that anticipates Said's theory of Orientalism.

Within the Malaysian context, *Myth* represents a retort foremost to the British colonialist's construction of Malay natives as lazy. It also serves as a critique to Mahathir's controversial book *The Malay Dilemma* written in English in 1970. Released a year after violent racial riots transpired between the Malays and the Chinese, *Dilemma* argues that the stark economic disparity between the two groups is the result of hereditary and environmental factors. It is these, says Mahathir, which make the Malays less prone to hard work as opposed to the Chinese. Mahathir recommends an affirmative action programme that "seeks to urbanize the Malays" by according them special privileges in areas like business and education.[12] His recommendations were later implemented under the New Economic Policy (NEP) programme during his tenure as Malaysia's fourth and longest serving prime minister between 1981 and 2003. It is Malaysia's national language academy *Dewan Bahasa dan Pustaka*, or the DBP, that undertakes the task of translating *Myth* into Malay in 1989, some 12 years after the publication of its original English version. Considering that Mahathir employs strict censorship measures to keep dissenting voices down,[13] it is imperative to ask: How

---

the Google Scholar's official website, accessed 29 August 2014, http://scholar.google.co.uk/scholar?hl=en&q=the+myth+of+the+lazy+native&btnG=&as_sdt=1%2C5&as_sdtp.

10 Edward Said, *Covering Islam: How the Media and Experts Determine How We See the Rest of the World* (London: Routledge and Kegan Paul, 1981), p. 166.

11 Edward Said, *Culture and Imperialism* (London: Chatto & Windus, 1993), p. 419.

12 Mahathir Mohamad, *The Malay Dilemma* (Singapore: Times Books, 1970), pp. 105–107, 112.

13 See, for instance, Barry Wain, *Malaysian Maverick: Mahathir Mohamad in Turbulent Times* (New York: Palgrave Macmillan, 2009), p. 81; and Edmund T. Gomez and Jomo K. S., *Malaysia's Political Economy: Politics, Patronage and Profits* (Cambridge: Cambridge University Press, 1999), pp. 2–3. In Wain, *Malaysian Maverick*, p. 40, the author cites the *Far Eastern Economic Review*'s comments that Mahathir was vying

can a book denigrating the authoritarian leader get translated during his rule?

Here, the timing of the translation is significant because it points to several factors that may have influenced the move. First, the political atmosphere in the years leading up to the translation was unfavourable to Mahathir. In 1997, he faced internal challenges to his leadership from politicians within UMNO. Inundated with criticisms over his pro-Malay NEP programme, Mahathir barely survived an internal party election after winning just over 50 percent of votes from UMNO cadres. Some dissenters later left UMNO to form a new political party known as *Semangat* '46 or the Spirit of '46.[14] This grouping was officially registered in mid-1989,[15] the same year that saw TTM published. Second, Mahathir suffered health problems in 1989. After experiencing a minor heart attack, he underwent a coronary bypass surgery in January but re-assumed his duties as prime minister in April.[16] At the time the TTM was published, Mahathir was thus not just seen to be politically weak, but also physically incapacitated.

A third factor relates to Alatas' status as a founder of an opposition political party known as Parti Gerakan Malaysia. Just a year before the TTM was published, Alatas returned to Malaysia to assume the post of vice-chancellor of a local university after spending nearly two decades in neighbouring Singapore as the head of the Malay Studies Department at the National University of Singapore.[17] While Alatas was no longer a member of the opposition party at that time, his searing criticisms against Mahathir and stature as a former opposition political member qualify

---

to "further bind an already cowed, pro-establishment media" by introducing the Printing Presses and Publications Act in 1987.

14 The name serves to invoke the original spirit of UMNO when it was formed in 1946. Members of this party believe that UMNO under the care of Mahathir has lost its way.

15 In-Won Hwang, *Personalized Politics: The Malaysian State under Mahathir* (Singapore: Institute of Southeast Asian Studies, 2003), p. 182.

16 Wain, *Malaysian Maverick*, pp. 57, 77.

17 Terenjit Sevea, "In Memoriam: Syed Hussein Alatas—The Postcolonial Oeuvre," *OpinionAsia*, 30 January 2007, http://archive.today/A4dEZ.

the TTM as a challenge to the latter's leadership. These factors suggest that *Myth* was translated at a time when Mahathir's position as Malaysia's top leader is seen to be wobbly. Given that the DBP is a government institution, the move to translate *Myth* can be seen as a clandestine literary coup d'état by certain quarters within UMNO to oust what they perceive to be a weak despot.

Patronage: Ideology Unmasked

I will first analyze the TTM by way of Lefevere's ideological component. A close reading of chapters 10 and 11 of the TTM reveals taints of the "*ketuanan Melayu*" ideology at play. My study will be directed at these two chapters because they deal primarily with Mahathir's views of the Malay Malaysians. There are two ways whereby the ideology of "*ketuanan Melayu*" in the TTM can be unmasked, namely, through semantic manipulations and omissions. Let me review each in turn.

Semantic Manipulations

To begin, the TTM is replete with semantic alterations that enhance the foreignness of the Chinese and Indian minorities in Malaysia. The translations of the following two excerpts from the English text will illustrate this:

> In colonial capitalism, the European community was the most valued, next came the *immigrant* population, and lastly the indigenous population.[18] [Emphasis by author]
>
> The British were accused of crippling the spirit of the Malays by various means, one of which was calling the Malays lazy while they brought *immigrants* from China and India to exploit the rich resources of the

18 Syed Hussein Alatas, *The Myth of the Lazy Native: A Study of the Image of the Malays, Filipinos, and Javanese from the 16th to the 20th Century and in the Ideology of Colonial Capitalism* (London: Frank Cass & Co., 1977), p. 151.

country for the benefit of the colonial power and the *immigrants*.[19] [Emphases by author]

The first excerpt represents a general observation. When translated, both the TTI[20] and TTM[21] use the word "*imigran*," which means "immigrant" in English.[22] This is not the case with the second excerpt, which pertains specifically to Malaysia. While the TTI still uses "*imigran*,"[23] TTM introduces the Malay word "*pendatang*" to refer to the Chinese and Indians.[24] Even though this term can be taken to mean "immigrant,"[25] it also has a derogatory connotation that is akin in meaning to "an intruder." This is repeated in another excerpt where Alatas summarizes Mahathir's point that the "immigrant population" has displaced the Malays.[26] Here again, TTI sticks to the term "*imigran*"[27] while TTM uses the more hostile "*pendatang*."[28]

Semantic manipulations are not only used to enhance the foreignness of the Chinese and Indians but to also entrench the idea that the Malays are the rightful inhabitants of Malaysia. Here, the translation of the term "Malaya"—the colonial name for Malaysia—is significant. The examples of two excerpts are instructive. In the first, Alatas uses "Malaya" to decry Mahathir's generalization positing that rice farmers across Malaysia see no need to be punctual because they only work for two months a year,

19 Alatas, *The Myth of the Lazy Native*, p. 152.

20 Syed Hussein Alatas, *Mitos Pribumi Malas* [The myth of the lazy native], trans. Akhmad Rofi'ie (Jakarta, Indonesia: LP3ES, 1988), p. 210.

21 Syed Hussein Alatas, *Mitos Peribumi Malas* [The myth of the lazy native], trans. Zainab Kassim (Selangor, Malaysia: Dewan Bahasa dan Pustaka, 1989), p. 145.

22 *Tuttle's Concise Indonesian Dictionary: Indonesian-English, English-Indonesian*, rev. ed. (Tokyo: Tuttle, 1993), s.v. "imigran." And *Collins English-Malay, Malay-English Dictionary*, 1st ed. (Glasgow: HarperCollins, 2005), s.v. "imigran."

23 Alatas, *Mitos Pribumi Malas*, p. 211.

24 Alatas, *Mitos Peribumi Malas*, p. 146.

25 *Collins English-Malay, Malay-English Dictionary*, s.v. "pendatang."

26 Alatas, *The Myth of the Lazy Native*, p. 158.

27 Alatas, *Mitos Pribumi Malas*, p. 39.

28 Alatas, *Mitos Peribumi Malas*, p. 153.

and are hence indolent.[29] In the second instance, Alatas summarizes Mahathir's argument that describes the Chinese such: "Chinese experience in graft and bribery at home served them in good stead in *Malaya*."[30] [Emphasis by author.] The first example, which does not compare the Malays to other races, sees "Malaya" being retained in both the TTI[31] and TTM.[32] With the second, however, "Malaya" is translated as "*Tanah Melayu*" in the TTM,[33] which means "land belonging to the Malays." By insinuating that the Malays own the land, the Chinese are again portrayed as intruders who have blemished Malaysia through their bad practices of "graft and bribery." Here, the idea of loyalty to a common land also helps to unite the Malays against the Chinese in an "us" versus "them" binary opposition that mirrors the colonizer/colonized dichotomy.

Omissions

Other than semantic manipulations, taints of the "*ketuanan Melayu*" ideology can be gleaned from ellipses in the TTM. The most telling instance comes from the following summary of Mahathir's views:

> The clash between the hereditarily and environmentally *weak* Malays and *strong* Chinese had an adverse effect on the Malays.[34] [Emphases by author]

When translated, the TTI retains the "weak" and "strong" juxtaposition between the two races[35] while the TTM omits them.[36] In doing so, the blame that Mahathir partly traces to the perceived weakness of the Malays is diminished in the TTM. Rather, the translated Malay sentence reads like there is a clash between the inherited traditions of the Chinese and

29 Alatas, *The Myth of the Lazy Native*, p. 172.
30 Ibid., p. 156.
31 Alatas, *Mitos Pribumi Malas*, p. 240.
32 Alatas, *Mitos Peribumi Malas*, p. 171.
33 Ibid., pp. 151–152.
34 Alatas, *The Myth of the Lazy Native*, p. 156.
35 Alatas, *Mitos Pribumi Malas*, p. 218.
36 Alatas, *Mitos Peribumi Malas*, p. 151.

the Malays, leading the former to take advantage of the latter. Perhaps the most obvious example of omission is the absence of the following sentence in TTM: "In his [Mahathir's] view, the Malays are by hereditary inferior to the Chinese."[37] This damning sentence is excluded in the TTM[38] but reproduced in the TTI.[39]

Patronage: Status and Economic Impetuses

I will now examine the TTM in relation to Lefevere's status and economic components of patronage, bearing in mind that the patron here refers to UMNO. As I will highlight, there are numerous instances in the TTM that cushion harsh criticisms against UMNO. Like my analysis of the ideological component, I shall again focus on semantic manipulations and omissions.

Semantic Manipulations

In the TTM, meanings have been manipulated to support UMNO. Take for instance the line where Alatas criticizes the party for championing an ideology that allows for "a *more thorough* degradation of the Malays than that expressed during the colonial period."[40] [Emphasis by author.] In the translations, the idea that UMNO's ideology as opposed to the colonialists' is more oppressive to the Malays is downplayed when "degradation" is translated as "irresponsible" instead of "more thorough."[41] The nuance here is striking. The word "irresponsible" implies a tinge of skepticism about the charge of "degradation," perhaps even calling into question its veracity. The phrase "more thorough," however, connotes a certain truth to the accusation. That this specific translation in the TTM does not depart from that in the TTI when most other passages concerning UMNO do strengthens the

37 Alatas, *The Myth of the Lazy Native*, p. 155.

38 Alatas, *Mitos Peribumi Malas*, p. 150.

39 Alatas, *Mitos Pribumi Malas*, p. 216.

40 Alatas, *The Myth of the Lazy Native*, p. 154.

41 Alatas, *Mitos Pribumi Malas*, p. 215. And Alatas, *Mitos Peribumi Malas*, p. 149.

postulation that there is an effort to diminish criticisms against the party.

Although other similar examples abound, the few that we have highlighted suggest that the TTM could be part of a wider attempt by individuals within UMNO to discredit Mahathir when he is seen to be at his most vulnerable. That is to say, the TTM's translator Zainab Kassim and her superiors at the DBP may possibly be anticipating a leadership change at UMNO and hedging their bets there. While the DBP translators have no qualms in criticizing Mahathir, they are more careful about translating antagonistic statements on UMNO. Their reluctance at denigrating the party delineates their belief that Mahathir can be replaced, but UMNO's stature as Malaysia's most powerful political party is more assured. To go against UMNO's ideology of Malay supremacy is therefore to endanger their careers.

Omissions

In terms of the status and economic components of Lefevere's theory, one of the clearest attempts where patronage is maintained can be illustrated through the omission of lines that allege corruption within UMNO's ranks as follows:

> The Secretary General [of UMNO] himself occupied an important position in a shipping company.[42]
>
> The fraternity between the top UMNO leadership and big business interest is a well-known fact.[43]
>
> They [UMNO politicians] are located on the other fringes of big business, on the boards of directors. The wealth and power of big business must have impressed them.[44]

While these lines are reproduced in the TTI,[45] they are starkly missing from the TTM.[46] This is significant considering that Alatas' criticisms

42 Alatas, *The Myth of the Lazy Native*, p. 153.

43 Ibid.

44 Ibid.

45 Alatas, *Mitos Pribumi Malas*, p. 213.

46 Alatas, *Mitos Peribumi Malas*, pp. 147–148.

of Mahathir's views in *Dilemma* are left intact (in fact, even enhanced) in the TTM. Take for instance the following damning sentences against Mahathir for arguing that "running amok" is a generically Malay trait:

> What Mahathir did was to use amok instead of *latah* as an element in the Malay community's psychological make-up; the suggestion has a *colonial ring* to it.[47]

> Mahathir's *unfamiliarity* with social sciences made him suggest amok to be a basic part of the Malay psychology.[48]

It is notable that the first sentence, which describes Mahathir as a pseudo-colonialist, is retained in both translations[49] while damaging sentences about UMNO like those presented earlier are omitted. With the second sentence, the TTM translates "unfamiliarity" as "*ketidaktahuan*" instead of "*ketidakbiasaan*."[50] The first Malay word connotes "ignorance" while the second one means, as its English equivalent, "unfamiliarity."[51] The translator therefore uses a much stronger term when describing Mahathir's poor grasp of social science concepts, making the UMNO leader appear incompetent. These examples imply that patronage with regard to the status and economic components, like ideology, is defined by loyalty to UMNO.

Neocolonial Elites: An Asian-Inspired Perspective

While this study stems from a context that makes up part of the "Asian translation traditions," the implications of its findings are not limited to translation practices in Malaysia or Asia. In this section, we explore its wider repercussions on post-colonial theory, specifically on the notion of neocolonialism. In contemporary post-colonial discourse, scholars have argued that neocolonialists, or powerbrokers in former colonies, are

47 Alatas, *The Myth of the Lazy Native*, p. 177.

48 Ibid.

49 Alatas, *Mitos Pribumi Malas*, p. 247. And Alatas, *Mitos Peribumi Malas*, p. 177.

50 Alatas, *Mitos Peribumi Malas*, p. 177.

51 *Collins English-Malay, Malay-English Dictionary*, s.v. "ketidakbiasaan."

defined by their dependence on Western powers. First theorized by Ghana revolutionary Kwame Nkrumah in his book *Neo-colonialism: The Last Stage of Imperialism* (1965), neocolonialism describes a condition where native elites occupy the position of "unwitting or even willing agents (compradors) for the former colonial rulers."[52] Since then, neocolonialism has been

> associated less with the influence of the former colonial powers and more with the role of the new superpower of the United States, whose expansionist policy past and present, it is argued, constitutes a new form of imperialism.[53]

Though the concept may have evolved, there is an implicit assumption in both definitions that neocolonial elites have a need to defer to a "Western" master. With the latter, Robert Young argues that neocolonialism is the product of development and dependency theory that sees elites from former colonies taking up loans from Western banks and nations to emulate the superior economies of First World nations, thereby entrenching their dependency.[54] This dependency continues, Young argues, with the advent of critical development theory that posits neocolonial elites as aiming to "develop" not just economics, but other areas such as politics, culture and society up to the standards of the Western world.[55]

Having unearthed manipulations in the Malay translation of *Myth*, our findings however run contrary to such Eurocentric perspectives. If there is deference in our case study, it is not directed at maintaining the interests of a "Western" master. Rather, dependency is predicated on serving a dominant native faction. In explaining this phenomenon, one can take credence from Hamid Dabashi's argument that the nature of neocolonialism in the contemporary world is the result of capitalism. He writes:

---

52 Bill Ashcroft, Gareth Griffiths and Helen Tiffin, *Post-Colonial Studies: The Key Concepts*, 2nd ed. (London: Routledge, 2000), p. 146.

53 Ibid.

54 Robert Young, *Postcolonialism: An Historical Introduction* (Oxford: Blackwell Publishing, 2001), p. 50.

55 Ibid., pp. 52–53.

> The defining function of the comprador intellectuals is to shore up that relation of commerce to power.... Capital will use whatever and whoever is convenient for each particular time, place and situation.[56]

Indeed, our analysis of the status and economic components of patronage in *Myth* has shown the single patron to be the local political party UMNO, not America or Malaysia's former colonial ruler, Britain. This renders inapt the concept of the neocolonial elites as dependent on Western nations to Malaysia. We believe that the manifestation of neocolonialism in Malaysia resonates better with aspects of Vilfredo Pareto's theory of the "circulation of elites." Pareto believes that an "elite exists in all societies and rules them, even when the regime is seemingly one with the most widespread democracy."[57] As a perpetual presence in society, elites can be divided into governing and non-governing groups who are engaged in a constant struggle to oust one another in the pursuit of power, he further argues. Over time, a society will see power changing hands between different groups of elites, thereby resulting in the circulation of elites.[58]

In line with Pareto's treatise, our analysis of *Myth* highlights the power struggle between two groups of elites within UMNO represented by the pro- and anti-Mahathir camps. Also pertinent to our thesis is Pareto's observation that a governing elite will apply force and persuasion to prolong its grip on power, though no elites have been successful at holding on to power forever.[59] Here again, we can see the manipulations of the Malay translation of *Myth* as an attempt by a ruling elite to "persuade" the masses to back UMNO in the translation's ideological enhancement of the party's exclusivist philosophy of "*ketuanan Melayu*." Despite the rift within the party on Mahathir's rule, the manipulations suggest an unwavering support towards UMNO.

---

56 Hamid Dabashi, *Brown Skin, White Masks* (London: Pluto Press, 2011), p. 45.

57 Vilfredo Pareto, *Manual of Political Economy*, trans. Ann S. Schweir (London: Macmillan, 1971), p. 91.

58 Vilfredo Pareto, *Trattato di Sociologia Generale* (Firenze: Barbera, 1916), trans. Andrew Bongiorno and Arthur Livingstone as *The Mind and Society: A Treatise on General Sociology* (New York: Dover Publications, 1935).

59 Pareto, *Manual of Political Economy*, pp. 90–94.

This implies that neocolonial elites are not always subservient to a more powerful "Western" master as theorized by Nkrumah and Young. In cases like Malaysia, they may already be at the top strata of a society's power hierarchy. This could also be true of other former colonies that have achieved economic independence with little help from Western nations. Included in this list are tiger economies like Singapore, the United Arab Emirates and India. It may therefore be worthwhile to explore if like-minded manipulations of translations in these societies are also designed to maintain the power of a ruling elite. There is some indication that such is the case in India if we consider Gopal Gandhi's 1998 Hindi translation of Vikram Seth's *A Suitable Boy* (1993). Pointing to the critic Enakshi Chatterjee's disproval of the Hindi translation for omitting instances of caste politics, Rashmi Sadana argues that the translation propagates the view that "something new has entered the Hindi literary field: the cultural pressure of Hindu nationalism, or Hindutva."[60] Like the manipulations in TTM, this could be read as an attempt at maintaining the interests of a ruling elite given that the Hindi translation of *Boy* was released during the reign of the pro-Hindutva Bharatiya Janata Party in the same way *Myth* was published at the height of UMNO's rule. If scholars like Vicente Rafael (1988), Eric Cheyfitz (1991) and Tejaswini Niranjana (1992) point to the role of translation in perpetuating colonization, I will argue that translations can also entrench neocolonialism, a condition reframed in this essay to include native elites who dispense the hegemony once practised by their former masters.

Post-colonial Translation: From Cannibalism to Incest?

A second generic implication of this study relates to the field of post-colonial translation. This has to do with metaphorics, a critical strategy of comprehending translations through analogies. Metaphorics is premised on the proposition that there exists an undeniable "parallel between *doing*

60 Rashmi Sadana, "A Suitable Text for a Vegetarian Audience: Questions of Authenticity and the Politics of Translation," *Public Culture* 19, no. 2 (2007), p. 324.

translation, and the business of *making metaphors*."[61] Hanne argues that this congruence hinges on the view that both, while mired in imperfections, are necessary human undertakings. Translations facilitate communication between people of different cultures, a task which would have been "even more fraught with difficulties than it is if we did not undertake translations."[62] Metaphors, meanwhile, help us "to express ideas and emotions which go beyond the resources of so-called literal language."[63]

If we could now describe the alterations performed on Alatas' *Myth* with a metaphor, the image of cannibalism can no longer suffice. Rather, it is an act akin to incest. The analogy of translation as incest is not alien to the field of translation studies. The poet and translator Serge Gavronsky first raised it when he describes the alterations performed by the cannibalistic translator such:

> The original has been captured, raped, and *incest performed* … The original is mutilated beyond recognition: the slave-master dialectic reversed.[64] [Emphasis by author]

If Lori Chamberlain seizes on the notion of rape in the above passage to develop a metaphorics of gender in translation,[65] I believe it is the image of incest that best describes a metaphorics of neocolonialism. Implicit in our metaphor are aspects culled from other analogies that have been used to describe alterations to translations. To begin, there is a sort of violence that has been committed on Alatas' *Myth*. The idea of translational violence, Chamberlain argues, can be traced to the philosopher George Steiner's second of a four-part translation process which sees the translator taking a

61 Michael Hanne, "Epilogue: Metaphors for the Translator," in *The Translator as Writer*, ed. Susan Bassnett and Peter Bush (London: Continuum, 2006), pp. 208–224.

62 Ibid., p. 209.

63 Ibid., p. 210.

64 Serge Gavronsky, "The Translator: From Piety to Cannibalism," *Substance* 16, no. 6–7 (1977), p. 60.

65 Lori Chamberlain, "Gender and the Metaphorics of Translation," *Signs* 13, no. 3 (1988), p. 462.

hostile stance reminiscent of rape by "'penetrating' and 'capturing' the text."[66] In considering the violence done unto *Myth*, there is merit in appropriating Chamberlain's treatise that posits translation as a gendered act. Our case suggests that Alatas as the author is feminized and rendered "relatively powerless in relation to the translator," who is here figured as a male.[67] With the TTM, the translator Zainab has indeed "quietly usurp … the role of the author"[68] possibly under the instruction of her superiors at DBP to make Alatas seemingly supportive of UMNO's ideological stance despite the fact that the Malaysian thinker was an opposition politician and a fierce critic of "*ketuanan Melayu*."

The metaphor of incest gains even more currency if I consider that *Myth* is not a source text foreign to its interpretive community.[69] Despite donning the garb of an academic treatise, the fact that Alatas' purposes for writing the book are to "correct a one-sided colonial view of the Asian native and his society" and "unmask the colonial ideology"[70] suggests that its target audience are not just international academics but also a segment of the Malaysian society who are literate in English, namely, its elites. In this light, the initiative to translate *Myth* into Malay must not figure as a trans-cultural initiative but an intra-cultural one. When rendered into Malay, the translation's target audience is now expanded to also include members of the Malay public who are not well-versed with English.[71]

Metaphorically speaking, *Myth* is confined to the same "house" even as it interacts with other "occupants." As members of the same "household,"

66 Chamberlain, "Gender and the Metaphorics of Translation," p. 463.

67 Ibid., p. 457.

68 Ibid., p. 462.

69 The phrase "interpretive community" here denotes not a nation-state but a community of peoples that upholds similar socio-economic qualities. This could be based on ethnicity or class. In our case, it is a mixture of both.

70 Alatas, *The Myth of the Lazy Native*, p. 9.

71 The post-colonial move to institutionalize Malay as the official language in education and administration in Malaysia began in 1965 and culminated in 1983 when Malay became the primary language of instruction in all public universities for all subjects except English. See Saran K. Gill, "Language Policy in Malaysia: Reversing Direction," *Language Policy* 4, no. 3 (2005), p. 257.

the text and its translation thus share a kinship that sees each leading unique but intertwined lives. Yet this is no ordinary household. The birth of the translation is the product of an act of "violence" committed by the translator as a trusted guardian, an adoptive parent if we may, upon the original text that is his charge. In the case of *Myth*, the translation is one born out of wedlock, the "bastard child" of the original. It has also turned out to be a case of violence begetting violence. The translation embodies the abuse it suffers as it assumes the oppressive disposition of its perpetrator. Indeed, the perversion that taints the Malay translation of *Myth* finds an outlet in oppressing Malaysia's minority groups in the service of maintaining the interests of the ruling Malay elites. The bastard child, as Gavronsky muses, is "mutilated beyond recognition." This unhappy household has seen "incest performed."

Conclusion

Our reading of *Myth* suggests a malicious façade to the "Empire translates back" revolution. In vying to upkeep their dominance as the new masters through translations, we have shown how Malaysia's neocolonial elites resort to oppressing other less powerful groups within their own society. This phenomenon, we argue, may not be limited to Malaysia if we consider the case of Gandhi's Hindi translation of *Boy* in India.

Yet our reading may also be construed as incongruent to the burgeoning move among scholars to problematize the source/target dichotomy by the likes of Bassnett.[72] While there is merit in distancing translation studies from subscribing to such a dichotomy, we believe that exceptions must be made when appraising translation in light of hegemony and subjugation. In analyzing translations from the perspective of power relations, it may be useful, even necessary, to uphold the source/target dichotomy.

72 Susan Bassnett, "Writing and Translating," in Bassnett and Bush, *The Translator as Writer*, pp. 173–174. And Susan Bassnett, "Writing Time, Writing Space," in *World Literature, World Culture*, ed. Karen-Margrethe Simonson and Jakob Stougaard-Nielsen (Aarhus: Aarhus University Press, 2008), pp. 81, 85.

Only then can the scholar comprehensively, fully capture the nuances of manipulations.

Our study can also be figured as an attempt at plugging a lacuna in the field of post-colonial translation, which has seen much theorizing about the impact of European colonization but little on neocolonialism. An apt path forward therefore is to study the translations of similar anti-imperialist texts produced from within, and for, the same interpretive community. Hence, one possible research could be to analyze whether the elite-sponsored translations of Frantz Fanon's *Peau Noire, Masques Blancs* (Black skin, white masks, 1952) into the native languages of black-majority countries—if any exists—display signs of manipulation. The case of South Africa could be apt because it is, like Malaysia, a cosmopolitan nation ravaged by racialism. Another could be to explore the government-linked translations—again, if they exist—of Edward Said's *Covering Islam* into Arabic in Arab-majority societies, especially those with ethnic and/or religious minorities such as Egypt and Syria.

In such attempts, one can latch on Lefevere's concept of patronage as a useful lens to draw out neocolonial tendencies. However, it must also be said that Lefevere's framework should not be applied too rigidly. For instance, while Lefevere has listed five control factors that affect translation—namely, language, the universe of discourse, poetics, the translation professionals, and patronage, the analysis of non-fictional works such as *Myth* is best performed according to just three of these factors—namely, language, the translation professionals, and most importantly, patronage. The researcher needs to consider that the boundaries between these classifications that Lefevere constructs are porous. In the case of *Myth*, for instance, translation professionals are themselves part of the patron. If such researches produce findings that are congruent with this paper's analysis of *Myth*, then there is a strong case for crying incest over texts that have hitherto cried freedom.

Bibliography

Alatas, Syed Hussein. *The Myth of the Lazy Native: A Study of the Image of the Malays, Filipinos, and Javanese from the 16th to the 20th Century and in the Ideology of Colonial Capitalism*. London: Frank Cass & Co, 1977.

———. *Mitos Pribumi Malas* [The myth of the lazy native]. Translated by Akhmad Rofi'ie. Jakarta, Indonesia: LP3ES, 1988.

———. *Mitos Peribumi Malas* [The myth of the lazy native]. Translated by Zainab Kassim. Selangor, Malaysia: Dewan Bahasa dan Pustaka, 1989.

Ashcroft, Bill, Gareth Griffiths, and Helen Tiffin. *Post-Colonial Studies: The Key Concepts*. 2nd ed. London: Routledge, 2000.

Bassnett, Susan. *Comparative Literature: A Critical Introduction*. Oxford: Blackwell, 1993.

———. "Writing and Translating." In *The Translator as Writer*, edited by Susan Bassnett and Peter Bush. London: Continuum, 2006, pp. 173–183.

———. "Writing Time, Writing Space." In *World Literature, World Culture*, edited by Karen-Margrethe Simonson and Jakob Stougaard-Nielsen. Aarhus: Aarhus University Press, 2008, pp. 75–86.

Bassnett, Susan, and Harish Trivedi. "Of Colonies, Cannibals and Vernaculars." In *Postcolonial Translation Theory: Theory and Practice*, edited by Susan Bassnett and Harish Trivedi. London: Routledge, 1999, pp. 1–18.

Chamberlain, Lori. "Gender and the Metaphorics of Translation." *Signs* 13, no. 3 (1988), pp. 454–472.

Cheyfitz, Eric. *The Poetics of Imperialism: Translation and Colonization from The Tempest to Tarzan*. New York and Oxford: Oxford University Press, 1991.

Collins English-Malay, Malay-English Dictionary. 1st ed. Glasgow: HarperCollins, 2005.

Dabashi, Hamid. *Brown Skin, White Masks*. London: Pluto Press, 2011.

Fanon, Frantz. *Peau Noire, Masques Blancs* [Black skin, white masks]. Paris: Les Éditions du Seuil, 1952.

Gavronsky, Serge. "The Translator: From Piety to Cannibalism." *Substance* 16, no. 6–7 (1977), pp. 53–62.

Gill, Saran K. "Language Policy in Malaysia: Reversing Direction." *Language Policy* 4, no. 3 (2005), pp. 241–260.

Gomez, Edmund T., and Jomo K. S. *Malaysia's Political Economy: Politics, Patronage and Profits*. Cambridge: Cambridge University Press, 1999.

Hanne, Michael. "Epilogue: Metaphors for the Translator." In *The Translator as Writer*, edited by Susan Bassnett and Peter Bush. London: Continuum, 2006, pp. 208–224.

Hwang, In-Won. *Personalized Politics: The Malaysian State under Mahathir*. Singapore: Institute of Southeast Asian Studies, 2003.

Lefevere, André. *Translation, Rewriting, and the Manipulation of Literary Fame*. London: Routledge, 1992.

Mohamad, Mahathir. *The Malay Dilemma*. Singapore: Times Books, 1970.

Nkrumah, Kwame. *Neo-colonialism: The Last Stage of Imperialism*. London: Nelson, 1965.

Niranjana, Tejaswini. *Siting Translation: History, Post-structuralism and the Colonial Context*. Los Angeles: University of California Press, 1992.

Pareto, Vilfredo. *Trattato di Sociologia Generale*. Firenze: Barbera, 1916. Translated by Andrew Bongiorno and Arthur Livingstone as *The Mind and Society: A Treatise on General Sociology* (New York: Dover Publications, 1935).

———. *Manual of Political Economy*. Translated by Ann S. Schweir. London: Macmillan, 1971.

Rafael, Vicente. *Contracting Colonialism: Translation and Christian Conversion in Tagalog Society under Early Spanish Rule*. Ithaca, New York: Cornell University Press, 1988.

Ramakrishna, Shantha. "Cultural Transmission through Translation: An Indian Perspective." In *Changing the Terms: Translating in the Postcolonial Era*, edited by Sherry Simon and Peter St-Pierre. Ottawa, Canada: University of Ottawa Press, 2000, pp. 87–100.

Sadana, Rashmi. "A Suitable Text for a Vegetarian Audience: Questions of Authenticity and the Politics of Translation." *Public Culture* 19, no. 2 (2007), pp. 307–328.

Said, Edward W. *Covering Islam: How the Media and Experts Determine How We See the Rest of the World*. London: Routledge and Kegan Paul, 1981.

———. *Culture and Imperialism*. London: Chatto & Windus, 1993.

Seth, Vikram. *A Suitable Boy*. London: HarperCollins, 1993.

———. *Koi Accha-sa Ladka*. Translated by Gopal Gandhi. New Delhi: Vani Prakashan, 1998.

Sevea, Terenjit. "In Memoriam: Syed Hussein Alatas—The Postcolonial Oeuvre." *OpinionAsia*, 30 January 2007. http://archive.today/A4dEZ.

Tuttle's Concise Indonesian Dictionary: Indonesian-English, English-Indonesian. Rev. ed. Tokyo: Tuttle, 1993.

Wain, Barry. *Malaysian Maverick: Mahathir Mohamad in Turbulent Times.* New York: Palgrave Macmillan, 2009.

Young, Robert. *Postcolonialism: An Historical Introduction.* Oxford: Blackwell Publishing, 2001.

Transnational Mobility, Translation, and Transference: The Cultural Identities of British Interpreters in Two Colonial Asian Cities (1840–1880)[1]

Uganda Sze-pui KWAN

Introduction

Interpreters were once perceived as passive intermediaries whose hands were tied by their commissions. However, they can be examined in a different light when placed in the colonial space in which "colonizer" and "colonized" were rigidly segregated. In the historical settings of colonial Hong Kong and the Strait Settlements during the period between 1840 and 1880, interpreters were agents capable of shifting stagnant power hierarchies and knowledge terrain. This period is remarkable because it was a time when the imperial force had just taken over the twin cities—Hong Kong and Singapore—which were heavily populated by Chinese whose language and culture were still largely unintelligible to their rulers. It was also a time when interpreters had to discharge their duties without any fixed ethical or professional guidance. In this study, we use a case in Hong Kong to illustrate an interpreter's ability to manoeuvre between the rulers and the ruled from their "designated" position, which led to suspicions of "Traduttore, traditore" (translator, traitor) in the eyes of the colonizer. Then, we follow a comparable case in the Straits Settlements during the same historical period, which reveals that translators were more protectors than traitors. Interpreters were the key element in the

1 The author owes many thanks to Professor Theo Hermans, who gave invaluable comments on an earlier draft of this article.

construction of colonial government, because when they performed linguistic transference, they could shift psychological transference and thus, empower cultural identification.

In an information network society, cultural exchange is no longer conditioned by the actual traffic of commodities or the travels of human beings. Even if we stay at home, we can still receive a huge influx of knowledge through the Internet.[2] The world before the advent of the modern was drastically different. With all kinds of factors governed by economic, technological, social, and cultural constraints, travel was restricted and the circulation of gold and goods was impeded. Even in the nineteenth century, when the world possessed uneven and incompatible views of modernities, intercultural exchange was still very restricted. This is well illustrated by the Sino-British relations. The British Empire was mesmerized by the spirit of international trade, global travel and worldwide expansion. China, whom the British viewed as a potential commercial partner, characteristically refused to make contact with the foreign world and maintained a closed-door policy. She had no need for British goods and capital. Furthermore, contact with foreigners was prohibited. As a result, cultural exchanges between the two sides were very limited before the Opium War—a watershed in China's modernity. Against this background, we can see how two British colonies along the trade route to China in the Far East acted as cultural bridges for both people and material goods. The discussion will focus on the important role interpreters played in facilitating communication in these two colonies.

Cultural Mobility between Colonies and Empires

In a strict sense, there were no Sino-British relations before the Opium War. Since the reign of Qianlong 乾隆 (1736–1795), China had maintained a closed-door policy, isolating itself from the outside world. Foreigners, foreign ideas and technological innovations were seen as a

2 Manuel Castells, *The Rise of the Network Society: The Information Age: Economy, Society and Culture* (1996; repr., Cambridge, MA: Blackwell Publishers, 2011), p. 15.

threat to internal stability and harmony. Emperor Qianlong's "Anti-Barbarian Edict" (1757) included five articles prohibiting interaction with foreigners. The purpose was to ban any exchange, tangible (goods and capital) or intangible (ideas and language), between the Chinese and foreigners.

Between 1760 and 1839, Sino-British contacts were limited to one region, Canton, under the "one-port trade" policy. All other ports, such as Xiamen and Fuzhou, were closed to foreigners. Trade with foreigners in Canton was regulated by the so-called "Canton trading system." It embodied China's effort to maintain social stability by limiting trade with foreigners to those who had either paid tribute or been quarantined at entrepôts on the Chinese frontier. Even within the system there were strict rules regarding personal contact. The foreign traders were not allowed to communicate directly with Chinese officials. They could only make contact with a few licensed Chinese merchants, known as the "Cohong." The Cohong members were subjected to the imperially appointed superintendent of maritime customs at Canton, known to Westerners as the "Hoppo."[3] All of their activities in Canton were supervised by the top officials in that province, the governor of Canton (Guangdong) and the governor-general (or "viceroy") of Guangdong (Kwangtung) and Guangxi (Kwangsi), who issued their orders and regulations or passed them from the Court to the Cohong members. If the merchants failed to follow the imperial orders and handle their affairs properly, they would face heavy punishment or even be dismissed from the monopolized trading system. The Western traders found it frustrating that their opinions, petitions and desires were not directly submitted to the central government.[4] More often, they were forced to use the linguistic markers that reflected their lower hierarchal position when writing official documents to the Chinese government. Under the imperial edict, Chinese people who offered

3 Paul A. Van Dyke, *The Canton Trade: Life and Enterprise on the China Coast, 1700–1845* (Hong Kong: Hong Kong University Press, 2005).

4 Frederick Wakeman, "The Canton Trade and the Opium War," in *The Cambridge History of China*, vol. 10, *Late Ch'ing 1800–1911, Part 1*, ed. John K. Fairbank (Cambridge: Cambridge University Press, 1978), pp. 163–212.

foreigners help or taught them Chinese were regarded as traitors and were liable to banishment. The most dramatic and illustrative example was Robert Morrison's native teacher of Chinese, who always carried a bottle of poison with him to take his own life if he were caught by the officials.[5] Even this simple description reveals that communications between Chinese officials and foreign traders were both intricate and laborious. After two diplomatic missions (Macartney Mission in 1793 and Amherst Mission in 1816) to negotiate more freedom on trade ended in failure, the British Empire resolved the prolonged discontent with military force.

On the Chinese side, as foreigners were seen as barbarians, Chinese people had no intention of facilitating any interaction. People believed that they were under the favour of the heavenly son—the Chinese emperor—and few entertained the idea of migration. Traditionally, only criminals or fugitives left their country deliberately, but in the late imperial period, stricken by poverty, social unrest and natural catastrophe, many people were reduced to wandering. The situation in remote coastal areas was especially lamentable because they were not usually given immediate attention by the central government. The two Opium Wars and the Taiping Rebellion in the mid-nineteenth century also exposed the Qing government's inability to protect their people. The harsher tax that was imposed on peasants to pay off the indemnity owed to the foreign powers after these conflicts forced many destitute people to risk their lives and try their luck abroad. In fact, the increasing human mobility from China to the colonies was caused not only by social unrest in the Chinese Empire, but also by the prospect of the colonies. Situated on the prominent trade route, Hong Kong and Singapore served as important gateposts to China. The two cities prospered under British rule and attracted an enormous inflow of British, Indian, and Portuguese businessmen.[6] Cheap Chinese labour was another important factor that made the seaport

5 Alexander Wylie, *Memorials of Protestant Missionaries to the Chinese: Giving a List of Their Publications, and Obituary Notices of the Deceased* (Shanghae [Shanghai]: American Presbyterian Mission Press, 1867), p. 3.

6 Anonymous, *India, Ceylon, Straits Settlements, British North Borneo, Hong Kong* (London: Kegan Paul, Trench, Trübner, 1899), pp. 457, 502.

colonies prosperous. In the first half of the nineteenth century, there was a constant influx of immigrants who were mainly employed for manual work such as the transportation of opium, tin, tea, rubber, and spices. In the second half of the nineteenth century, Chinese businessmen brought their families and capital along to seek out less tumultuous environment on which to develop their businesses. The administration of the colonies encouraged and facilitated the blending of human capital, entrepreneurial ideas and material goods to generate wealth. The effectiveness of the judicial system was also crucial in the success of colonial rule, yet for the Western concepts of legal system, legislature, and public policy to be successfully transplanted, a good crop of competent and trustworthy interpreters was needed. In the first few decades of colonial governance, the British rule was plagued by an insufficient quantity of good-quality interpreters. The lack of capable and trustworthy interpreters who could translate between Chinese and English was a recurrent predicament in the Sino-British relations of the nineteenth century.

After the Opium War in 1842, Hong Kong was ceded to the British as a crown colony. In the newly established Hong Kong government, interpreters and translators were required at every step to implement the British rule. The functional and official language of the regime was English, but the local people did not speak that foreign tongue. No smooth interaction between the ruled and the ruling class was possible unless the huge linguistic and cultural gaps could be bridged. The colonizer was well aware of the problem:

> [I]t is not too much to say that for the last fifty years we have been content to go on in almost total ignorance of the language, habits and feelings of a great and, at any rate, the most important part of the population of our colonies in the Far East.[7]

---

7 James William Norton-Kyshe, *A Judicial History of the Straits Settlements 1786–1890*, which was originally published as the Preface of the four-volume work *Cases Heard and Determined in Her Majesty's Supreme Court of the Straits Settlements, 1808–1890*, reprinted with an introduction by M. B. Hooker in *Malaya Law Review* 11, no. 1 (1969), pp. 1–36, 107.

The British never attempted to completely uproot the Chinese element in Hong Kong and in the Straits Settlements, or to implement full-scale English education. Once a new law was issued, its announcement, proclamation, and execution were out of the hands of the ruling class. The success or failure of a public policy rested on the public's reception. Lamentably, the colonial government frequently faced the situation in which the proclamations were wrongly translated and thus misunderstood by the ruled. As a result of such miscommunication and various other grievances, the city was always on the verge of a riot and mired in a state of anarchy.

The British judicial and legal systems were not easy to implement. The Chinese and the British harboured different views of justice and consequently had different trial and prosecution procedures. To effectively transplant and execute the British rule in the colonies, the government had to have highly competent interpreters. Only after they fully grasped and transferred the ideas behind the British justice system could the stakeholders understand how to do business under British law. The task, however, was more daunting than anyone had imagined, and the chronic lack of interpreters had afflicted the British Empire for some time. The establishment of the colonial government only intensified the problem as the various quarters battled for the few capable interpreters. The extant interpreting team inherited from the Opium War was divided into two sections: one to conduct diplomatic relations in China and the other to take up the colonial administration in Hong Kong. Both diplomacy and colonial rule were supervised by the Hong Kong governor at the time, as he was also the plenipotentiary and chief superintendent of British trade in China. The former position had been under the jurisdiction of the Foreign Office and later the Colonial Office. It was only when the British established an embassy in Beijing under the Peking Convention (1860) that the diplomatic role played by the Hong Kong governor began to subside. In the exchange between British officials posted in the Far East and those in the British government, the lack of interpreters was a constant theme, indicating that it was one of the most formidable problems for the British at that time.

Indeed, the shortage of interpreters was ubiquitous in the Far East. The same want of interpreters was felt as early as in the 1820s when Singapore was ceded to the British, but the problem was not solved until the 1870s.[8] The need for interpreters at that time is well-documented in colonial correspondences, government annual reports, and judicial records. The governor-generals exploited every possible means to seek British citizens or foreigners who could undertake Chinese-English interpreting. They wrote to China, to the Colonial Office and to local missionary institutions.[9] Sir Robert Fullerton (1773–1831), the governor of Penang at the time, wrote on 18 June 1828 to "the Select Committee of Supra Cargoes" in Canton for assistance with and advice on the search for interpreters:

> It is with much regret we have to state that while we entertain every wish to comply with the request contained in the communication above referred to, we are unable to recommend any plan which promises hopes of succeeding in the desired object of employing the natives of this country in the situation of Interpreters.[10]

It is evident that the routine administration of the Straits was seriously compromised due to the lack of competent interpreters. However, this predicament had still not been resolved by 1858, when the East India Company (EIC) was abolished and the sovereignty of the Straits Settlements was transferred from the Company to the British government's India Office. The Straits Settlements, comprising three different possessions acquired from different sources by the British in different periods and combined in 1826—Penang, gained by the EIC's Captain Francis Light (1740–1794) from the Sultanate (King) of Kedah in 1790; Singapore by the EIC's Sir Stamford Raffles (1781–1826) from the Sultanate of Johor in 1824; and Malacca from the Netherlands in 1824—were declared a separate British Crown Colony in 1867. Lord Canning, the once Parliamentary Under-Secretary of State

8 Great Britain, Colonial Office (hereafter CO), CO 273/81/131–135, 15 August 1875.

9 C. B. Buckley, *An Anecdotal History of Old Times in Singapore*, vol. 1 (London: S.I., 1903), p. 205.

10 Norton-Kyshe, *A Judicial History of the Straits Settlements 1786–1890*, p. 107.

for Foreign Affairs but the then Governor-General of India, in a minute written in 1859 on the proposed transfer of the Straits to the India Office, stated clearly that the Straits were, as far as civil administration was concerned, a positive evil. The officers dealing with the Indian Empire had never foreseen that they would have to rule the Chinese. Therefore, while the Straits were to be transferred, little was known about the subjects to be ruled. The large part of the population of the Straits Settlements was different from any people that the India officers had dealt with before.[11]

From the perspective of the colonizer, Hong Kong and the Straits Settlements were like mirror cities that shared numerous similarities, both in geographical location and demographic composition. Even the perplexities of administering the colonial cities seemed the same. The colonial correspondences (CO 129 and CO 273), which were written by respective governors to the same colonial secretary in his London headquarters, reveal why a similar governmental structure was imposed in two different places. It was largely due to the fact that the Colonial Office projected the problems of one city onto the other. In addition, there was no far-sighted solution for dealing with the problems in the Far East colonies, and it was perceived that the most economical approach would be to use one method to deal with similar problems in both places. That is probably why similar offices, both in duty, name, and even personnel (by reposting the officers and governors), were created in the nineteenth century in both Hong Kong and Singapore. We return to this through the prism of the interpreters' job portfolios in the twin cities in later sections.

Social Mobility and the Profile of Imperial Interpreters in Asia

In this section, we show how imperial careers influenced the social structure and stability of Victorian Britain, which was a notoriously rigorous class society. Social historian François Bedarida argues that in the middle of the

11 Great Britain, India Office, *Correspondence Respecting the Transfer of Control over the Straits Settlements from the India Office to the Colonial Department* (London: H. M. Stationery Office, 1866), p. 13.

nineteenth century, the traditional distinctions of "upper" and "lower" classes were no longer as useful as they had been before when Karl Marx's class struggle was firstly introduced in England. Instead, it had become a common practice to define the British social system in terms of three layers when the middle class emerged. The three layers were: the bottom included the lower or working class, such as manual workers; next up was the middle class, the bourgeoisies; the top was the aristocracy (the upper class). This social stratification was the result of both tangible and intangible features: (1) one's position in the system of production, i.e. occupation, income, and standard of living; (2) a collective consciousness of belonging to a certain class; and (3) the sharing of common values in life, education, and status.[12] It functioned well because the stratification was so distinctive that almost every Victorian citizen knew his place and understood the rules of the game. Although education was recognized as a valuable tool for enhancing social mobility, the cost and the right to enter a public school or university were discriminative and restrictive. Education was a long-term investment, with no immediate harvest promised—an entrance ticket to upper social circles rather than a window to social change. In Victorian Britain, whether a self-made man could truly prosper depended on the type of business or career they pursued.[13] In this historical junction, British imperial power not only forged the colonies into new entities under colonial administration; it also produced a huge social reservoir that fuelled internal societal change. During the high tide of colonialism in the mid-nineteenth century, Britain had a population of 34.5 million colonized people all over the world, which amounted to approximately 70 percent of the total number of people colonized at that time.[14] The Empire required a substantial number of officials to run colonial administrations in large and small overseas possessions. Colonial careers opened unprecedented avenues for internal social mobility and

12 François Bédarida, *Social History of England 1851–1990*, trans. A. S. Forster and Jeffrey Hodgkinson (London: Routledge, 1991), p. 38.

13 Howard L. Malchow, *Gentlemen Capitalists: The Social and Political World of the Victorian Businessman* (Basingstoke: Macmillan, 1991).

14 Robert Delavignette, *Christianity and Colonialism* (London: Burns & Oates, 1964), p. 16.

external transnational mobility.[15] The continued successes in global wars by the nineteenth-century British "military-fiscal state" run by a group of able and ambitious aristocrats also promoted an idea of powerful government and effective bureaucratic system of civil servants.[16] Hence, in a time when traditional society was undergoing further change due to internal urbanization and overseas expansion, the "rising industry" of civil servant became a promising and profitable career that attracted new social forces and manpower. However prosperous it looked, the period between the 1830s and 1870s was a time when a permanent and secure bureaucratic apparatus had not yet been constructed. Although the government had a huge need of competent officials to run the state and its overseas colonies and the ambitious mind had a great wish to join the bureaucratic machinery, the government had not developed structures for their training, induction, and perpetuation in government.[17]

If the governmental system at home was not yet matured, we could well imagine that the ruling order given to the overseas colonial government could hardly be precise and clear. Britain had no predetermined blueprint for colonial affairs in the Far East, but a set of vague instructions for the administrators. Colonial careers, though undoubtedly an opportunity for upward mobility, were very much a gamble. One might pay a high price instead of gaining, perhaps even the ultimate price of one's own life. Most of the time the government just left the colonial possessions in the hands of administrators called the colonial governors, who came from diverse backgrounds—mostly military, but also non-military cultural enthusiast. Wherever they came from, these people were often without

15 Martin Daunton and Rick Halpern, eds., *Empire and Others, British Encounters with Indigenous Peoples, 1600–1850* (London: UCL Press, 1999).

16 Peter Mandler, *Aristocratic Government in the Age of Reform: Whigs and Liberals, 1830–1852* (Oxford: Clarendon Press, 1990).

17 Lawrence Goldman, *Science, Reform, and Politics in Victorian Britain* (Cambridge: Cambridge University Press, 2002), pp. 14–15; Richard Johnston, "Administration in Education before 1870: Patronage, Social Position and Role," in *Studies in the Growth of Nineteenth Century Government*, ed. Gillian Sutherland (London: Routledge and K. Paul, 1972), pp. 130–138.

administrative experience or long-term governance vision. Many policies and governmental structures were put in place on a trial-and-error basis. When a certain officer proved to be efficient or indispensable, they would enjoy a chance to get promoted to an unprecedentedly high position, and vice versa. Sir Charles Elliot, Hong Kong's first administrator, was a good example. He was sent to resolve the escalating conflicts between the Qing government and the British merchants in Canton in 1839. Unable to diplomatically resolve the issue, Britain declared war on China, which led to the cession of Hong Kong to the British under the Convention of Chuenpee in 1841. Elliot was dismissed afterwards due to the Foreign Secretary's fury over receiving "a barren island" at such a high cost.

Due to the harsh working environment which included poor living conditions, poor hygiene, and insufficient social infrastructure in the colonies, many officials suffered from epidemic diseases, resulting in a high attrition rate or early retirement. Thus, the governments in the Far East colonies always suffered from a constantly changing personnel profiling. Moreover, colonies were usually acquired through military means and maintained by political coercion. This meant that the British almost always settled into an unstable political environment in which their lives might be jeopardized by resistance against British rule. Therefore, individuals who were resourceful enough at home might be unwilling to face the risks associated with an expatriate life overseas. Sir John Bowring was a perfect example. For many years he had been a widely acclaimed envoy and diplomat for European politics, but because he was heavily indebted, he chose to take up a career in China with an exceptionally high salary as consul in 1849 to repay his debt.[18] If some young, adventurous gentlemen did choose a colonial career in the East, it was typically in India, for many ambitious individuals had managed to make their dreams come true under the more effectively structured India Civil Service. Simply due to these reasons, a colonial career in the Far East could yield the most unexpected rise and fall in one's wheel of fortune.

Among all of the jobs available for a colonial career, interpreter was

18 John Bowring and Lewin Bentham Bowring, *Autobiographical Recollections of Sir John Bowring* (London: H. S. King & Co., 1877).

perhaps the one with the highest potential for upward mobility. First, in a time when interpreter was not yet a professionalized career, the threshold of entering the job was not exceptionally difficult, as compared with an imperial career such as an administrator or military officer. Second, the Empire was suffering from a chronic lack of interpreters between Chinese and English. The demand was far higher than the supply. We can use the salary scale to indicate the social need for interpreters, both at home and abroad. According to the records of the Foreign Office,[19] the annual salary for a translator in 1809 was £300, and it was increased to £500 in 1854 for the Spanish, Portuguese, Italian, and Danish languages.[20] There is no record of the salary for a Chinese-speaking interpreter before the Opium War. In the Colonial Office, the salary was far less than that in the Foreign Office for a similar position, and an interpreter was only regarded as contingent, for translation and interpretation were largely done by their overseas counterparts. The salary was set at £200 in 1814 but increased to £280 in 1819.[21] In other parts of the world, the salary for an interpreter was higher. Take Hong Kong as an example. In 1843, the starting salary for an English/Chinese interpreter was about £400, and it was raised to £700 or more in only a few years' time. We are only indicating the interpreters who are of European descent. To make the comparison more evident, consider people who possessed similar language competency. The salary provided to an inaugural professor of Chinese in Britain was £60 in 1837, with a slight increase to £100 per annum in 1847. The monetary reward was attractive enough, and if one managed to enter the imperial machinery, it could lead to an even more splendid career and social status. Accepting a career as an interpreter at the Foreign Office was just an entry ticket to the more prosperous future of a diplomatic career.

---

19 Thomas G. Otte, *The Foreign Office Mind: The Making of British Foreign Policy, 1865–1914* (Cambridge: Cambridge University Press, 2011).

20 Great Britain, Foreign Office (hereafter FO), FO 366/671/362–3.

21 John C. Sainty, *Colonial Office Officials: Officials of the Secretary of State for War, 1794–1801, of the Secretary of State for War and Colonies, 1801–54, and of the Secretary of State for Colonies, 1854–70*, vol. 6 (London: University of London, Institute of Historical Research, 1976), p. 21.

To specify the social mobility generated by an interpreter career in the context of colonial rule, we can categorize the types of interpreter to be found in Asia around the time of the First Opium War. The inclusion of names below is of course not exhaustive. Nevertheless, this will help us to reflect on the essential qualities required by the Empire. Studying this group of interpreters is particularly meaningful, as they were the pioneers who not only informed the Empire on how to build an interpreter office and programme in the coming years, but also broadened the channel of Chinese studies in England. The way the Empire facilitated resources for certain categories of interpreters to enable them rise to social prominence also reflected the national, social, and cultural identities that the Empire chose to construct for its interpreters. In other words, the Empire acted as an institutional patron. Whether different kinds of interpreters could differentiate themselves from their colleagues largely depended on how they used (or, exploited) the freedom, resources, and restrictions offered to them under this patronage. The people named here, while not an exhaustive sample, are representative enough to offer an overview. To achieve this, we use the tripartite model suggested by François Bedarida for social categorization. One aspect of note is the issue of ethnic background. In Victorian expansionist Britain, a person's value was largely determined by their descent, which comprised their class (blue blood) and Englishness (pure blood).[22] This added extra weight to the value of a person devoted to an imperial career, as it might safeguard his adherence to the Empire's core values and interests. This factor was also important for imperial interpreters because they were at the front line in handling national and political intelligence, which meant that the British government had to be sure that they were trustworthy and bound by the right kind of ethics.

Among all of the interpreters in the newly opened Sinophone world in the nineteenth century, the names of the people in the first group may be familiar: Sir George Thomas Staunton (1781–1859), Robert

22 Amelia Hadfield-Amkhan, *British Foreign Policy, National Identity, and Neoclassical Realism* (Lanham: Rowman & Littlefield, 2010).

Morrison (1782–1834) and his son John Robert Morrison (1814–1843), Thomas Francis Wade (1818–1895), William Henry Medhurst, Jr. (1822–1885), Samuel Turner Fearon (1819–1854), and Robert Thom (1816–1846). Some of them, such as Sir George Thomas Staunton, Robert Thom, and Samuel Fearon, had been engaged with the EIC and the Canton General Chamber of Commerce. Regardless of their initial aspiration, they all ultimately helped the Empire's interpreting business, especially during times of war and the signing of treaties. After retiring from their interpreter careers in the EIC, superintendent trade office or colonial government, they brought back with them to England not only their local knowledge but also a large number of books. This group of interpreters formed the core cohort and went on to change the environment of Chinese learning in their homeland. Under their endeavour, the professionalization of interpreters was realized that was shaped through the built-up of Chinese studies in the various academic institutions. Their most concrete, direct and long-term achievement, however, was the creation of the student and cadet interpreter programmes for the Foreign and Colonial Offices, respectively. Their endeavour to change the knowledge terrain was not merely a response to the growing interest in Britain for books about China in England, the books are meant to provide a sufficient resource to train the next generation of interpreters. These programmes produced some 300 qualified interpreters for the Colonial and Foreign Offices before the decline of the Empire in World War I.

A second group of interpreters who served the British government also deserves our attention. They made their way to prominence purely through their Chinese competency, although there were certainly hybridity and humbleness in their ethnic origin, social class, and educational backgrounds. Some came from continental Europe, such as the well-known missionaries Karl Friedrich August Gützlaff (1803–1851) and E. J. Eitel (1838–1908), who assumed the head of the interpreter office in colonial Hong Kong in the 1870s. To demonstrate their dedication to the British Empire, in the course of their careers, they converted their religious denomination to the London

Missionary Society and even became naturalized British subjects. In this group, there were also dedicated missionaries and individuals who were of British origin, such as William Milne (1785–1822), Walter Henry Medhurst (1796–1857), and James Legge (1815–1897). They did not forget their sacred duties, but had to forge an interdepended relationship with the regime that could provide them financial and imperium patronage to carry out secular work for themselves and the government. Missionaries would not necessarily work in concordance with the Empire if the interest or goal to emancipate the Chinese was divergent. Hence, in the course of making a team of the imperial interpreter, the reliance on the missionaries was gradually reduced. There were also some people who came from very insignificant social backgrounds and achieved social recognition only through their interpreter careers and unswerving loyalties. Sir Harry Smith Parkes (1828–1885) was an orphan who had no better alternative than to follow his brother-in-law, Gützlaff, to seek a career in Asia and William Alexander Pickering (1840–1907) was a sailor apprentice and tidewaiter. He later became the chief of the office of interpreters and also the chief of the office in charge of all of the Chinese in a colony, the Protector of Chinese in Singapore. We revisit this below at greater length. Also in this group were those who were of humble origin and of foreign ethnic background, such as Daniel Richard Caldwell (1816–1875) who was borne on the island of St. Helena, of mixed race. Like Pickering, Caldwell began his career as an interpreter but later took the helm of the office tasked with managing all Chinese affairs in Hong Kong.

The members of the third and last group were the collaborators of the British translators, typically called Chinese or native assistants. On many occasions, they were the ones who actually penned the Chinese versions of treaties, correspondences, and memoranda to Chinese officials and proclamations to the local people. Their job was to make sure that these documents were written in a readable and intelligible style. However, this group of interpreters is the most difficult to identify, as most of them have been forgotten by history. They also intentionally hid behind the scenes lest their work for foreigners endangered their families or clans who still lived in China. We can only get a glimpse of their identities through the nicknames and aliases used in the various imperial records. For example, the two Chinese interpreters who helped to draft the Treaty of Nanking in 1842—awarded with Chinese medals in the First Opium War by the Empire—are only known as Atchie and Apoon, which indicates that their surnames were omitted even though they were given the highest possible honour for an interpreter in the British Empire.

I use the examples of Daniel Richard Caldwell from Hong Kong and William Alexander Pickering from Singapore to demonstrate the extent of the power acquired by an interpreter in the colonial government. They obtained the same kind of power from the same type of institutional framework, but the consequences of their power differed significantly. Comparing their careers in a colonial network is illustrative not only because it gives us a more complete view of the colonial structure,[23] but also because their life histories had a certain interconnection.

Translator, Traitor: Caldwell in Hong Kong

Daniel Richard Caldwell, like many interpreters in the translation history, did not leave behind clear biographical details. His background was obscure. Fortunately for us, but unfortunately for him, he was involved in a controversial translation scandal in Hong Kong that led to an inquiry into civil service abuse in the British Parliament in the 1860s, during which much of his background was revealed.[24] As mentioned, he was borne on the island of St. Helena, of no significant social background. Following the trade route to the Far East, he was at one point stationed in Singapore to seek opportunities with British traders. It is believed

23 Stephen Howe, ed., *The New Imperial Histories Reader* (London: Routledge, 2010), p. 137.

24 Daniel Richard Caldwell, *A Vindication of the Character of the Undersigned from the Aspersions of Mr Thomas Chisholm Anstey* (Hong Kong: Noronha's Office, 1860).

that he learned Chinese from the locals,[25] and when China opened, he followed the British traders to Canton in the hope of pursuing a lucrative business. He only managed to secure a job as a bookkeeper in the China trade companies, which he despised as menial work. In 1838, dissatisfied, he left Canton and returned to Singapore. On his return journey, his multilingual competency impressed the passengers on board, some of whom were British colonial officials heading to Hong Kong. In addition to Malay, Hindustani, and Portuguese, he had acquired the language skill in great demand at the time—Chinese. When they arrived in Hong Kong, Caldwell was invited to join the government.

He joined the British Hong Kong government on 19 January 1843, employed as an interpreter for the Supreme Court and Chief Magistrate Office.[26] The magistrate, police, and the Supreme Court were separate institutions, and to maintain judicial independence, each held different areas of jurisdiction with separate teams of officials, especially interpreters. However, the lack of competent interpreters in Hong Kong made the situation complicated. Caldwell was employed by all of the courts and sometimes the prosecutor had to postpone the trial because there was no interpreter. In some instances, when Caldwell attended a court as a civilian to observe the legal proceedings, he was summoned to replace the court interpreter, due to the latter's incapability.

In 1850, during Caldwell's leave of absence back to Singapore, the judicial department fell into a state of near paralysis. The colonial court had no choice but to use local Chinese as interpreters. In one trial, while waiting for the verdict, the jurors questioned the accuracy of the

25 E. J. Eitel, *Europe in China* (Hong Kong: University of Hong Kong, 1961); G. B. Endacott, *A Biographical Sketch-Book* (Hong Kong: Hong Kong University Press, 2005); Christopher Munn, *Anglo-China: Chinese People and British Rule in Hong Kong, 1841–1880* (Hong Kong: Hong Kong University Press, 2009); Christopher Munn, "Colonialism 'in a Chinese Atmosphere': The Caldwell Affair and the Perils of Collaboration in Early Colonial Hong Kong," in *New Frontiers: Imperialism's New Communities in East Asia, 1842–1953*, ed. Robert A. Bickers and Christian Henriot (Manchester and New York: Manchester University Press, 2000), pp. 12–37.

26 Great Britain, Colonial Office, Bluebook of 1844, CO 133/1.

translation and demanded a retrial. The judge refused, as it was not in compliance with the judicial procedure. This resulted in a vigorous debate between the jurors and the judge. Instead of a retrial, the judge ruled that the translation in question should be replaced. Due to this incident, the judicial procedure and spirit of law were greatly tainted.[27] In 1855, Caldwell resigned from the government after his failed attempt to secure a salary increment, and the government assigned a European to be his successor. A similar courtroom incident occurred some time afterwards. Another trial had to be adjourned, and the courtroom fell victim to a bizarre atmosphere of mistrust and disbelief.

The local newspaper began to ridicule the impotence of a government that seemed unable to operate without Caldwell, and there appears to have been some truth to the criticism. Caldwell's importance was such that he could hijack the daily administration of the government, but that was not the extent of his power. His influence was quickly felt in other departments related to the Chinese communities. Beginning in 1847, he served as assistant superintendent of police and tax collector, which gave him direct authority over intelligence gathering and tax collection from Chinese population. He was popular and much revered among the Chinese, as he was seen as the main source of authority. The local communities called him *daren* 大人, which means "Your Highness" or "Your Honour," to indicate the power he possessed even in the beginning, when he had begun to approach them as an interpreter.

With the help of local communities, he made breakthroughs in the investigation of many deadlocked cases. One case in particular is worth mentioning. In 1854, an American businessman was sent from his parent company in the United States to deal with transactions in Macao and Canton, using Hong Kong as a stop enroute. He was declared missing after his arrival in Hong Kong.[28] Caldwell discovered that a fisherman had murdered the US businessman when he boarded the fisherman's

27 Great Britain, Colonial Office, Bluebook of 1850, CO 129/34/198–205.

28 James William Norton-Kyshe, *The History of the Laws and Courts of Hong Kong from the Earliest Period to 1898*, vol. 1 (Hong Kong: Vetch and Lee, 1971), p. 349.

boat. Caldwell's service was highly acclaimed by the American Embassy, which wrote directly to the colonial Secretary of Hong Kong to praise his efficiency.[29]

In 1856, Caldwell was promoted to Registrar General, the highest position related to the colonial population. The duties encompassed everything about the Chinese: population registration, census, license issuance, hygiene, and healthcare, etc. The office's most prominent duty was to communicate with the Chinese people, thus the holder needed superb communication skills.[30] During the governance of Sir John Bowring (Hong Kong governorship: 1854–1859), Caldwell was given a more distinguished position, Protector of Chinese.[31] The new system was in line with the new policy issued on 2 July 1855 by the Foreign Secretary, Lord John Russell (1792–1878), which stated that officials who knew Chinese would have a higher chance of promotion. More resources would also be allocated by the government to language learning courses right before or after office hours. It was hoped that better communication with the local Chinese people could be fostered. One of Caldwell's duties as Protector was to make regular appointments with the Chinese community. He explained the new government policy and law, and listened to any grievances.[32] The Protector's title was rendered by the Chinese community as Fuhuadao 撫華道 in Hong Kong and Huweisi 護衛司 in Singapore. "Dao" and "si" were a Chinese rank and the terms as a whole meant the office to pacify and protect the Chinese population.

The Protector of Chinese was a special position in the colonial governments of the British Empire in the nineteenth and twentieth centuries. It was not found in every British colony, but only in places where the population was overwhelmingly Chinese but the Chinese were treated as a separate community within the colony. The Protector's position was established as a senior office in the government and served as the chief

29 Great Britain, Colonial Office, Bluebook of 1854, CO 129/46/304–307.

30 CO 129/202/136, 20 July 1882; CO 129/202/447, 28 August 1882.

31 *The Hong Kong Government Gazette*, 22 November 1856.

32 *The Hong Kong Government Gazette*, 4 December 1856; Norton-Kyshe, *The History of the Laws and Courts of Hong Kong from the Earliest Period to 1898*, p. 410.

adviser to the governor on questions involving Chinese law, customs or opinion. He was also responsible for the employment and deployment of interpreters to other departments, especially those who were desperately in need of interpreters to ensure the accuracy and efficiency of translation in matters of law. That is why the justice department and the law enforcement units were always the Protector's closest partners. The Protector's main function was to improve the communication between the colonial government and the native people and in this capacity he was responsible for presenting official policies to the Chinese. Most importantly, while he solicited information and enhanced communication, he also collected intelligence for the government. Therefore, the censorship of Chinese newspapers, publications, textbooks, and even postal mail was also conducted by this office. His job thus had two sides. Many events in the early stages of the colonial government showed that the Protector, as the person who possessed the necessary local knowledge and communication skills and whose official duties included matters of interpretation and translation, should be seen as more than just a mediator between the colonizer and the colonized. His position was crucial to successful and efficient colonial administration.[33]

In 1857, Caldwell faced his greatest challenge. When the new Attorney General Thomas Chisholm Anstey (1816–1873) reported for duty in Hong Kong, he was stunned by the skulduggery of the colonial government. There were no checks or balances of power in the system. Many officials had their hands in three supposedly independent departments—legislative, administrative, and judicial—and Caldwell was one of them. Bribery seemed rampant. Anstey decided that Caldwell was one of the culprits, as his influence was great within the government as a whole, and his income was not proportional to his salary.[34] The most unforgivable crime he allegedly committed was accepting money from and

33 Hugh Tinker, "Structure of the British Imperial Heritage," in *Asian Bureaucratic Systems Emergent from the British Imperial Tradition*, ed. Ralph Braibanti (Durham, N. C.: Duke University Press, 1966), p. 23.

34 T. Chisholm Anstey, *Crime and Government at Hong Kong: A Letter to the Editor of the "Times" Newspaper* (London: Effingham Wilson, 1859).

passing information to the most notorious pirate at the time. Hong Kong was an island without serious military defences, and all of its inhabitants were placed in danger if someone in the government was in the pocket of the pirates.[35] It might even provoke a rebellion against British rule. Caldwell's ethnic and racial identities were questioned. In fact, apart from calling him *daren*, he was also nicknamed Cald Sangui,[36] an allusion to Wu Sangui 吳三桂 (1612–1678), a famous traitor in Chinese history. Wu Sangui was a high-ranking military officer of the Ming dynasty and of Han-Chinese ethnicity, but he colluded with the Manchu people, who had been enemies of the Ming dynasty for decades. He opened the gate to let them in China which led to the fall of the Ming dynasty. To nickname Caldwell "Sangui" was to imply that he had betrayed the British colonial government.

Anstey wrote to the *Times* newspaper to complain about the misconduct of the civil servants and the colonial government. He also insinuated that Caldwell had polluted the racial purity of the British, as he was of mixed race (African and British) and had married a local Chinese prostitute. The translator's scandal led to an inquiry into civil service abuse by the British Parliament.[37] At that time, the British were busy waging the Second Opium War (1856–1860), which led to the annexation of the Kowloon Peninsula. Almost all capable interpreters and translators had to spare some time to deal with the inquiry brought about by the scandal when they were drafting the Treaty of Tianjin (June 1858), marching with military force to Beijing and handling the Taiping Rebellion (1850–1864).[38]

35 CO 129/30/255, 3 November 1849.

36 CO 129/74/327, 2 December 1859.

37 CO 129/81/376, 20 June 1861; CO 129/90/258, 8 December 1862; Hong Kong, Commission to Enquire into the Charges Against Mr D. R. Caldwell, Registrar General, Daniel Richard Caldwell, *Report of the Commission, with Minutes of Evidences, etc.* (London: H.M.S.O., 1858), p. 159; Hong Kong Government, *Supplement to the Minutes of Inquiry into Civil Service Abuses Before the Executive Council 1860–61* (Hong Kong: Hong Kong Government Printer, 1862).

38 John Scarth, *Twelve Years in China: The People, the Rebels, and the Mandarins, by a British Resident* (Edinburgh: T. Constable and Co., 1860), p. 124.

In the end, four out of the eight people involved in the scandal were convicted. In December 1886, Caldwell was suspended whilst his alleged bribery was being investigated. All of the other officials involved were either suspended or had their positions terminated, including Anstey, whom the British government accused of casting aspersion through ungrounded accusations. Anstey himself was also seen as an unpopular political figure as he was one of the first Catholic parliamentarians in the nineteenth century. It was difficult to determine the sources of corruption. Caldwell was surely not the only official who used his power to buy and build estates. However, it was only with the government's support that Caldwell was able to stretch his influence across the legal department and the police force. He resigned three times but he was awarded better terms after each negotiation. The government alone gave him a pay rise and awarded him for his dedicated service.[39] If Caldwell was guilty of corruption, then the government had to bear certain responsibilities. Caldwell was eventually reinstated—censured but not convicted—and returned to his position as an interpreter. Even those who did not believe that he leaked information to the pirates accused him of partiality, cronyism, financial mismanagement, and other misdemeanours. He was held responsible for despotism and political imposture.

The charge of Caldwell had further divided up the cohesion of the government and the society. During the investigation, some of his colleagues vouched for him,[40] and 918 natives sent petition letters to the government in his support,[41] including local businessmen, philanthropists, the sick, the poor, and the orphaned. He almost appeared to be a Robin Hood of the colony, which explained to some extent how he had acquired such a large amount of money. He married a converted prostitute, Chan Ayow, and they adopted more than 10 orphans in Hong Kong, giving them the best possible education. Some grew to become prominent figures

39 Norton-Kyshe, *The History of the Laws and Courts of Hong Kong from the Earliest Period to 1898*, p. 286.

40 Ibid., p. 587.

41 CO 129/73/214–218, 22 January 1859; CO 129/114/475–494, 27 August 1866.

in the colony at the end of the century, especially in bringing Chinese voices to the Legislative Council and mending the differences between East and West.[42] Caldwell also gifted the church with land in the island's most expensive area that was presumably acquired through bribery. Apart from the church, he also contributed in building the hospital. In early Hong Kong, the locals were sceptical about Western medicine and the sick preferred to stay in very primitive Chinese waiting rooms for recovery and medical attention. The hygiene was far from satisfactory and the rooms sometimes caused disease outbreaks. The Chinese refused post-mortem examinations of those who died, as it was their cultural belief that the body should be kept intact. On many occasions, Caldwell was there to help the colonial surgeons or policemen in resolving conflicts with the locals as to whether there was the need for post-mortem examination. Also, if he found that a poor family was unable to bury the dead, he would give them money for the burial and alleviate the situation.[43] The first hospital for the local Chinese, the Tung Wah Hospital 東華醫院, was established with his support.[44] Yet some of his deeds appeared suspicious to ordinary people, and his membership in the secret society of Freemasons probably added to his mystique.

It may be argued that Caldwell was simply an adventurer, seizing every opportunity available to further his career, be it for material gain or reputation. Beyond his professional realm, he transgressed the cultural and ethnic boundaries in marrying a Chinese woman of the lower class and adopting orphans, which provoked the upper-class white people. There was evidence suggesting that his sympathy lay with the locals, with whom he identified, to an extent. After all, he was lower-born himself. He was a good example of how an interpreter could shift allegiance and end up in

42 Guan Zhaoshuo 關肇碩 and Rong Yingyu 容應萸, eds., *Xianggang kaibu yu Guanjia* 香港開埠與關家 [The opening of Hong Kong and Kwan family] (Hong Kong: Wide Angle Press Limited, 1997); Susan Hoe, *The Private Life of Old Hong Kong: Western Women in the British Colony, 1841–1941* (Hong Kong: Oxford University Press, 1991), pp. 65, 69–70, 137.

43 "Chinese Hospital Case," *Hong Kong Daily Press*, 26 April and 29 April 1869.

44 CO 129/202/136–198, 20 July 1882; CO 129/202/447–451, 28 August 1882.

a very delicate position. Ironically, it was only when he demonstrated his loyalty and dedication as Protector of Chinese, the title the Empire gave him, that he was condemned.

Translator, Protector: Pickering in the Straits Settlements

Pickering's story was not much different from that of Caldwell. Born in Nottingham, Pickering was already leading a wandering life at the age of 16 as a sailor apprentice. Malaya, Siam, and Burma were often on his sailing route, as they were by the famous monsoon trade route in Asia. In 1862, he followed a tea vessel arriving in Fuzhou, which had been opened for trade since the First Opium War. Then, when the opportunity arose, he entered into the Chinese Maritime Custom Service as a tide-waiter at the monthly salary of £15. Imperial Chinese Custom was a body set up by the Chinese government immediately after the First Opium War to replace the old custom system. For many years, the first Inspector-General was British for the sake of keeping tax evasion and smuggling at bay. Pickering spent his free time learning Chinese after work. Using his finger to imitate the strokes of the Chinese characters printed around him, such as on the carton of Chinese tea, he learned the language gradually. Whenever he came across an unknown character and its pronunciation, he would ask the Chinese labourer and the headman. His diligence and self-awareness in learning Chinese were greatly appreciated by the chief of the Imperial Chinese Custom, Sir Robert Hart. Hart came to China through the Student Interpreter Programme in 1854. He himself went through a painstaking learning process to acquire the language. As the Student Interpreter Programme was set up to guarantee the British Empire's interest in China would not suffer due to the poor quality of translations, Hart must have known the importance of his staff having good Chinese. Hart gave Pickering an extra allowance and encouraged him to attend proper tutorials with Chinese scholars after work. In this primitive way, Pickering learned many southern Chinese dialects such as Fujian (Hokkien), Guangdong (Cantonese), Chaozhou (Teochew), and Kejia (Hakka). After the Treaty of Tianjin in 1858, more ports were opened in China. Pickering then went to the newly opened treaty ports in the southern part of Taiwan to continue his service. He never ceased to challenge himself. In his new position he spent his free time on expeditions to the most remote inner parts of the island where the aboriginal people lived. Such adventures were partially motivated by his ethnographical curiosity, but they were also for the sake of exploring the business potential of natural herbs and bio-resources such as spices, herbs, and camphor for the Empire. He even wrote a book, *Pioneering in Formosa: Recollections of Adventures among Mandarins, Wreckers, & Head-Hunting Savage,*[45] in which he recorded his observations and the tensions between the Chinese, the foreigners, and the island's natives. During his short spell back in England for a leave of absence in 1871, Pickering met Sir Harry Ord (1867–1873), the forthcoming governor of the Straits Settlements. Ord was impressed by Pickering's Chinese competence and he invited him to join the new British Crown Colony. Pickering was first appointed as an interpreter and a teacher of Chinese to government interpreters, and then Chief Interpreter of various offices. His salary began at £500, almost double that of those who worked as interpreters in the Colonial Office in London.[46] As he worked his way up to a position in the central administration, it is fair to say that it was the Empire made him, and more importantly he made the Empire.

Pickering was appointed Protector of Chinese on 3 May 1877 under the Chinese Immigrants' Ordinance (the purpose of which was to check on the legality of new immigrants' employment contracts) and the Crimping Ordinance. These Ordinances were designed to prevent any illegal recruitment of emigrants for service in the Straits. Immigrant and foreign labour provided society with huge manpower, but it also created many social problems. It was a criminal triad and not the

45 William Pickering, *Pioneering in Formosa: Recollections of Adventures among Mandarins, Wreckers, & Head-Hunting Savage* (London: Hurst & Blackett, 1898).

46 CO 273/57/409, 17 May 1872; Sir Harry Ord to the Earl of Kimberley, CO 273/409, no. 6155, 6 December 1871.

immigrants who were to blame, as the former monopolized the businesses and manipulated the inflow of new labour. When new labourers or the new immigrants (locally called "Sin-keh," meaning "fresh off boat") arrived in Singapore, they were detained by the headman to await local and foreign employment opportunities. During this period, social evils proliferated. Many headmen were themselves members of the triad, which was segmented into dialect groups. The newcomers, who were deprived of information and opportunities, naturally clung to and were mobilized by the people who came from the same villages and lineages in South China and who spoke the same tongue. In contrast, the diasporic nature of the Straits encouraged the conglomeration of different labour gangs. To sustain their lives in a fiercely competitive situation, people from diverse linguistic backgrounds, left to their own devices, naturally gathered to form a solid, centripetal power that supported clannishness. In this competitive yet exploitative environment, new labour often fell prey to the inhuman treatment of the triad.

The triad (locally called T'ian Tay Hoey 天地會, or Heaven and Earth Society) was not forcefully eradicated in a sweeping gesture. It claimed to be fraternalistic, its motto being "Obey heaven and work righteousness." This claim undoubtedly had a special appeal among the Chinese commoners, especially those who were deprived and destitute. In the late-Qing China context, the triad as a political society grew from a group of adamant patriots with the goal of overthrowing the Manchurians, who had invaded China and seized the Ming dynasty throne in 1644. However, given the encroaching military contact between Westerners and China, the meaning of the term "barbarian" had shifted and was now used to denote the Westerners. As the British were well aware, Chinese people in the Straits were so xenophobic that they would call every Westerner a "red-haired barbarian." Previously, the sporadic Hokkien-Teochew riot, which broke out in Larut (in Penang) and in Malacca in 1854, comprised gang fights between two separate dialect groups: the Hokkien (Ghee Hok society) and the Teochew (Ghee Hin society). If the British rulers were to deal recklessly with the triad problem at large before obtaining the absolute and reliable intelligence required to deploy their

and consultation, as they had no intention of or interest in learning what the local people wanted and felt. In a report written by a special committee created to deal with the Chinese after the suppression of the riots, society was described as being divided in two: "The government knows little or nothing of the Chinese … and the immense majority of them know still less of government."[48] Despite expressing the desire to listen to the local voice, they would have found themselves lacking the intermediary, especially those interpreters who could help them succeed.[49]

If the case of Caldwell in Hong Kong showed that the colonial rule was vulnerable, often at the mercy of the deployment and recruitment of capable and trustworthy interpreters, then the case of Pickering in the Straits Settlements is even more illustrative of this fact. The composition of society in the Straits was more segregated, diversified and complicated. The right hand of the Singapore governor, Major Samuel Dunlop (1838–1917), followed a visit to Hong Kong with the suggestion that the Straits appoint a Chinese-speaking official in the institutional power structures to oversee all issues related to the Chinese people, similar to the Protector of Chinese office. In this proposal, which had an epochal effect on the administrative history of the Straits, Dunlop wrote,

> What is wanted is, not so much new or amended laws, as a strong personal government, in which the administrations are brought into intimate relations with the people. To effect this, I am of opinion that, in each Settlement, a system of Registration of Chinese should be instituted, and a Protector of Chinese appointed, who should be a thoroughly trustworthy European conversant with some dialect of Chinese and able to write the language.[50]

---

48 Peter Hodge, *Community Problems and Social Work in Southeast Asia: The Hong Kong and Singapore Experience* (Hong Kong: Hong Kong University Press, 1980), p. 11.

49 Benjamin N. Lawrance, Emily Lynn Osborn, and Richard L. Roberts, *Intermediaries, Interpreters, and Clerks: African Employees in the Making of Colonial Africa* (Madison, Wisconsin: University of Wisconsin Press, 2006).

50 Straits Settlements, Legislative Council. *Proceedings of the Legislative Council of the Straits Settlements in 1876 Appendix I9*, Samuel Dunlop, "Report of the Inspector General of Police, Straits Settlements, for the year 1875" (Singapore: The Government Printing Office, 1876).

To maximize the jurisdiction of the Singapore Chinese protectorate office, which was the first of its kind in the Settlements, the same departments were also established in Penang, Malacca, and the Malay States. To tackle the triad's core, the British sought to gain sufficient intelligence from a handful of interpreters through the protectorate office. The colonizer could also use this as a gesture to demonstrate that the ruling class was opening up channels to listen to and communicate with the Chinese, especially the emerging social elite and Chinese businessmen, who had always been marginalized in traditional Chinese society. In a new social setting, their power and influence could be easily co-opted into the British regime.

Pickering's multilingual skills, his experience in the government and his popularity among the majority of the Chinese community all suggested that he was the right candidate for the position. A centralized office to oversee all Chinese affairs would also mean an augmentation of duties and powers. Once Pickering took up the office, his work spectrum widened dramatically. He not only had to communicate with the Chinese, but he also made sure that each proclamation, notice, and ordinance translated into Chinese was correct and free of any technical errors, promoted the new policy and consulted the opinion of the Chinese. The governor made it clear that "[a]ll Chinese notices published by Government should pass through his hands, and all Chinese publications and notices, issued by private chops or persons, should be submitted to and stamped by him, before publication, under a penalty."[51] Moreover, he had to fight battles with the Colonial Office about the pensions, salaries and welfare for the subordinates in his department.[52] Pickering was politically astute in his recognition that only a secured and respectable civil servant income could prevent extortion and abuse of power. This was especially true for those handling highly sensitive intelligence.

---

51 Straits Settlements, Legislative Council. *Proceedings of the Legislative Council of the Straits Settlements in 1876 Appendix 19*, Samuel Dunlop, "Report of the Inspector General of Police, Straits Settlements, for the year 1875."

52 CO 273/134/217, 6 May 1885.

Having learned from Caldwell's case in Hong Kong, the Colonial Office was more alarmed than ever about the over-expansion of one single individual and his department. However, the new crops of student interpreters and interpreter cadets trained through the Foreign Office in the year of 1854 and Colonial Office in 1861 were ready to be deployed in the Straits. Student interpreters were the crème de la crème of society, selected from Britain's seven top-tier universities. They went through a stringent competitive examination and while their practical experience was undoubtedly no match to Pickering's, their positions were intended to provide on-the-job training with the promise of a senior position in the future. Their education, social backgrounds and job prospects all fostered a fundamentally different outlook on how to administer the natives. They also had different ideas regarding good translation, as it reflected their literacy and aesthetic appreciation. To Pickering, language competency was just one aspect of the job, with the other indispensable features being experience, good listening skills, and patience in handling Chinese affairs. The tensions between him and the newly arriving interpreters increased even as the Colonial and Foreign Offices—run by the social elite—grew increasingly dissatisfied with Pickering's performance.

Pickering was forced to retire in 1888, after being in office for more than a decade. The imminent reason for his retirement, however, was not the aforementioned internal conflicts. He was ambushed by a triad member who claimed to be submitting a petition and then attacked Pickering with an axe, almost killing him.[53] Pickering was in a critical condition and suffered as an invalid for almost a year. After convalescence, he retired and returned to England. Despite being a dedicated person who devoted his time and energy to living up to the expectations of his position, the people he was sworn to protect did not see him as a protector, but rather as someone upsetting the social harmony of Chinese society. Pickering was definitely a scapegoat for the grievances in that colonial setting. Ironically, following his attack, his reputation and social status escalated in Britain. He was awarded the honourable knighthood G.C.M.G. title to praise his devotion to the Empire and a street in Singapore was

53 CO 273/148/393, 17 October 1887.

named after him to commemorate his contribution to the colony. When he retired and relocated to England, he was invited to help the Foreign Office train and examine student interpreters.

Conclusion

The Empire's efficiency was hampered by the lack of interpreters, the ensuing mistranslations, and the potential betrayal the interpreters represented. Those in power finally came to the stark awareness that the only way to combat the problem was to design the interpreter training programmes to train trustworthy interpreters that would be at the Empire's full disposal. To disarm the potential threat posed by go-betweens and interpreters, the Empire only invested in those thought to be in line with the Empire's interests and capable of sharing its glory and mission. People who were largely groomed and moulded from the same academic and aristocratic background would tend to believe that administration efficiency was to be achieved by the social elite despite individuals having different political views.[54] Beginning in 1854, the Foreign Office sought the help of King's College London to train its interpreters. The programme tagged along with the existing Chinese programme in the College, and the entrance requirement was highly selective and competitive. The Vice-Chancellor would nominate its best students to the secretary of the Foreign Office. Once approved, they would undergo a two-year study of Chinese at King's College before going to China. The training programme was consolidated further in 1860 when there was a structural change in the way the government recruited civil servants. This change involved standardizing the salary levels, eligibility, and recruitment channels of all civil servants to ensure that all new recruits were of similar class, social, and educational backgrounds—those whose allegiance to the Empire would less likely be shifted even though working in a demanding overseas environment.

54 Kathleen Wilson, *The Sense of the People: Politics, Culture and Imperialism in England, 1715–1785* (Cambridge: Cambridge University Press, 1995); Mandler, *Aristocratic Government in the Age of Reform*.

Bibliography

Anonymous. *India, Ceylon, Straits Settlements, British North Borneo, Hong Kong.* London: Kegan Paul, Trench, Trübner, 1899.

Anstey, T. Chisholm. *Crime and Government at Hong Kong: A Letter to the Editor of the "Times" Newspaper.* London: Effingham Wilson, 1859.

Bédarida, François. *Social History of England 1851–1990.* Translated by A. S. Forster and Jeffrey Hodgkinson. London: Routledge, 1991.

Bowring, John, and Lewin Bentham Bowring. *Autobiographical Recollections of Sir John Bowring.* London: H. S. King & Co., 1877.

Buckley, C. B. *An Anecdotal History of Old Times in Singapore.* Vol. 1. London: S.I., 1903.

Caldwell, Daniel Richard. *A Vindication of the Character of the Undersigned from the Aspersions of Mr Thomas Chisholm Anstey.* Hong Kong: Noronha's Office, 1860.

Castells, Manuel. *The Rise of the Network Society: The Information Age: Economy, Society and Culture.* 1996. Reprint, Cambridge, MA: Blackwell Publishers, 2011.

"Chinese Hospital Case." *Hong Kong Daily Press.* 26 April and 29 April 1869.

Daunton, Martin, and Rick Halpern, eds. *Empire and Others, British Encounters with Indigenous Peoples, 1600–1850.* London: UCL Press, 1999.

Delavignette, Robert. *Christianity and Colonialism.* London: Burns & Oates, 1964.

Eitel, E. J. *Europe in China.* Hong Kong: University of Hong Kong, 1961.

Endacott, G. B. *A Biographical Sketch-Book.* Hong Kong: Hong Kong University Press, 2005.

Goldman, Lawrence. *Science, Reform, and Politics in Victorian Britain.* Cambridge: Cambridge University Press, 2002.

Great Britain. India Office. *Correspondence Respecting the Transfer of Control over the Straits Settlements from the India Office to the Colonial Department.* London: H. M. Stationery Office, 1866.

Guan, Zhaoshuo 關肇碩, and Rong Yingyu 容應萸, eds. *Xianggang kaibu yu Guanjia* 香港開埠與關家 [The opening of Hong Kong and Kwan family]. Hong Kong: Wide Angle Press Limited, 1997.

Hadfield-Amkhan, Amelia. *British Foreign Policy, National Identity, and Neoclassical Realism.* Lanham: Rowman & Littlefield, 2010.

Hodge, Peter. *Community Problems and Social Work in Southeast Asia: The Hong Kong and Singapore Experience.* Hong Kong: Hong Kong University Press, 1980.

Hoe, Susan. *The Private Life of Old Hong Kong: Western Women in the British Colony, 1841–1941*. Hong Kong: Oxford University Press, 1991.

Hong Kong. *The Hong Kong Government Gazette*. 22 November 1856.

———. *The Hong Kong Government Gazette*. 4 December 1856.

———. Commission to Enquire into the Charges Against Mr D. R. Caldwell, Registrar General, Daniel Richard Caldwell. *Report of the Commission, with Minutes of Evidences, etc*. London: H.M.S.O., 1858.

———. *Supplement to the Minutes of Inquiry into Civil Service Abuses Before the Executive Council 1860–61*. Hong Kong: Hong Kong Government Printer, 1862.

Howe, Stephen, ed. *The New Imperial Histories Reader*. London: Routledge, 2010.

Johnston, Richard. "Administration in Education before 1870: Patronage, Social Position and Role." In *Studies in the Growth of Nineteenth Century Government*, edited by Gillian Sutherland. London: Routledge and K. Paul, 1972, pp. 110–138.

Lawrance, Benjamin N., Emily Lynn Osborn, and Richard L. Roberts. *Intermediaries, Interpreters, and Clerks: African Employees in the Making of Colonial Africa*. Madison, Wisconsin: University of Wisconsin Press, 2006.

Malchow, Howard L. *Gentlemen Capitalists: The Social and Political World of the Victorian Businessman*. Basingstoke: Macmillan, 1991.

Mandler, Peter. *Aristocratic Government in the Age of Reform: Whigs and Liberals, 1830–1852*. Oxford: Clarendon Press, 1990.

Munn, Christopher. "Colonialism 'in a Chinese Atmosphere': The Caldwell Affair and the Perils of Collaboration in Early Colonial Hong Kong." In *New Frontiers: Imperialism's New Communities in East Asia, 1842–1953*, edited by Robert A. Bickers and Christian Henriot. Manchester and New York: Manchester University Press, 2000, pp. 12–37.

———. *Anglo-China: Chinese People and British Rule in Hong Kong, 1841–1880*. Hong Kong: Hong Kong University Press, 2009.

Norton-Kyshe, James William. *A Judicial History of the Straits Settlements 1786–1890*. Collected and reprinted in *Malaya Law Review* 11, no. 1 (1969), pp. 1–36, 107.

———. *The History of the Laws and Courts of Hong Kong from the Earliest Period to 1898*. Vol. 1. Hong Kong: Vetch and Lee, 1971.

Otte, Thomas G. *The Foreign Office Mind: The Making of British Foreign Policy, 1865–1914*. Cambridge: Cambridge University Press, 2011.

Pickering, William. *Pioneering in Formosa: Recollections of Adventures among Mandarins, Wreckers, & Head-Hunting Savage*. London: Hurst & Blackett, 1898.

Public Record Office, the National Archive of the United Kingdom. CO 129. Colonial Office, Original Correspondence: Hong Kong. 1841–1951.

———. CO 133/1. Colonial Office, Bluebooks of Statistics. 1844.

———. CO 273. Colonial Office, Original Correspondence: The Straits Settlements. 1838–1946.

———. FO 366. Foreign Office and Diplomatic Service Administration Office: Chief Clerk's Department and Successors. 1719–1967.

Sainty, John C. *Colonial Office Officials: Officials of the Secretary of State for War, 1794–1801, of the Secretary of State for War and Colonies, 1801–54, and of the Secretary of State for Colonies, 1854–70*. Vol. 6. London: University of London, Institute of Historical Research, 1976.

Scarth, John. *Twelve Years in China: The People, the Rebels, and the Mandarins, by a British Resident*. Edinburgh: T. Constable and Co., 1860.

Straits Settlements. Legislative Council. *Proceedings of the Legislative Council of the Straits Settlements in 1876*. Singapore: The Government Printing Office, 1876.

Tinker, Hugh. "Structure of the British Imperial Heritage." In *Asian Bureaucratic Systems Emergent from the British Imperial Tradition,* edited by Ralph Braibanti. Durham, N. C.: Duke University Press, 1966, pp. 23–86.

Van Dyke, Paul A. *The Canton Trade: Life and Enterprise on the China Coast, 1700–1845*. Hong Kong: Hong Kong University Press, 2005.

Wakeman, Frederick. "The Canton Trade and the Opium War." In *The Cambridge History of China*. Vol. 10, *Late Ch'ing 1800–1911, Part 1,* edited by John K. Fairbank. Cambridge: Cambridge University Press, 1978, pp. 163–212.

Wilson, Kathleen. *The Sense of the People: Politics, Culture and Imperialism in England, 1715–1785*. Cambridge: Cambridge University Press, 1995.

Wylie, Alexander. *Memorials of Protestant Missionaries to the Chinese: Giving a List of Their Publications, and Obituary Notices of the Deceased*. Shanghae [Shanghai]: American Presbyterian Mission Press, 1867.

Contributors

Nazry BAHRAWI is a literary and cultural critic at the Singapore University of Technology and Design, and a research fellow at the Middle East Institute, National University of Singapore. He is also a contributing editor for *Critical Muslim*, a UK-based quarterly by Hurst Publishers. He has published essays on utopianism and postsecular Islam (*Literature and Theology*, 2011), ecotheology of Margaret Atwood's *MaddAddam* novels (*Green Letters*, 2014), and translation and postsecular dissent in Jose Saramago's *Cain* (2014). His research interests include world literature and literary translation, the intersections between literature, theology, and philosophy in Western and Islamic thoughts, as well as literary and cultural theory.

Phrae CHITTIPHALANGSRI is currently a lecturer in Comparative Literature and Translation Studies at Chulalongkorn University, Thailand. She received a BA in English in 2003, and was then granted the Anandamahidol Foundation Royal Scholarship to continue her postgraduate study in the UK. In 2009, she completed her doctoral thesis "Translation, Orientalism, Virtuality: English and French Translations of the Bhagavad Gītā and Śakuntalā, 1784–1884" at University College London. She served as co-editor of the online journal *New Voices in Translation Studies* from 2009–2012. Her current research includes studies of Thai translation history, with a particular focus on Thai translation concepts and traditions. The article "On the Virtuality of Translation in Orientalism," in which she develops the concept of virtuality in translation and representation initiated in her thesis, was published in Routledge's *Translation Studies* in 2014.

Joshua A. FOGEL received his Ph.D. from Columbia University in 1980. He is Canada Research Chair in Modern Chinese History and Professor of History at York University in Toronto. He is also an Honorary Senior Research Fellow at the Research Centre for Translation, The Chinese University of Hong Kong. His research concerns Sino-Japanese cultural interactions over the past two centuries. His most recent publications include: *Japanese Historiography and the Gold Seal of 57 C.E.: Relic, Text, Object, Fake* (2013); an edited volume, *The Role of Japan in Modern Chinese Art* (2012); a translation, *Just a Scholar: The Memoirs of Zhou Yiliang* (2013); and *Maiden Voyage: The* Senzaimaru *and the Creation of Modern Sino-Japanese Relations* (2014).

Georgios T. HALKIAS is currently Assistant Professor of Buddhism at the University of Hong Kong and a fellow at the Oxford Centre of Buddhist Studies. He received his D.Phil. in Oriental Studies at University of Oxford in 2006 and has held several research posts in interdisciplinary projects as Research Assistant at the Warburg Institute, University of London; British Academy Post-Doctoral Fellow at SOAS, University of London; Research Fellow and Coordinator of Religions of Central Asia at Ruhr-Universität in Germany. He specializes on the religious history of early Tibetan Buddhist translations and Tibetan Pure Land Buddhism. His research interests focus on regional and transnational histories of Buddhist "texts, rituals, and practices" in India, Tibet, and Hellenistic Central Asia. He is the author of several research articles on Indo-Tibetan Buddhism and Himalayan religious history and a book based on his dissertation, *Luminous Bliss: A Religious History of Pure Land Buddhism in Tibet* (2013).

Theresa HYUN was a member of the College of Foreign Languages at Kyung Hee University, Seoul for a number of years before taking her position at York University, Toronto where she teaches Korean Studies. She has been actively involved in organizing international conferences on Korean culture in a comparative perspective. Her publications focus on Korean literature and culture and translation studies. Representative publications include *Writing Women in Korea: Translation and Feminism in the Colonial Period* (2004) and a book of original poetry *P'anmunjom eso ui Ch'a Han Chan* (A Cup of Tea at P'anmunjom, 2012). Her current research deals with literary translation in North Korea from the late 1940s to the late 1960s.

Uganda Sze-pui KWAN is Associate Professor at the Chinese Division of Nanyang Technological University, Singapore. Her research interests include Chinese knowledge production by the British interpreter in the nineteenth century, literary translation of modern Chinese literature, and Sino-Japanese comparative literary and cultural studies. She is currently working on a book manuscript that is a revisionist history of British Sinology in the nineteenth century. Her other book projects include *Scholars and Interpreters* (2015) and *Bridging the Language Gaps: Translation and Interpretation Activities in the Early Hong Kong Government (1842–1860)* (2015). She has published over 50 articles in leading journals in English, Chinese, and Japanese. Apart from the honorary research appointment at the Research Centre for Translation (RCT), The Chinese University of Hong Kong, she has taken visiting appointments in the University of Tokyo, University College London, and Harvard University.

Megha PANSARE is Assistant Professor of Russian at the Department of Foreign Languages, Shivaji University, Kolhapur in India. Her doctoral thesis studies the literary translations from Russian into Marathi from the polysystem theory approach and attempts to find out the socio-political connections of these translations in a historical perspective. She has participated in international and national conferences on translation studies and has worked widely in the field of literary translation between Russian and Marathi. Her translations of 40 short stories/articles/interviews/poems have been published in various Marathi newspapers and journals, including works like *Letters of Lev Tolstoi to Mahatma Gandhi, Gospodin iz Sanfransisco* by Ivan Bunin, extracts from *Russkaya Ideya* by Nikolai Berdyaev, one-act play *Predlozheniye* by Anton Chekhov, *Sud'ba Cheloveka* by Mikhail Sholokhov, and a short novel *Seryozha* by Vera Panova. She has written articles on Russia, which include "The Changing Status of Russian Woman during the Pre-Soviet, Soviet and Post-Soviet Eras." Her recent publication *Talghar* (2011) is the Marathi translation of the four-act play *Na Dne* by Maksim Gorky. She has completed a UGC-Major Research Project on "Introducing Culture and Civilization of Russia to the Russian language learners." She is also an activist in the women's movement.

E. V. RAMAKRISHNAN is a bilingual writer who has published criticism and poetry in Malayalam, his mother tongue (a language spoken in the South Indian state of Kerala), and English. He also translates between Indian languages and English. His research interests are comparative literature, translation studies, Indian literature, and South Asian literature. He has published over 100 research papers in these areas. Among his books in English are *Interdisciplinary Alter-natives in Comparative Literature* (co-edited, 2013), *Locating Indian Literature: Texts, Traditions and Translations* (2011), and *Making It New: Modernism in Malayalam, Marathi and Hindi Poetry* (1995), besides three volumes of poetry in English. He was awarded Kerala Sahitya Akademi Award for the critical work in Malayalam, *Aksharavum Aadhunikatayum* (1994). He has also published four other critical studies in Malayalam, among which are *Desheeyatakalum Sahityavum* (2001) and *Anubhavangale Aarkkanu Peti?* (2012). He is presently Professor and Dean of School of Language, Literature and Culture Studies at Central University of Gujarat, Gandhinagar, Gujarat.

Jae-ho SHIN is a Ph.D. candidate in the University of Pennsylvania and is now working as a research fellow at National Institute of Korean History in Korea. His concentration is transnational interactions between premodern Korea and its neighbours, mainly focusing on border-crossing exchanges of religion, ideas, and commodities in late medieval period.

Corazon D. VILLAREAL is Professor at the Department of English and Comparative Literature at the University of the Philippines Diliman, of which she was former chair. She is the recipient of a number of grants, among them a Fulbright research fellowship at Columbia University, a research grant on semiotics at Indiana University in Bloomington, and a workshop grant at the Nida School of Translation Studies in Misano, Italy. Her research and teaching interests are eclectic but her major publications are in translation and intercultural studies and Philippine vernacular literatures. Among her publications are "Enacting Hybridity: The Philippine Diaspora" in *The Global-Local Interface and Hybridity* (2014), "Looking for Melayu: Translators and Seafarers" in *Kritika Kultura* (August 2013), and "Review of Doctoral Research on English Language Education in the Philippines, Singapore, and Malaysia (2007–2010)" in *Language Teaching* (January 2012). She is a co-convenor of the Sixth Asian Translation Traditions International Conference on "Translating Asia: Migrations and Transgressions" (October 2014).

Lawrence Wang-chi WONG received his Ph.D. from SOAS, University of London. He is Chairman and Professor of Humanities at the Department of Translation, and Director of the Research Centre for Translation, The Chinese University of Hong Kong. He was formerly Associate Dean (Research) of the Faculty of Arts, Director of Research Institute of Humanities, and Director of the Centre for Hong Kong Cultural Studies, CUHK. His research interests include translation history of China in the early modern and modern period (eighteenth century onwards), modern Chinese literature, and Hong Kong cultural studies. He has single-authored 14 books and over 130 academic articles and book chapters in these fields, including *Fanyi yu jindai Zhongguo* (Translation and Early Modern China, 2014), *Fanyi yu wenxue zhijian* (Between Translation and Literature, 2011 & 2013), *Chongshi "xin da ya": Ershi shiji Zhongguo fanyi yanjiu* (Reinterpreting *Xin Da Ya*: Translation Studies of the Twentieth-century China, 1999 & 2007), *Lu Xun yu "Zuo Lian"* (Lu Xun and the Left League, 1991 & 2006), and *Lishi de chenzhong: Cong Xianggang kan Zhongguo dalu Xianggang shi lunshu* (The Burden of History: On the Hong Kong Histories Published in Mainland China, 2000 & 2001). He is also Executive Editor of *Renditions* and Chief Editor of *Journal of Translation Studies* and *Studies in Translation History*.

best-known "divide and rule" strategy, it might only incur an opposite outcome. The gangs, no matter to which society or dialect group they belonged, would unite and call for a justifiable revolt to "expel barbarians."

Practically speaking, to tackle the triad's core, the British would have had to possess sufficient intelligence gained from a handful of interpreters who knew the various local Chinese dialects. However, this problem had long bedevilled ruling parties in the Straits. The entire multilingual situation was incomprehensible to the British—a fact that was well recorded as early as the 1820s when the British arrived in the colony:

> The second objection [against forming the Straits] which offers itself to our notice, arises from the variety of *dialects spoken by the inhabitants of the different provinces who compose the Emigrants to the Straits*, the greater part of whom are stranger to the dialect of Canton, the natives of which province alone are acquainted in any manner, with the English language, the knowledge possessed however by these persons, is perfectly inadequate to interpret the explanations and evidence upon general subjects.[47] [Emphasis by author]

The triad's existence was not solely to blame for the lawlessness and chaotic situation in the Straits. The ruler's apathy and ignorance of its subjects was another factor that contributed to the government's downfall. The main driving force behind Chinese labourers enduring the hardships of the various menial industries in an exploitative environment was the belief that they would be able to sustain and support their families in China. A regular remittance of their hard-earned money to their hometown was all they wanted. The remittance was usually sent with a well-penned letter written by a jobless literate person stationed at the remittance booth near the harbour. Although the remitting agents operated on board the many Chinese junks that called at Singapore, they were not registered with or regulated by any statutory power and the remittance company sometimes absconded with the remittance money. Local business scions, known as "towkays" locally, stepped in and took over. Inevitably, a monopolization

47 Norton-Kyshe, *A Judicial History of the Straits Settlements 1786–1890*, p. 108.

gradually took shape—another form of clannish power—and triad protection and money laundering also became commonplace.

To combat the uncontrolled postal and monetary circulation and inhibit the excessive outflow of money, Governor Sir William Jervois (1821–1897; governorship 1875–1877) proposed to modernize the local practice by establishing a sub-post office run by a Chinese agent through the existing postal service. Under this new mechanism, all letters would be sent through this agent, who was appointed by the government, and likewise all remittances had to be transmitted through this proper and recorded channel. To the locals, exposing their financial situations and personal correspondence to this centralized ruling machinery would mean opening the floodgates to censorship and taxation. In addition, an operational cost was to be incurred by a stamp duty. The towkays opposed the new policy, as it promised to strip them of their vested interest. All of the aforementioned details made the new administrative method repugnant to the Chinese, which increased the tension between the rulers and the ruled. The locals felt exploited and more tightly controlled by the rulers at every turn. To make matters worse, when the new postal system was launched, mistranslation intensified the tension. The original idea was to allow the Chinese to choose whether or not to send their remittance through this new sub-post office. The merit of making the choice was that they could be sure that their money was kept safe by a company registered with the government. Some distrustful middlemen took advantage of the situation and quickly disseminated misinformation among the people, knowing that the government would not be able to find or take immediate action against the leak to ratify the translation. This event, called the Post Office Riot (December 1876), reflected Chinese feeling towards the authorities and the government's presumptuous attitude that their policy could be implemented without broad consultation. During the early colonial history of the Straits and Hong Kong, these types of miscommunication between government and the people were only too frequent. Society lacked the proper channels of effective communication and its people were deprived of any chance to voice their opinions, anger or grievances. In truth, the colonizer might not even have recognized the need for communication